Exploring DraftSight

Randy H. Shih
Oregon Institute of Technology

ISBN: 978-1-58503-755-1

SDC
PUBLICATIONS

Mission, Kansas

Schroff Development Corporation

P.O. Box 1334
Mission KS 66222
(913) 262-2664
www.SDCpublications.com

Publisher: Stephen Schroff

Trademarks

The following are registered trademarks of *Dassault Systèmes*, Inc.: CATIA, SolidWorks, and DraftSight.
Microsoft, Windows are either registered trademarks or trademarks of Microsoft Corporation.
All other trademarks are trademarks of their respective holders.

Examination Copies:

Books received as examination copies are for review purposes only and may not be made available for student use. Resale of examination copies is prohibited.

Electronic Files:

Any electronic files associated with this book are licensed to the original user only. These files may not be transferred to any other party.

Shih, Randy H.
  Exploring DraftSight

Randy H. Shih

ISBN 978-1-58503-755-1

The author and publisher of this book have used their best efforts in preparing this book. These efforts include the development, research and testing of the material presented. The author and publisher shall not be liable in any event for incidental or consequential damages with, or arising out of, the furnishing, performance, or use of the material.

Printed and bound in the United States of America.

Preface

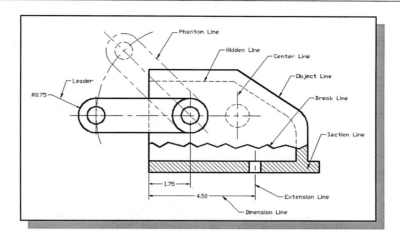

The primary goal of *Exploring DraftSight* is to introduce the aspects of Engineering Graphics with the use of modern Computer Aided Design package – DraftSight. This text is intended to be used as a training guide for students and professionals. The chapters in this text proceed in a pedagogical fashion to guide you from constructing basic shapes to making complete sets of engineering drawings. This text takes a hands-on, exercise-intensive approach to all the important concepts of Engineering Graphics, as well as in-depth discussions of CAD techniques. This textbook contains a series of twelve chapters, with detailed step-by-step tutorial style lessons, designed to introduce beginning CAD users to the graphic language used in all branches of technical industry. The CAD techniques and concepts discussed in this text are also designed to serve as the foundation to the more advanced parametric feature-based CAD packages such as SolidWorks and CATIA. This book does not attempt to cover all of DraftSight's features, only to provide an introduction to the software. It is intended to help you establish a good basis for exploring and growing in the exciting field of Computer Aided Engineering.

Acknowledgments

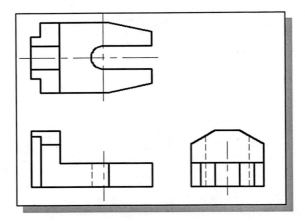

This book would not have been possible without a great deal of support. First, special thanks to two great teachers, Prof. George R. Schade of University of Nebraska-Lincoln and Mr. Denwu Lee, who taught me the fundamentals, the intrigue and the sheer fun of Computer Aided Engineering.

The effort and support of the editorial and production staff of Schroff Development Corporation is gratefully acknowledged. I would especially like to thank Stephen Schroff for his support and helpful suggestions during this project.

I am grateful that the Mechanical and Manufacturing Engineering Technology Department of Oregon Institute of Technology has provided me with an excellent environment in which to pursue my interests in teaching and research. I would especially like to thank Professor Brian Moravec and Emeritus Professor Charles Hermach for helpful comments and encouragement.

Finally, truly unbounded thanks are due to my wife Hsiu-Ling and our daughter Casandra for their understanding and encouragement throughout this project.

Randy H. Shih
Klamath Falls, Oregon
Spring, 2012

Table of Contents

Chapter 2
Geometric Constructions

Chapter 3
Object Properties and Organization in DraftSight

Chapter 4
Orthographic Projections and Multiview Constructions

Chapter 5
Pictorials and Sketching

Chapter 6

Dimensioning and Notes

Chapter 7

Tolerancing and Fits

Chapter 8
Symmetrical Features in Designs

Chapter 9
Auxiliary Views

Chapter 10
Section Views

Chapter 11
Threads and Fasteners

Chapter 12
Working Drawings

Appendix

Index

Notes:

Introduction:

Transition from AutoCAD® to DraftSight™

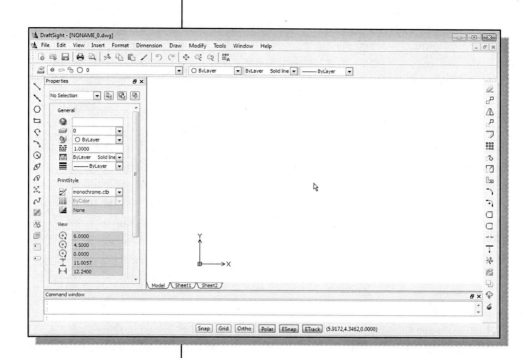

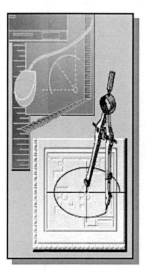

Key DraftSight Advantages

- ♦ **Free, professional-grade CAD product to create, edit and view DWG/DXF files.**
- ♦ **Compatibility with Windows®, Mac®, and Linux.**
- ♦ **Easy transition for AutoCAD users.**

Ease of Use without the overhead

DraftSight™ is designed to allow professionals to quickly create/edit 2D drawings. (Note that DraftSight can also be used to view 3D DWG/DXF drawings.) DraftSight is not AutoCAD®, but most AutoCAD users will feel right at home with DraftSight for several reasons. The user interfaces on both systems are quite similar. The footprint of DraftSight is relatively small (200 MBytes) and will start much faster than AutoCAD (1.6 GBytes). DraftSight is available on multiple platforms such as Windows®, Mac® and Linux. The same DWG/DXF file can be viewed/edited on any system running DraftSight. Last and not least, DraftSight is freeware for engineers, architects, designers, students and educators.

In this text, we will concentrate on learning the principles of engineering graphics and creating designs using two-dimensional geometric construction techniques. The fundamental concepts and use of different **DraftSight** commands are presented using step-by-step tutorials. We will begin with creating simple geometric entities and then move toward creating detailed working drawings and assembly drawings. The techniques presented in this text will also serve as the foundation for entering the world of three-dimensional solid modeling using packages such as **SolidWorks, CATIA, Creo Parametric** and **Autodesk Inventor**.

What is DraftSight?

DraftSight is a freeware 2D CADD (computer-aided design and computer-aided drafting) product for engineers, architects, designers, students and educators. The product was developed by Dassault Systèmes and lets users create, edit and view AutoCAD DWG and DXF files.

DWG files contain the binary data for CAD design and it is the drawing format for many CAD programs. DWG is a long-time abbreviation for "Drawing." A DXF, or Drawing Exchange File, is used to convert CAD files into a generic format that can be read by other CAD software products. DraftSight lets professional CAD users, students and educators create, edit and view DWG files. DraftSight runs on Windows®, Mac® and Linux.

DraftSight competes against more than three dozen 2D or 2D/3D hybrid products on the market. General availability of DraftSight for Windows was released in February 2011 and was downloaded more than 1.8 million times as of December 2011. Note that the DraftSight software can be downloaded via the DraftSight Web page:

http://www.3ds.com/products/draftsight

DraftSight and AutoCAD

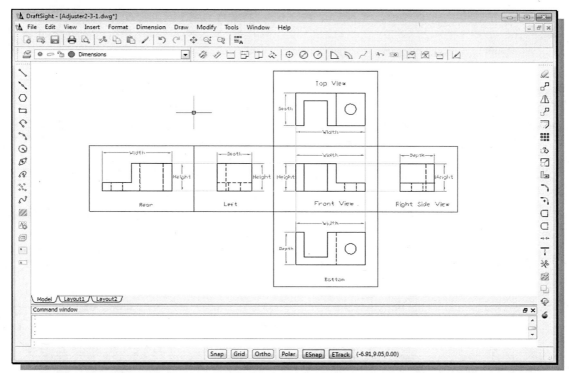

An AutoCAD DWG drawing opened in DraftSight with all *layers*, *linetypes*, *lineweight*, and *color* supports.

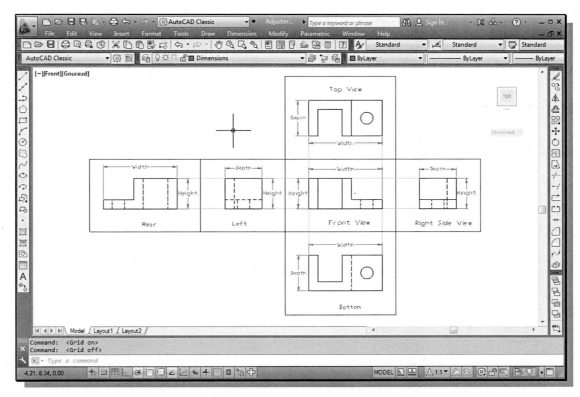

The same DWG drawing was edited in DraftSight and then opened in AutoCAD.

AutoCAD® is a software application for both 2D and 3D designs. The software is developed by Autodesk, Inc., first released in December 1982. Since 1984, **AutoCAD®** has established the reputation for being the most widely used PC-based CAD software around the world. By 2007, it was estimated that there were over 6 million **AutoCAD®** users in more than 150 countries worldwide.

AutoCAD® has been considered as the industry leader in the 2D CAD software and its DWG file format has been widely adopted for 2D designs. The native file format of AutoCAD is the DWG format. The DWG format and the other AutoCAD file format (DXF: *Drawing Exchange Format*) have become de facto standards for 2D CAD data interoperability. In 2006, Autodesk estimated the number of active 2D and 3D DWG files are in excess of one billion. Currently in the CAD industry, many efforts are placed on transferring existing 2D drawings into 3D solid models. Both the DWG and DXF drawings can be imported directly into many of the 3D parametric modeling software, such as SolidWorks, Creo Parametric, and Autodesk Inventor.

Chapter 1
Introduction and DraftSight Fundamentals

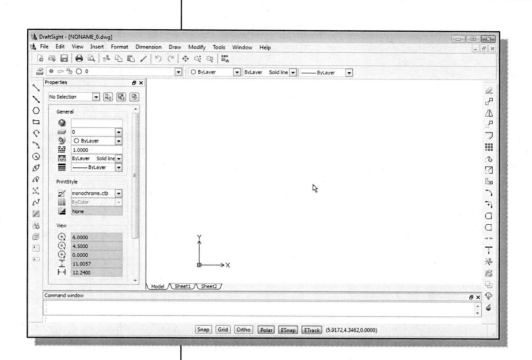

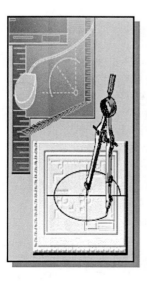

Learning Objectives

- ◆ **The History and Importance of Engineering Graphics**
- ◆ **Be familiar with the DraftSight Toolbars**
- ◆ **Use the DraftSight Visual Reference Commands**
- ◆ **Draw, Using the LINE and CIRCLE Commands**
- ◆ **Use the DELETE Command**
- ◆ **Define Positions Using the Basic Entry Methods**
- ◆ **Create and Save a DraftSight Drawing**

Introduction

Engineering Graphics, also known as **Technical Drawing**, is the technique of creating accurate representations of designs, an *engineering drawing*, for construction and manufacturing. An **engineering drawing** is a type of drawing that is technical in nature, used to fully and clearly define requirements for engineered items, and is usually created in accordance with standardized conventions for layout, nomenclature, interpretation, appearance, size, etc. A skilled practitioner of the art of engineering drawing is known as a *draftsman* or *draftsperson*.

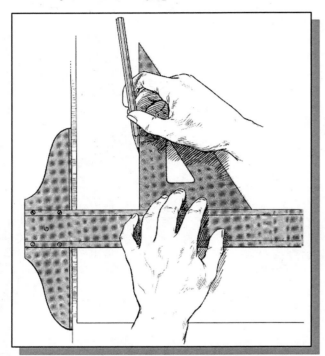

The basic mechanics of drafting are to use a pencil and draw on a piece of paper. For engineering drawings, papers are generally placed on a drafting table and additional tools are used. A T-square is one of the standard tools commonly used with a drafting table.

A T-square is also known as a *sliding straightedge*; parallel lines can be drawn simply by moving the T-square and running a pencil along the T-square's straightedge. The T-square is more typically used as a tool to hold other tools such as triangles. For example, one or more triangles can be placed on the T-square and lines can be drawn at the chosen angle on the paper.

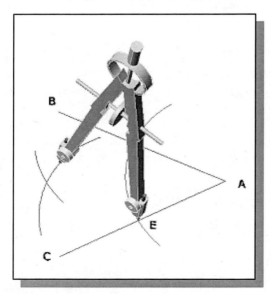

In addition to the triangles, other tools are used to draw curves and circles. Primary among these are the compass, used for drawing simple arcs and circles, and the French curve, typically a piece of plastic with a complex curve on it. A spline is a rubber coated articulated metal that can be manually bent to almost any curve.

This basic drafting system requires an accurate table and constant attention to the positioning of the tools. A common error is to allow the triangles to push the top of the T-square down slightly, thereby throwing off all angles. And in general, drafting was a time consuming process.

A solution to these problems was the introduction of the **"drafting machine"**, which is a device that allowed the draftsperson to have an accurate right angle at any point on the page quite quickly. These machines often included the ability to change the angle, thereby removing the need for triangles as well.

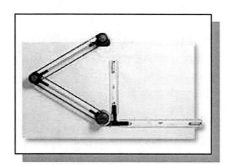

In addition to the mechanics of drawing the lines onto a piece of paper, drafting requires an understanding of geometry and the professional skills of the specific designer. At one time, drafting was a sought-after job, considered one of the more demanding and highly-skilled of the trades. Today the mechanics of the drafting task have been largely automated, and greatly accelerated, through the use of **computer aided design** (CAD) systems. Proficiency in using CAD systems has also become one of the more important requirements for engineers and designers.

Computer Aided Design

Computer Aided Design (CAD) is the process of doing designs with the aid of computers. This includes the generation of computer models, analysis of design data and the creation of the necessary drawings. **DraftSight**® is a computer-aided-design software developed by *Dassault Systèmes*. The **DraftSight**® software is a tool that can be used for design and drafting activities. The two-dimensional and three-dimensional models created in **DraftSight**® can be transferred to other computer programs for further analysis and testing. The computer models can also be used in manufacturing equipment such as machining centers, lathes, mills or rapid prototyping machines to manufacture the product.

The rapid changes in the field of **computer aided engineering** (CAE) have brought exciting advances in industry. Recent advances have made the long-sought goal of reducing design time, producing prototypes faster, and achieving higher product quality closer to a reality.

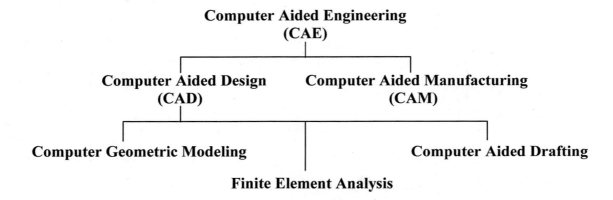

Development of Computer Geometric Modeling

Computer aided design is a relatively new technology and its rapid expansion in the last fifty years is truly amazing. Computer modeling technology advanced along with the development of computer hardware. The first generation CAD programs, developed in the 1950s, were mostly non-interactive; CAD users were required to create program codes to generate the desired two-dimensional (2D) geometric shapes. Initially, the development of CAD technology occurred mostly in academic research facilities. The Massachusetts Institute of Technology, Carnegie-Mellon University, and Cambridge University were the lead pioneers at that time. The interest in CAD technology spread quickly and several major industry companies, such as General Motors, Lockheed, McDonnell, IBM and Ford Motor Co., participated in the development of interactive CAD programs in the 1960s. Usage of CAD systems was primarily in the automotive industry, aerospace industry, and government agencies that developed their own programs for their specific needs. The 1960s also marked the beginning of the development of finite element analysis methods for computer stress analysis and computer aided manufacturing for generating machine tool-paths.

The 1970s are generally viewed as the years of the most significant progress in the development of computer hardware, namely the invention and development of **microprocessors**. With the improvement in computing power, new types of 3D CAD programs that were user-friendly and interactive became reality. CAD technology quickly expanded from very simple **computer aided drafting** to very complex **computer aided design**. The use of 2D and 3D wireframe modelers was accepted as the leading edge technology that could increase productivity in industry. The developments of surface modeling and solid modeling technology were taking shape by the late 1970s; but the high cost of computer hardware and programming slowed the development of such technology. During this time period, the available CAD systems all required extremely expensive room-sized mainframe computers.

In the 1980s, improvements in computer hardware brought the power of mainframes to the desktop at less cost and with more accessibility to the general public. By the mid-1980s, CAD technology had become the main focus of a variety of manufacturing industries and was very competitive with traditional design/drafting methods. It was during this period of time that 3D solid modeling technology had major advancements, which boosted the usage of CAE technology in industry.

In the 1990s, CAD programs evolved into powerful design/manufacturing/management tools. CAD technology has come a long way, and during these years of development, modeling schemes progressed from two-dimensional (2D) wireframe to three-dimensional (3D) wireframe, to surface modeling, to solid modeling and, finally, to feature-based parametric solid modeling.

The first generation CAD packages were simply 2D **computer aided drafting** programs, basically the electronic equivalents of the drafting board. For typical models, the use of this type of program would require that several to many views of the objects be created individually as they would be on the drafting board. The 3D designs remained in the designer's mind, not in the computer database. The mental translation of 3D objects to 2D views is required throughout the use of the packages. Although such systems have some advantages over traditional board drafting, they are still tedious and labor intensive. The need for the development of 3D modelers came quite naturally, given the limitations of the 2D drafting packages.

The development of the 3D wireframe modeler was a major leap in the area of computer modeling. The computer database in the 3D wireframe modeler contains the locations of all the points in space coordinates and it is sufficient to create just one model rather than multiple models. This single 3D model can then be viewed from any direction as needed. The 3D wireframe modelers require the least computer power and achieve reasonably good representation of 3D models. But because surface definition is not part of a wireframe model, all wireframe images have the inherent problem of ambiguity.

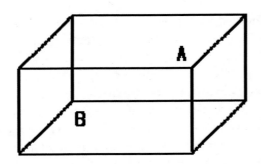

Wireframe Ambiguity: Which corner is in front, A or B?

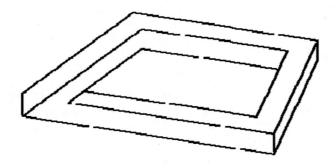

A non-realizable object: Wireframe models contain no surface definitions.

Surface modeling is the logical development in computer geometry modeling to follow the 3D wireframe modeling scheme by organizing and grouping edges that define polygonal surfaces. Surface modeling describes the part's surfaces but not its interiors. Designers are still required to interactively examine surface models to insure that the various surfaces on a model are contiguous throughout. Many of the concepts used in 3D wireframe and surface modelers are incorporated in the solid modeling scheme, but it is solid modeling that offers the most advantages as a design tool.

In the solid modeling presentation scheme, the solid definitions include nodes, edges and surfaces, and it is a complete and unambiguous mathematical representation of a precisely enclosed and filled volume. Unlike the surface modeling method, solid modelers start with a solid or use topology rules to guarantee that all of the surfaces are stitched together properly. Two predominant methods for representing solid models are **constructive solid geometry** (CSG) representation and **boundary representation** (B-rep).

The CSG representation method can be defined as the combination of 3D solid primitives. What constitutes a "primitive" varies somewhat with the software but typically includes a rectangular prism, a cylinder, a cone, a wedge, and a sphere. Most solid modelers allow the user to define additional primitives, which can be very complex.

In the B-rep representation method, objects are represented in terms of their spatial boundaries. This method defines the points, edges, and surfaces of a volume, and/or issues commands that sweep or rotate a defined face into a third dimension to form a solid. The object is then made up of the unions of these surfaces that completely and precisely enclose a volume.

By the 1990s, a new paradigm called *concurrent engineering* had emerged. With concurrent engineering, designers, design engineers, analysts, manufacturing engineers, and management engineers all work closely right from the initial stages of the design. In this way, all aspects of the design can be evaluated and any potential problems can be identified right from the start and throughout the design process. Using the principles of concurrent engineering, a new type of computer modeling technique appeared. The technique is known as the *feature-based parametric modeling technique.* The key advantage of the *feature-based parametric modeling technique* is its capability to produce very flexible designs. Changes can be made easily and design alternatives can be evaluated with minimum effort. Various software packages offer different approaches to feature-based parametric modeling, yet the end result is a flexible design defined by its design variables and parametric features.

In this text, we will concentrate on creating designs using two-dimensional geometric construction techniques. The fundamental concepts and use of different **DraftSight**® commands are presented using step-by-step tutorials. We will begin with creating simple geometric entities and then move toward creating detailed working drawings and assembly drawings. The techniques presented in this text will also serve as the foundation for entering the world of three-dimensional solid modeling using packages such as **Dassault Systèmes CATIA** and **Dassault Systèmes SolidWorks**.

Why use a PC-Based CAD System?

DraftSight® was first introduced to the public in 2010, and is one of the PC-based CAD software products that are available for individual use. Today, PC-based CAD software has become the most widely used CAD/CAE software around the world. By 2007, it was estimated that there were over 4.5 million PC-Based CAD users in more than 150 countries worldwide.

CAD provides us with a wide range of benefits; in most cases, the result of using CAD is increased accuracy and productivity. First of all, the computer offers much higher accuracy than the traditional methods of drafting and design. Traditionally, drafting and detailing are the most expensive cost element in a project and the biggest bottleneck. With CAD systems, such as **DraftSight**®, the tedious drafting and detailing tasks are simplified through the use of many of the CAD geometric construction tools, such as *grids*, *snap*, *trim*, and *auto-dimensioning*. Dimensions and notes are always legible in CAD drawings, and in most cases CAD systems can produce higher quality prints compared to traditional hand drawings.

CAD also offers much-needed flexibility in design and drafting. A CAD model generated on a computer consists of numeric data that describe the geometry of the object. This allows the designers and clients to see something tangible and to interpret the ramifications of the design. In many cases, it is also possible to simulate operating conditions on the computer and observe the results. Any kind of geometric shape stored in the database can be easily duplicated. For large and complex designs and drawings, particularly those involving similar shapes and repetitive operations, CAD approaches are very efficient and effective. Because computer designs and models can be altered easily, a multitude of design options can be examined and presented to a client before any construction or manufacturing actually takes place. Making changes to a CAD model is generally much faster than making changes to a traditional hand drawing. Only the affected components of the design need to be modified and the drawings can be plotted again. In addition, the greatest benefit is that, once the CAD model is created, it can be used over and over again. The CAD models can also be transferred into manufacturing equipment such as machining centers, lathes, mills, or rapid prototyping machines to manufacture the product directly.

CAD, however, does not replace every design activity. CAD may help, but it does not replace the designer's experience with geometry and graphical conventions and standards for the specific field. CAD is a powerful tool, but the use of this tool does not guarantee correct results; the designer is still responsible for using good design practice and applying good judgment. CAD will supplement these skills to ensure that the best design is obtained.

CAD designs and drawings are stored in binary form, usually as CAD files, to magnetic devices such as diskettes and hard disks. The information stored in CAD files usually requires much less physical space in comparison to traditional hand drawings. However, the information stored inside the computer is not indestructible. On the contrary, the electronic format of information is very fragile and sensitive to the environment. Heat or cold can damage the information stored on magnetic storage devices. A power failure while you are creating a design could wipe out the many hours you spend working in front of the computer monitor. It is a good habit to save your work periodically, just in case something might go wrong while you are working on your design. In general, one should save one's work onto a storage device at an interval of every 15 to 20 minutes. You should also save your work before you make any major modifications to the design. It is also a good habit to periodically make backup copies of your work and put them in a safe place.

Getting started with DraftSight

How to start DraftSight depends on the type of workstation and the particular software configuration you are using. With most *Windows* systems, you may select the **DraftSight** option on the *Start* menu or select the **DraftSight** icon on the *Desktop*. Consult with your instructor or technical support personnel if you have difficulty starting the software.

The program takes a while to load, so be patient. Eventually the DraftSight main *drawing screen* will appear on the screen. The tutorials in this text are based on the assumption that you are using DraftSight's default settings. If your system has been customized for other uses, some of the settings may not work with the step-by-step instructions in the tutorials. Contact your instructor and/or technical support personnel to restore the default software configuration.

DraftSight Screen Layout

The default DraftSight *drawing screen* contains the *Main Menu*, the *Standard* toolbar, the *command window*, the *Status Bar*, and the *Ribbon Tabs* and *Panels* that contain several *control panels* such as the *Draw and Modify* panel and the *Annotation* panel. You may resize the DraftSight drawing window by clicking and dragging at the edges of the window, or relocate the window by clicking and dragging at the window title area.

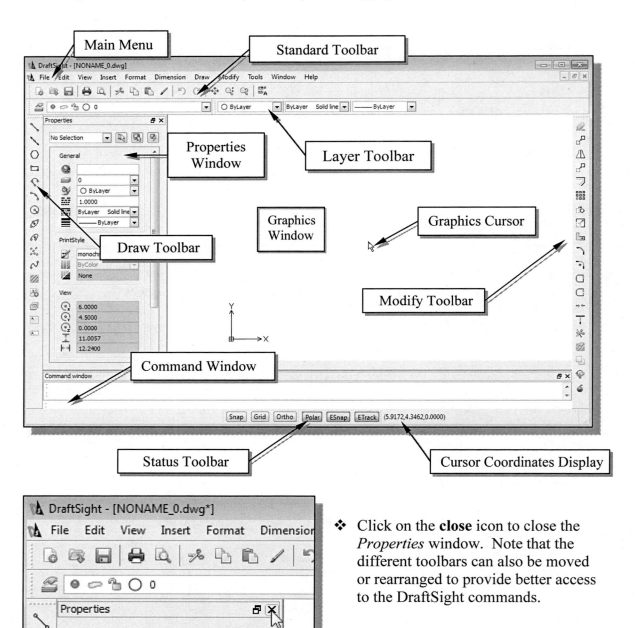

❖ Click on the **close** icon to close the *Properties* window. Note that the different toolbars can also be moved or rearranged to provide better access to the DraftSight commands.

- **Main Menu**

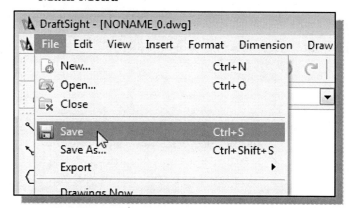

The *Main Menu* provides an easy access to the majority commands of DraftSight.

- **Standard Toolbar**

The *Standard Access* toolbar at the top of the *DraftSight* window allows us quick access to frequently used commands, such as New, Open, Save, Copy, Paste, Undo and also the View related commands. Note that we can customize the toolbars by adding and removing sets of options or individual commands.

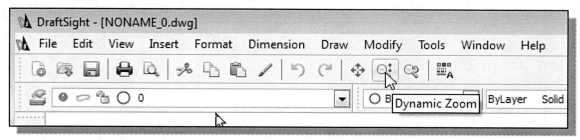

- **Graphics Window**

The *graphics window* is the area where models and drawings are displayed.

- **Graphics Cursor or Crosshairs**

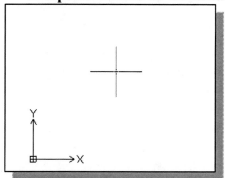

The *graphics cursor*, or *crosshairs*, shows the location of the pointing device in the graphics window. The coordinates of the cursor are displayed at the bottom of the screen layout. The cursor's appearance can be set through the available *DraftSight* Options.

- **Command window**

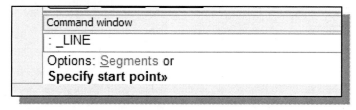

The bottom section of the screen layout provides status information for an operation and it is also the area for command and data input.

- **Cursor Coordinates**

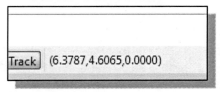

The bottom right side of the screen layout displays the coordinate information of the cursor.

- **Status Toolbar**

Next to the cursor coordinate display is the *Status* toolbar, showing the status of several commonly used display and construction options.

- **Draw and Modify Toolbar Panels**

The *Draw* and *Modify* toolbar panels contain icons for basic draw and modify commands.

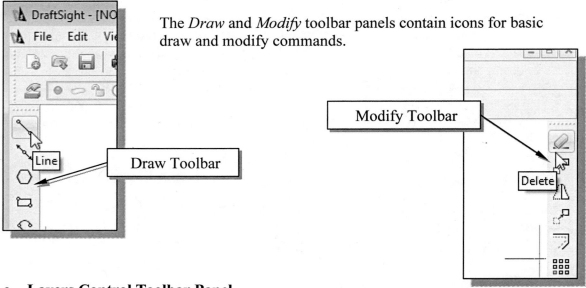

- **Layers Control Toolbar Panel**

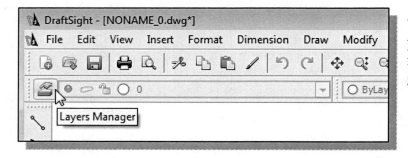

The *Layers Control* toolbar panel contains tools to help manipulate the properties of graphical objects.

- **Drawing Layout/Model tabs**

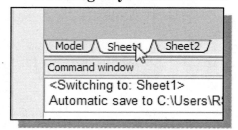

The *Drawing Layout* tabs can be used to quickly switch to the drawing sheets for printing.

Mouse Buttons

DraftSight utilizes the mouse buttons extensively. In learning DraftSight's interactive environment, it is important to understand the basic functions of the mouse buttons. It is highly recommended that you use a mouse or a tablet with DraftSight since the package uses the buttons for various functions.

- **Left mouse button**
  The **left-mouse-button** is used for most operations, such as selecting menus and icons, or picking graphic entities. One click of the button is used to select icons, menus and form entries, and to pick graphic items.

- **Right mouse button**
  The **right-mouse-button** is used to bring up additional available options. The software also utilizes the **right-mouse-button** as the same as the [**ENTER**] key, and is often used to accept the default setting to a prompt or to end a process. In DraftSight, **right-click configuration** can be done through the DraftSight **Options** command.

- **Middle mouse button/wheel**
  The middle mouse button/wheel can be used to Pan (hold down the wheel button and drag the mouse) or Zoom (rotate the wheel) dynamically.

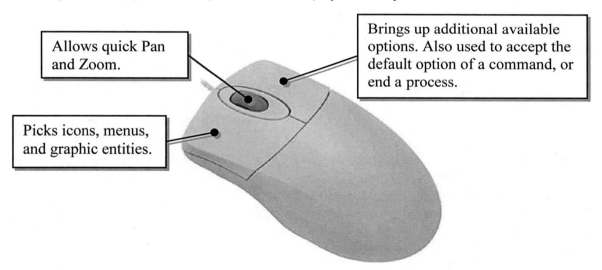

Allows quick Pan and Zoom.

Brings up additional available options. Also used to accept the default option of a command, or end a process.

Picks icons, menus, and graphic entities.

[Esc] – Canceling commands

The [**Esc**] key is used to cancel a command in DraftSight. The [**Esc**] key is located near the top left corner of the keyboard. Sometimes, it may be necessary to press the [**Esc**] key twice to cancel a command; it depends on where we are in the command sequence. For some commands, the [**Esc**] key is used to exit the command.

DraftSight Help System

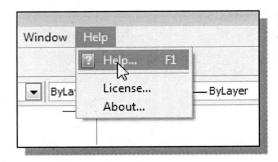

By default, the *Help* system can be accessed through the *Main Menu* or by pressing the [**F1**] function key.

- A list of the search options appears in the *DraftSight Help* window; and we can choose the type of information through the available tabs, or use the Search option.

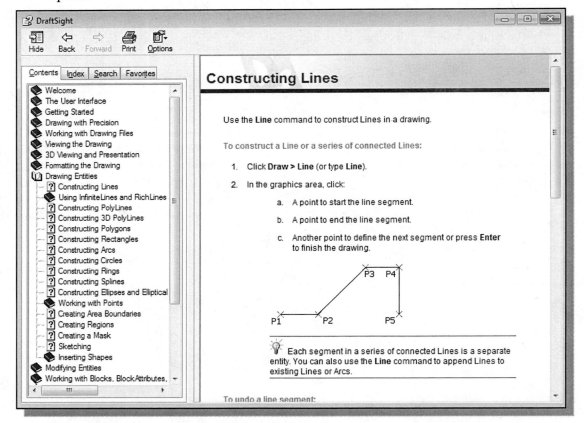

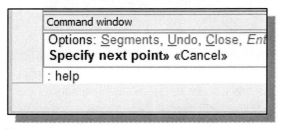

- Note the *Help* system can also be accessed through the command window.

Leaving DraftSight

➤ To leave DraftSight, use the left-mouse-button and click the **File** button at the top of the *DraftSight* screen window, then choose **Exit** from the *Main Menu* or type **QUIT/EXIT** in the command window.

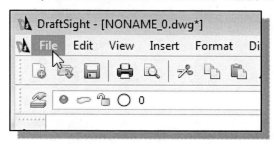 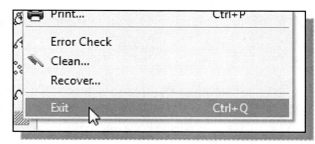

Creating a CAD file folder

❖ It is a good practice to create a separate folder to store your CAD files. You should not save your CAD files in the same folder where the DraftSight application is located. It is much easier to organize and back up your project files if they are in a separate folder. Making folders within this folder for different types of projects will help you organize your CAD files even further. When creating CAD files in DraftSight, it is strongly recommended that you *save* your CAD files on the hard drive.

➤ To create a new folder in the *Windows* environment:

1. In *My Computer*, or start the **Windows Explorer** under the *Start* menu, open the folder in which you want to create a new folder.

2. On the **File** menu, point to **New**, and then click **Folder**. The new folder appears with a temporary name.

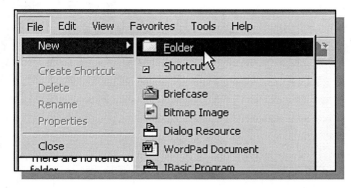

3. Type a name for the new folder, and then press [**ENTER**].

Drawing in DraftSight

Learning to use a CAD system is similar to learning a new language. It is necessary to begin with the basic alphabet and learn how to use it correctly and effectively through practice. This will require learning some new concepts and skills as well as learning a different vocabulary. All CAD systems create designs using basic geometric entities. Many of the constructions used in technical designs are based upon two-dimensional planar geometry. The method and number of operations that are required to accomplish the constructions are different from one system to another.

In order to become effective in using a CAD system, we must learn to create geometric entities quickly and accurately. In learning to use a CAD system, **lines** and **circles** are the first two, and perhaps the most important two, geometric entities that one should master the skills of creating and modifying. Straight lines and circles are used in almost all technical designs. In examining the different types of planar geometric entities, the importance of lines and circles becomes obvious. Triangles and polygons are planar figures bounded by straight lines. And ellipses and splines can be constructed by connecting arcs with different radii. As one gains some experience in creating lines and circles, similar procedures can be applied to create other geometric entities. In this chapter, the different ways of creating lines and circles in DraftSight are examined.

Starting Up DraftSight

1. Select the **DraftSight** option on the *Program* menu or select the **DraftSight** icon on the *Desktop*.

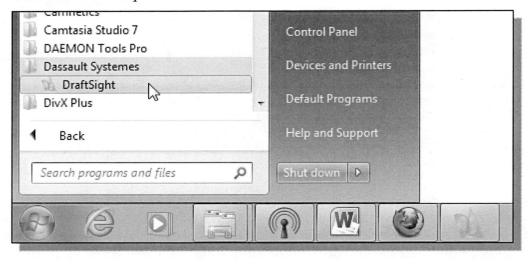

❖ Once the program is loaded into memory, the **DraftSight** drawing screen will appear on the screen.

> Note that DraftSight automatically assigns generic name, *Drawing X*, as new drawings are created. In our example, DraftSight opened the graphics window using the default system units and assigned the drawing name *NoName_0*.

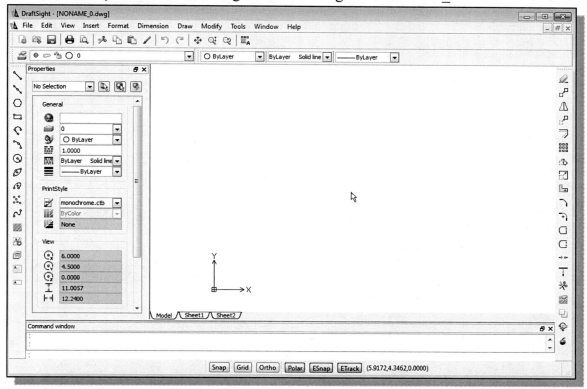

Drawing Units Setup

> Every object we construct in a CAD system is measured in **units**. We should determine the system of units within the CAD system before creating the first geometric entities.

1. In the *Menu Bar* select:
   [Format] → [Units]

- The DraftSight *Menu Bar* contains multiple *Main Menus*, where all of the DraftSight commands can be accessed. Note that many of the menu items listed in the *Main Menus* can also be accessed through the *Quick Access* toolbar and/or *Ribbon* panels.

2. Click on the *Length Type* option to display the different types of length units available. By default, the *Length Type* is set to **Decimal**.

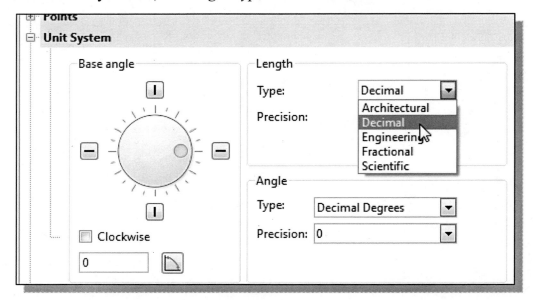

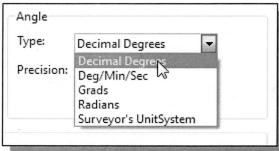

3. On your own, examine the other settings that are available.

4. In the *Drawing Units* dialog box, set the *Length Type* to **Decimal**. This will set the measurement to the default *English* units, inches.

5. Set the *Precision* to **two digits** after the decimal point as shown in the figure to the right.

6. Pick **OK** to exit the *Options* dialog box.

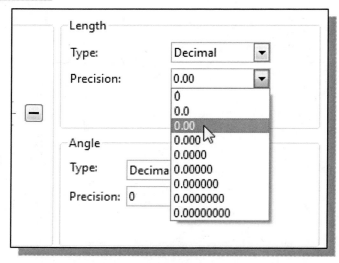

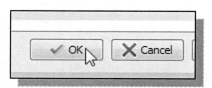

Drawing Area Setup

❖ Next, we will set up the **Drawing Boundary** by entering a command in the command window. Setting the Drawing Boundary controls the extents of the display of the *grid*. It also serves as a visual reference that marks the working area. It can also be used to prevent construction outside the grid limits and as a plot option that defines an area to be plotted/printed. Note that this setting does not limit the region for geometry construction.

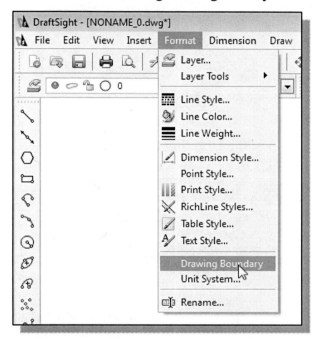

1. In the *Menu Bar* select:
   [Format] → [Drawing Boundary]

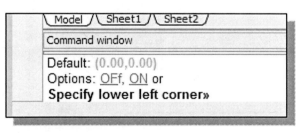

2. In the command window, the message *"Reset Model Space Limits: Specify lower left corner or [On/Off] <0.00,0.00>:"* is displayed. Press the [**ENTER**] key once to accept the default coordinates <**0.00,0.00**>.

3. In the command window, the message *"Specify upper right corner <12.00,9.00>:"* is displayed. Press the [**ENTER**] key again to accept the default coordinates <**12.00,9.00**>.

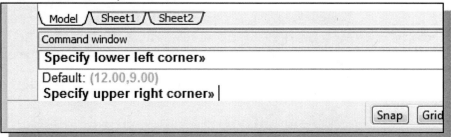

Drawing lines with the *LINE* command

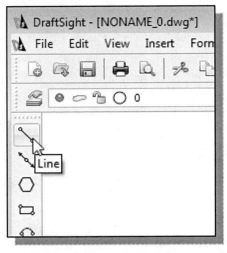

1. Move the graphics cursor to the first icon in the *Draw* toolbar. This icon is the **Line** icon.

2. Select the icon by clicking once with the **left-mouse-button**, which will activate the Line command.

3. In the command window, near the bottom of the DraftSight drawing screen, the message "*_line Specify first point:*" is displayed. DraftSight expects us to identify the starting location of a straight line. Move the graphics cursor inside the graphics window and watch the display of the coordinates of the graphics cursor at the bottom of the DraftSight drawing screen. The three numbers represent the location of the cursor in the X, Y, and Z directions. We can treat the graphics window as if it were a piece of paper and we are using the graphics cursor as if it were a pencil with which to draw.

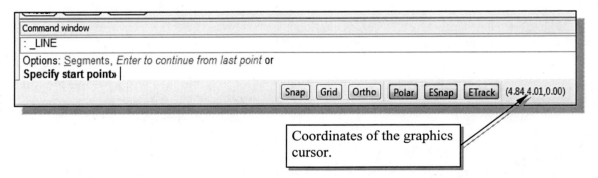

Coordinates of the graphics cursor.

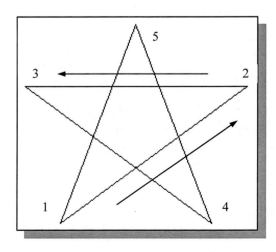

❖ We will create a freehand sketch of a five-point star using the Line command. Do not be overly concerned with the actual size or the accuracy of your freehand sketch. This exercise is to give you a feel for the DraftSight user interface.

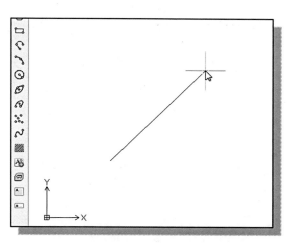

4. We will start at a location about one-third from the bottom of the graphics window. Left-click once to position the starting point of our first line. This will be *point 1* of our sketch. Next move the cursor upward and toward the right side of *point 1*. Notice the rubber-band line that follows the graphics cursor in the graphics window. Left-click again (*point 2*) and we have created the first line of our sketch.

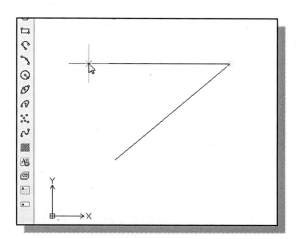

5. Move the cursor to the left of *point 2* and create a horizontal line about the same length as the first line on the screen.

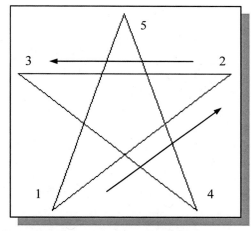

6. Repeat the above steps and complete the freehand sketch by adding three more lines (from *point 3* to *point 4*, *point 4* to *point 5*, and then connect to *point 5* back to *point 1*).

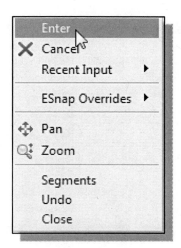

7. Notice that the **Line** command remains activated even after we connected the last segment of the line to the starting point *(point 1)* of our sketch. Inside the graphics window, **click once** with the **right-mouse-button** and a popup menu appears on the screen.

8. Select **Enter** with the left-mouse-button to end the **Line** command. (This is equivalent to hitting the [**ENTER**] key on the keyboard.)

9. Move the cursor near *point 2* and *point 3*, and estimate the length of the horizontal line by watching the displayed coordinates for each point.

Visual reference

The method we just used to create the freehand sketch is known as the **interactive method**, where we use the cursor to specify locations on the screen. This method is perhaps the fastest way to specify locations on the screen. However, it is rather difficult to try to create a line of a specific length by watching the displayed coordinates. It would be helpful to know what one inch or one meter looks like on the screen while we are creating entities. DraftSight provides us with many tools to aid the construction of our designs. For example, the **GRID** and **SNAP MODE** options can be used to get a visual reference as to the size of objects and learn to restrict the movement of the cursor to a set increment on the screen.

The **GRID** and **SNAP MODE** options can be turned *ON* or *OFF* through the *Status Bar*. The *Status Bar* area is located at the bottom left of the DraftSight drawing screen, next to the cursor coordinates.

The first button in the *Status Bar* is the *SNAP MODE* option and the second button is the *GRID DISPLAY* option. Note that the buttons in the *Status Bar* area serve two functions: (1) to display the status of the specific option, and (2) as toggle switches that can be used to turn these special options *ON* and *OFF*. When the corresponding button is *highlighted*, the specific option is turned *ON*. Use the buttons is a quick and easy way to make changes to these *drawing aid* options. Another aspect of the buttons in the *Status Bar* is these options can be switched *ON* and *OFF* in the middle of another command.

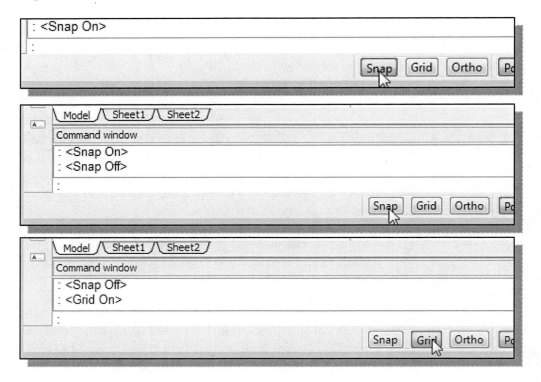

GRID ON

1. Left-click the **GRID** button in the *Status Bar* to turn **ON** the *GRID DISPLAY* option. (Notice in the command window, the message "*<Grid on>*" is also displayed.)

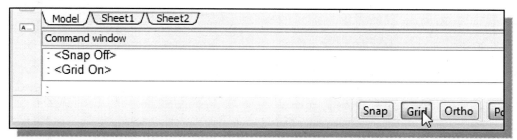

2. Move the cursor inside the graphics window, and estimate the distance in between the grid lines by watching the coordinates display at the bottom of the screen.

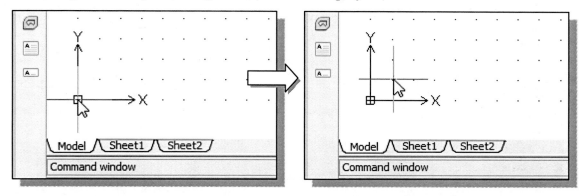

➢ The *GRID* option creates a pattern of lines that extends over an area on the screen. Using the grid is similar to placing a sheet of grid paper under a drawing. The grid helps you align objects and visualize the distance between them. The grid is not displayed in the plotted drawing. The default grid spacing, which means the distance in between two lines on the screen, is 0.5 inches. We can see that the sketched horizontal line in the sketch is about 5.5 inches long.

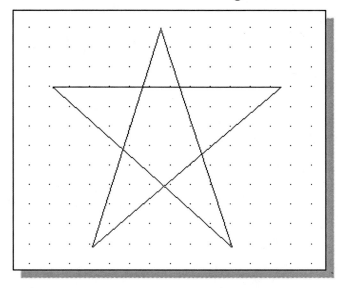

SNAP MODE ON

1. Left-click the ***SNAP MODE*** button in the *Status Bar* to turn ***ON*** the *SNAP* option.

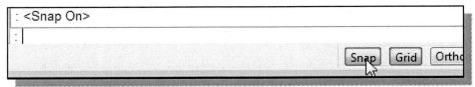

2. Move the cursor inside the graphics window, and move the cursor diagonally on the screen. Observe the movement of the cursor and watch the *coordinates display* at the bottom of the screen.

➢ The *SNAP* option controls an invisible rectangular grid that restricts cursor movement to specified intervals. When *SNAP* mode is on, the screen cursor and all input coordinates are snapped to the nearest point on the grid. The default snap interval is 0.5 inches, and aligned to the grid points on the screen.

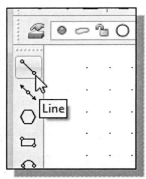

3. Click on the **Line** icon in the *Draw* toolbar. In the command window, the message "*_line Specify first point:*" is displayed.

4. On your own, create another sketch of the five-point star with the *GRID* and *SNAP* options switched *ON*.

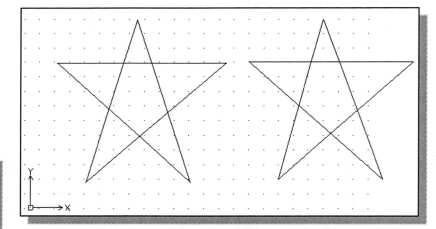

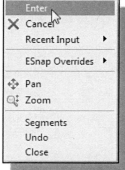

5. Use the **right-mouse-button** and select **Enter** in the popup menu to end the **Line** command if you have not done so.

Using the *DELETE* command

❖ One of the advantages of using a CAD system is the ability to remove entities without leaving any marks. We will delete two of the lines using the **Delete** command.

1. Pick **Delete** in the *Modify* toolbar. (The icon is a picture of an eraser at the end of a pencil.) The message *"Select objects"* is displayed in the command window and DraftSight awaits us to select the objects to delete.

2. Left-click the ***SNAP MODE*** button on the *Status Bar* to turn ***OFF*** the *SNAP MODE* option so that we can more easily move the cursor on top of objects. We can toggle the *Status Bar* options *ON* or *OFF* in the middle of another command.

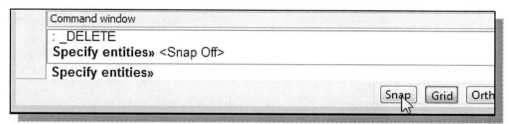

3. Select any two lines on the screen; the selected lines are displayed as dashed lines as shown in the figure below.

➤ To **deselect** an object from the selection set, hold down the [**SHIFT**] key and select the object again.

4. **Right-mouse-click** once to accept the selections. The selected two lines are deleted.

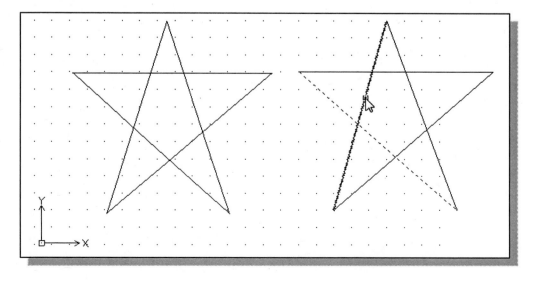

Repeat the last command

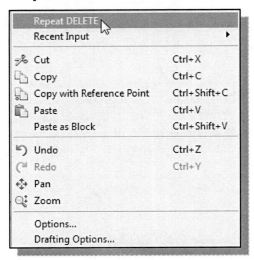

1. Inside the graphics window, click once with the right-mouse-button to bring up the popup option menu.

2. Pick **Repeat Delete**, with the left-mouse-button, in the popup menu to repeat the last command. Notice the other options available in the popup menu.

➤   DraftSight offers many options to accomplish the same task. Throughout this text, we will emphasize the use of the DraftSight heads-up interface, which means we focus on the screen, not on the keyboard.

3. Move the cursor to a location that is above and toward the left side of the entities on the screen. Left-mouse-click once to start a corner of a rubber-band window.

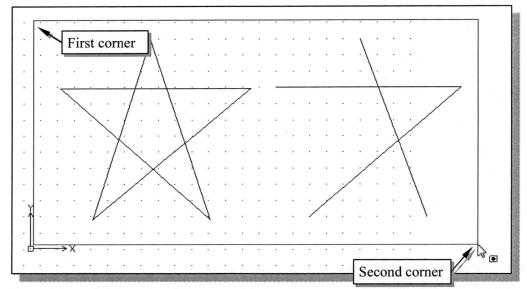

4. Move the cursor towards the right and below the entities, and then left-mouse-click to enclose all the entities inside the **selection window**. Notice all entities that are inside the window are selected.

5. Inside the graphics window, right-mouse-click once to proceed with erasing the selected entities.

➤   On your own, create a free-hand sketch of your choice using the **Line** command. Experiment with using the different commands we have discussed so far. Reset the status buttons so that only the **_GRID DISPLAY_** option is turned **_ON_** as shown.

The CAD Database and the User Coordinate System

❖ Designs and drawings created in a CAD system are usually defined and stored using sets of points in what is called **world space**. In most CAD systems, the world space is defined using a three-dimensional *Cartesian coordinate system*. Three mutually perpendicular axes, usually referred to as the X-, Y-, and Z-axes, define this system. The intersection of the three coordinate axes forms a point called the **origin**. Any point in world space can then be defined as the distance from the origin in the X-, Y- and Z-directions. In most CAD systems, the directions of the arrows shown on the axes identify the positive sides of the coordinates.

A CAD file, which is the electronic version of the design, contains data that describes the entities created in the CAD system. Information such as the coordinate values in world space for all endpoints, center points, etc., along with the descriptions of the types of entities are all stored in the file. Knowing that DraftSight stores designs by keeping coordinate data helps us understand the inputs required to create entities.

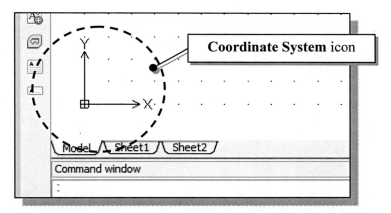

The icon near the bottom left corner of the default DraftSight graphics window shows the positive X-direction and positive Y-direction of the coordinate system that is active. In DraftSight, the coordinate system that is used to create entities is called the **custom coordinate system** (CCS). By default, the **user coordinate system** is aligned to the **world coordinate system** (WCS). The **world coordinate system** is a coordinate system used by DraftSight as the basis for defining all objects and other coordinate systems defined by the users. We can think of the **origin** of the **world coordinate system** as a fixed point being used as a reference for all measurements. The default orientation of the Z-axis can be considered as positive values in front of the monitor and negative values inside the monitor.

Cartesian and Polar Coordinate Systems

In a two-dimensional space, a point can be represented using different coordinate systems. The point can be located, using a *Cartesian coordinate system*, as X and Y units away from the origin. The same point can also be located using the *polar coordinate system*, as r and θ units away from the origin.

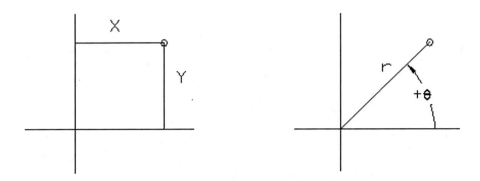

For planar geometry, the polar coordinate system is very useful for certain applications. In the polar coordinate system, points are defined in terms of a radial distance, r, from the origin and an angle, θ, between the direction of r and the positive X axis. The default system for measuring angles in DraftSight defines positive angular values as counter-clockwise from the positive X-axis.

Absolute and Relative Coordinates

- DraftSight also allows us to use *absolute* and *relative coordinates* to quickly construct objects. **Absolute coordinate values** are measured from the current coordinate system's origin point. **Relative coordinate values** are specified in relation to previous coordinates.

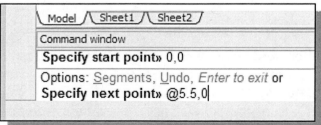

- In DraftSight, the *absolute* coordinates and the *relative* coordinates can be used in conjunction with the *Cartesian* and *polar* coordinate systems. By default, DraftSight expects us to enter values in *absolute Cartesian coordinates*, distances measured from the current coordinate system's origin point. We can switch to using the *relative coordinates* by using the @ symbol. The @ symbol is used as the *relative coordinates specifier*, which means that we can specify the position of a point in relation to the previous point.

Defining Positions

In DraftSight there are five methods for specifying the locations of points when we create planar geometric entities.

> **Interactive method**: Use the cursor to select on the screen.

> **Absolute coordinates (Format: X,Y)**: Type the X and Y coordinates to locate the point on the current coordinate system relative to the origin.

> **Relative rectangular coordinates (Format: @X,Y)**: Type the X and Y coordinates relative to the last point.

> **Relative polar coordinates (Format: @Distance<angle)**: Type a distance and angle relative to the last point.

> **Direct Distance entry technique**: Specify a second point by first moving the cursor to indicate direction and then entering a distance.

The *GuidePlate*

We will next create a mechanical design using the different coordinate entry methods.

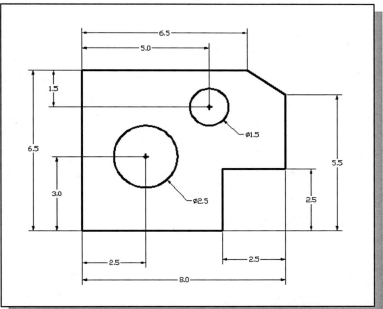

❖ The rule for creating CAD designs and drawings is that they should be created at **full size** using real-world units. The CAD database contains all the definitions of the geometric entities and the design is considered as a virtual, full-sized object. Only when a printer or plotter transfers the CAD design to paper is the design scaled to fit on a sheet. The tedious task of determining a scale factor so that the design will fit on a sheet of paper is taken care of by the CAD system. This allows the designers and CAD operators to concentrate their attention on the more important issues – the design.

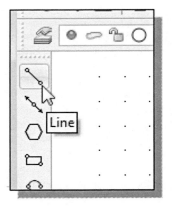

1. Select the **Line** command icon in the *Draw* toolbar. In the command window, near the bottom of the DraftSight graphics window, the message "*_line Specify start point:*" is displayed. DraftSight expects us to identify the starting location of a straight line.

2. We will locate the starting point of our design at the origin of the *world coordinate system*.

   Command: _line Specify first point: **0,0**
   (Type **0,0** and press the [**ENTER**] key once.)

3. We will create a horizontal line by entering the absolute coordinates of the second point.
   Specify next point: **5.5,0** [**ENTER**]

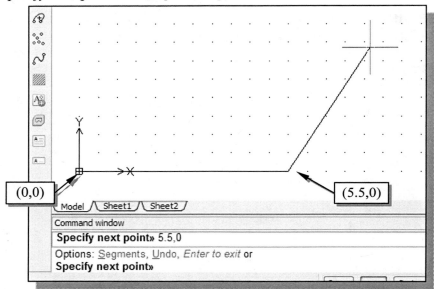

- Note that the line we created is aligned to the bottom edge of the drawing window. Let us adjust the view of the line by using the **Pan Dynamic** command.

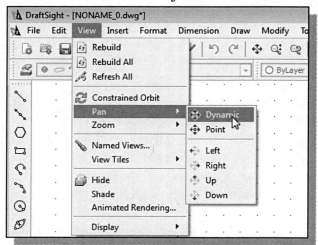

4. In the *Main Menu* select:
   [**View**] → [**Pan**] → [**Dynamic**]

❖ The available **Pan** commands enable us to move the view to a different position. The **Pan-Dynamic** function acts as if you are using a video camera.

5. Move the cursor, which appears as a hand inside the graphics window, near the center of the drawing window, then push down the left-mouse-button and drag the display toward the right and top side.

6. Press the **[Esc]** key once to exit the **Pan-Dynamic** command. Notice that DraftSight goes back to the **Line** command.

7. We will create a vertical line by using the *relative rectangular coordinates entry method*, relative to the last point we specified:
   Specify next point or [Close/Undo]: **@0,2.5 [ENTER]**

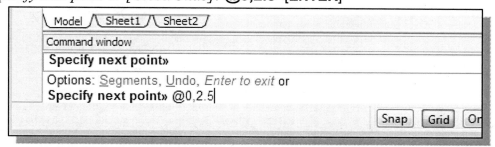

8. We can mix any of the entry methods in positioning the locations of the endpoints. Move the cursor to the *Status Bar* area, and turn **ON** the *SNAP MODE* option.

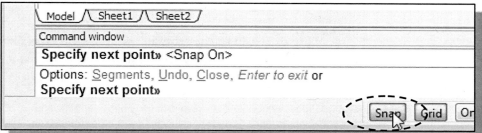

❖ Note that the **Line** command is resumed as the settings are adjusted.

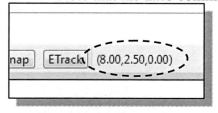

9. Create the next line by picking the location, world coordinates (**8,2.5**), on the screen.

❖ We will next use the *relative polar coordinates entry method*, relative to the last point we specified:
   Specify next point or [Close/Undo]: **@3<90 [ENTER]**
   (Distance is **3** inches with an angle of **90** degrees.)

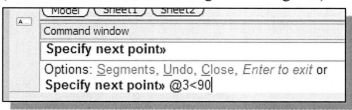

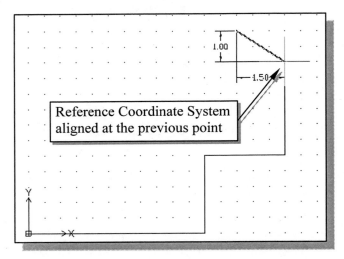

Reference Coordinate System
aligned at the previous point

10. Using the *relative rectangular coordinates entry method* to create the next line, we can imagine a *reference coordinate system* aligned at the previous point. Coordinates are measured along the two reference axes.

Specify next point or [Close/ Undo]: **@-1.5,1 [ENTER]**

(**-1.5** and **1** inches are measured relative to the reference point.)

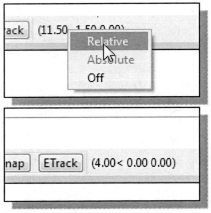

11. Right-click once on the coordinates display area to bring up the option menu and notice the display is set to the default **Absolute** option. Select **Relative** to switch to the relative coordinates display option.

• Note the coordinates display area has changed to show the length of the new line and its angle.

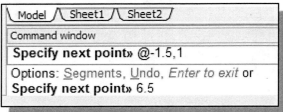

12. Move the cursor directly to the left of the last point and use the *direct distance entry technique* by entering **6.5 [ENTER]**.

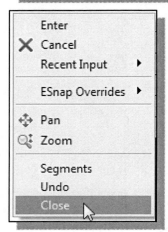

13. For the last segment of the sketch, we can use the **Close** option to connect back to the starting point. Inside the graphics window, **right-mouse-click** and a *popup menu* appears on the screen.

14. Select **Close** with the left-mouse-button to connect back to the starting point and end the **Line** command.

Creating *Circles*

- The menus and toolbars in DraftSight are designed to allow the CAD operators to quickly activate the desired commands.

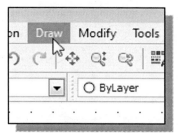

1. In the *Draw* toolbar, click on the little triangle below the circle icon. Note that the little triangle indicates additional options are available.

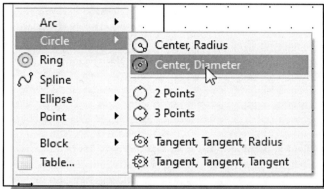

2. In the option list, select:
   [Circle] → [Center, Diameter]

Notice the different options available under the *Circle* submenu:

- **Center, Radius**: Draws a circle based on a center point and a radius.

- **Center, Diameter**: Draws a circle based on a center point and a diameter.

- **2 Points**: Draws a circle based on two endpoints of the diameter.

- **3 Points**: Draws a circle based on three points on the circumference.

- **Tangent, Tangent, Radius**: Draws a circle with a specified radius tangent to two objects.

- **Tangent, Tangent, Tangent**: Draws a circle tangent to three objects.

3. In the command window, the message *"Specify center point:"* is displayed. DraftSight expects us to identify the location of a point or enter an option. We can use any of the four coordinate entry methods to identify the desired location. We will enter the **world coordinates (2.5,3)** as the center point for the first circle. *Specify center point:* **2.5,3 [ENTER]**

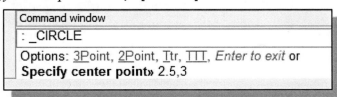

4. In the command window, the message "*Specify diameter of circle:*" is displayed.
    Specify diameter of circle: **2.5 [ENTER]**

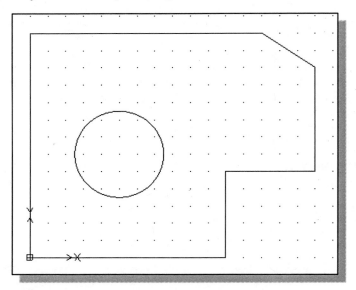

5. Inside the graphics window, right-mouse-click to bring up the popup option menu.

6. Pick **Repeat CIRCLE** with the left-mouse-button in the popup menu to repeat the last command.

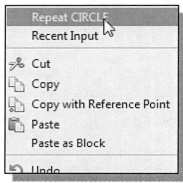

7. Using the *relative rectangular coordinates entry method*, relative to the center-point coordinates of the first circle, we specify the location as (**2.5,2**).
    Specify center point for circle: **@2.5,2 [ENTER]**

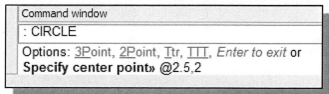

8. In the command window, the message "*Specify Radius*" is displayed. The default option for the Circle command in DraftSight is to specify the *radius*.

9. Inside the graphics window, **right-mouse-click** to bring up the popup option menu and select **Diameter** as shown.

10. In the command window, enter **1.5** as the diameter.

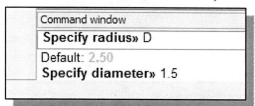

Specify Diameter of circle<2.50>: **1.5**
[ENTER]

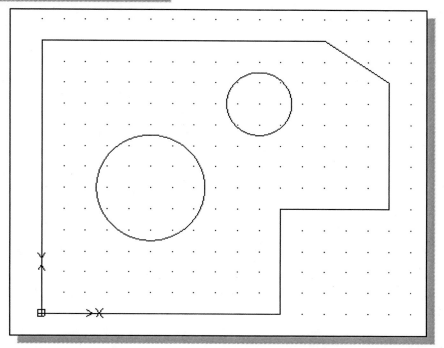

Saving the CAD Design

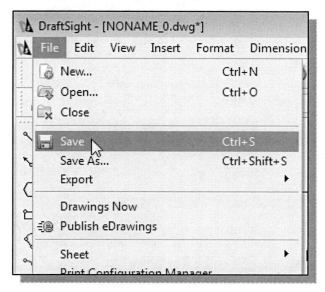

1. In the *Main Menu*, select:

   [File] → [Save]

❖ Note the command can also be activated with quick-key combination of **[Ctrl]+[S]**.

2. In the *Save Drawing As* dialog box, select the folder in which you want to store the CAD file and enter **GuidePlate** in the *File name* box.

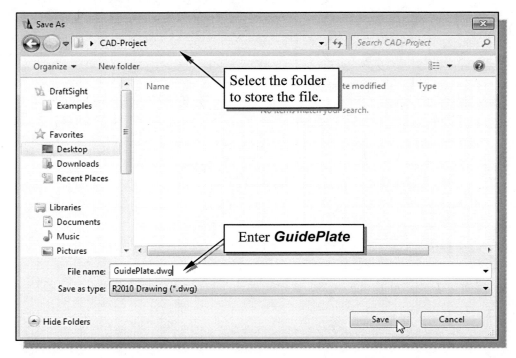

3. Click **Save** in the *Save Drawing As* dialog box to accept the selections and save the file. Note the default file type is DWG, which is the standard DraftSight drawing format.

Close the Current Drawing

❖ Several options are available to close the current drawing:

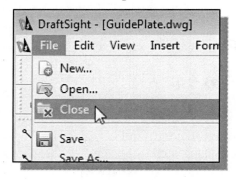

➢ Select **[File] → [Close]** in the *Main Menu Bar* as shown.

➢ Enter **Close** at the command window.

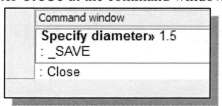

➢ The third option is to click on the **Close** icon, located at the upper-right-hand corner of the drawing window.

The *Spacer* design

❖ We will next create the *Spacer* design using more of the DraftSight's drawing tools.

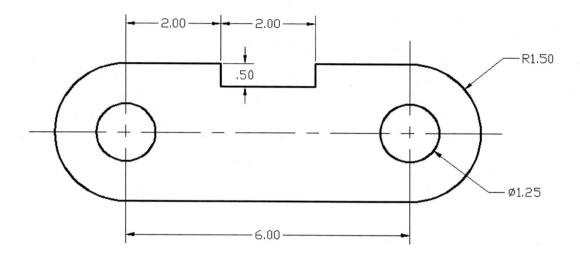

Start a New Drawing

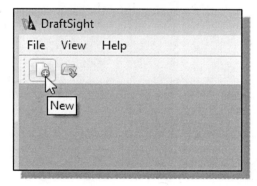

1. In the *Standard* toolbar area, select **[New]** to start a new drawing.

2. The ***Specify Template*** dialog box appears on the screen. Accept the default **Standard.dwt** as the template to open.

➤ The dwt file type is the DraftSight template file format. A DraftSight template file contains pre-defined settings to reduce the amount of tedious repetitions.

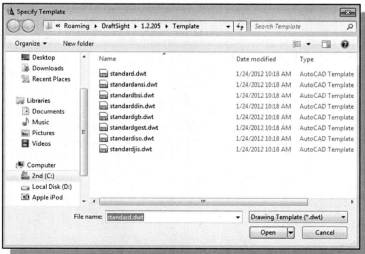

Drawing Units Setup

➢ Every object we construct in a CAD system is measured in **units**. We should determine the system of units within the CAD system before creating the first geometric entities.

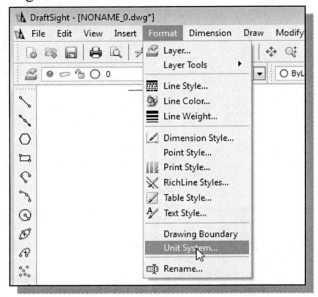

1. In the *Menu Bar* select:
   [Format] → [Units]

2. In the *Drawing Units* dialog box, set the *Length Type* to **Decimal**. This will set the measurement to the default *English* units, inches.

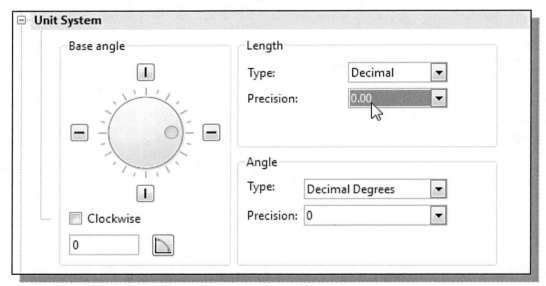

3. Set the *Precision* to **two digits** after the decimal point as shown in the figure above.

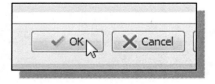

4. Pick **OK** to exit the *Options* dialog box.

Drawing Area Setup

❖ Next, we will set up the **Drawing Boundary** by entering a command in the command window. Setting the Drawing Boundary controls the extents of the display of the *grid.* It also serves as a visual reference that marks the working area.

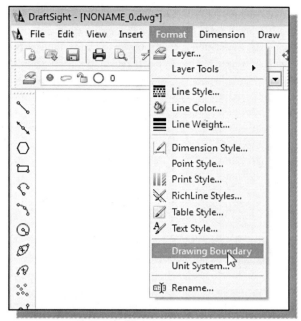

1. In the *Menu Bar* select:
[Format] → [Drawing Boundary]

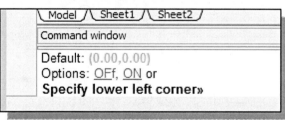

2. In the command window, the message "*Reset Model Space Limits: Specify lower left corner or [On/Off] <0.00,0.00>:*" is displayed. Press the **[ENTER]** key once to accept the default coordinates **<0.00,0.00>**.

3. In the command window, the message "*Specify upper right corner <12.00,9.00>:*" is displayed. Press the **[ENTER]** key again to accept the default coordinates **<12.00,9.00>**.

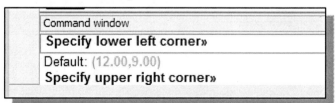

➢ On your own, reset the status buttons so that only **GRID DISPLAY** and **SNAP MODE** are turned **ON** as shown.

Using the Line Command

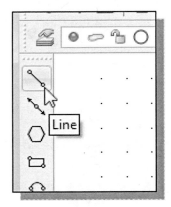

1. Select the **Line** command icon in the *Draw* toolbar. In the command window, near the bottom of the *DraftSight* graphics window, the message "*_line Specify first point:*" is displayed. DraftSight expects us to identify the starting location of a straight line.

2. To further illustrate the usage of the different input methods and tools available in *DraftSight*, we will start the line segments at an arbitrary location. Start at a location that is somewhere in the lower left side of the graphics window.

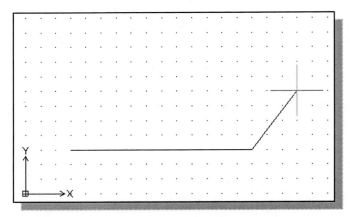

3. We will create a horizontal line by using the *relative rectangular coordinates entry method*, relative to the last point we specified: **@6,0 [ENTER]**

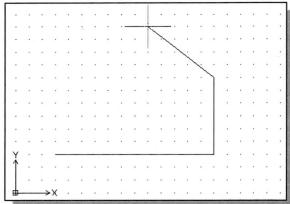

4. Next, create a vertical line by using the *relative polar coordinates entry method*, relative to the last point we specified: **@3<90 [ENTER]**

5. Next, we will use the *direct input method*; first, move the cursor directly to the left of the last endpoint of the line segments.

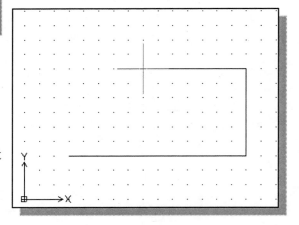

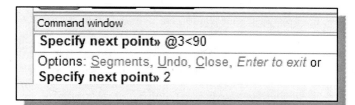

6. Use the *direct distance entry technique* by entering **2** [**ENTER**].

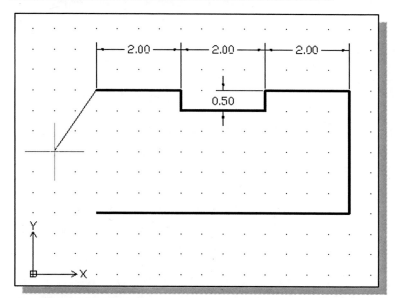

7. On your own, repeat the above steps and create the four additional line segments, using the dimensions as shown.

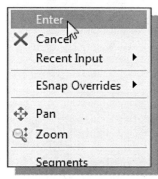

8. To end the Line command, we can either hit the [**ENTER**] key on the keyboard or use the **Enter** option; **right-mouse-click** and a *popup menu* appears on the screen.

9. Select **Enter** with the left-mouse-button to end the Line command.

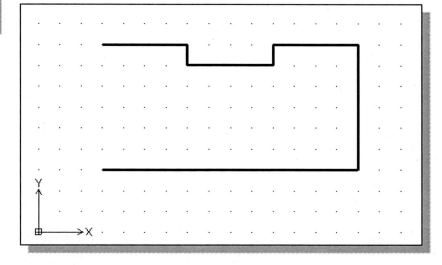

Using the *DELETE* command

❖ The vertical line on the right was created as a construction line, to aid the construction of the rest of the lines for the design. We will use the Delete command to remove it.

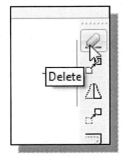

1. Pick **Delete** in the *Modify* toolbar. The message *"Select objects"* is displayed in the command window and DraftSight awaits us to select the objects to delete.

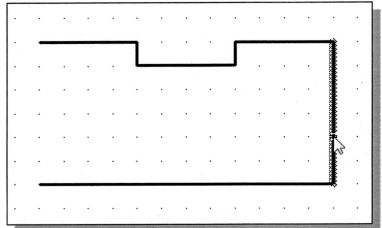

2. Select the vertical line as shown.

3. Click once with the **right-mouse-button** to accept the selection and delete the line.

Using the Arc Command

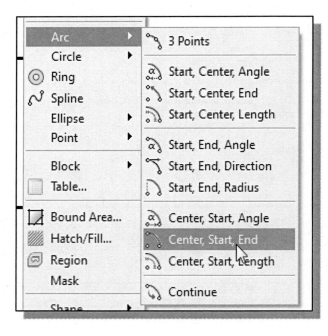

1. Click the **Arc** command in the *Draw* main menu and display the different Arc construction options.

➢ DraftSight provides eleven different ways to create arcs. Note that the different options are used based on the geometry conditions of the design. The more commonly used options are the **3-Points** option and the **Center, Start, End** option.

2. Select the **Center, Start, End** option as shown. This option requires the selection of the center point, start point and end point locations, in that order, of the arc.

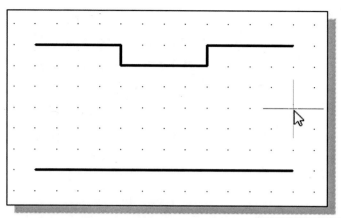

3. Move the cursor to the middle of the two horizontal lines and align the cursor to the two endpoints as shown. Click once with the **right-mouse-button** to select the location as the center point of the new arc.

4. Move the cursor downward and select the right endpoint of the bottom horizontal line as the start point of the arc.

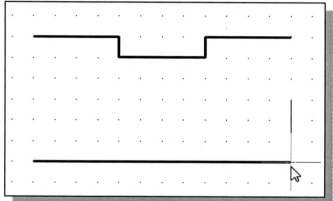

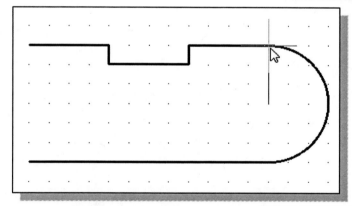

5. Move the cursor to the right endpoint of the top horizontal line as shown. Pick this point as the endpoint of the new arc.

6. On your own, repeat the above steps and create the other arc as shown. Note that in most CAD packages, positive angles are defined as going counterclockwise; therefore the starting point of the second arc is the endpoint on top.

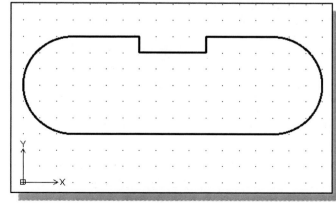

Using the *CIRCLE* command

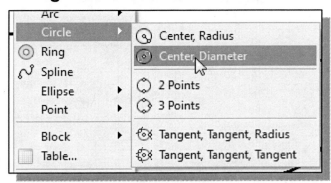

1. Select the **[Circle]** → **[Center, Diameter]** option as shown.

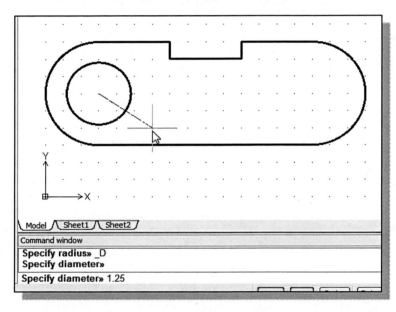

2. Select the same location for the arc center as the center point for the new circle.

3. In the command window, the message "*Specify diameter of circle:*" is displayed. *Specify diameter of circle:* **1.25** **[ENTER]**

4. On your own, create the other circle and complete the drawing as shown.

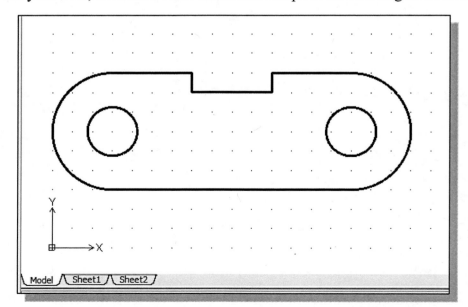

Saving the CAD Design

1. In the *Standard* toolbar, select: **[Save]**

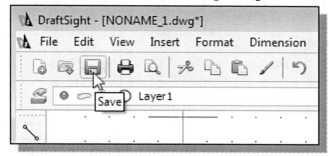

❖ Note the command can also be activated with quick-key combination of **[Ctrl]+[S]**.

2. In the *Save Drawing As* dialog box, select the folder in which you want to store the CAD file and enter **Spacer** in the *File name* box.

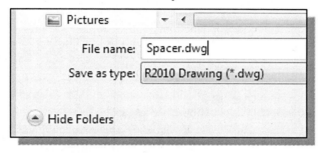

3. Click **Save** in the *Save Drawing As* dialog box to accept the selections and save the file. Note the default file type is DWG, which is the standard DraftSight drawing format.

Exit DraftSight

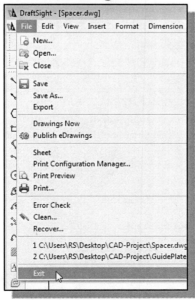

❖ To exit DraftSight, select **Exit DraftSight** in the *Menu Bar* or type **QUIT** at the command prompt. Note the command can also be activated with the quick-key combination of **[Ctrl]+[Q]**.

Review Questions:

1. What are the advantages and disadvantages of using CAD systems to create engineering drawings?

2. What is the default DraftSight filename extension?

3. How do the **GRID** and **SNAP** options assist us in sketching?

4. List and describe the different **coordinate entry methods** available in DraftSight.

5. When using the Line command, which option allows us to quickly create a line-segment connecting back to the starting point?

6. List and describe the two types of coordinate systems commonly used for planar geometry.

7. Which key do you use to quickly cancel a command?

8. When you use the Pan command, do the coordinates of objects get changed?

9. Find information on how to draw ellipses in DraftSight through the *help system* and create the following ellipse. If it is desired to position the center of the ellipse at a specific location, which ellipse command is more suitable?

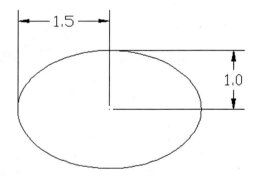

10. Find information on how to draw arcs in DraftSight through the *help system* and create the following arc. List and describe two methods to create arcs in DraftSight.

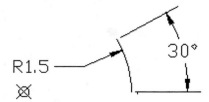

Exercises: (All dimensions are in inches.)

1. Angle Spacer

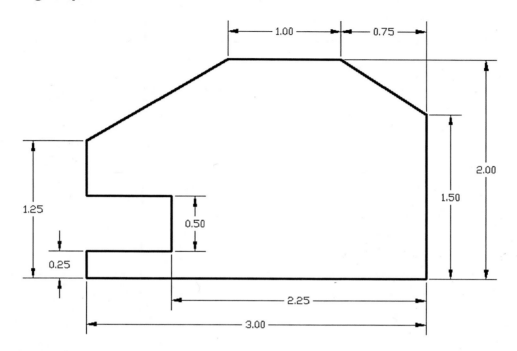

2. Base Plate

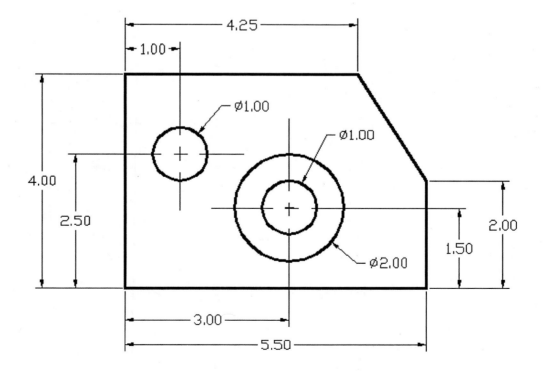

3. T-Clip

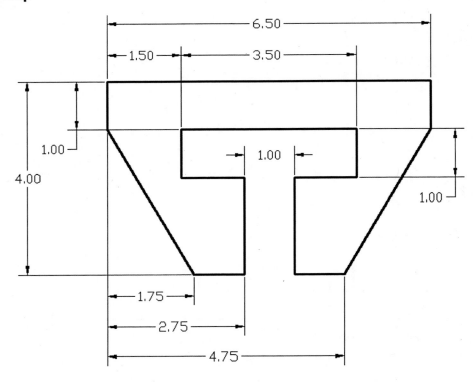

4. Channel Plate

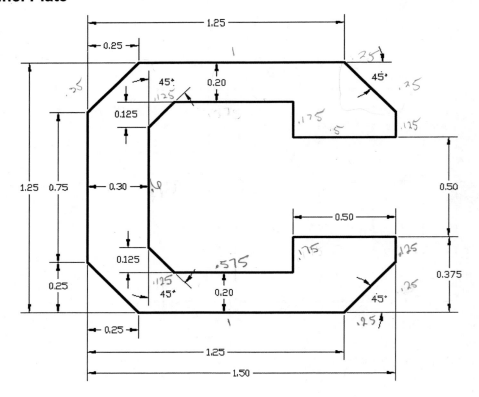

Chapter 2
Geometric Constructions

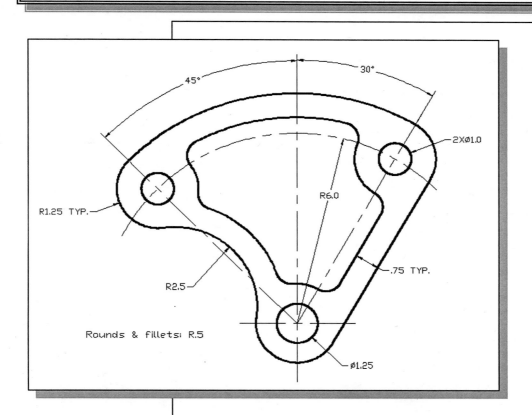

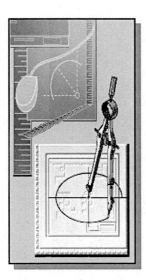

Learning Objectives

- ◆ **Understand the Classic Geometric Construction Tools and Methods**
- ◆ **Reference the WCS**
- ◆ **Use the Startup Dialog Box**
- ◆ **Set Up GRID & SNAP Intervals**
- ◆ **Display DraftSight's Toolbars**
- ◆ **Set Up and Use ENTITY SNAPS**
- ◆ **Edit, Using the TRIM Command**
- ◆ **Use the Polygon Command**
- ◆ **Create Tangent Lines**

Geometric Constructions

The creation of designs usually involves the manipulations of geometric shapes. Traditionally, manual graphical construction uses simple hand tools like T-square, straightedge, scales, triangles, compass, dividers, pencils, and paper. The manual drafting tools are designed specifically to assist the construction of geometric shapes. For example, a T-square and drafting machine can be used to construct parallel and perpendicular lines very easily and quickly. Today, modern CAD systems provide designers much better control and accuracy in the constructions of geometric shapes.

In technical drawings, many of the geometric shapes are constructed with specific geometric properties, such as perpendicularity, parallelism and tangency. For example, in the drawing below, quite a few **implied** geometric properties are present.

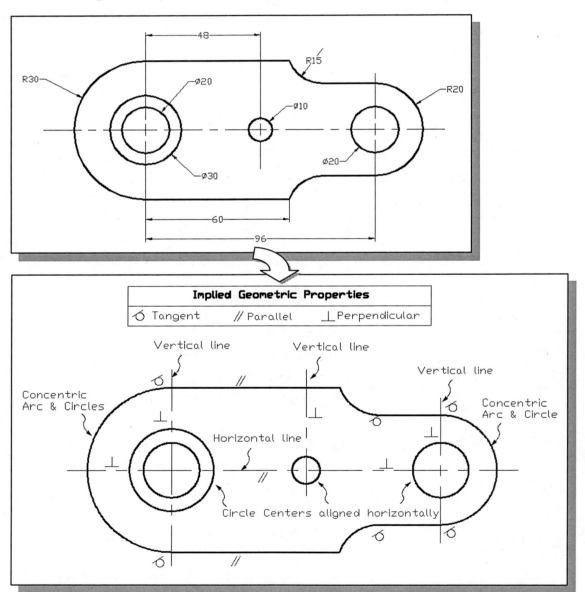

Geometric Constructions – Classical Methods

Geometric constructions are done by applying geometric rules to graphics entities. Knowledge of the principles of geometric construction and its applications are essential to Designers, Engineers and CAD users.

For 2D drawings, it is crucial to be able to construct geometry entities at specified angles to each other, various plane figures, and other graphic representations. In this section, we will examine both the traditional graphical methods and the CAD methods of the basic geometric constructions commonly used in engineering graphics. This chapter provides information that will aid you in drawing different types of geometric constructions.

- **Bisection of a Line or Arc**

    1. Given a line or an arc AB.

    2. From A and B draw two equal arcs with a radius that is greater than one half of line AB.

    3. Construct a line by connecting the intersection points, D and E, with a straight line to locate the midpoint of line AB.

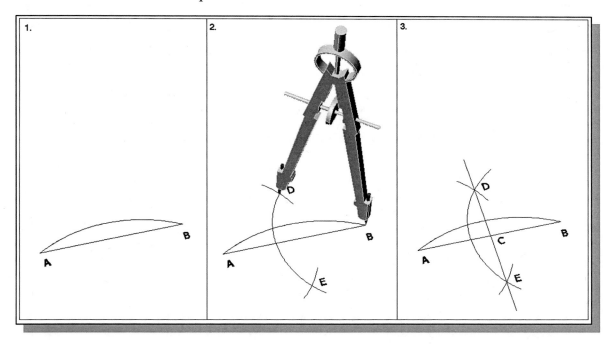

   ❖ Note that the constructed bisecting line DE is also perpendicular to the given line AB at the midpoint C.

• **Bisection of an Angle**

1. Given an angle ABC.

2. From A draw an arc with an arbitrary radius.

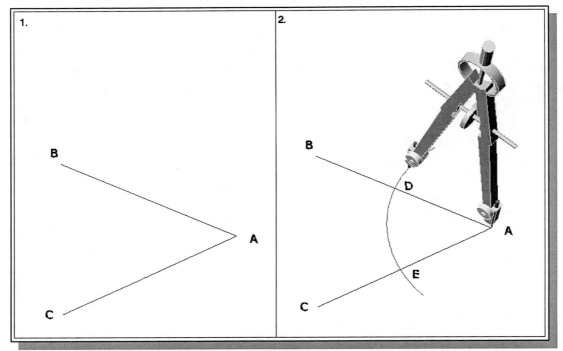

3. Construct two equal radius arcs at D and E.

4. Construct a straight line by connecting point A to the intersection of the two arcs.

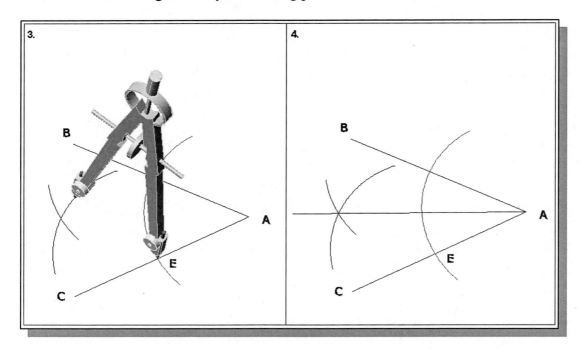

• Transfer of an Angle

1. Given an angle ABC, transfer the angle to line XY.

2. Create two arcs, at A and X, with an arbitrary radius R.

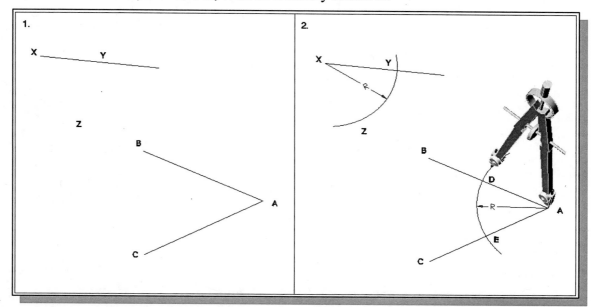

3. Measure the distance between point D and E, using a compass.

4. Construct an arc at Y, using the distance measured in the previous step.

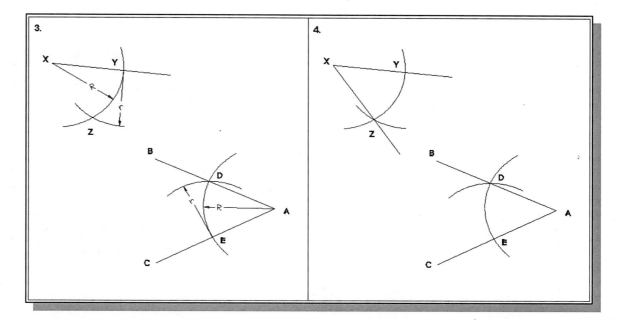

• Dividing a Given Line into a Number of Equal Parts

1. Given a line AB; the line is to be divided into five equal parts.

2. Construct another line at an arbitrary angle. Measure and mark five units along the line.

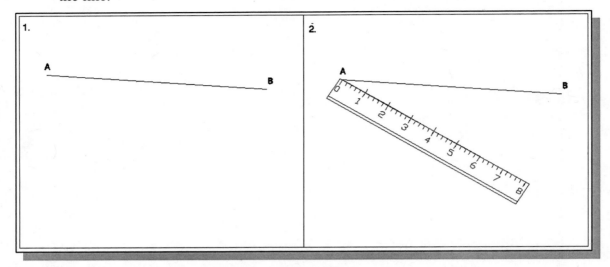

3. Construct a line connecting the fifth mark to point B.

4. Create four lines parallel to the constructed line through the marks.

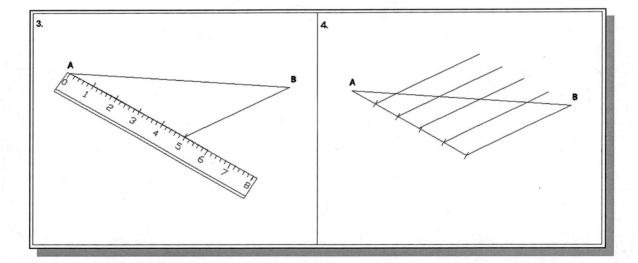

- ## Circle through Three Points

    1. Given three points A, B and C.

    2. Construct a bisecting line through line AB.

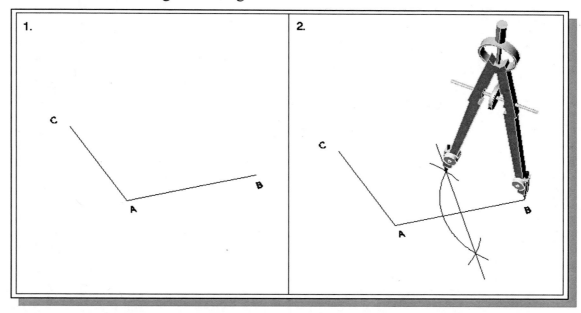

    3. Construct a second bisecting line through line AC. The two bisecting lines
        intersect at point D.

    4. Create the circle at point D, using DA, DB or DC as radius.

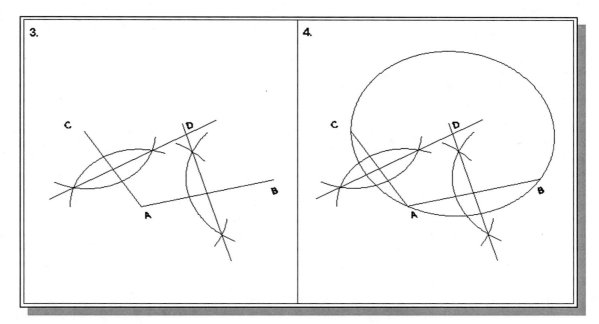

- ## Line Tangent to a Circle from a Given Point

   1. Given a circle, center point C and a point A.

   2. Create a bisecting line through line AC.

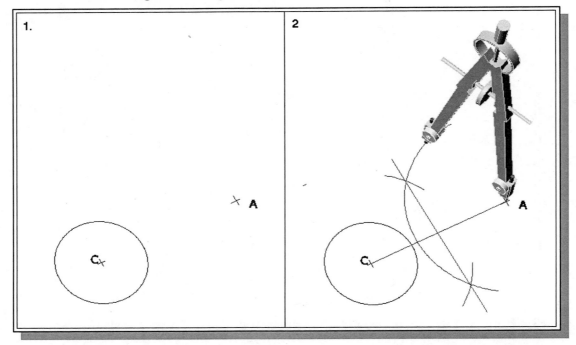

   3. Create an arc at point B (midpoint on line AC), with AB or BC as the radius.

   4. Construct the tangent line by connecting point A at the intersection of the arc and the circle.

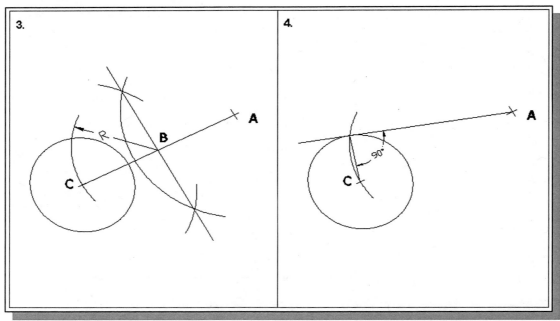

- **Circle of a Given Radius Tangent to Two Given Lines**

    1. Given two lines and a given radius R.

    2. Create a parallel line by creating two arcs of radius R, and draw a line tangent to the two arcs.

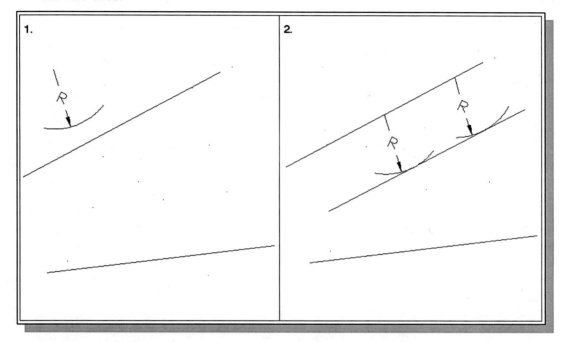

    3. Create another line parallel to the bottom edge by first drawing two arcs.

    4. Construct the required circle at the intersection of the two lines using the given radius R.

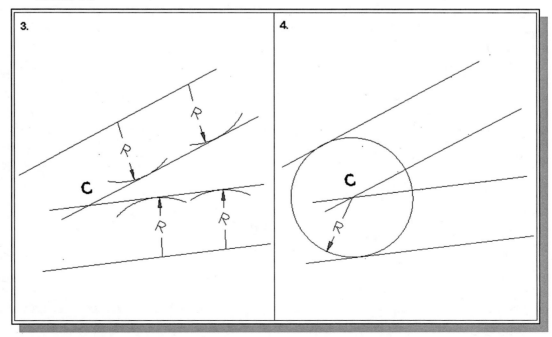

- **Circle of a Given Radius Tangent to an Arc and a Line**

   1. Given a radius R, a line and an arc.

   2. Create a parallel line by creating two arcs of radius R, and draw a line tangent to the two arcs.

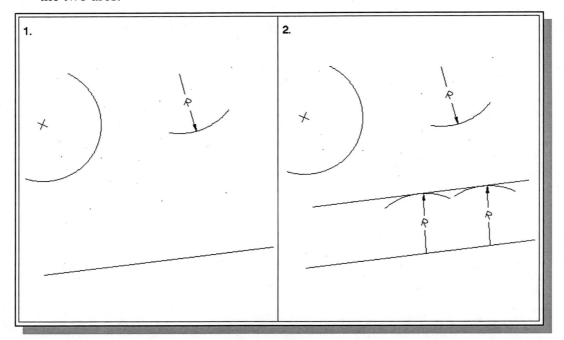

   3. Create a concentric arc at the center of the given arc, using a radius that is r+R.

   4. Create the desired circle at the intersection using the given radius R.

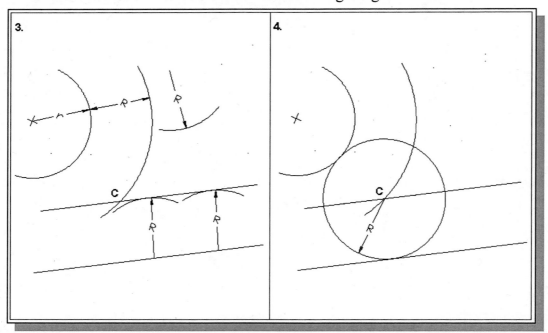

• Circle of a Given Radius Tangent to Two Arcs

1. Given a radius R and two arcs.

2. Create a concentric arc at the center of the small arc, using a radius that is R distance more than the original radius.

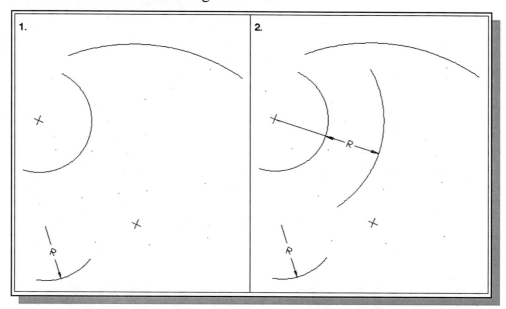

3. Create another concentric arc at the center of the large arc, using a radius that is R distance smaller than the original radius.

4. Create the desired circle at the intersection using the given radius R.

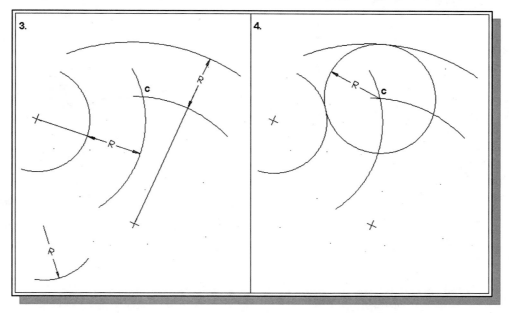

Starting Up DraftSight

1. Start DraftSight by selecting through the **Start** menu as shown. Once the program is loaded into memory, the *DraftSight* drawing screen will appear on the screen.

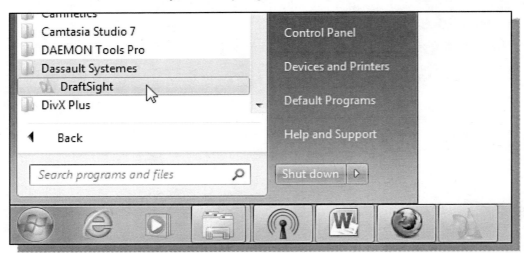

Entity Snap Toolbar

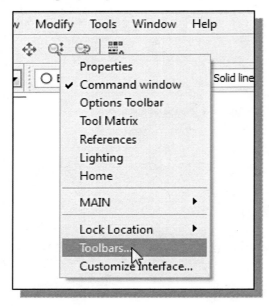

1. Move the cursor on top of any icon in the *Standard* toolbar and right-mouse-click once to display the option menu.

2. In the option list, choose **Toolbars**.

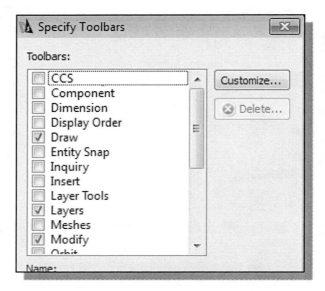

❖ DraftSight provides 22 predefined toolbars for access to frequently used commands, settings, and modes. A *checkmark* (next to the item) in the list identifies the toolbars that are currently displayed on the screen.

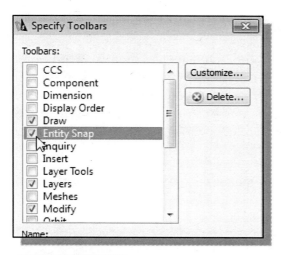

3. Select **Entity Snap**, with the left-mouse-button, to display the *Entity Snap* toolbar on the screen.

❖ **Entity Snap** is an extremely powerful construction tool available on most CAD systems. During an entity's creation operations, we can snap the cursor to points on objects such as endpoints, midpoints, centers, and intersections. For example, we can quickly draw a line to the center of a circle, the midpoint of a line segment, or the intersection of two lines.

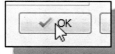

4. Click **OK** to accept the settings.

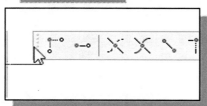

5. On your own, drag the *Entity Snap* toolbar, with the left-mouse-button, to the center of the graphics area.

6. Move the cursor over the icons in the *Entity Snap* toolbar and read the description of each icon.

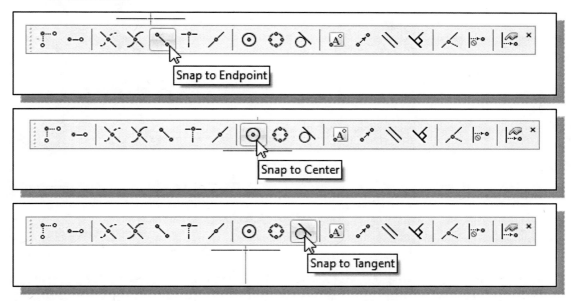

7. On your own, in the *Status Bar* area, reset the option buttons so that only the *GRID DISPLAY* is switched *ON*.

Geometric Construction – CAD Method

The main characteristic of any CAD system is its ability to create and modify 2D/3D geometric entities quickly and accurately. Most CAD systems provide a variety of object construction and editing tools to relieve the designer of the tedious drudgery of this task, so that the designer can concentrate more on design content. A good understanding of the computer geometric construction techniques will enable the CAD user to fully utilize the capability of the CAD system.

➢ Note that with CAD systems, besides following the classic geometric construction methods, quite a few options are also feasible.

• Bisection of a Line or Arc

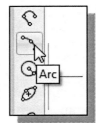

1. Select the **Arc** command icon in the *Draw* toolbar. Create an arbitrary arc **AB** by selecting three locations on the screen.

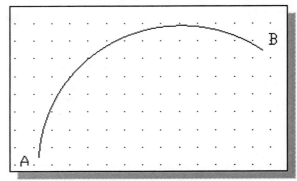

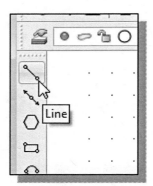

2. Select the **Line** command icon in the *Draw* toolbar.

3. Pick **Snap to Endpoint** in the *Entity Snap* toolbar. In the command window, the message "*_ENDP of*" is displayed

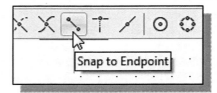

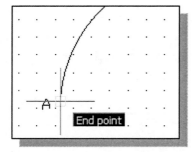

4. Select the left endpoint of the arc to attach the start location for the new line.

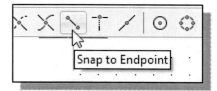

5. Pick **Snap to Endpoint** in the *Entity Snap* toolbar. In the command window, the message "*_ENDP of*" is displayed

6. Select the right endpoint of the arc to attach the end location for the new line.

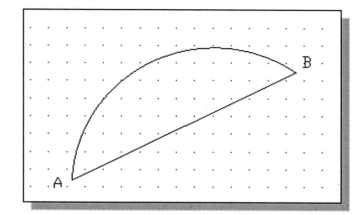

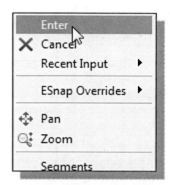

7. To end the Line command, select the **Enter** option by **right-mouse-clicking** in the graphics area.

8. Select the **Line** command icon in the *Draw* toolbar.

9. Pick **Snap to Perpendicular** in the *Entity Snap* toolbar. In the command window, the message "*_per to*" is displayed.

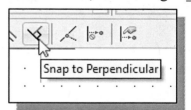

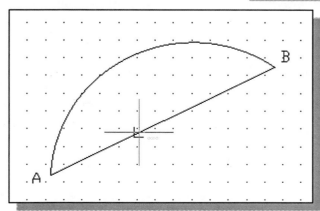

10. Select line **AB** at any position.

❖ Note the ***Perpendicular*** icon is displayed next to the cursor indicating the construction type.

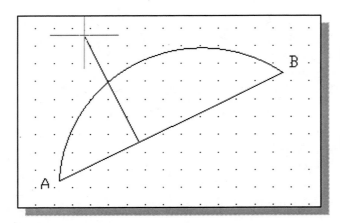

11. Select an arbitrary point above and create a perpendicular line as shown.

12. Hit the [**ENTER**] key once to end the Line command.

13. Select **Move** in the *Modify* toolbar as shown.

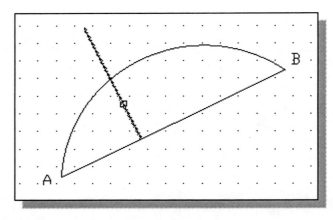

14. Select the perpendicular line we just created.

15. Click once with the right-mouse-button to accept the selection.

❖ In the command window, the message: "*Displacement or Specify from point]*" is displayed. DraftSight expects us to select a reference point as the base point for moving the selected object.

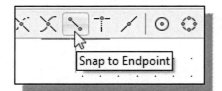

16. Pick **Snap to Endpoint** in the *Entity Snap* toolbar.

17. Select the lower **Endpoint** of the selected line as shown.

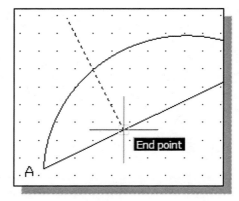

18. Move the cursor inside the graphics window, and notice the line can be moved to any location on the screen,

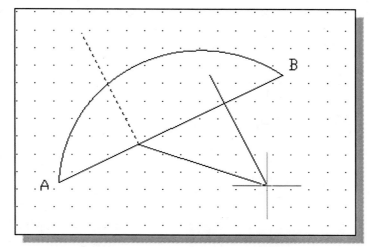

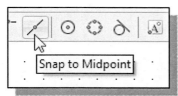

19. Pick **Snap to Midpoint** in the *Entity Snap* toolbar.

❖ In the command window, the message "*_mid to*" is displayed.

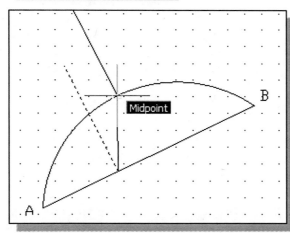

20. Move the cursor on top of the arc and notice the midpoint of the arc is indicated.

• Note that the midpoint of an arc or a line is displayed when the cursor is on top of the object.

21. On your own, move the perpendicular line to the midpoint of line **AB** as shown.

➢ The constructed bisecting line is perpendicular to line **AB** and it also passes through the midpoint of the line or arc **AB**.

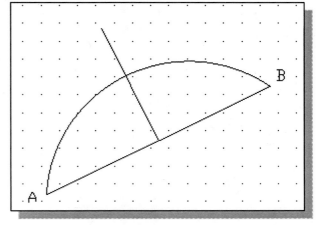

- ## Bisection of an Angle

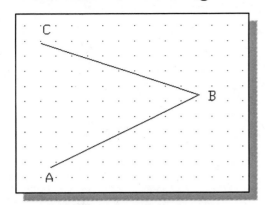

1. Create an arbitrary angle **ABC** as shown in the figure.

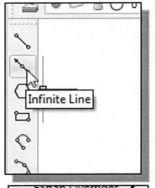

2. Select the **Infinite Line** icon in the *Draw* toolbar. In the command window, the message "*Specify position*" is displayed.

   ➢ *Construction lines* are lines that extend to infinity. Construction lines are usually used as references for creating other objects.

3. Inside the graphics window, **right-mouse-click** once to bring up the option menu.

4. Select **Bisect** from the option list as shown. In the command window, the message "*Specify angle vertex point:*" is displayed.

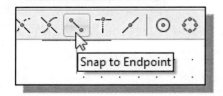

5. Pick **Snap to Endpoint** in the *Entity Snap* toolbar.

6. Select the vertex point of the angle as shown. In the command window, the message "*Specify first angle:*" is displayed.

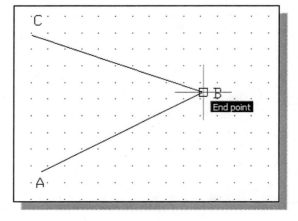

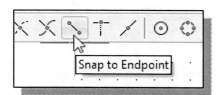

7. Pick **Snap to Endpoint** in the *Entity Snap* toolbar.

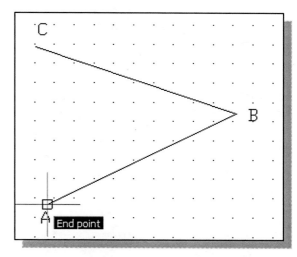

8. Select one of the endpoints of the angle.

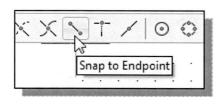

9. Pick **Snap to Endpoint** in the *Entity Snap* toolbar.

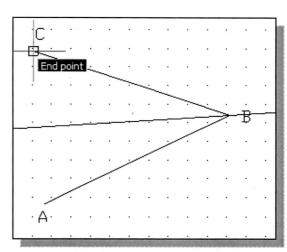

10. Select the other endpoint of the angle.

➤ Note that the constructed bisection line divides the angle into two equal parts.

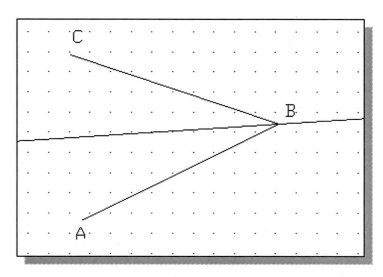

• Dividing a Given Line into a Number of Equal Parts

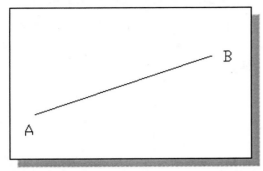

1. Create a line **AB** at an arbitrary angle; the line is to be divided into five equal parts.

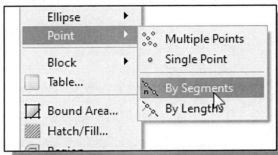

2. From the *Draw* main menu, select:
   [Point] → [By Segments]

3. Select line **AB**. In the command window, the message "*Specify number of segments:*" is displayed.

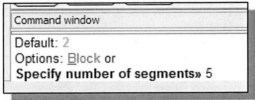

4. Enter **5** as the number of segments needed.

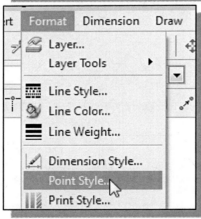

5. From the *Format* main menu, select:
   [Point Style]

6. Select the *point type* as shown.

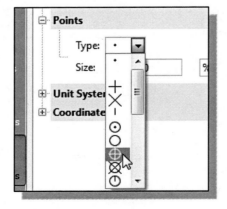

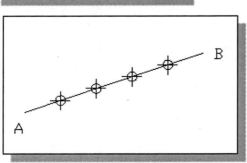

• Circle through Three Points

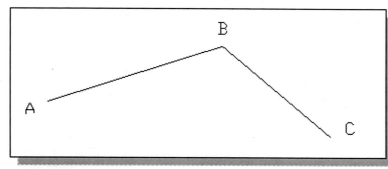

1. Create two arbitrary line segments, **AB** and **BC**, as shown.

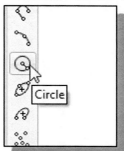

2. Select the **Circle** command in the *Draw* toolbar as shown.

3. Select the **3Point** option in the option menu as shown.

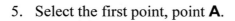

4. Pick **Snap to Endpoint** in the *Entity Snap* toolbar.

5. Select the first point, point **A**.

6. Repeat the above steps and select points **B** and **C** to create the circle that passes through all three points.

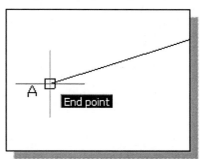

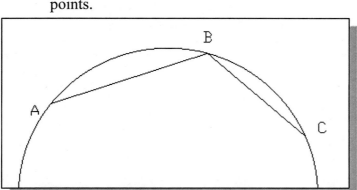

• Line Tangent to a Circle from a Given Point

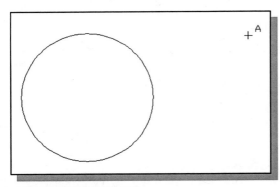

1. Create a circle and a point **A**. (Use the Single Point command to create point **A**.)

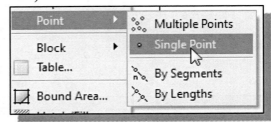

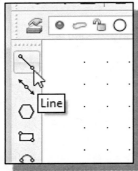

2. Select the **Line** command icon in the *Draw* toolbar. DraftSight expects us to identify the starting location of a straight line.

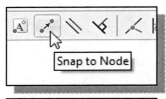

3. Pick **Snap to Node** in the *Entity Snap* toolbar.

4. Select point **A** as the starting point of the new line.

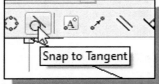

5. Pick **Snap to Tangent** in the *Entity Snap* toolbar.

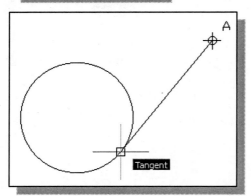

6. Select the circle near the lower right side to create the tangent line as shown.

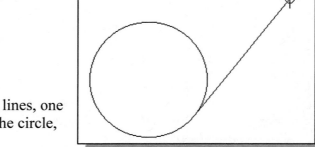

➢ Note that we can create two tangent lines, one to the top and one to the bottom of the circle, from point **A**.

- ## Circle of a Given Radius Tangent to two Given Lines

Option I: TTR circle

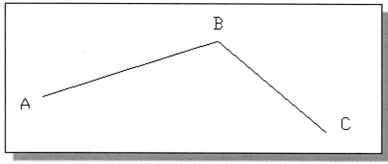

1. Create two arbitrary line segments as shown.

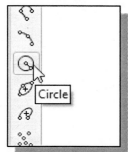

2. Select the **Circle** command in the *Draw* toolbar as shown.

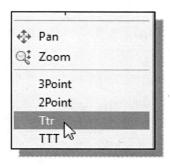

3. Select **Ttr** option in the option menu as shown.

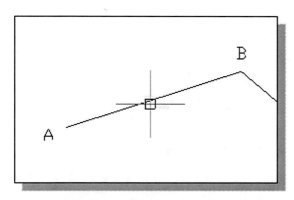

4. Select one of the line segments; note the tangency is deferred until all inputs are completed.

5. Select the other line segment; note the circle is still deferred until all inputs are completed.

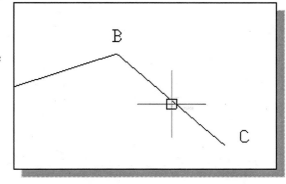

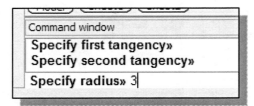

6. Enter **3** as the radius of the circle.

➢ The circle is constructed exactly tangent to both lines.

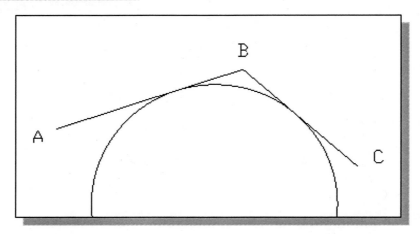

Option II: Fillet command

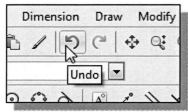

1. Select the **Undo** icon in the *Standard* toolbar as shown. This will undo the last step, the circle.

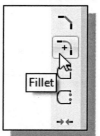

2. Select **Fillet** in the *Modify* toolbar as shown.

3. In the command window, the message "*Select first entity*" is displayed. By default *Mode* is set to **TRIM** and the current arc *Radius* is set to **0.0000** as shown.

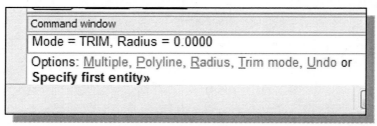

4. Inside the graphics window, **right-mouse-click** once to bring up the option menu.

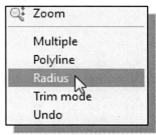

5. Select **Radius** to adjust the radius of the fillet.

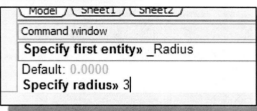

6. Enter **3** as the new radius of the **Fillet** command.

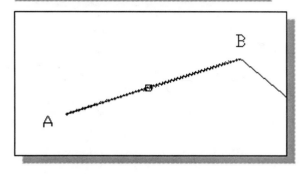

7. Select one of the lines as the first object.

8. Select the other line as the second object.

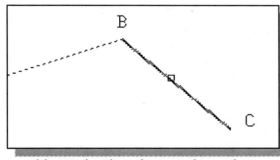

➢ Note that the default setting of the **Fillet** command is to trim the edges as shown in the figure below.

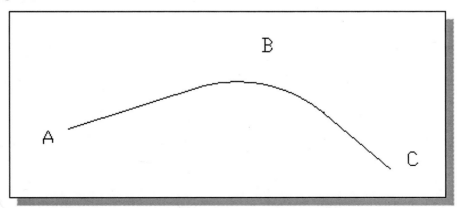

• Note that all of the classical methods for geometric construction, such as the one shown on page 2-10, can also be used in CAD systems.

The *RockerArm* Design

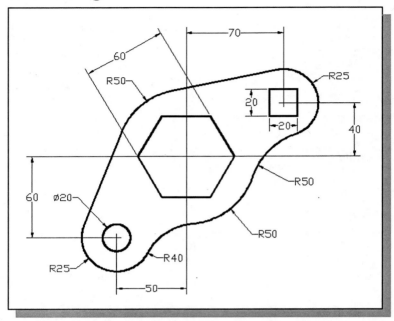

❖ Before continuing to the next page, on your own, make a rough sketch showing the steps that can be used to create the design. Be aware that there are many different approaches to accomplishing the same task.

Start a New File using the StandardISO Template

In DraftSight, we can use the predefined *Templates* to establish different types of drawing settings.

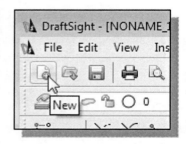

1. In the *Standard* toolbar, select **New** to start a new file.

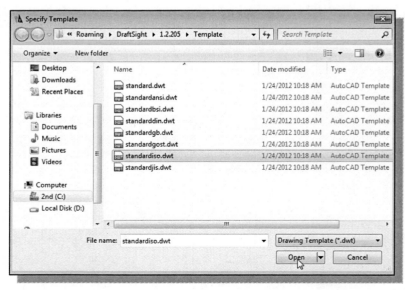

2. In the specify template dialog box, select the metric template, ***StandardISO.dwt*** as shown.

Drawing Units Display Setup

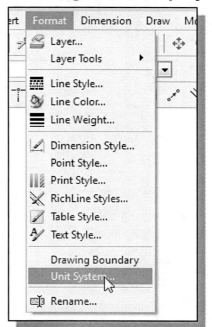

1. In the *Main Menu*, select:
   [Format] → [Unit System]

2. Set the *Precision* to **no digits** after the decimal point.

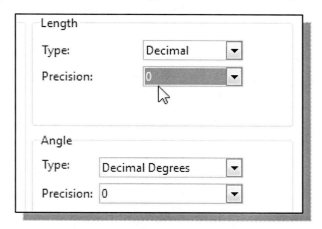

3. Click **OK** to exit the *Drawing Settings* dialog box.

GRID and *SNAP* Intervals Setup

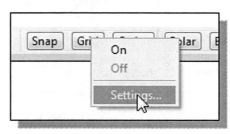

1. In the *Status Bar* area, **right-mouse-click** on *Snap Mode* and choose **[Settings]**.

2. Confirm the *Grid Spacing* is set to **10** for both horizontal and vertical directions.

3. Switch *ON* the *Grid Display* and *Match Snap Spacing* options as shown.

4. Pick **OK** to exit the *User Preferences* dialog box.

5. Switch *ON* the *Snap* option as shown.

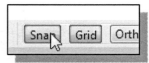

Drawing Area Setup

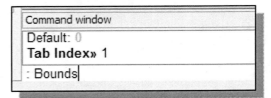

1. Click inside the command window.

2. Inside the command window, enter **Bounds** and press the [**ENTER**] key.

3. In the command window, near the bottom of the DraftSight drawing screen, the message "*Specify lower left corner:*" is displayed. Enter **-200,-100** as shown.

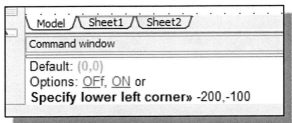

4. In the command window, the message "*Specify upper right corner:*" is displayed. Enter **200,100** as the new upper right coordinates as shown.

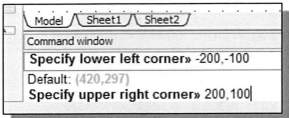

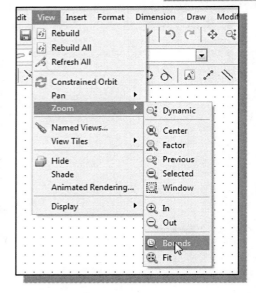

5. In the *Main Menu* select the [**View**] → [**Zoom**] → [**Bounds**] option to adjust the display based on the established drawing boundary.

❖ Notice the *CCS Icon*, which is aligned to the origin of the world coordinate system, is displayed at the center of the graphics window.

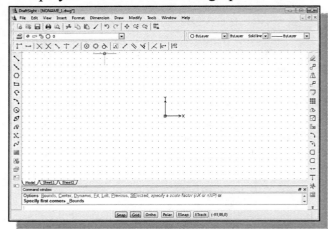

Creating *Circles*

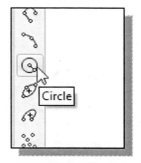

1. Select the **Circle** command icon in the *Draw* toolbar. Note the default Circle command expects the input of the center location and radius of the circle.

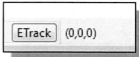

2. Select the **origin** of the world coordinate system as the center point location.

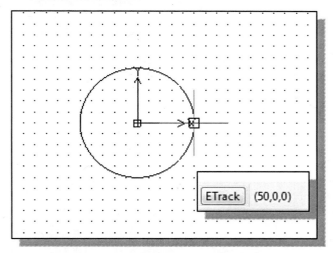

3. In the command window, the message "*Specify radius of circle or [Diameter]:*" is displayed. DraftSight expects us to identify the radius of the circle. Set the radius to **50** by observing the tooltips as shown.

4. Hit the **[SPACE BAR]** once to repeat the **Circle** command.

5. On your own, select **70,40** as the absolute coordinate values of the center point coordinates of the second circle.

6. Set the value of the radius to **25**.

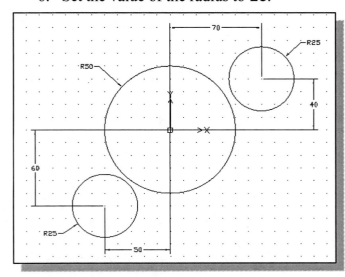

7. On your own, repeat the above procedure and create another circle (radius **25**) at absolute coordinates of **-50,-60** as shown in the figure.

8. On your own, reset the option buttons in the *Status Bar* area, so that only the *GRID DISPLAY* option is switched *ON*.

Using the *LINE* command

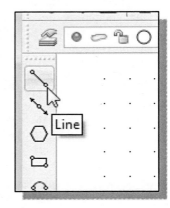

1. Select the **Line** command icon in the *Draw* toolbar. In the command window, near the bottom of the DraftSight drawing screen, the message "*Specify start point:*" is displayed.

2. Pick **Snap to Tangent** in the *Entity Snap* toolbar. DraftSight now expects us to select a circle or an arc on the screen.

❖   The **Snap to Tangent** option allows us to snap to the point on a circle or arc that, when connected to the last point, forms a line tangent to that object.

3. Pick a location that is near the top left side of the smaller circle on the right; note the tangent symbol is displayed as shown.

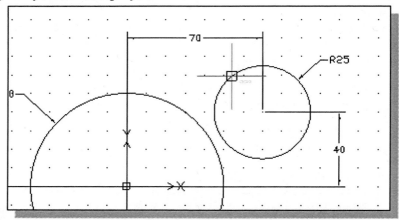

❖   Note that the line segment will be adjusted as the cursor is moved; DraftSight will finalize the tangent location when the other endpoint of the line is defined.

4. Pick **Snap to Tangent** in the *Entity Snap* toolbar. DraftSight now expects us to select a circle or an arc on the screen.

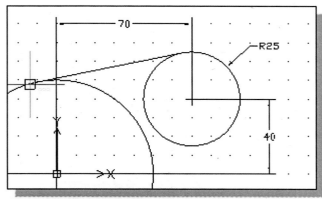

5. Pick a location that is near the top left side of the center circle; note the tangent symbol is displayed as shown.

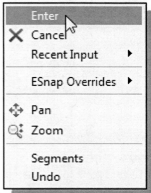

6. Inside the graphics window, **right-mouse-click** to activate the option menu and select **Enter** with the left-mouse-button to end the Line command.

❖ A line tangent to both circles is constructed as shown in the figure.

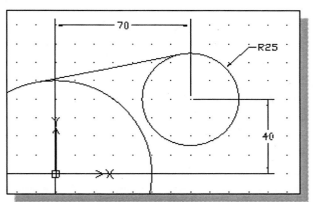

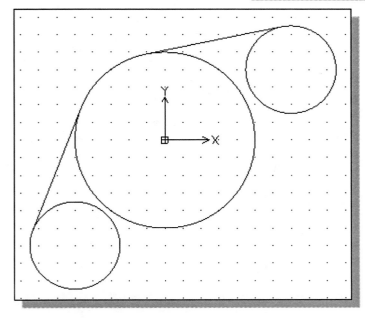

7. On your own, repeat the above steps and create the other tangent line between the center circle and the circle on the left. Your drawing should appear as the figure.

Creating *TTR Circles*

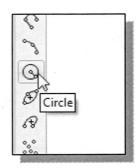

1. Select the **Circle** command in the *Draw* toolbar as shown.

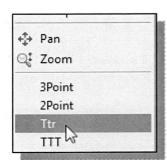

2. Inside the graphics window, right-mouse-click to activate the option menu and select the **Ttr (tan tan radius)** option. This option allows us to create a circle that is tangent to two objects.

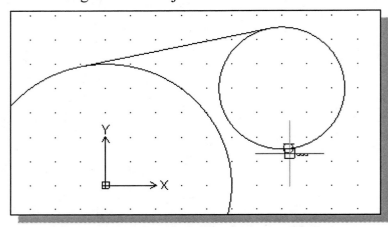

3. Pick a location near the **bottom of the smaller circle** on the right. We will create a circle that is tangent to this circle and the center circle.

4. Pick the **center circle** by selecting a location that is near the right side of the circle. DraftSight interprets the locations we selected as being near the tangency.

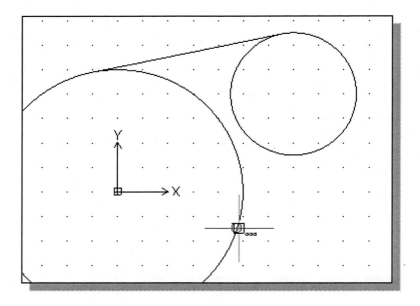

5. In the command window, the message "*Specify radius of circle*" is displayed. Enter **50** as the radius of the circle.

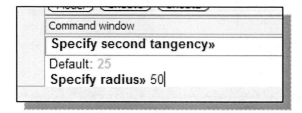

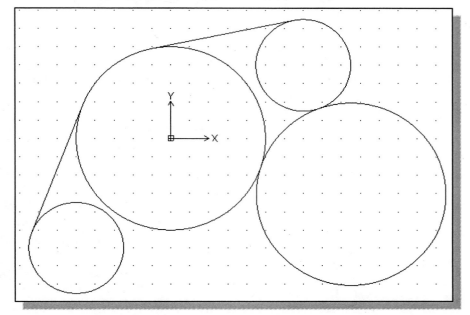

6. On your own, repeat the above steps and create the other **Ttr** circle (radius **40**). Your drawing should appear as the figure below.

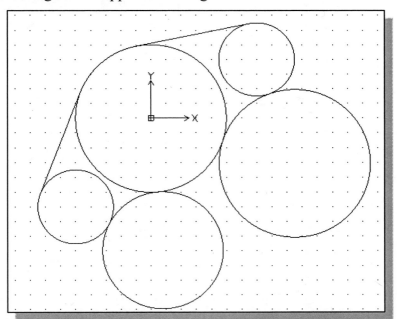

Using the *TRIM* Command

- The **Trim** command shortens an object so that it ends precisely at a selected boundary.

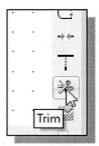

1. Select the **Trim** command icon in the *Modify* toolbar; click on the down-triangle to display additional icons as shown. In the command window, the message "*Specify cutting edges:*" is displayed.

- First, we will select the objects that define the boundary edges to which we want to trim the object.

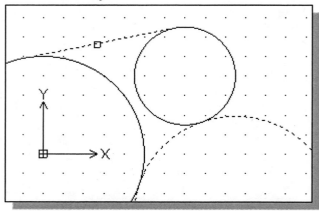

2. Pick the tangent line connecting the center circle and the top right circle.

3. Pick the lower right circle. The two selected entities are highlighted as shown in the figure.

4. Inside the graphics window, **right-mouse-click** once to proceed with the Trim command.

5. The message "*Specify segments to remove:*" is displayed in the command window. Pick the **left** section of the upper right circle and note the selected portion is trimmed as shown.

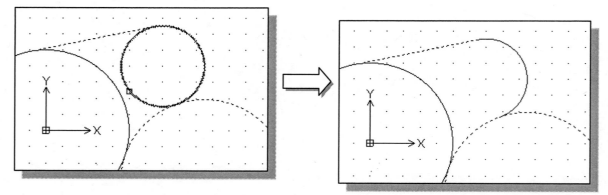

- ❖ In DraftSight, the Trim command requires first selection of objects that define the cutting edges at which an object is to stop. Valid cutting edge objects include most 2D geometry such as lines, arcs, circles, ellipses, polylines, splines, and text. For 3D objects, a 2D projection method is used where objects are projected onto the XY plane of the current custom coordinate system (CCS).

6. Select the upper right side of the center circle to remove the selected portion.

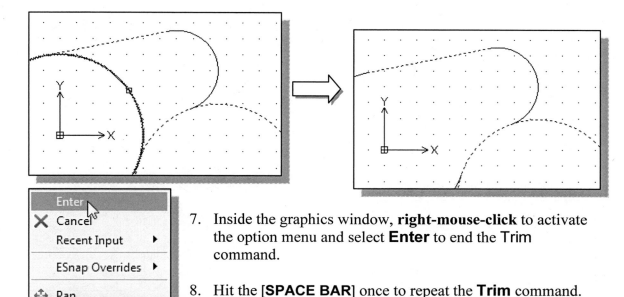

7. Inside the graphics window, **right-mouse-click** to activate the option menu and select **Enter** to end the Trim command.

8. Hit the **[SPACE BAR]** once to repeat the **Trim** command.

9. Select the two arcs that were trimmed as the two cutting edges and trim the lower section of the TTR circle as shown.

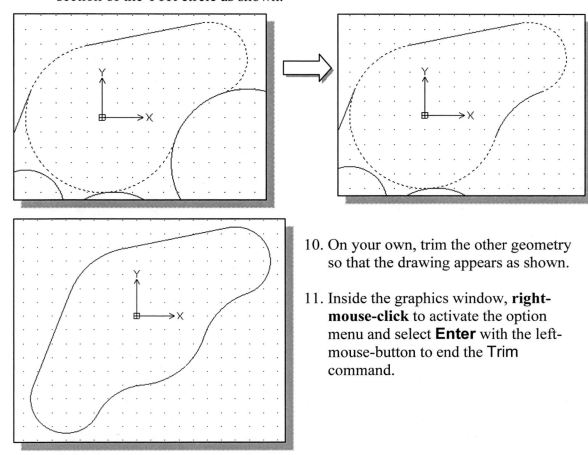

10. On your own, trim the other geometry so that the drawing appears as shown.

11. Inside the graphics window, **right-mouse-click** to activate the option menu and select **Enter** with the left-mouse-button to end the Trim command.

Using the *POLYGON* command

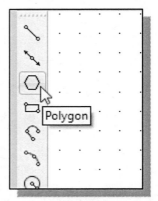

1. Select the **Polygon** command icon in the *Draw* toolbar.

2. Enter **6** to create a six-sided hexagon.
   Specify number of sides: **6** [ENTER]

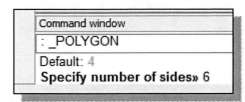

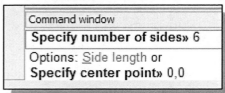

3. The message *"Specify center point:"* is displayed. Since the center of the large circle is aligned to the origin of the WCS. Set the center point to the origin by entering the absolute coordinates.

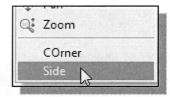

4. In the command window, the message *"Specify distance option:"* is displayed. Use the option menu and select the **Side** option.

5. In the command window, the message *"Specify distance:"* is displayed.
   Specify distance: **0,30** [ENTER]

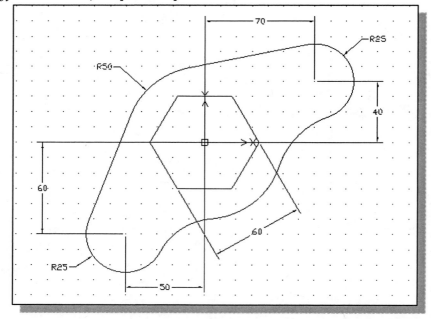

❖ Note that the polygon option [**COrner** /**Side**] allows us to create either **corner to corner** or **flat to flat** distance.

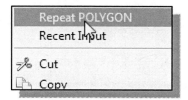

6. Inside the graphics window, **right-mouse-click** to activate the option menu and select **Repeat POLYGON**. In the command window, the message *"Specify number of sides:"* is displayed.

7. Enter **4** to create a four-sided polygon.
    Specify number of sides: **4** [ENTER]

8. In the command window, the message *"Specify center point:"* is displayed. Let's use the *Entity Snap* options to locate its center location. Pick **Snap to Center** in the *Entity Snap* toolbar as shown.

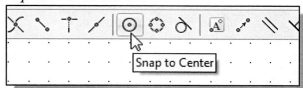

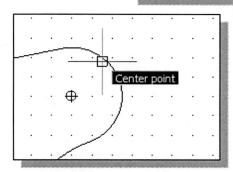

9. Move the cursor on top of the arc on the right and notice the center point is automatically highlighted. Select the arc to accept the highlighted location.

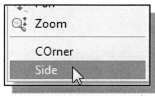

10. In the command window, the message *"Specify distance option:"* is displayed. Use the option menu and select the **Side** option.

11. Switch **ON** the **SNAP** option in the *Status Bar* as shown.

12. Create a square by selecting one of the adjacent grid points next to the center point as shown. Note that the orientation of the polygon can also be adjusted as the cursor is moved to other locations.

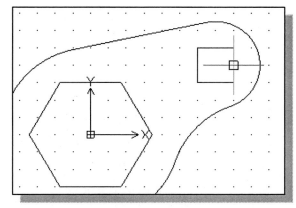

Create a Concentric *Circle*

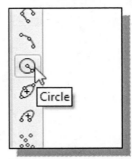

1. Select the **Circle** command icon in the *Draw* toolbar. In the command window, the message "*Specify center point for circle or [3P/2P/Ttr (tan tan radius)]:*" is displayed.

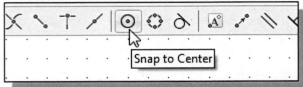

2. Let's use the *Entity Snap* options to assure the center location is aligned properly. Pick **Snap to Center** in the *Entity Snap* toolbar as shown.

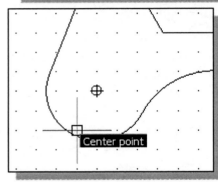

3. Move the cursor on top of the lower arc on the left and notice the center point is automatically highlighted. Select the arc to accept the highlighted location.

4. In the command window, the message "*Specify radius*" is displayed. Enter **10** to complete the **Circle** command.
    Specify radius: **10** **[ENTER]**

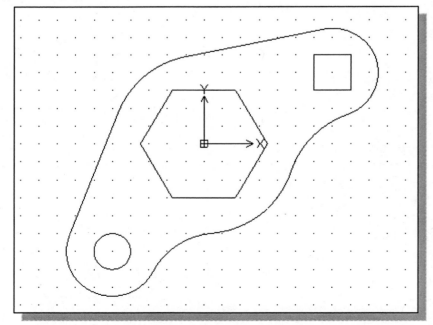

Measure Distance

- DraftSight also provides several tools that will allow us to measure distance, area, perimeter. With the use of the *Entity Snap* options, getting measurements of the completed design can be done very quickly.

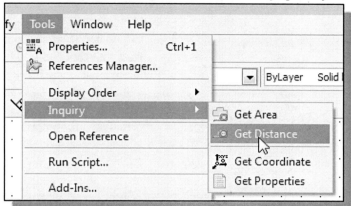

1. Select **Get Distance** in the *Tools* main menu as shown.

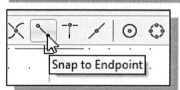

2. Pick **Snap to Endpoint** in the *Entity Snap* toolbar.

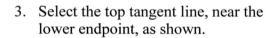

3. Select the top tangent line, near the lower endpoint, as shown.

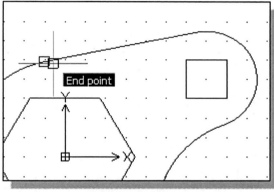

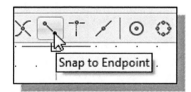

4. Pick **Snap to Endpoint** in the *Entity Snap* toolbar.

5. Select the tangent line, near the upper endpoint, as shown.

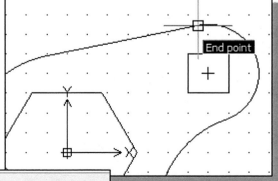

❖ The length of the line is displayed in the command window as shown.

Command window

Distance = 77, Angle in XY Plane = 12, Angle from XY Plane = 0
Delta X = 75, Delta Y = 16, Delta Z = 0

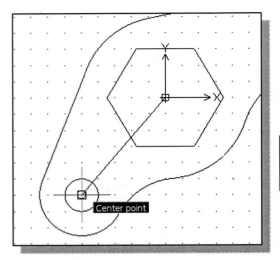

6. On your own, repeat the above steps and measure the center to center distance of the lower region of the design as shown. (Hint: use the **Snap to Center** option.)

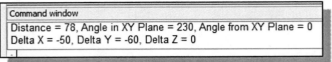

Command window

Distance = 78, Angle in XY Plane = 230, Angle from XY Plane = 0
Delta X = -50, Delta Y = -60, Delta Z = 0

Saving the CAD file

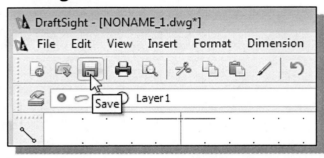

1. In the *Standard* toolbar, select: **Save**.

❖ Note the command can also be activated with the quick-key combination of **[Ctrl]+[S]**.

2. In the *Save As* dialog box, select the folder in which you want to store the CAD file and enter **RockerArm** in the *File name* box.

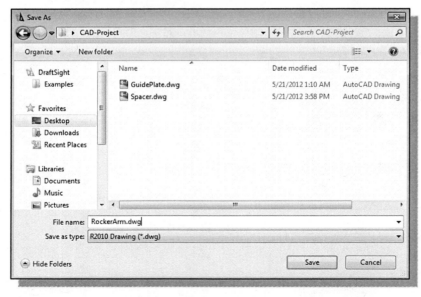

3. Pick **Save** in the *Save Drawing As* dialog box to accept the selections and save the file.

Review Questions:

1. List and describe three options in the DraftSight *Entity Snap* toolbar.

2. Which DraftSight command can we use to remove a portion of an existing entity?

3. Describe the difference between the *circumscribed* and *inscribed* options when using the DraftSight **Polygon** command.

4. Create the following triangle and fill in the blanks: Length = _____, Angle = _____. (Dimensions are in inches.)

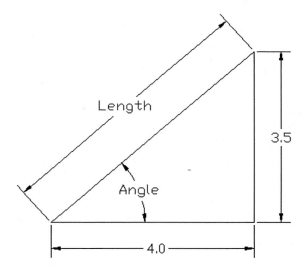

5. Create the following drawing; line **AB** is tangent to both circles. Fill in the blanks: Length = _____, Angle = _____. (Dimensions are in inches.)

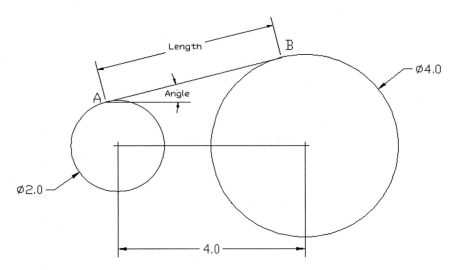

Exercises:

(Unless otherwise specified, dimensions are in inches.)

1. Adjustable Support

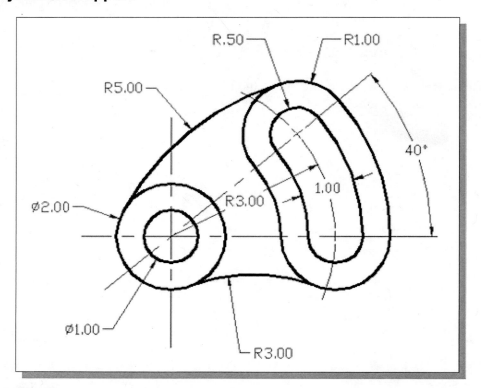

2. V-Slide Plate (The design has two sets of parallel lines with implied tangency.)

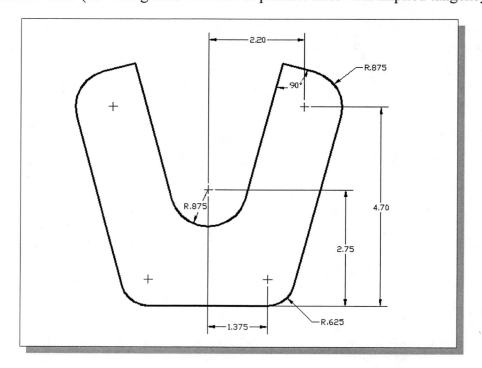

3. Swivel Base (Dimensions are in Millimeters.)

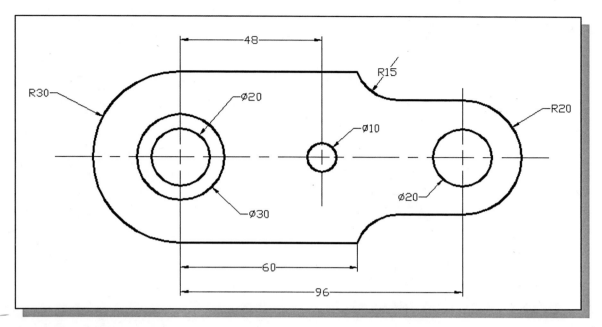

4. Sensor Mount

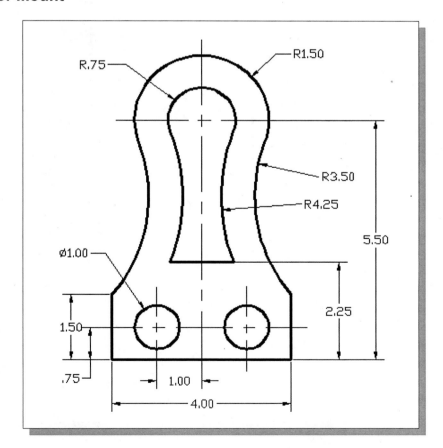

5. Flat Hook (Dimensions are in Millimeters. Thickness: 25 mm.)

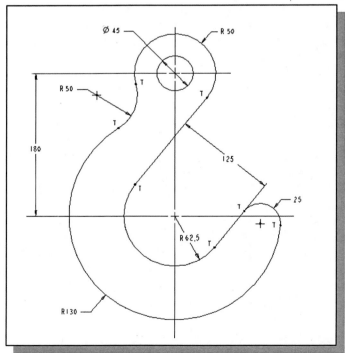

Chapter 3
Object Properties and Organization in DraftSight

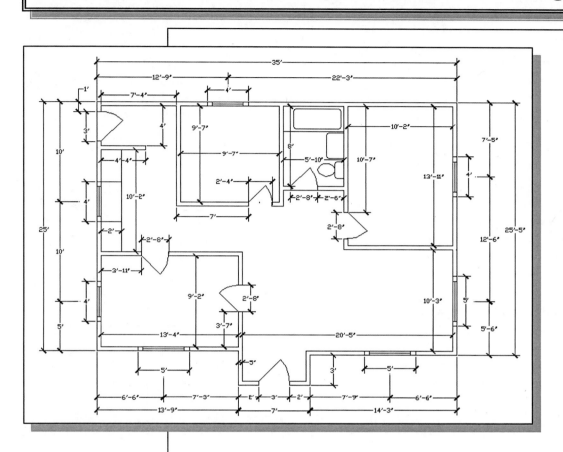

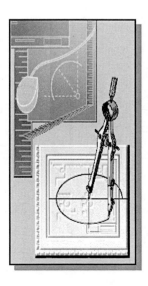

Learning Objectives

- ♦ Use the DraftSight Unit System
- ♦ Create new Richline Styles
- ♦ Draw, Using the RICHLINE Command
- ♦ Use the ZOOM BOUNDS Command
- ♦ Create New Layers
- ♦ Pre-selection of Objects
- ♦ Control Layer Visibility
- ♦ Move Objects to a Different Layer

Introduction

The CAD database of a design may contain information regarding the hundreds of CAD entities that are used to create the CAD model. One of the advantages of using a CAD system is its ability to organize and manage the database so that the designer can access the information quickly and easily. Typically, CAD entities that are created to describe one feature, function, or process of a design are perceived as related information and therefore are organized into the same group. In DraftSight, the **Layer** command is used extensively for this purpose. For example, an architectural drawing typically will show walls, doors, windows, and dimensions. Using layers, we can choose to display or hide sub-systems for clarity; we can also change object properties, such as colors and linetypes, quickly and easily.

In this chapter, we will continue to explore the different construction and editing tools that are available in DraftSight. We will demonstrate the use of the **Limits**, **Mline**, **Medit**, and **Layer** commands. As you become proficient with the CAD tools and understand the underlying CAD modeling concepts, you are encouraged to experiment with new ideas in using the CAD tools and develop your own style of using the system.

The *Floor Plan* design

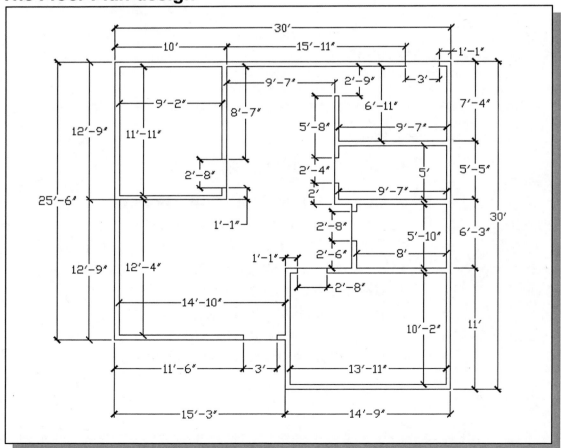

Starting Up DraftSight

1. Select the **DraftSight** option on the *Program* menu or select the **DraftSight** icon on the *Desktop*. Once the program is loaded into the memory, the *DraftSight* drawing screen will appear on the screen.

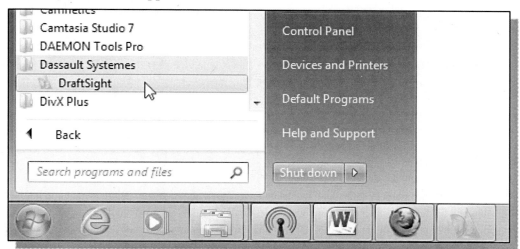

Use the Unit System to Setup an Architectural Drawing

*   DraftSight's *Unit System* allows us to customize the default DraftSight settings depending on the options we choose. Choices for units include *Decimal*, *Engineering*, *Architectural*, *Fractional*, and *Scientific*.

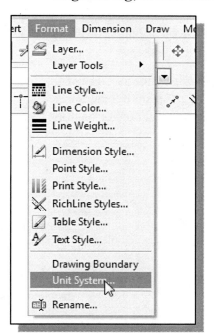

1. In the *Main Menu*, select:
    [Format] → [Unit System]

2. Set the *Length Type* to **Architectural**.

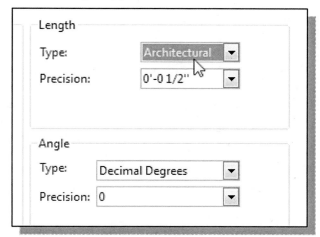

3. Set the *Precision* to **1/2″** as shown.

4. Click **OK** to exit the *Drawing Settings* dialog box.

Drawing Area Setup

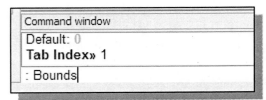

1. Click inside the command window.

2. Inside the command window, enter **Bounds** and press the [**ENTER**] key.

3. In the command window, near the bottom of the DraftSight drawing screen, the message "*Specify lower left corner:*" is displayed. Enter **0,0** as shown.

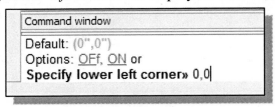

4. In the command window, the message "*Specify upper right corner:*" is displayed. Enter **60´,40´** as the new upper right coordinates as shown.

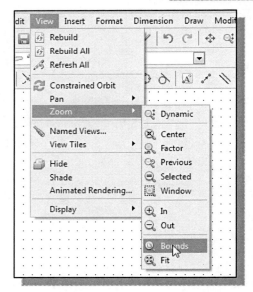

5. In the *Main Menu* select the [**View**] → [**Zoom**] → [**Bounds**] option to adjust the display based on the established drawing boundary.

❖ Notice the *CCS Icon*, which is aligned to the origin of the world coordinate system, is displayed at the lower left corner of the graphics window.

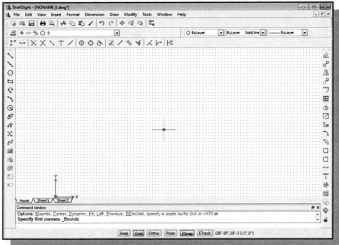

GRID and *SNAP* Intervals Setup

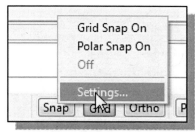

1. In the *Status* toolbar, right-mouse-click once on the *SNAP* button to bring up the option menu.

2. Select **Settings** to bring up the setup dialog box as shown.

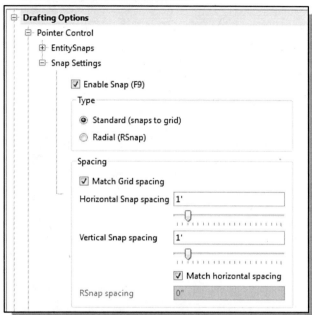

3. In the *Drafting Options* list, adjust the *Snap Spacing* to *1'* for both *Horizontal* and *Vertical* directions.

4. Activate the **Match Grid spacing** option as shown.

5. Activate the snap option by clicking on the **Enable Snap** box. Note function key [**F9**] can also be used to toggle *ON* and *OFF* the *SNAP* option.

6. On your own, switch to the *Grid Settings* list and confirm the *Grid Spacing* has been updated to *1'* as shown.

7. Pick **OK** to exit the *Drafting Settings* dialog box.

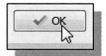

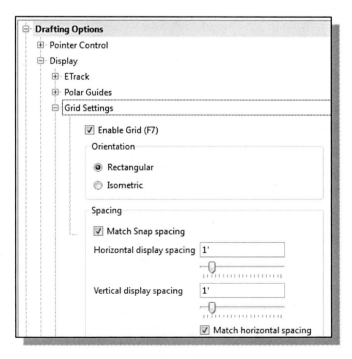

The DraftSight *RICHLINE* command

- The **RichLine** command in DraftSight is used to create multiple parallel lines. This command is very useful for creating designs that contain multiple parallel lines, such as walls for architectural designs and for highway designs in civil engineering. The RichLine command creates a set of parallel lines (up to 16 lines) and all line segments are grouped together to form a single *RichLine object*, which can be modified using the Explode command. We will first create a new *RichLine style* for our floor plan design.

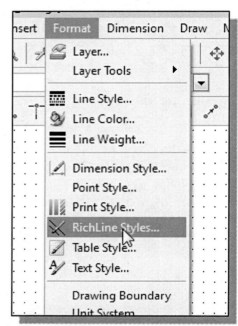

1. In the *Main Menu*, select:

   [Format] → [RichLine Styles]

❖ The default DraftSight RichLine style is called *STANDARD*, and it consists of two elements (two parallel lines) with an offset distance of 0.50 inch.

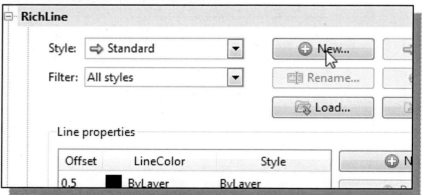

2. In the *RichLine Style* area, choose **New** to create a new RichLine style.

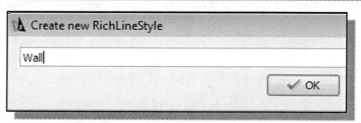

3. In the *New Style Name* box, enter **Wall** as the new RichLine style name.

4. Click **OK** to create the new style.

❖ All line elements in the RichLine style are defined by an offset from a reference line, the *RichLine origin*.

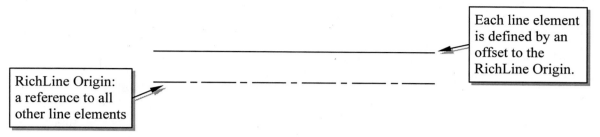

Each line element is defined by an offset to the RichLine Origin.

RichLine Origin: a reference to all other line elements

❖ Note that, in the *Elements* section, all the line elements are listed in descending order with respect to their offsets. We will create two line elements representing a six-inch wall (offsetting on both sides of the reference location).

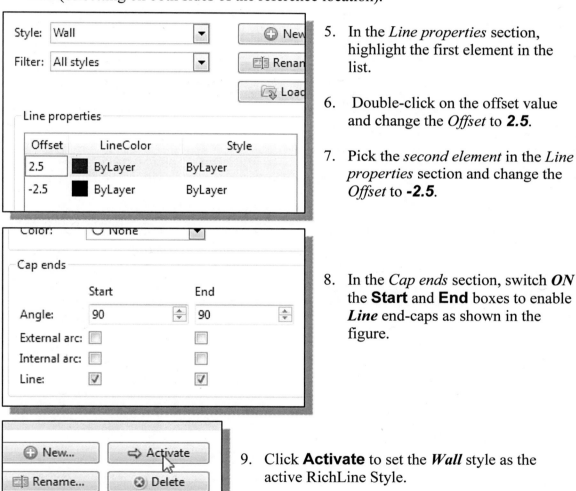

5. In the *Line properties* section, highlight the first element in the list.

6. Double-click on the offset value and change the *Offset* to **2.5**.

7. Pick the *second element* in the *Line properties* section and change the *Offset* to **-2.5**.

8. In the *Cap ends* section, switch **ON** the **Start** and **End** boxes to enable *Line* end-caps as shown in the figure.

9. Click **Activate** to set the *Wall* style as the active RichLine Style.

10. Choose **OK** to exit the *Drafting Styles* dialog box.

Entity Snap Toolbar

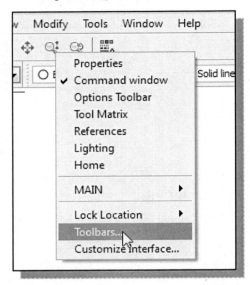

1. Move the cursor on top of any icon in the *Standard* toolbar and right-mouse-click once to display the option menu.

2. In the option list, choose **Toolbars**.

❖ DraftSight provides 22 predefined toolbars for access to frequently used commands, settings, and modes. A *checkmark* (next to the item) in the list identifies the toolbars that are currently displayed on the screen.

3. Select **Entity Snap**, with the left-mouse-button, to display the *Entity Snap* toolbar on the screen.

❖ **Entity Snap** is an extremely powerful construction tool available on most CAD systems. During an entity's creation operations, we can snap the cursor to points on objects such as endpoints, midpoints, centers, and intersections. For example, we can quickly draw a line to the center of a circle, the midpoint of a line segment, or the intersection of two lines.

4. Click **OK** to accept the settings.

5. On your own, in the *Status* toolbar area, reset the option buttons so that *Snap*, *Grid Display* and *Ortho* are switched **ON**.

- The **Ortho** mode limits the line construction to be paralleled to the axes of the current coordinate system. *Ortho mode* makes it easier to design and place parallel or collinear lines on entities. By default, with the standard World Coordinate System (WCS), orthogonal lines are either horizontal or vertical.

Drawing RichLines

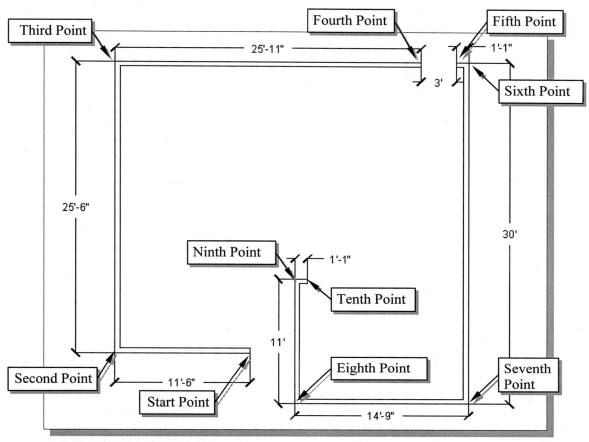

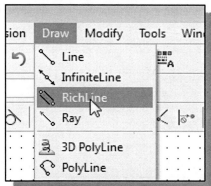

1. In the *Main Menu,* select **RichLine** under the *Draw* list as shown.

2. Inside the graphics window, **right-mouse-click** and select **Scale** to adjust the Scale.

3. Enter **1** as the new scale value.

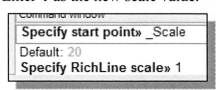

4. On your own, confirm the *Scale* is set to **1.00**, the *Styles* set to **Wall** and the *Justification* to **Top**, by examining the list in the command window.

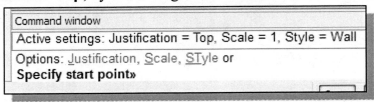

Command window
Active settings: Justification = Top, Scale = 1, Style = Wall
Options: Justification, Scale, STyle or
Specify start point»

5. In the command window, the message *"Specify start point"* is displayed. Select a location **near** the bottom center of the graphics window, coordinates (24',11',0) as the **start point** of the new RichLine.

6. Create a horizontal line by using the *Dynamic Input* option or the *relative rectangular coordinates entry method* in the command window:
Specify next point: **@-11'6",0 [ENTER]**

7. Create a vertical line by using the *Dynamic Input* option or the *relative rectangular coordinates entry method* in the command window:
Specify next point: **@25'6"<90 [ENTER]**

8. Create a horizontal line by using the *Direct Input* option; move the cursor to the right and enter the distance:
Specify next point: **25'11" [ENTER]**

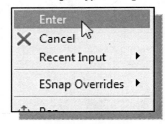

9. Inside the graphics window, **right-mouse-click** and select **Enter** to end the RichLine command.

10. Hit the **[Spacebar]** once to repeat the last command, the **RichLine** command. In the command window, the current settings *"Justification = **Top**, Scale = **1.00**, Style = **Wall**"* are displayed.

11. We will use the **Snap from** option to continue creating the exterior walls. In the *Entity Snap* toolbar, pick **Snap From**. In the command window, the message *"Base point"* is displayed. DraftSight now expects us to select a point on the existing geometric entity on the screen.

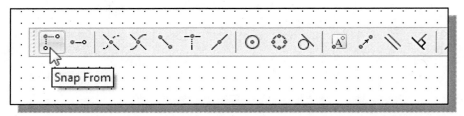

12. We will position the starting point relative to the last position of the previous RichLine. To assure the selection of the endpoint, choose the **Snap to Endpoint** option as shown.

13. Pick the upper corner of the top horizontal RichLine as shown. (Hint: Use the **Dynamic Pan** and **Zoom** functions, the mouse wheel, to aid the selection.)

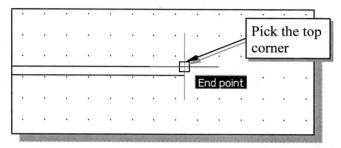

➢ Note that it is feasible to stack snap options for precise positioning/selecting of geometry.

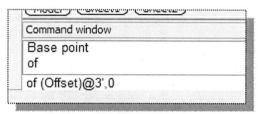

14. The position of the starting point of the new *RichLine* segments is 3′ to the right of the reference point we just picked. At the command window, enter **@3′,0″[ENTER]**.

15. Now enter **@1′1″,0** to define the top corner of the exterior wall.

16. On your own, complete the RichLine segments by specifying the rest of the corners using the dimensions as shown in the figure below.

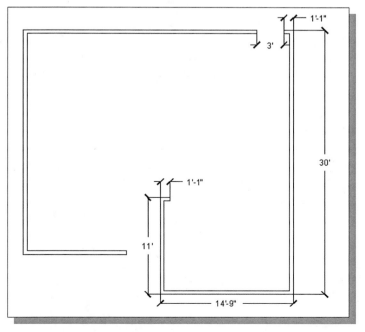

- Note that the points we have specified are defining the outside corners of the floor plan design.

17. Inside the graphics window, right-mouse-click and select **Enter** to end the RichLine command.

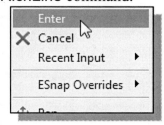

Creating interior walls

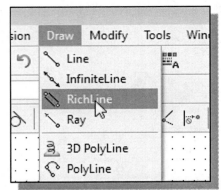

1. Select the **RichLine** command in the *Draw* main menu as shown. In the command window, the current settings "*Justification = **Top**, Scale = **1.00**, Style = **Wall**"* are displayed. In the command window, the message "*Specify start point:*" is displayed.

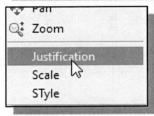

2. Inside the graphics window, **right-mouse-click** to display the option menu.

3. Pick **Justification** in the option menu. In the command window, the message "*Specify option:*" is displayed.

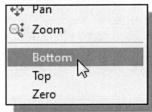

4. Inside the graphics window, right-mouse-click to display the option menu and select **Bottom** so that the points we select will be set as alignments for the bottom element.

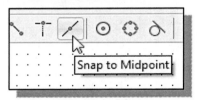

5. In the *Entity Snap* toolbar, pick **Snap to Midpoint**. DraftSight now expects us to select a geometric entity on the screen.

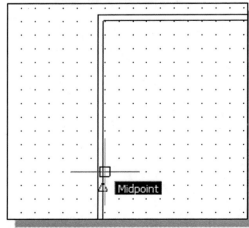

6. Select the inside **left vertical line** as shown.

7. Using the *Direct Input* option, create a **9′7″** inside wall toward the right.

8. Now enter **@0,1′1″** to define the vertical stub wall.

9. Inside the graphics window, right-mouse-click once and select **Enter** to end the command.

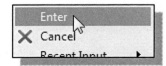

- Next, we will create a vertical wall directly above the last corner.

10. Hit the [**Spacebar**] once to repeat the last command, the **RichLine** command. Since the last position used is directly below the new location, we will just enter the relative coordinates. At the command window, enter **@0,2'8"**.

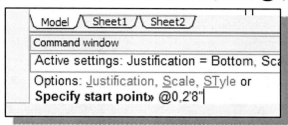

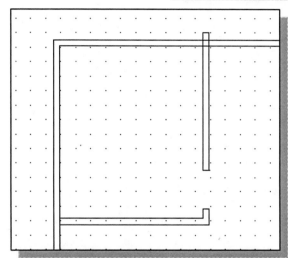

11. Place the other end above the top horizontal line as shown in the figure. In the next section, we will adjust these constructions.

12. Inside the graphics window, right-mouse-click and select **Enter** to end the RichLine command.

13. Hit the [**Spacebar**] once to repeat the last command, the **RichLine** command. In the text window, the current settings "*Justification = **Bottom**, Scale = **1.00**, Style = **Wall***" are displayed. In the command window, the message "*Specify start point:*" is displayed.

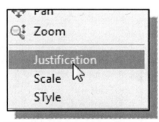

14. Inside the graphics window, **right-mouse-click** to display the option menu.

15. Pick **Justification** in the option menu. In the command window, the message "*Specify option:*" is displayed.

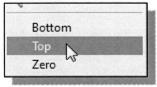

16. Inside the graphics window, right-mouse-click to display the option menu and select **Top** so that the points we select will align to the top element.

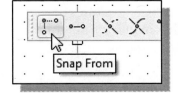

17. In the *Entity Snap* toolbar, pick **Snap From**. DraftSight now expects us to select a geometric entity on the screen.

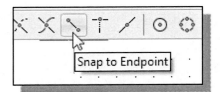

18. In the *Entity Snap* toolbar, pick **Snap to Endpoint**. In the command window, the message "*_endp of*" is displayed.

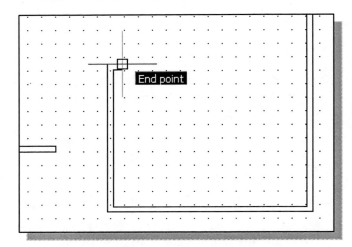

19. We will create another inside wall on the right side. Pick the corner as shown.

20. At the command window, enter **@2'8",0 [ENTER]**.

21. Pick a location that is to the right of the right-vertical exterior wall. The drawing should appear as shown in the figure below.

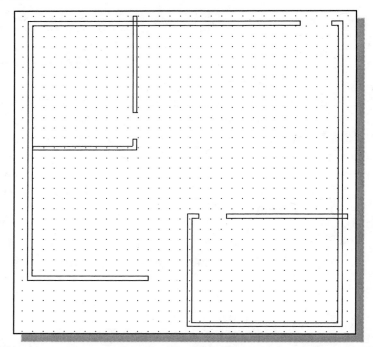

❖ One of the main advantages of using a CAD system to create drawings is the ability to create and/or modify geometric entities quickly, using many of the available tools. Unlike traditional board drafting, where typically only the necessary entities are created, CAD provides a much more flexible environment that requires a slightly different way of thinking, as well as taking a different view of the tasks at hand.

Using the *EXPLODE* command

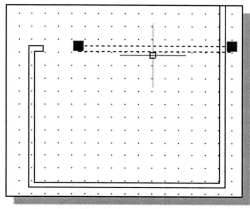

1. Select the last **RichLine** we just created and notice the four edges forming the RichLine entity are highlighted.

2. In the *Modify toolbar*, select **Explode** as shown. Notice the selected RichLine has been broken into individual line segments.

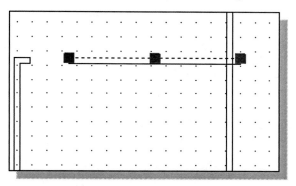

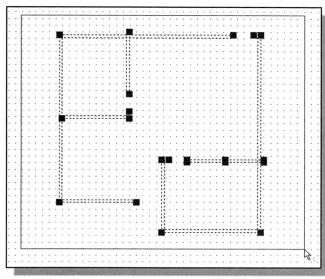

3. Select all of the created entities by enclosing the entities inside a selection window. (Hint: Define the selection from left to right.)

4. In the *Modify* toolbar, select **Explode** to ungroup all of the RichLines into individual line segments.

➢   The **Explode** command can be used to break a complex object into its component entities. We can explode Blocks and other complex objects like PolyLines, Richlines, Hatches, and Dimensions.

Using the *TRIM* Command

- The **Trim** command shortens an object so that it ends precisely at a selected boundary.

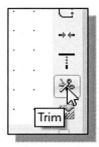

1. Select the **Trim** command icon in the *Modify* toolbar, click on the down-triangle to display additional icons as shown. In the command window, the message "*Specify cutting edges:*" is displayed.

- First, we will select the objects that define the boundary edges to which we want to trim the object.

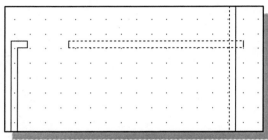

2. Pick the two horizontal lines and the right edge as shown.

3. Inside the graphics window, **right-mouse-click** once to proceed with the Trim command.

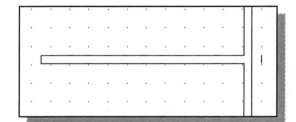

4. On your own, remove the sections not needed.

5. Note there is an extra vertical line segment that should be deleted.

6. On your own, complete the additional walls and doorways as shown.

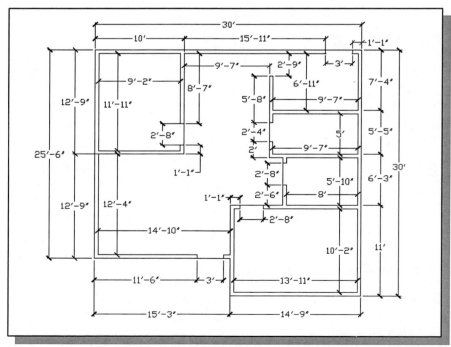

Using *Layers* and Object Properties

In DraftSight, *layers* can be thought of as transparent overlays on which we organize different kinds of design information. Typically, CAD entities that are created to describe one feature or function of a design are considered as related information and therefore can be organized into the same group. The objects we organized into the same group will usually have common properties such as colors, linetypes, and lineweights. Color helps us visually distinguish similar elements in our designs. Linetype helps us identify easily the different drafting elements, such as centerlines or hidden lines. Lineweight increases the legibility of an object through width. Consider the floor plan we are currently working on. The floor plan can be placed on one layer, electrical layout on another, and plumbing on a third layer. Organizing layers and the objects on layers makes it easier to manage the information in our designs. Layers can be used as a method to control the visibility of objects. We can temporarily switch *ON* or *OFF* any layer to help construction and editing of our designs.

DraftSight allows us to create an infinite number of layers. In general, twenty to thirty layers are sufficient for most designs. Most companies also require designers and CAD operators to follow the company standards in organizing objects in layers.

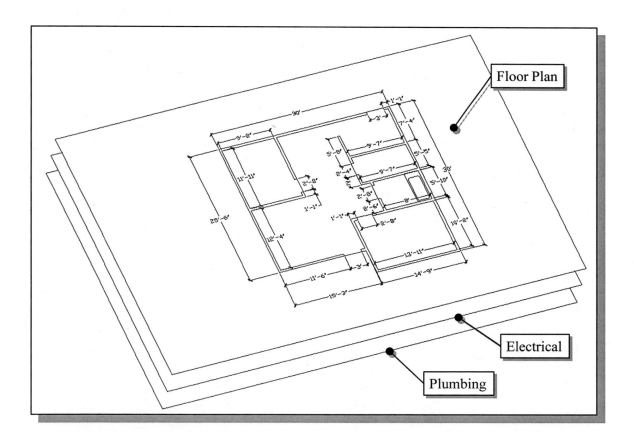

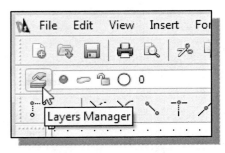

1. Pick **Layers Manager** in the *Layers* toolbar as shown.

❖ The *Layers Properties Manager* dialog box appears. DraftSight creates a default layer, *Layer 0*, which we cannot rename or delete. Note that *Layer 0* has special properties which are used by the system.

❖ In DraftSight, we always construct entities on a layer. It may be the default layer or a layer that we create. Each layer has associated properties such as the visibility setting, color, linetype, lineweight, and print style.

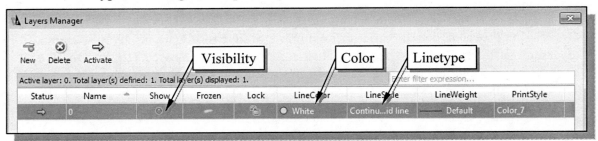

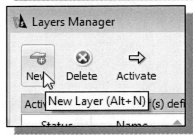

2. Click on the **New Layer** button. Notice a layer is automatically added to the list of layers.

➢ Note that we can create an unlimited number of layers in a drawing.

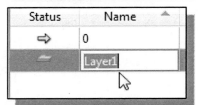

3. DraftSight will assign a generic name to the new layer (*Layer1*). Enter **BathRoom** as the name of the new layer as shown in the figure below.

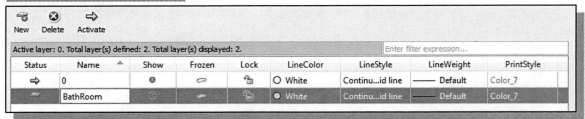

❖ Layer properties can be adjusted by clicking on the icon or name of a property. For example, clicking on the *Show* icon toggles the visibility of the layer *ON* or *OFF*.

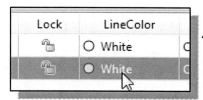

4. Pick the color swatch or the color name (**White**) of the *BathRoom* layer. The *Select Color* dialog box appears.

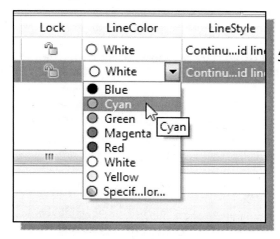

5. Pick **Cyan** *(Index color: 4)* in the *Color List* section. Notice the current color setting is displayed at the top of the list.

6. Click on the **Activate** button to make *BathRoom* the *Active Layer*. There can only be one *Active Layer*, and new entities are automatically placed on the layer that is set to be the *Active Layer*.

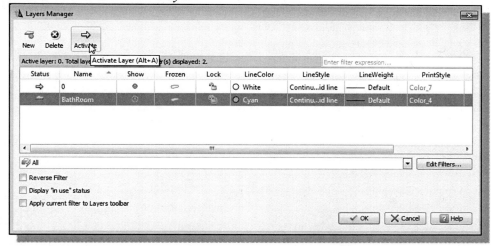

7. Click on the **OK** button, at the lower right corner of the dialog box, to accept the settings and exit the *Layer Manager* dialog box.

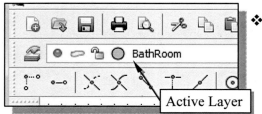

Active Layer

❖ The *Layer Control* toolbar located below the *Standard* toolbar shows the status of the active layer. The *BathRoom* layer is shown as the current active layer. Note that this *Layer* toolbar can also be used to control the settings of individual layers.

Using the *Dynamic Zoom* command

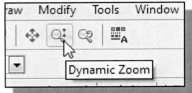

1. Click on the **Dynamic Zoom** icon in the *Standard* toolbar located above the top side of the graphics window.

2. Inside the graphics window **push and hold down the left-mouse-button,** then move upward to enlarge the current display scale factor.

3. Inside the graphics window, right-mouse-click to bring up the option menu and notice the different dynamic viewing functions as shown.

4. On your own, use the **Dynamic Pan** option to reposition the display so that we can work on the bathroom of the floor plan. (Press the [**Esc**] key to exit the Dynamic Viewing command.)

➢ Note that the mouse-wheel can also be used to Dynamic Zoom; turning the wheel forward will enlarge the current display scale factor.

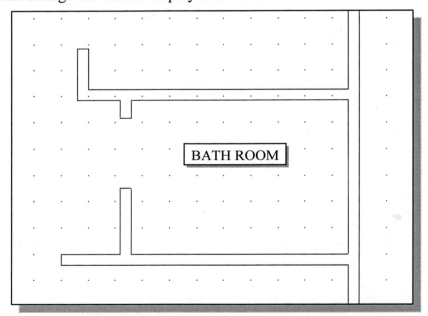

5. In the *Status* toolbar area, reset the option buttons so that all of the buttons are switched *OFF*.

Modeling the bathroom

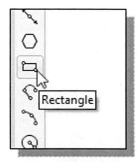

1. Click on the **Rectangle** command icon in the *Draw* toolbar. In the command window, the message *"Specify first corner point:"* is displayed.

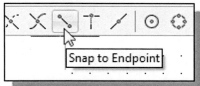

2. In the *Entity Snap* toolbar, pick **Snap to Endpoint**. DraftSight now expects us to select a geometric entity on the screen.

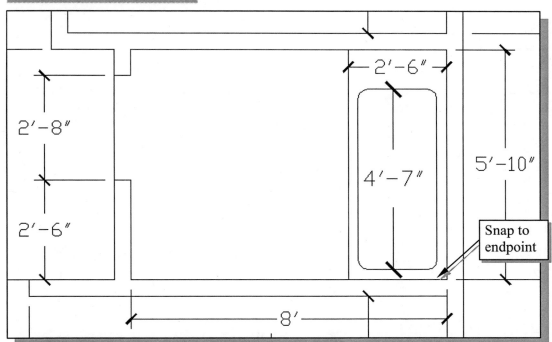

3. On your own, create the outer rectangle of the tub (*2'-6" x 5'-10"*).

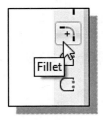

4. Complete the inner shape by creating a rectangle with a distance of 3" from the outer rectangle and rounded corners of 3" radius.

5. Create two rectangles (*10″×20″* and *20″×30″*) with rounded corners (radius **3″**) and position them as shown.

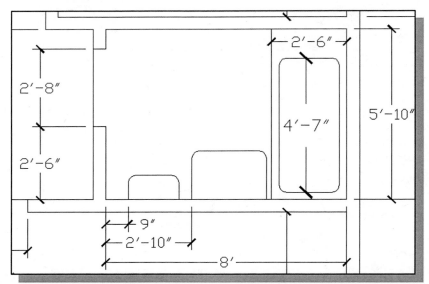

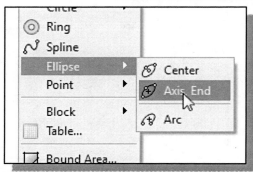

6. Select the **Ellipse → Axis, End** command icon in the *Draw* toolbar. In the command window, the message "*Specify axis endpoint:*" is displayed.

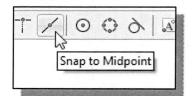

7. In the *Entity Snap* toolbar, pick **Snap to Midpoint** as shown.

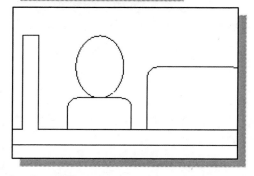

8. Pick the **top horizontal line** of the small rectangle we just created.

9. For the second point location, enter **@0,20″** **[ENTER]**.

10. For the third point, enter **@7.5″,0 [ENTER]**.

❖ An ellipse has a major axis, the longest distance between two points on the ellipse, and a minor axis, the shorter distance across the ellipse. The three points we specified identify these two axes.

Controlling *Layer Visibility*

DraftSight does not display or plot the objects that are on invisible layers. To make layers invisible, we can *freeze* or *turn off* those layers. Turning off layers only temporarily removes the objects from the screen; the objects remain active in the CAD database. Freezing layers will make the objects invisible and also disable the objects in the CAD database. Freezing layers will improve object selection performance and reduce regeneration time for complex designs. When we *thaw* a frozen layer, DraftSight updates the CAD database with the screen coordinates for all objects in the design.

1. On the *Layers* toolbar panel, choose the triangle next to the **Layer Control** box with a click of the left-mouse-button.

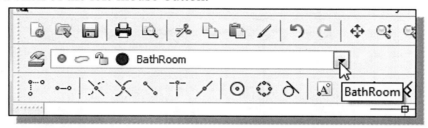

2. Move the cursor over the **Show** icon for *Layer 0*.

3. **Left-mouse-click once** and notice the icon color is changed to a grey color, representing the layer (*Layer 0*) is turned *OFF*.

4. Move the cursor into the graphics window and **left-mouse-click once** to accept the layer control settings.

➢ On your own, practice turning on *Layer 0* and freezing/thawing *Layer 0*. What would happen if we turn off all layers?

Adding a New Layer

1. Pick **Layer Manager** in the *Layers* toolbar panel. The *Layer Manager* dialog box appears.

2. Create a new layer (layer name: *Walls*) and change the layer color to **Green**.

3. Turn *ON* the *0* layer, turn *OFF* the *BathRoom* layer, and set the *Walls* layer as the *Active Layer*. Click on the **OK** button to exit *Layer Properties*.

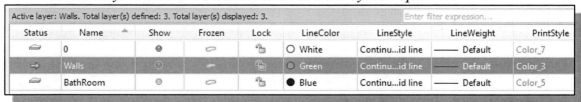

Status	Name	Show	Frozen	Lock	LineColor	LineStyle	LineWeight	PrintStyle
	0				○ White	Continu...id line	—— Default	Color_7
	Walls				○ Green	Continu...id line	—— Default	Color_3
	BathRoom				● Blue	Continu...id line	—— Default	Color_5

Active layer: Walls. Total layer(s) defined: 3. Total layer(s) displayed: 3.

Moving objects to a different layer

❖ DraftSight provides a flexible graphical user interface that allows users to select graphical entities BEFORE the command is selected (*pre-selection*), or AFTER the command is selected (*post-selection*). The procedure we have used so far is the *post-selection* option. We can pre-select one or more objects by clicking on the objects at the command window (**Command:**). To deselect the selected items, press the **[Esc]** key twice.

1. Inside the graphics window, pre-select all objects by enclosing all objects inside a **selection window** as shown.

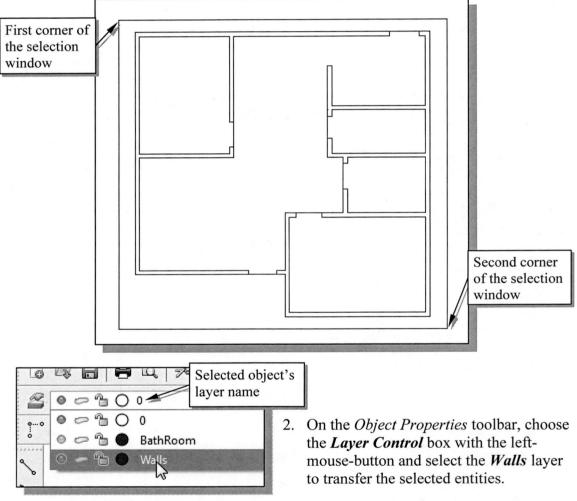

First corner of the selection window

Second corner of the selection window

Selected object's layer name

2. On the *Object Properties* toolbar, choose the **Layer Control** box with the left-mouse-button and select the **Walls** layer to transfer the selected entities.

❖ Notice the layer name displayed in the *Layer Control* box is the selected object's assigned layer and layer properties.

3. On your own, switch the **Walls** layer **on** and **off** to confirm the setup.

4. Before continuing to the next page, switch **ON** both *Walls* and *Bathroom* layers.

Matching Entity Properties

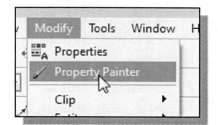

1. In the *Main Menu*, choose **Property Painter** in the *Modify* toolbar panel. In the command window, the message "*Specify source entity:*" is displayed.

2. Select any object on the ***Walls*** layer.

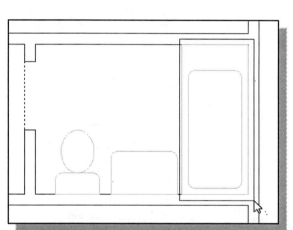

3. Select the **bathtub** using a selection window as shown.

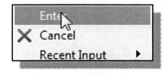

4. Inside the graphics window, **right-mouse-click** once and select **Enter** to accept the selection.

➢ In the graphics window, notice the color of the selected objects have changed to the same color as the *Walls* layer.

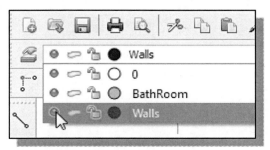

5. On your own, switch ***ON*** and ***OFF*** the ***Walls*** and ***BathRoom*** layers to examine the results of the Match Layer Properties command.

➢ On your own, complete the floor plan by creating the 4′ and 5′ windows in a new
layer *Windows*. The dimensions are as shown in the figure below.

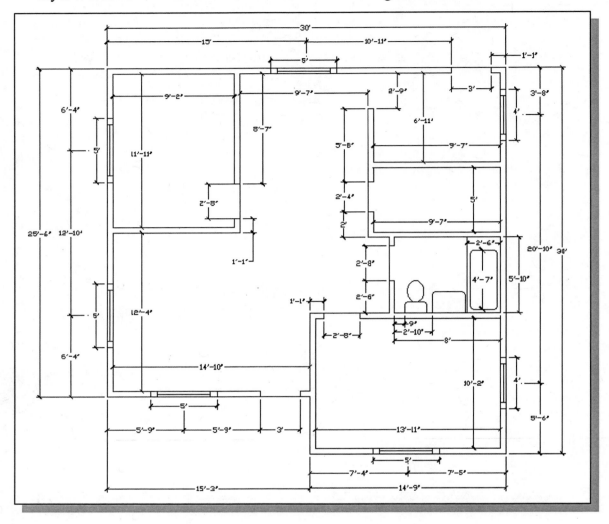

Review Questions:

1. List some of the advantages of using *layers*.

2. List two methods to control the *layer visibility* in DraftSight.

3. Describe the procedure to move objects from one layer to another.

4. When and why should you use the RichLine command?

5. Is there a limitation to how many layers we can set up in DraftSight?

6. List and describe the two options available in DraftSight to create ellipses.

7. Is there a limitation to how many parallel lines we can set up when using DraftSight RichLine objects?

8. What is the name of the layer that DraftSight creates as the default layer (the layer that we cannot rename or delete)?

9. When and why would you use the **Property Painter** command?

10. A **chamfer** connects two objects with an angled line. A chamfer is usually used to represent a beveled edge on a corner. Construct the following corners by using the **Chamfer** command.

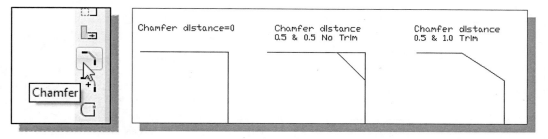

Exercises:

1. Floor Plan A (Wall thickness: 5 inch)

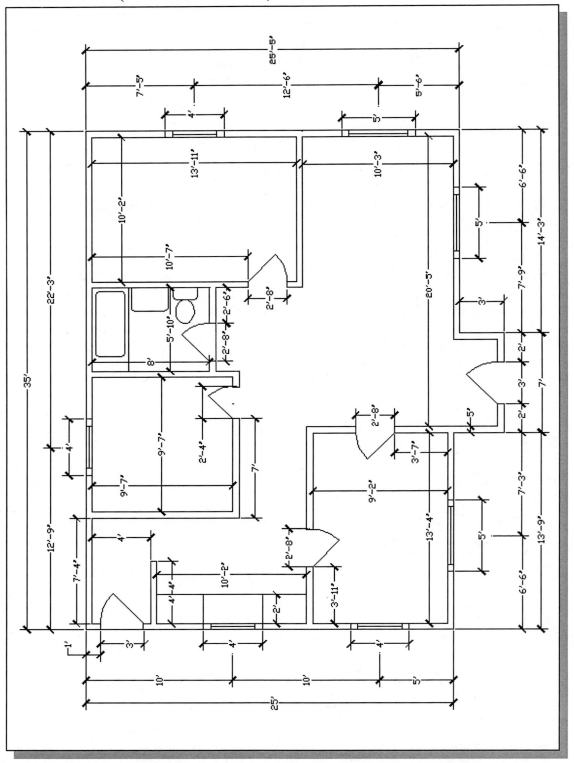

2. Floor Plan B (Wall thickness: 5 inch)

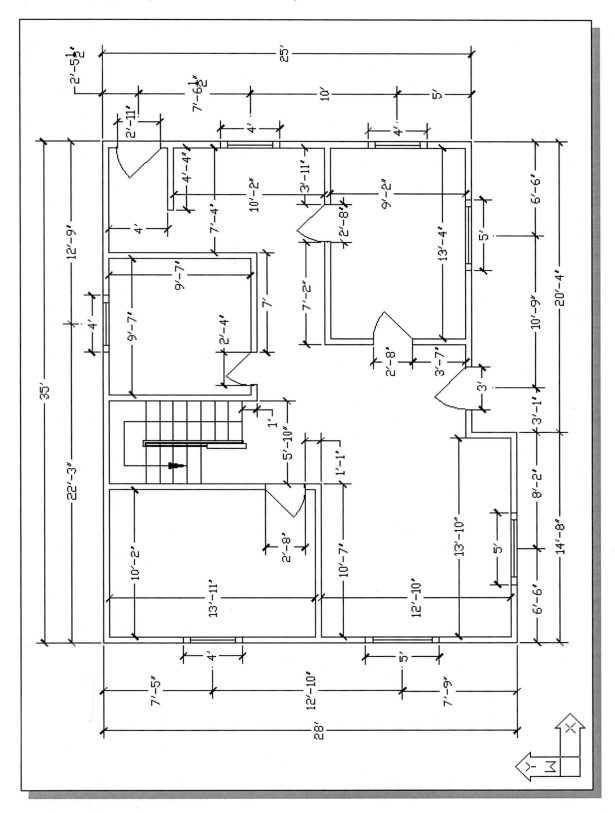

Notes:

Chapter 4
Orthographic Projection and Multiview Constructions

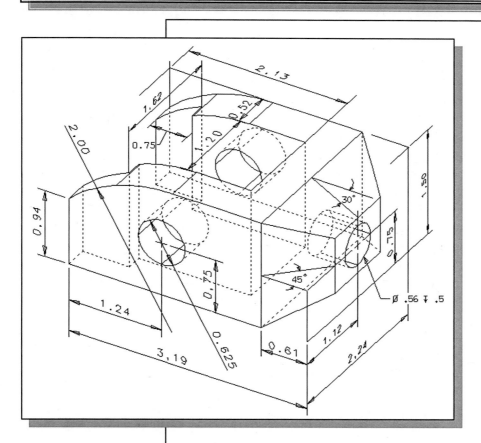

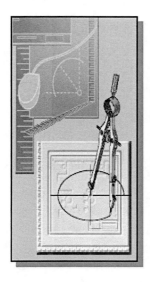

Learning Objectives

- **Understand the Basic Orthographic Projection Principles**
- **Be able to Perform 1st and 3rd Angle Projections**
- **Use the INFINITE LINE Command in DraftSight to Draw**
- **Use the DraftSight Running Object Snaps Options**
- **Use DraftSight's *ESnap* and *ETrack* Features**
- **Use the Miter Line Method**

Introduction

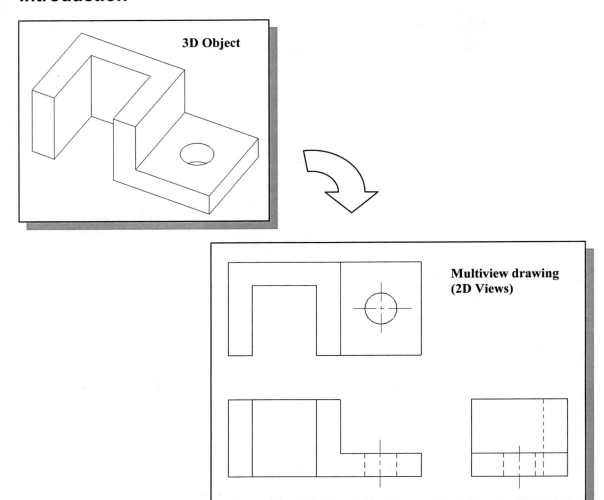

Most drawings produced and used in industry are ***multiview drawings***. Multiview drawings are used to provide accurate three-dimensional object information on two-dimensional media, a means of communicating all of the information necessary to transform an idea or concept into reality. The standards and conventions of multiview drawings have been developed over many years, which equip us with a universally understood method of communication.

Multiview drawings usually require several orthographic projections to define the shape of a three-dimensional object. Each orthographic view is a two-dimensional drawing showing only two of the three dimensions of the three-dimensional object. Consequently, no individual view contains sufficient information to completely define the shape of the three-dimensional object. All orthographic views must be looked at together to comprehend the shape of the three-dimensional object. The arrangement and relationship between the views are therefore very important in multiview drawings. Before taking a more in-depth look into the multiview drawings, we will first look at the concepts and principles of projections.

Basic Principles of Projection

To better understand the theory of projection, one must become familiar with the elements that are common to the principles of **projection**. First of all, the **POINT OF SIGHT** (aka **STATION POINT**) is the position of the observer in relation to the object and the plane of projection. It is from this point that the view of the object is taken. Secondly, the observer views the features of the object through an imaginary PLANE OF PROJECTION (or IMAGE PLANE). Imagine yourself standing in front of a glass window, IMAGE PLANE, looking outward; the image of a house at a distance is sketched onto the glass which is a 2D view of a 3D house.

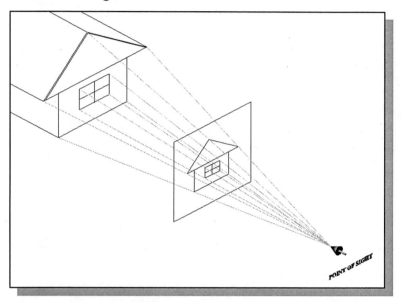

Orthographic Projection

The lines connecting from the *Point of Sight* to the 3D object are called the **Projection Lines** or **Lines of Sight**. Note that in the above figure, the projection lines are connected at the point of sight, and the projected 2D image is smaller than the actual size of the 3D object.

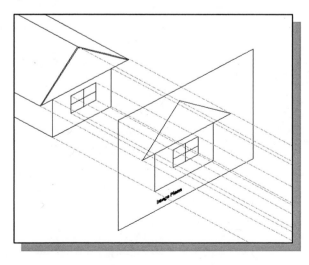

Now, if the *projection lines* are **parallel** to each other and the image plane is also **perpendicular** (*normal*) to the projection lines, the result is what is known as an **orthographic projection**. When the projection lines are parallel to each other, an accurate outline of the visible face of the object is obtained.

The term **orthographic** is derived from the word *orthos* meaning **perpendicular** or **90°**.

In *Engineering Graphics*, the projection of one face of an object usually will not provide an overall description of the object; other planes of projection must be used. To create the necessary 2D views, the *point of sight* is changed to project different views of the same object; hence, each view is from a different point of sight. If the point of sight is moved to the front of the object, this will result in the front view of the object. And then move the point of sight to the top of the object and looking down at the top, and then move to the right side of the object, as the case may be. Each additional view requires a new point of sight.

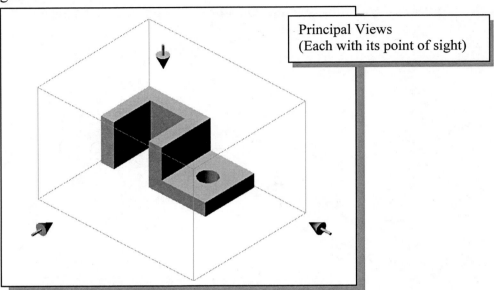

Principal Views
(Each with its point of sight)

Multiview Orthographic Projection

In creating multiview orthographic projection, different systems of projection can be used to create the necessary views to fully describe the 3D object. In the figure below, two perpendicular planes are established to form the image planes for a multiview orthographic projection.

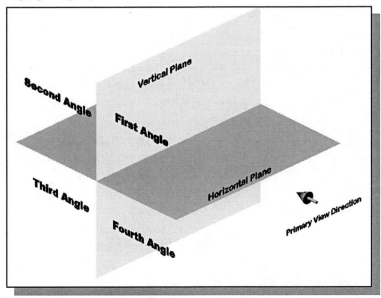

The angles formed between the horizontal and the vertical planes are called the **first, second, third** and **fourth angles**, as indicated in the figure. For engineering drawings, both **first angle projection** and **third angle projection** are commonly used.

FIRST-ANGLE PROJECTION

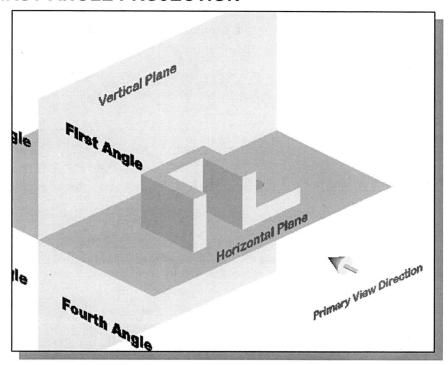

❖ In first-angle projection, the object is placed in **front** of the image planes. And the views are formed by projecting to the image plane located at the back.

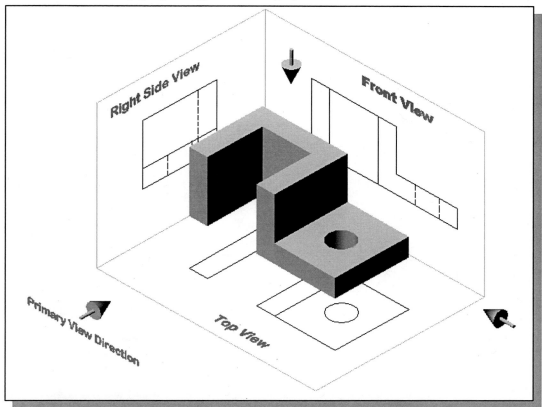

Rotation of the Horizontal and Profile Planes

In order to draw all three views of the object on the same plane, the horizontal (Top View) and profile (Right Side view) are rotated into the same plane as the primary image plane (Front View).

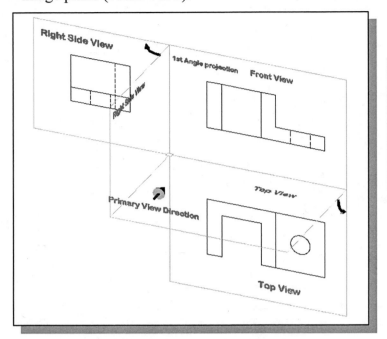

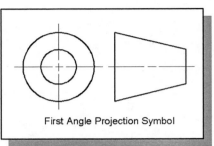

First Angle Projection Symbol

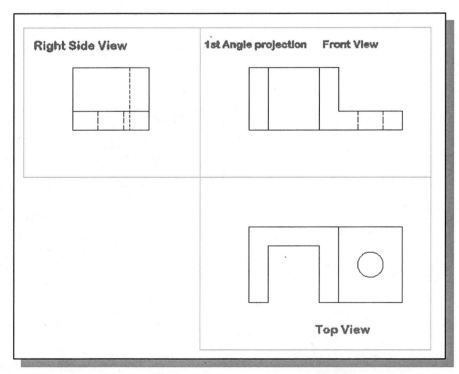

Getting the *3D Adjuster* Model through the Internet

DraftSight allows us to share files and resources through the Internet. Drawings can be placed and opened to an Internet location, blocks inserted by dragging drawings from a web site, and hyperlinks inserted in drawings so that others can access related documents. Note that to use the DraftSight Internet features, *Microsoft Internet Explorer 6.0* (or a later version) and Internet or Intranet connections are required.

We will illustrate the procedure to open a DraftSight file from the Internet by *Uniform Resource Locator* (URL).

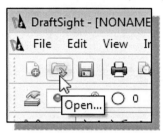

1. Select the **DraftSight** option on the *Program* menu or select the **DraftSight** icon on the *Desktop*.

2. In the DraftSight *Standard* toolbar, select **Open a Drawing** with a single click of the left-mouse-button.

3. In the *Open File* dialog box, enter **http://www.schroff.com/DraftSight/Adjuster1stAngle.dwg** as shown in the figure below.

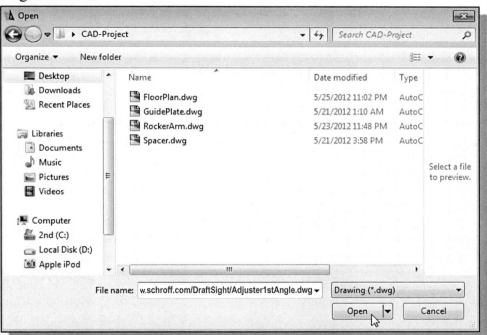

4. Click the **Open** icon and the file is downloaded from the www.schroff.com website to the local computer.

➤ The URL entered must be of the *Hypertext Transfer Protocol* (http://) and the complete filename must be entered including the filename extension (such as .dwg or .dwt).

Dynamic Rotation – Constrained Orbit

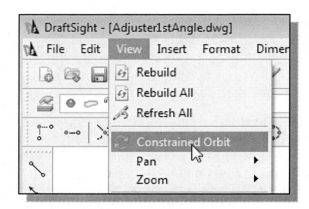

1. In the *Main Menu,* select **Constrained Orbit** under the *View* list as shown.

❖ Constrained Orbit enables us to manipulate the view of 3D objects by clicking and dragging with the left-mouse-button.

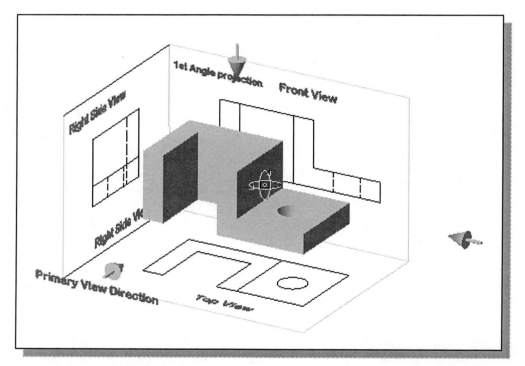

2. Inside the graphics window, press down the left-mouse-button and drag it up and down to rotate about the screen X-axis. Dragging the mouse left and right will rotate about the screen Y-axis.

3. On your own, use the real-time dynamic rotation feature of the Constrained Orbit command and examine the relations of the 2D views, projection planes and the 3D object.

Third-Angle Projection

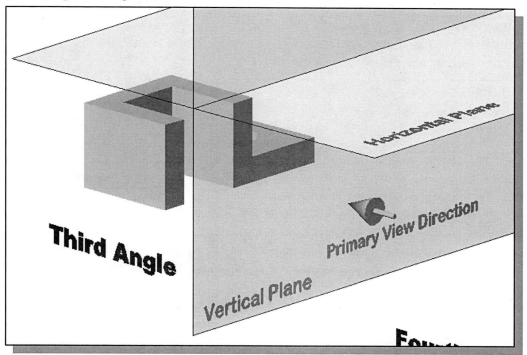

❖ In *third-angle projection*, the image planes are placed in between the object and the observer. And the views are formed by projecting to the image plane located in front of the object.

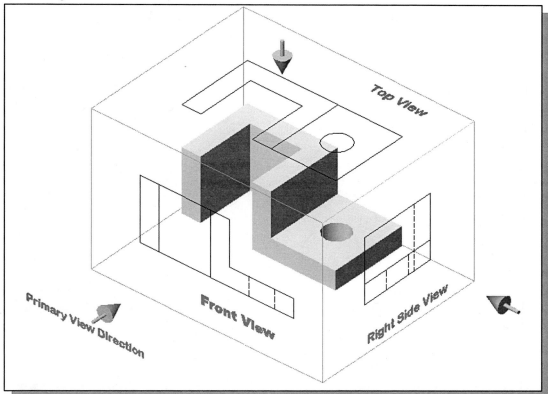

Rotation of the Horizontal and Profile Planes

In order to draw all three views of the object on the same plane, the horizontal (*Top View*) and profile (*Right Side View*) are rotated into the same plane as the primary image plane (*Front View*).

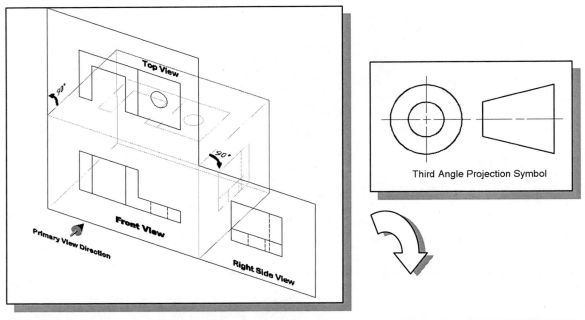

Third Angle Projection Symbol

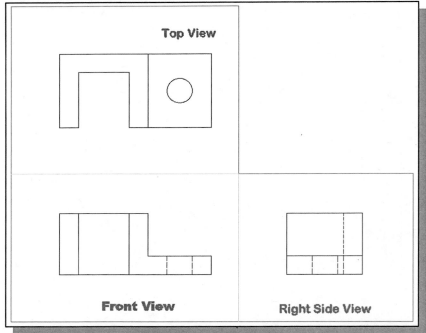

> Using *Internet Explorer*, open the following **avi** file to view the rotation of the projection planes:
> ***http://www.schroff.com/DraftSight/AdjusterRTOP.avi***

Examining the 3rd Angle Projection

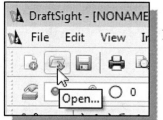

1. Click the **Open** icon in the *Standard* toolbar area as shown.

2. In the *Open File* dialog box, enter the following file name:
   http://www.schroff.com/DraftSight/Adjuster3rdAngle.dwg

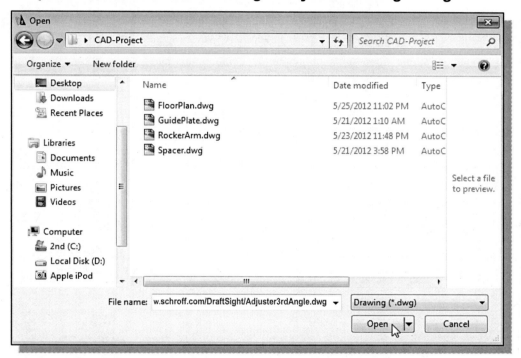

3. Click the **Open** icon and the ***Adjuster3rdAngle*** file is downloaded from the www.schroff.com web site to the local computer.

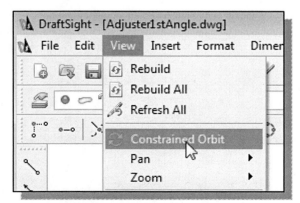

4. Select **Constrained Orbit** in the *Main Menu* area.
   [View] → [Constrained Orbit]

5. On your own, examine the relations of the 2D views, projection planes and the 3D object.

The Glass Box and the Six Principal Views

Considering the third angle projection described in the previous section further, we find that the object can be entirely surrounded by a set of six planes, a Glass box. On these planes, views can be obtained of the object as it is seen from the top, front, right side, left side, bottom, and rear.

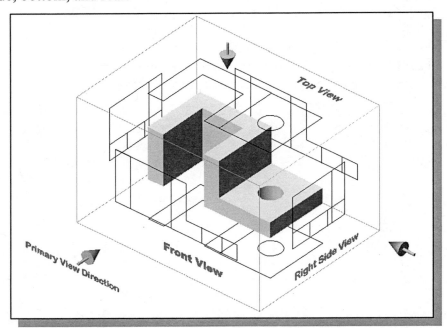

❖ Consider how the six sides of the glass box are being opened up into one plane. The front is the primary plane, and the other sides are hinged and rotated into position.

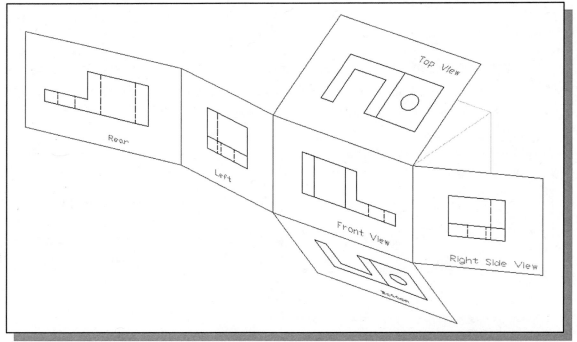

❖ In actual work, there is rarely an occasion when all six principal views are needed on one drawing, but no matter how many are required, their relative positions need to be maintained. These six views are known as the **six principal views**. In performing orthographic projection, each of 2D views shows only two of the three dimensions (**height**, **width**, and **depth**) of the 3D object.

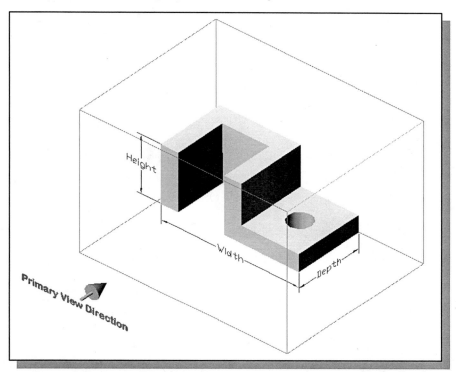

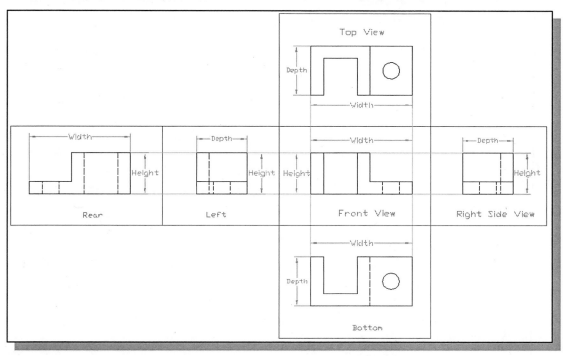

Examining the Glass Box Model

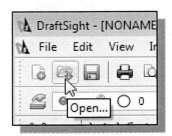

1. Click the **Open** icon in the *Standard* toolbar area as shown.

2. In the *Select File* dialog box, enter the following file name:
   http://www.schroff.com/DraftSight/AdjusterGlassBox.dwg

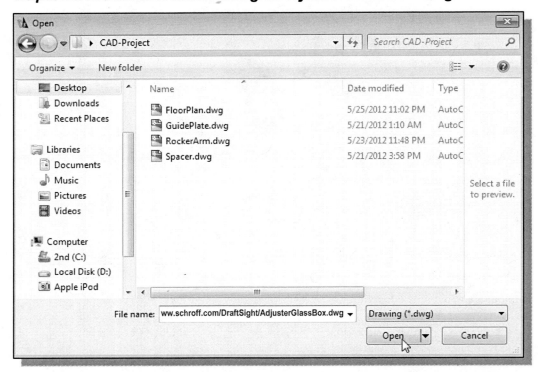

3. Click the **Open** icon and the ***AdjusterGlassBox*** file is downloaded from the www.schroff.com web site to the local computer.

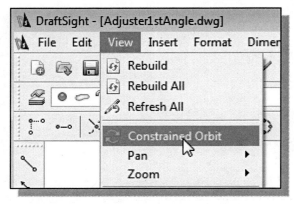

4. Select **Constrained Orbit** in the *Menu Bar*.
   [View] → **[Constrained Orbit]**

5. On your own, examine the relations of the 2D views, projection planes and the 3D object.

Alphabet of Lines

In Technical Engineering Drawings, each line has a definite meaning and is drawn in accordance to the line conventions as illustrated in the figure below. Two widths of lines are typically used on drawings; the thick line width should be 0.6 mm and the thin line width should be 0.3 mm.

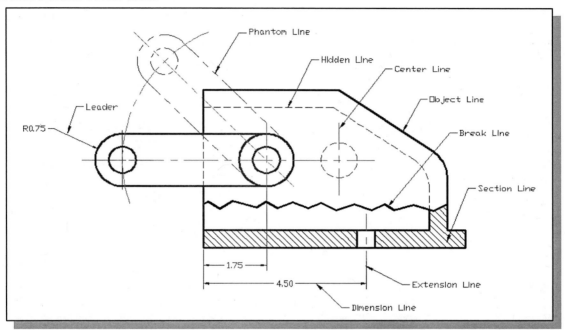

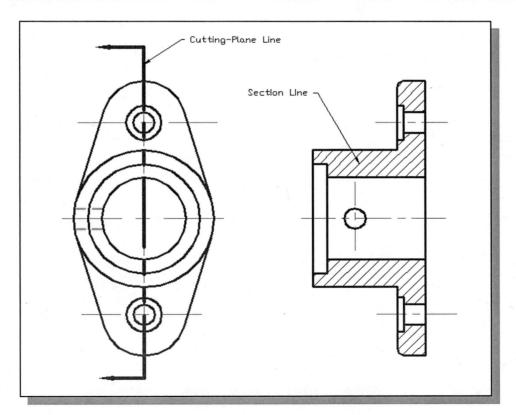

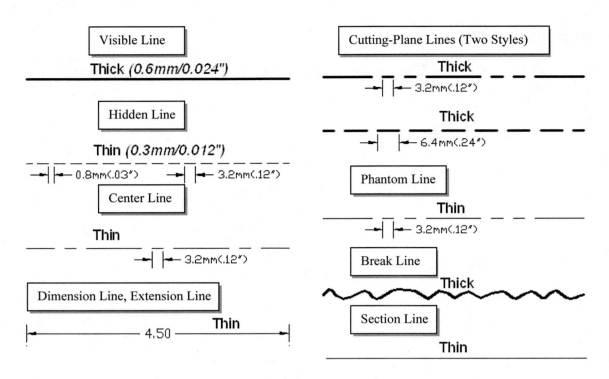

Visible Line Visible lines are used to represent visible edges and boundaries. The line weight is thick, 0.6mm/0.024″).

Hidden Line Hidden lines are used to represent edges and boundaries that are not visible from the viewing direction. The line weight is thin, 0.3mm/0.012″.

Center Line Center lines are used to represent axes of symmetry. The line weight is thin, 0.3mm/0.012″.

Dimension Line, Extension Line and Leader Dimension lines are used to show the sizes and locations of objects. The line weight is thin, 0.3mm/0.012″.

Cutting Plane Lines Cutting Plane lines are used to represent the location of an imaginary cut has been made, so that the interior of the object can be viewed. The line weight is thick, 0.6mm/0.024″. (Note that two forms of line type can be used.)

Phantom Line Phantom lines are used to represent imaginary features or objects, such as a rotated position of a part. The line weight is thin, 0.3mm/0.012″.

Break Line Break lines are used to represent imaginary cut, so that the interior of the object can be viewed. . The line weight is thick, 0.6mm/0.024″.

Section Line Section lines are used to represent the regions that have been cut with the *break lines* or *cutting plane lines*. The line weight is thin, 0.3mm/0.012″.

Precedence of Lines

In multiview drawings, coincidence lines may exist within the same view. For example, hidden features may project lines to coincide with the visible object lines. And center lines may occur where there is a visible or hidden outline.

In creating a multiview drawing, the features of the design are to be represented, therefore object and hidden lines take precedence over all other lines. And since the visible outline is more important than hidden features, the visible object lines take precedence over hidden lines. As shown in the below figure.

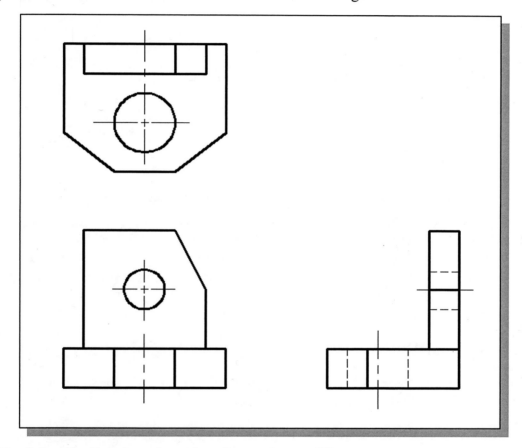

The following list gives the order of precedence of lines:

1. **Visible object lines**
2. **Hidden lines**
3. **Center line or cutting-plane line**
4. **Break lines**
5. **Dimension and extension lines**
6. **Crosshatch/section lines**

In the following sections, the general procedure of creating a 3rd angle three-view orthographic projection using DraftSight is presented.

The *Locator* part

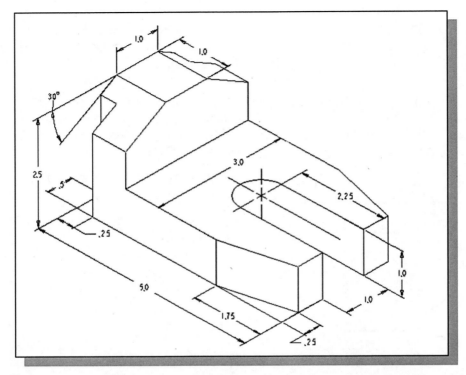

> ➤ Before going through the tutorial, make a rough sketch of a multiview drawing of the part. How many 2D views will be necessary to fully describe the part? Based on your knowledge of **DraftSight** so far, how would you arrange and construct these 2D views? Take a few minutes to consider these questions and do preliminary planning by sketching on a piece of paper. You are also encouraged to construct the orthographic views on your own prior to following through the tutorial.

Starting Up DraftSight

1. Select the **DraftSight** option on the *Program* menu or select the **DraftSight** icon on the *Desktop*.

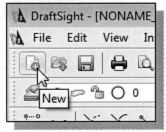

2. In the *Standard* toolbar, select the **New File** option with a single click of the left-mouse-button.

3. In the *Specify Template* dialog box, pick **Standard.dwt** as the template file to use.

4. On your own, open up the *Drafting Options* dialog box, and confirm **Grid Spacing** is set to **0.5** for both X and Y directions.

5. Also set the *Snap Spacing* to Match Grid spacing.

Layers setup

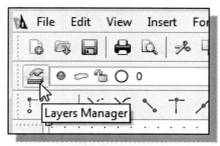

1. Pick **Layers Manager** in the *Layers* toolbar.

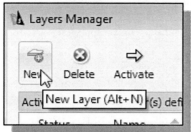

2. Click on the **New** icon to create new layers.

3. Create two **new** layers with the following settings:

Layer	Color	LineStyle
Construction	White	Continuous
Object	Blue	Continuous

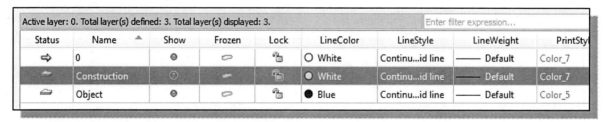

4. Highlight the layer *Construction* in the list of layers.

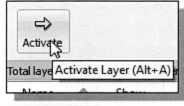

5. Click on the **Activate** button to set layer *Construction* as the *Current Layer*.

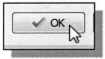

6. Click on the **OK** button to accept the settings and exit the *Layers Manager* dialog box.

7. In the *Status Bar* area, reset the option buttons so that only *SNAP Mode* and *GRID Display* are switched *ON*.

Drawing *Infinite Line*s

❖ *Infinite Lines* are lines that extend to infinity. Infinite Lines are usually used as references for creating other objects. We will also place the Infinite Lines on the *Construction* layer so that the layer can later be frozen or turned off.

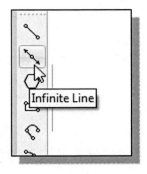

1. Select the **Infinite Line** icon in the *Draw* toolbar. In the command window, the message "*_Infiniteline Specify position:*" is displayed.

   • To orient Infinite Lines, we generally specify two points. Note that other orientation options are also available.

2. Select a location near the lower left corner of the graphics window, near the origin of the WCS. It is not necessary to align objects to the world coordinate origin. CAD systems provide us with many powerful tools to manipulate geometry. Our main goal is to use the CAD system as a flexible and powerful tool, and to be very efficient and effective with the system.

3. Pick a location above the last point to create a **vertical Infinite Line**.

4. Move the cursor toward the right of the first point and pick a location to create a **horizontal Infinite Line**.

5. Inside the graphics window, **right-mouse-click** to end the Infinite Line command.

6. In the *Status* toolbar area, turn **OFF** the *SNAP* option.

Using the *OFFSET* command

1. Select the **Offset** icon in the *Modify* toolbar. In the command window, the message "*Specify offset distance or [Through/Erase/Layer]:*" is displayed.

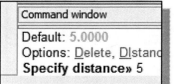

2. In the command window, enter: **5.0** [ENTER].

3. In the command window, the message "*Select source entity:*" is displayed. Pick the **vertical line** on the screen.

4. DraftSight next asks us to identify the direction of the offset. Pick a location that is to the **right** of the vertical line.

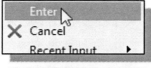

5. Inside the graphics window, **right-mouse-click** and choose **Enter** to end the Offset command.

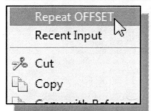

6. Inside the graphics window, **right-mouse-click** to bring up the option menu.

7. Select **Repeat Offset** in the popup list to repeat the Offset command.

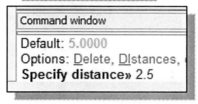

8. In the command window, enter: *1.5* [ENTER].

9. In the command window, the message "*Select source entity:*" is displayed. Pick the **horizontal line** on the screen.

10. DraftSight next asks us to identify the direction of the offset. Pick a location that is **above** the horizontal line.

11. Inside the graphics window, **right-mouse-click** to end the Offset command.

12. Repeat the **Offset** command and create the offset lines as shown.

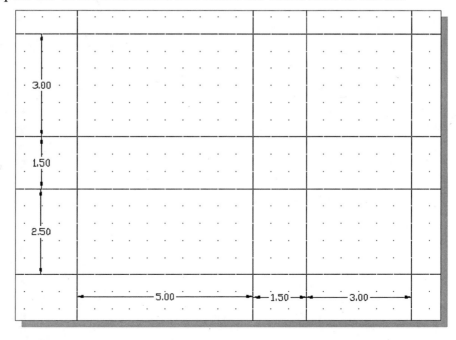

Set layer *Object* as the current layer

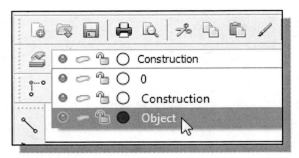

1. On the *Layers* toolbar panel, choose the **Layer Control** box with the left-mouse-button.

2. Move the cursor over the name of the layer *Object*. **Left-mouse-click once** and the *Object* layer is set as the *Current Layer*.

Using the *Running Entity Snaps*

In DraftSight, while using geometry construction commands, the cursor can be placed at points on objects such as endpoints, midpoints, centers, and intersections. In DraftSight this tool is called the ***Entity Snap***.

Entity Snaps can be turned *ON* in one of two ways:
- **Single Point (or override) Entity Snaps**: Sets an Entity Snap for one use.
- **Running Entity Snaps**: Sets Entity Snaps *active* until we turn them *OFF*.

The procedure we have used so far is the *Single Point Entity Snaps* option, where we select the specific Entity Snap from the *Entity Snap* toolbar for one use only. The use of the *Running Entity Snaps* option to assist the construction is illustrated next.

1. In the *Status* toolbar, right-mouse-click on **ESnap** to bring up the option menu and select **[Settings]**.

- Notice the different symbols associated with the different *Entity Snap* options. The *Running Entity Snap* options can be turned *ON* or *OFF* by clicking the different options listed.

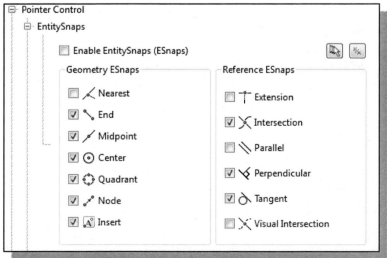

2. Turn **ON** the *Running Entity Snap* by clicking the **Enable EntitySnaps (ESnaps)** box, or hit the **[F3]** key once.

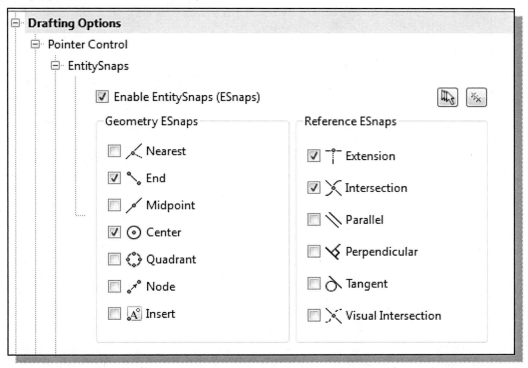

3. Reset the ESnaps options so that the ***Endpoint, Center, Extension*** and ***Intersection*** options are switched **ON**.

4. Click on the **OK** button to accept the settings and exit from the *Drafting Options* dialog box.

❖ Notice in the *Status Bar* area the ***ESnap*** button is switched **ON**. We can toggle the *Running Entity Snap* option *ON* or *OFF* by clicking the *ESnap* button.

5. Press the **[F3]** key once and notice the ***ESnap*** button is switched **OFF** in the *Status* toolbar area.

6. Press the **[F3]** key again and notice the ***ESnap*** button is now switched **ON** in the *Status* toolbar area.

➢ **DraftSight** provides many input methods and shortcuts; you are encouraged to examine the different options and choose the option that best fits your own style.

Creating *Object* lines

> ➤ We will define the areas for the front view, top view and side view by adding object lines using the *Running Entity Snap* option.

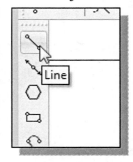

1. Select the **Line** command icon in the *Draw* toolbar. In the command window, the message *"Specify start point:"* is displayed.

2. Move the cursor to the **intersection** of any two lines and notice the visual aid automatically displayed at the intersection.

3. Pick the four intersection points closest to the lower left corner to create the four sides of the area of the front view.

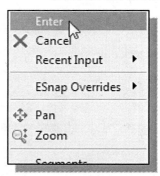

4. Inside the graphics window, right-mouse-click to activate the option menu and select **Enter** with the left-mouse-button to end the **Line** command.

5. Repeat the **Line** command to define the *Top View* and *Side View* as shown.

```
                        Top View

        3.00


        1.50


        2.50      Front View        Side View


              |----- 5.00 -----|-1.50-|-- 3.00 --|
```

Turn *OFF* the Infinite Lines layer

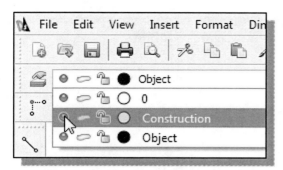

1. On the **Layer Control** toolbar, choose the down arrow with the left-mouse-button.

2. Move the cursor over the **Show** icon for the **Construction** layer. Left-mouse-click once and notice the icon color is changed to gray, representing the layer (layer *Construction*) is turned *OFF*.

Adding more objects in the Front View

1. Use the **Offset** command and create the two parallel lines in the *Front View* as shown.

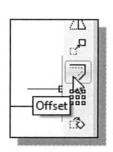

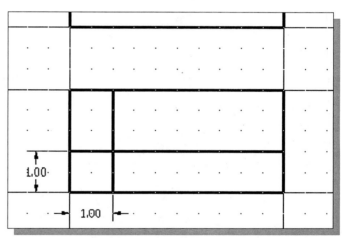

2. Use the **Trim** command and modify the *Front View* as shown.

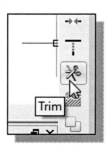

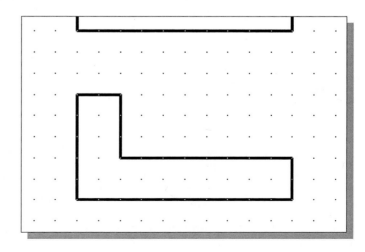

DraftSight's *ESnap* and *ETrack* features

DraftSight's *ESnap* and *ETrack* provide visual aids when the *Entity Snap* options are switched *ON*. The main advantages of *ESnap* and *ETrack* are as follows:

- **Symbols**: Automatically displays the *Entity Snap* type at the *Entity Snap* location.

- **ToolTips**: Automatically displays the *Entity Snap* type next to the cursor.

- **Magnet**: Locks the cursor onto a snap point when the cursor is near the point.

With **Entity Snap Tracking**, the cursor can track along alignment paths based on other *Entity Snap* points when specifying points in a command. To use *Entity Snap Tracking*, one or more *Entity Snaps* must be switched *ON*. The basic rules of using the **Entity Snap Tracking** option are as follows:

- To track from a *Running Entity Snap* point, pause over the point while in a command.

- A tracking vector appears when we move the cursor.

- To stop tracking, pause over the point again.

1. In the *Status* toolbar area, turn *ON* the *ETrack* option.

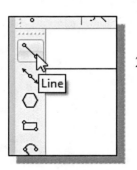

2. Select the **Line** command icon in the *Draw* toolbar. In the command window, the message "*Specify start point:*" is displayed.

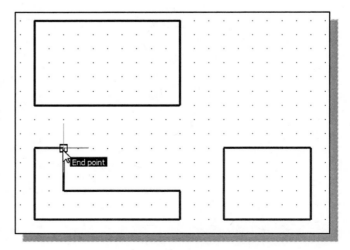

3. Move the cursor near the top right corner of the vertical protrusion in the *Front View*. Notice that *ESnap* automatically locks the cursor to the corner and displays the **Endpoint** symbol.

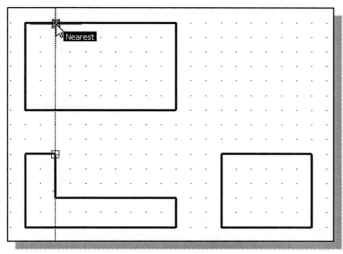

4. Move the cursor upward and notice that *Entity Tracking* displays a dashed line, showing the alignment to the top right corner of the vertical protrusion in the *Front View*. Move the cursor near the top horizontal line of the *Top View* and notice that *ESnap* displays the nearest point. Left-mouse-click to place the starting point at this location.

5. Move the cursor to the bottom edge of the *Top View* to activate the tracking feature.

6. Create the line as shown in the figure.

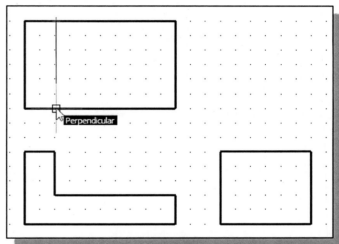

Adding more objects in the Top View

1. Use the **Offset** command and create the two parallel lines in the *Top View* as shown.

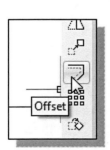

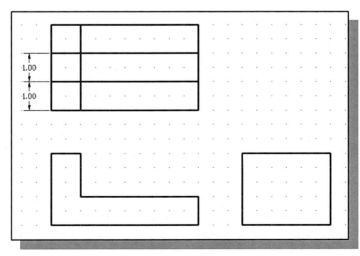

2. On your own, display the *Entity Snap* toolbar on the screen.

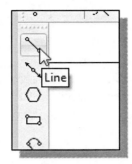

3. Select the **Line** command icon in the *Draw* toolbar. In the command window, the message "*_line Specify first point:*" is displayed.

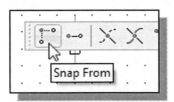

4. In the *Entity Snap* toolbar, pick **Snap From**. DraftSight now expects us to select a reference point on the screen.

➢ Note the ***Single Point Entity Snap*** overrides the ***Running Entity Snap*** options.

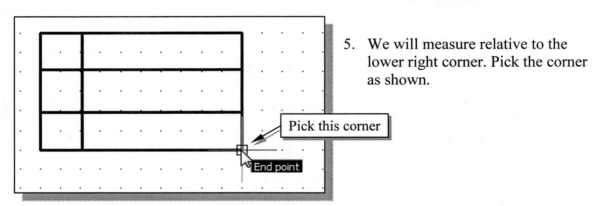

5. We will measure relative to the lower right corner. Pick the corner as shown.

6. In the command window, enter **@0,0.25** [ENTER].

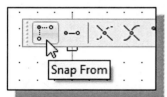

7. In the *Entity Snap* toolbar, pick **Snap From**.

8. Pick the **lower right corner** of the *Top View* again.

9. In the command window, enter **@-1.75,0** [ENTER].

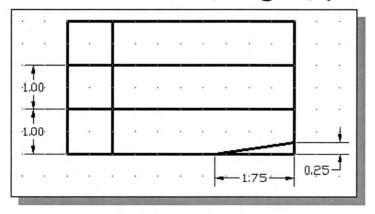

10. Inside the graphics window, right-mouse-click to activate the option menu and select **Enter** with the left-mouse-button to end the Line command.

11. Repeat the procedure and create the line on the top right corner as shown.

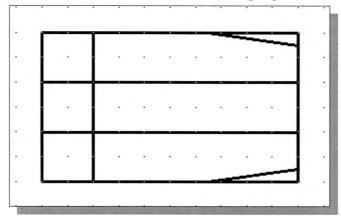

12. Using the *Snap From* option, create the circle (diameter **1.0**) as shown.

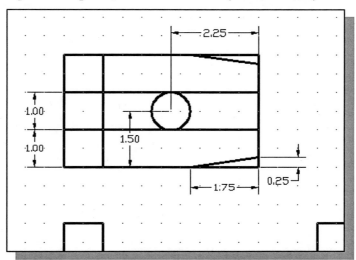

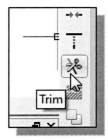

13. Select the **Trim** icon in the *Modify* toolbar. In the command window, the message "*Select boundary edges... Select objects:*" is displayed.

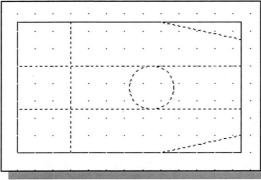

14. Pick the following objects as boundary edges: the circle and the lines that are near the circle.

15. Inside the graphics window, **right-mouse-click** to accept the selected objects.

16. Select the unwanted portions and modify the objects as shown.

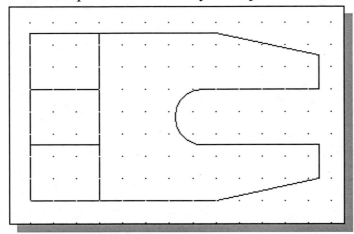

17. On your own, use the **Offset** and **Trim** commands and modify the *Top View* as shown.

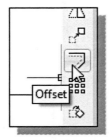
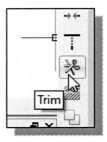

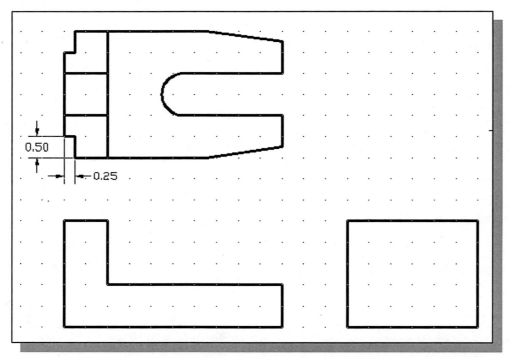

Drawing using the *Miter Line* method

❖ The *45° miter line* method is a simple and straightforward procedure to transfer measurements in between the *Top View* and the *Side View*.

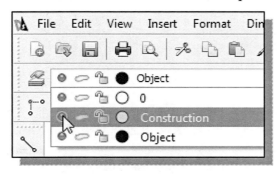

1. On the *Layers* toolbar panel, choose the *Layer Control* box by clicking once with the left-mouse-button.

2. Move the cursor over the **Show** icon for layer *Construction*.

3. **Left-mouse-click once** and notice the icon color is changed to a light color, representing the layer (layer *Construction*) is turned *ON*.

4. **Left-mouse-click once** over the name of the layer *Construction* to set it as the *Current Layer*.

5. Use the **Line** command and create the *miter line* by connecting the two intersections of the *Infinite Lines* as shown.

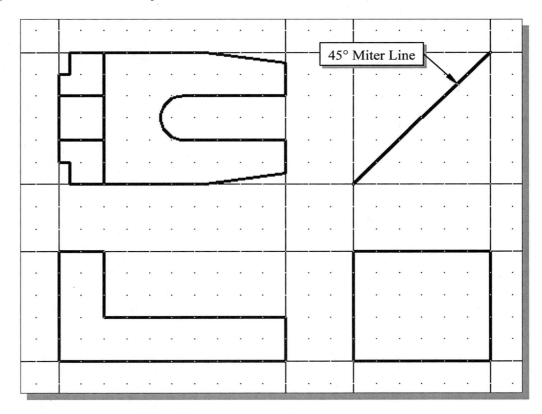

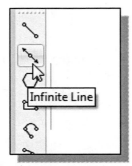

6. Select the **Infinite Line** command in the *Draw* toolbar as shown.

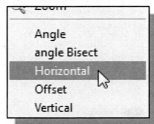

7. In the option menu, select the **Horizontal** option as shown.

8. On your own, create horizontal projection lines through all the corners in the *Top View* as shown.

9. Use the **Trim** command and trim the projection lines as shown in the figure below.

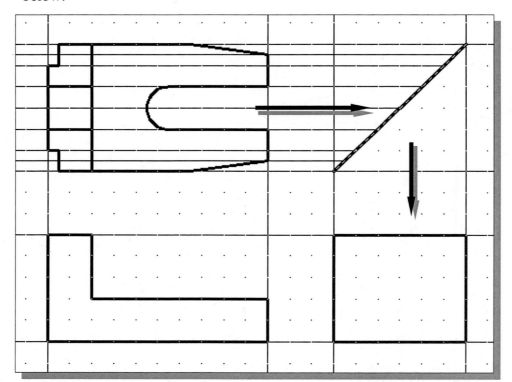

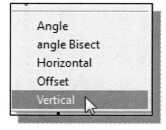

10. On your own, create additional Infinite Lines (Vertical option) through all the intersection points that are on the *miter line*.

More Layers setup

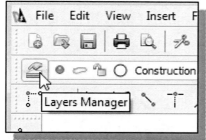

1. Pick **Layers Manager** in the *Layers* toolbar panel as shown in the figure.

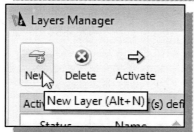

2. Click on the **New** icon to create new layers.

3. Create two **new layers** with the following settings:

Layer	*Color*	*LineStyle*
Hidden	**Cyan**	**HIDDEN**
Center	**Red**	**CENTER**

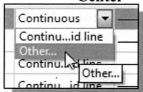

- The default *LineStyle* is *Continuous*. To use other *LineStyles*, click on the **Load** button in the *LineStyle* dialog box and select the desired *LineStyles*.

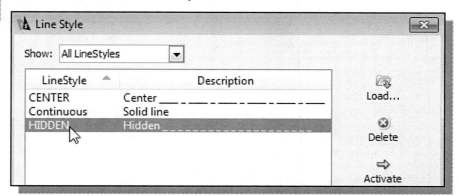

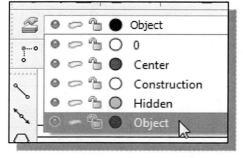

4. On your own, set the layer **Object** as the *Current Layer*.

Top View to Side View Projection

1. Using the *Running Entity Snaps*, create the necessary **object lines** in the *Side View*.

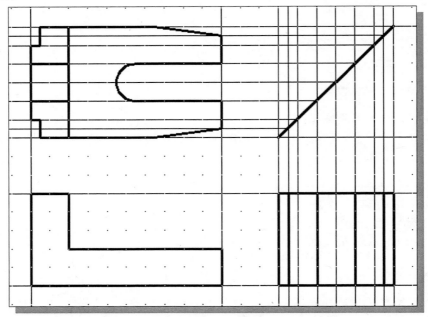

2. Set layer **Hidden** as the *Current Layer* and create the two necessary hidden lines in the *Side View*.

3. Set layer **Center** as the *Current Layer* and create the necessary centerlines in the *Side View*.

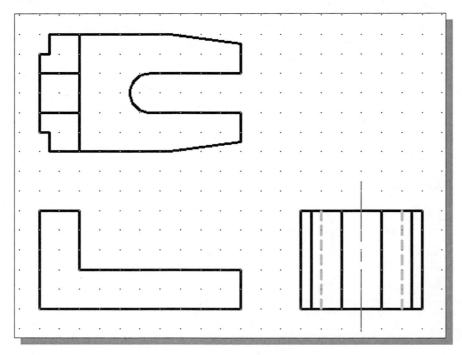

4. In the *Layer Control* box, turn **OFF** the ***Infinite Lines***.

5. Set layer ***Object*** as the *Current Layer*.

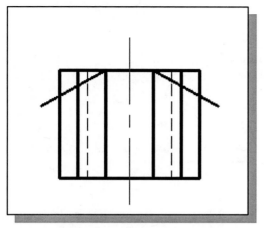

6. Use the **Line** command and create the two 30° inclined lines as shown.

   (Hint: Relative coordinate entries of **@2.0<-30** and **@2.0<210**.)

7. Use the **Line** command and create a horizontal line in the *Side View* as shown.

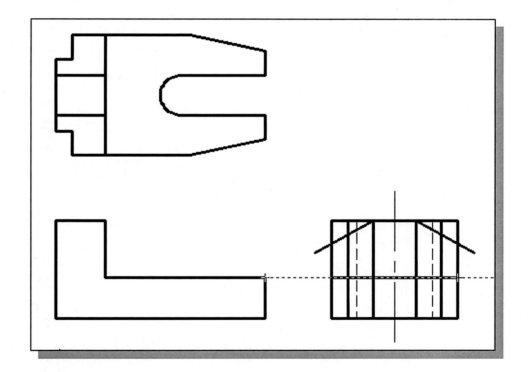

8. On your own, use the **Trim** command and remove the unwanted portions in the *Side View*. Refer to the image shown on the next page if necessary.

Completing the Front View

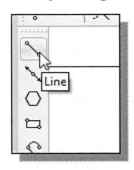

1. Select the **Line** command icon in the *Draw* toolbar. In the command window, the message "*_line Specify first point:*" is displayed.

2. Move the cursor to the top left corner in the *Side View* and the bottom left corner in the *Top View* to activate the *Entity Tracking* option to both corners.

3. Left-mouse-click once when the cursor is aligned to both corners as shown.

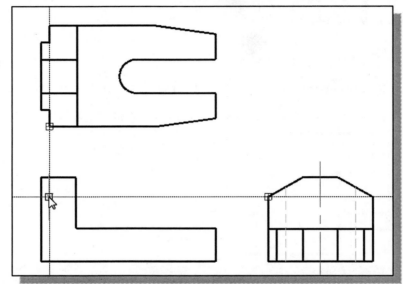

4. Create the **horizontal line** as shown.

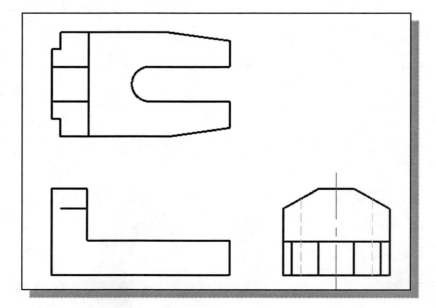

5. Repeat the procedure and create the lines in the *Front View* as shown.

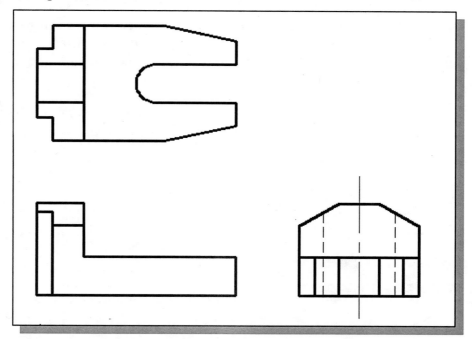

6. Add in any additional object lines that are necessary.

7. Set layer **Hidden** as the *Current Layer* and create the necessary hidden lines in the *Front View*.

8. Set layer **Center** as the *Current Layer* and create the necessary centerlines in the *Top View* and *Front View*.

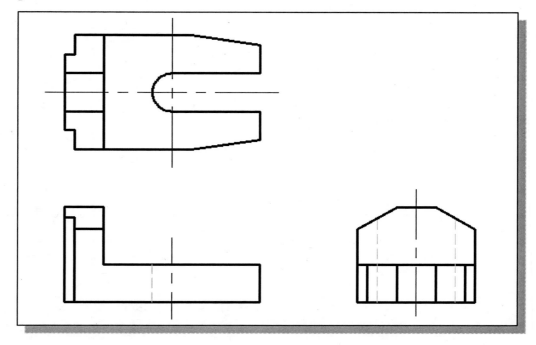

Object Information using the *LIST* command

- DraftSight provides several tools that will allow us to get information about constructed geometric objects. The **List** command can be used to show detailed information about geometric objects.

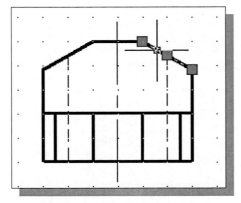

1. Move the cursor to the *Side View* and select the inclined line on the right, as shown in the figure.

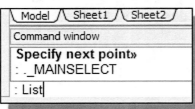

2. In the command window, enter **List** to activate the command.

- Note the information regarding the selected object is displayed in the DraftSight *Command Window* as shown.

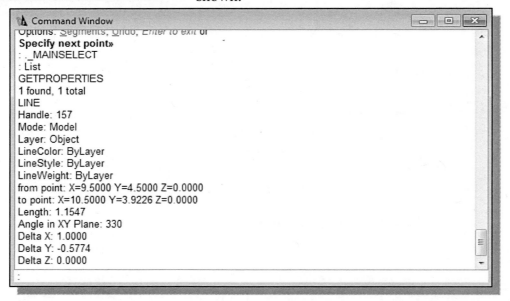

- Note the **List** command can be used to show detailed information about the selected line. The angle and length of the line, as well as the X, Y and Z components between the two endpoints are all listed in a separate window.

3. Press the [**F2**] key once to close the DraftSight command window.

Object Information using the *PROPERTIES* command

- DraftSight also provides tools that allow us to display and change properties of constructed geometric objects. The **Properties** command not only provides the detailed information about geometric objects; modifications can also be done very quickly.

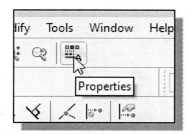

1. In the *Main Menu* area, left-mouse-click once on the **Properties** icon to activate the command.

2. Note the *Properties* panel appears on the screen. The "*No selection*" on top of the panel indicates no object has been selected.

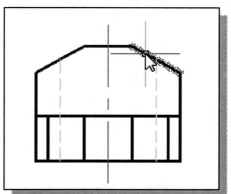

3. Move the cursor to the *Side View* and select the inclined line on the right, as shown in the figure.

4. The geometry information is listed at the bottom section. Note the line length is *1.1547* and at the angle of *330* degrees.

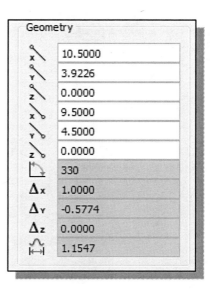

Review Questions:

1. Explain what an orthographic view is and why it is important to engineering graphics.

2. What does the *Running Entity Snaps* option allow us to do?

3. Explain how a *miter line* can assist us in creating orthographic views.

4. Describe the DraftSight *ESnap* and *ETrack* options.

5. List and describe two DraftSight commands that can be used to get geometric information about constructed objects.

6. List and describe two options you could use to quickly create a 2-inch line attached to a 2-inch circle, as shown in the below figure.

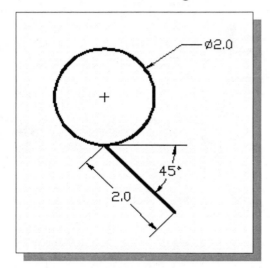

7. What are the length and angle of the inclined line, highlighted in the figure below, in the *Top View* of the *Locator* design?

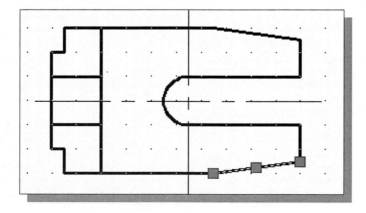

Exercises:

(Unless otherwise specified, dimensions are in inches.)

1. Saddle Bracket

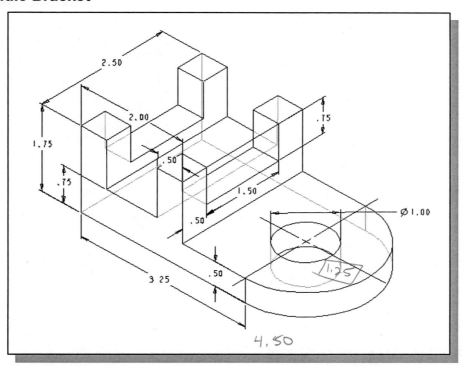

2. Anchor Base

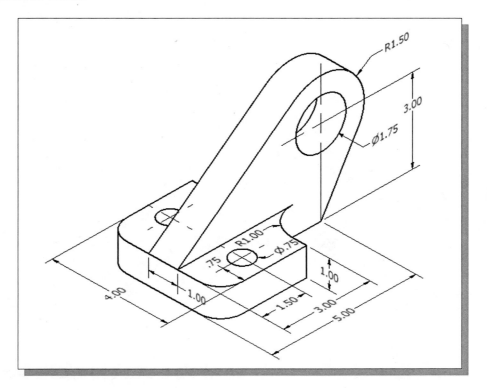

3. Bearing Base

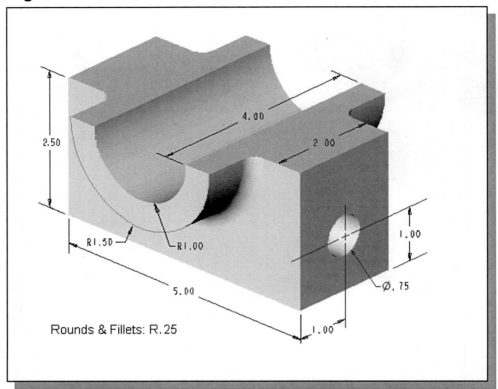

Rounds & Fillets: R.25

4. Shaft Support (Dimensions are in Millimeters.)

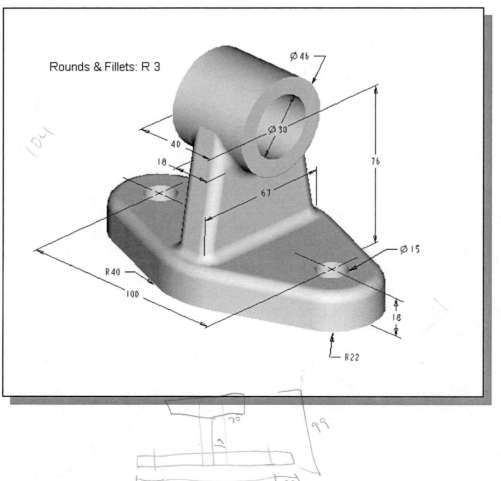

Rounds & Fillets: R 3

5. Connecting Rod

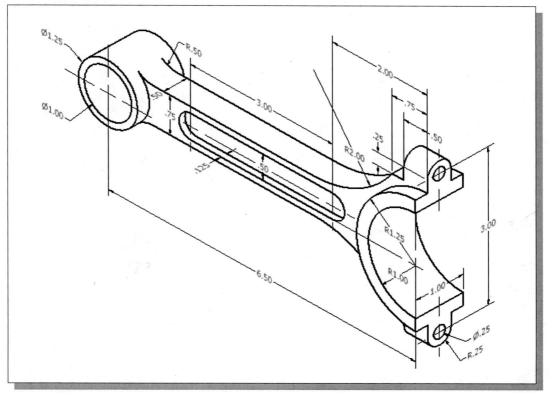

6. Tube Hanger

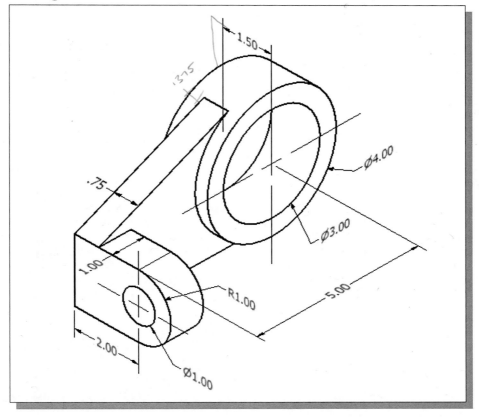

Notes:

Chapter 5
Pictorials and Sketching

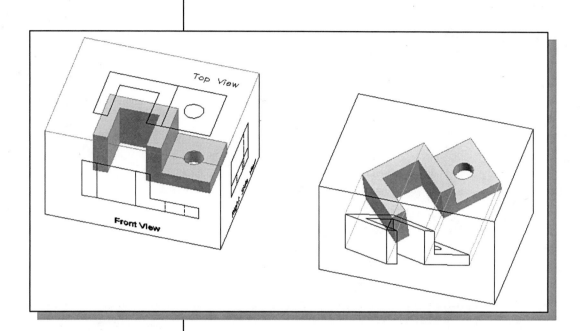

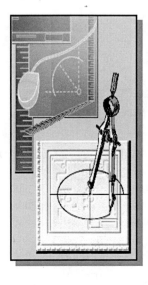

Learning Objectives

- ◆ **Understand the Importance of Freehand Sketching**
- ◆ **Understand the Terminology Used in Pictorial Drawings**
- ◆ **Understand the Basics of the Following Projection Methods: Axnonometric, Oblique and Perspective**
- ◆ **Be Able to Create Freehand 3D Pictorials**

Engineering Drawings, Pictorials and Sketching

One of the best ways to communicate one's ideas is through the use of a picture or a drawing. This is especially true for engineers and designers. Without the ability to communicate well, engineers and designers will not be able to function in a team environment and therefore will have only limited value in the profession.

For many centuries, artists and engineers used drawings to express their ideas and inventions. The two figures below are drawings by da Vinci (1453-1528) illustrating some of his engineering inventions.

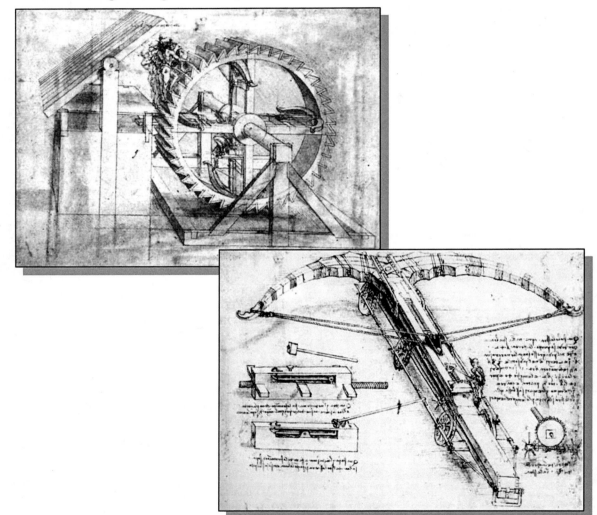

Engineering design is a process to create and transform ideas and concepts into a product definition that meet the desired objective. The engineering design process typically involves three stages: (1) Ideation/conceptual design stage: this is the beginning of a engineering design process, where basic ideas and concepts take shapes. (2) Design development stage: the basic ideas are elaborated and further developed. During this stage, prototypes and testing are commonly used to ensure the developed design meet the desired objective. (3) Refine and finalize design stage: This stage of the design process is the last stage of the design process, where the finer details of the design are further refined. Detailed information of the finalized design is documented to assure the design is ready for production.

Two types of drawings are generally associated with the three stages of the engineering process: (1) Freehand Sketches and (2) Detailed Engineering Drawings.

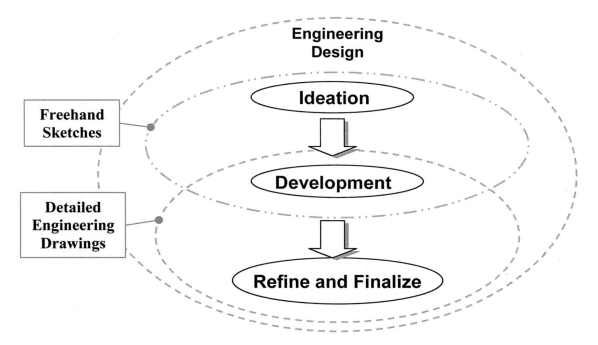

Freehand sketches are generally used in the beginning stages of a design process: (1) to quickly record designer's ideas and help formulating different possibilities, (2) to communicate the designer's basic ideas with others and (3) to develop and elaborate further the designer's ideas/concepts.

During the initial design stage, an engineer will generally picture the ideas in his/her head as three-dimensional images. The ability to think visually, specifically three-dimensional visualization, is one of the most essential skills for an engineer/designer. And freehand sketching is considered as one of the most powerful method to help develop visualization skills.

Detailed engineering drawings are generally created during the second and third stages of a design process. The detailed engineering drawings are used to help refine and finalize the design and also to document the finalized design for production. Engineering drawings typically require the use of drawing instruments, from compasses to computers, to bring precision to the drawings.

Freehand Sketches and Detailed Engineering Drawings are essential communication tools for engineers. By using the established conventions, such as perspective and isometric drawings, engineers/designers are able to quickly convey their design ideas to others.

The ability to sketch ideas is absolutely essential to engineers. The ability to sketch is helpful, not just to communicate with others, but also to work out details in ideas and to identify any potential problems. Freehand sketching requires only simple tools, a pencil and a piece of paper, and can be accomplished almost anywhere and anytime. Creating freehand sketches does not require any artistic ability. Detailed engineering drawing is employed only for those ideas deserving a permanent record.

Freehand sketches and engineering drawings are generally composed of similar information, but there is a tradeoff between time required to generate a sketch/drawing verses the level of design detail and accuracy. In industry, freehand sketching is used to quickly document rough ideas and identify general needs for improvement in a team environment.

Besides the 2D views, described in the previous chapter, there are three main divisions commonly used in freehand engineering sketches and detailed engineering drawings: (1) **Axonometric**, with its divisions into **isometric, dimetric** and **trimetric**; (2) **Oblique**; and (3) **Perspective**.

1. **Axonometric projection**: The word *Axonometric* means "to measure along axes". Axonometric projection is a special *orthographic projection* technique used to generate *pictorials*. **Pictorials** show a 2D image of an object as viewed from a direction that reveals three directions of space. In the figure below, the adjuster model is rotated so that a *pictorial* is generated using *orthographic projection* (projection lines perpendicular to the projection plane) as described in the previous chapter. There are three types of axonometric projections: isometric projection, dimetric projection, and trimetric projection. Typically in an axonometric drawing, one axis is drawn vertically.

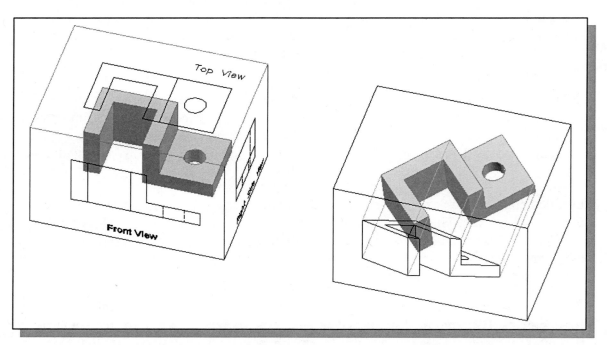

In **isometric projections**, the direction of viewing is such that the three axes of space appear equally foreshortened, and therefore the angles between the axes are equal. In **dimetric projections**, the directions of viewing are such that two of the three axes of space appear equally foreshortened. In **trimetric projections**, the direction of viewing is such that the three axes of space appear unequally foreshortened.

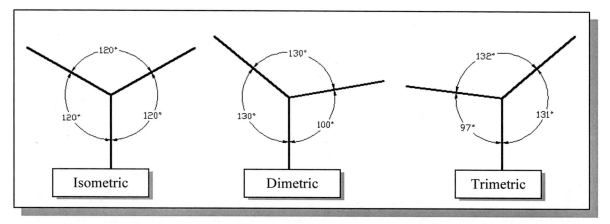

Isometric projection is perhaps the most widely used for pictorials in engineering graphics, mainly because isometric views are the most convenient to draw. Note that the different projection options described here are not particular critical in freehand sketching as the emphasis is generally placed on the proportions of the design, not the precision measurements. The general procedure to constructing isometric views is illustrated in the following sections.

2. **Oblique Projection** represents a simple technique of keeping the front face of an object parallel to the projection plane and still reveals three directions of space. An **orthographic projection** is a parallel projection in which the projection lines are perpendicular to the plane of projection. An **oblique projection** is one in which the projection lines are other than perpendicular to the plane of projection.

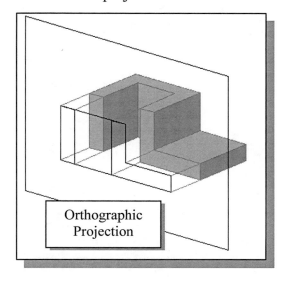

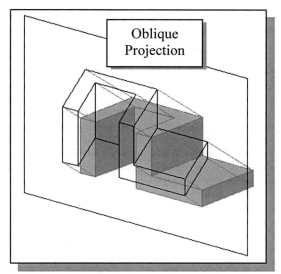

In an oblique drawing, geometry that are parallel to the frontal plane of projection are drawn true size and shape. This is the main advantage of the oblique drawing over the axonometric drawings. The three axes of the oblique sketch are drawn horizontal, vertical, and the third axis can be at any convenient angle (typically between 30 and 60 degrees.) The proportional scale along the 3rd axis is typically a scale anywhere between ½ and 1. If the scale is ½, then it is a **Cabinet** oblique. If the scale is 1, then it is a **Cavalier** oblique.

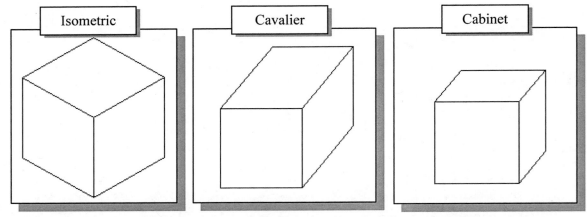

3. **Perspective Projection** adds realism to the three-dimensional pictorial representation; a perspective drawing represents an object as it appears to an observer; objects that are closer to the observer will appear larger to the observer. The key to the perspective projection is that parallel edges converge to a single point, known as the **vanishing point**. If there is just one vanishing point, then it is called a one-point perspective. If two sets of parallel edge lines converge to their respective vanishing points, then it is called a two-point perspective. There is also the case of a three-point perspective in which all three sets of parallel lines converge to their respective vanishing points.

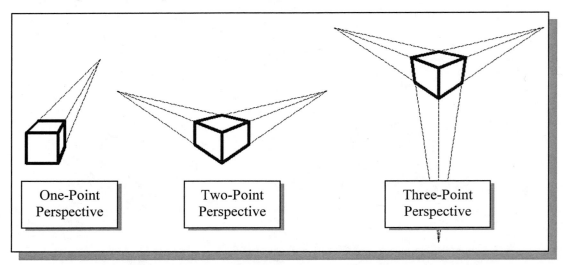

- Although there are specific techniques available to create precise pictorials with known dimensions, in the following sections, the basic concepts and procedures relating to freehand sketching are illustrated.

Isometric Sketching

Isometric drawings are generally done with one axis aligned to the vertical direction. A **regular isometric** is when the viewpoint is looking down on the top of the object, and a **reversed isometric** is when the viewpoint is looking up on the bottom of the object.

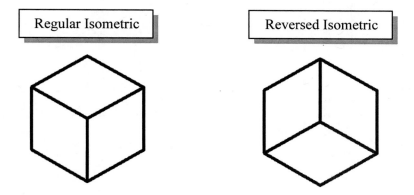

Two commonly used approaches in creating isometric sketches are: (1) the **enclosing box** method and (2) the **adjacent surface** method. The enclosing box method begins with the construction of an isometric box showing the overall size of the object. The visible portions of the individual 2D-views are then constructed on the corresponding sides of the box. Adjustments of the locations of surfaces are then made, by moving the edges, to complete the isometric sketch.

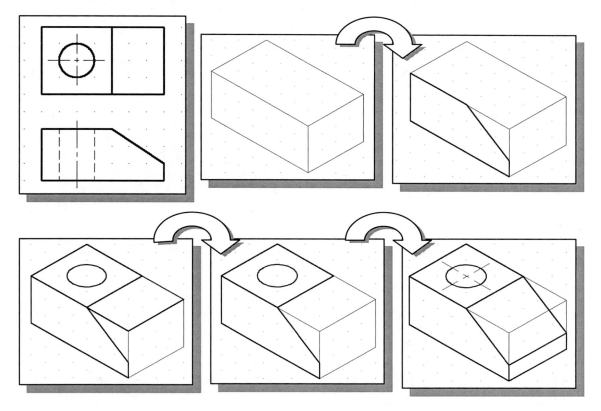

The adjacent surface method begins with one side of the isometric drawing, again with the visible portion of the corresponding 2D-view. The isometric sketch is completed by identifying and adding the adjacent surfaces.

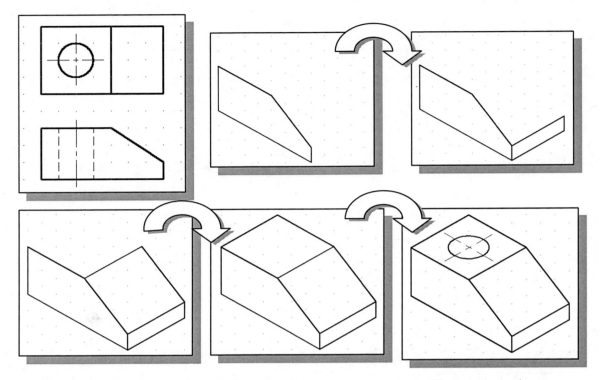

In an isometric drawing, cylindrical or circular shapes appear as ellipses. It can be confusing in drawing the ellipses in an isometric view; one simple rule to remember is the **major axis** of the ellipse is always **perpendicular** to the **center axis** of the cylinder as shown in the figures below.

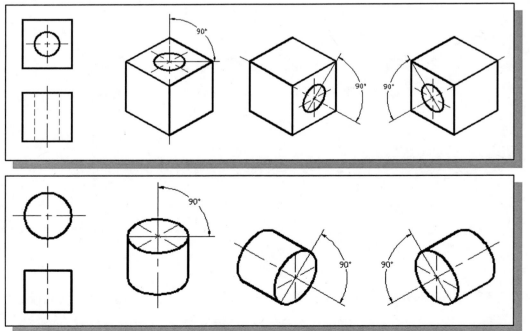

Isometric Sketching Exercises:
Given the Orthographic Top view and Front view, create the isometric view.

1.

2.

3.

Oblique Sketching

Keeping the geometry that is parallel to the frontal plane true size and shape is
the main advantage of the oblique drawing over the axonometric drawings. Unlike
isometric drawings, circular shapes that are paralleled to the frontal view will remain as
circles in oblique drawings. Generally speaking, an oblique drawing can be created very
quickly by using a 2D view as the starting point. For designs with most of the circular
shapes in one direction, an oblique sketch is the ideal choice over the other pictorial
methods.

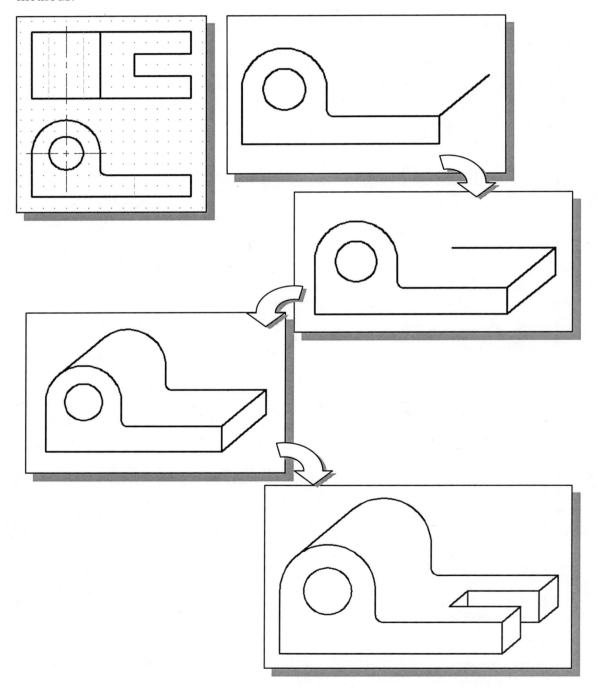

Oblique Sketching Exercises:

Given the Orthographic Top view and Front view, create the oblique view.

1.

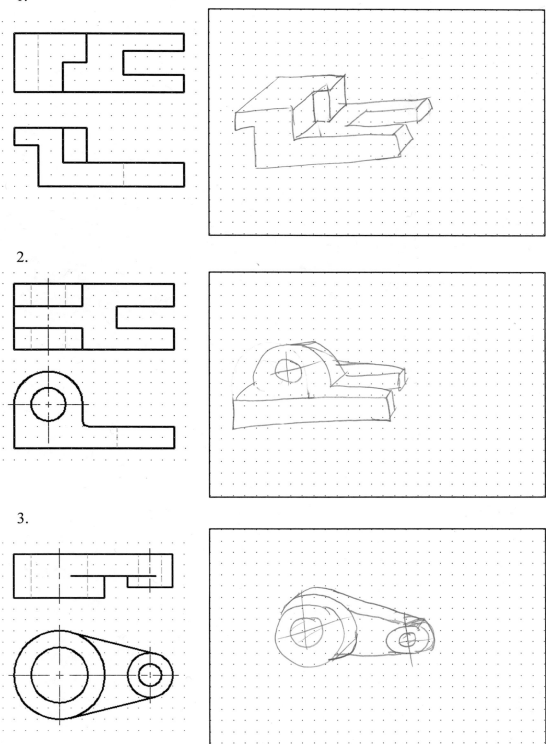

2.

3.

Perspective Sketching

A perspective drawing represents an object as it appears to an observer; objects that are closer to the observer will appear larger to the observer. The key to the perspective projection is that parallel edges converge to a single point, known as the **vanishing point**. The vanishing point represents the position where projection lines converge.

The selection of the locations of the vanishing points, which is the first step in creating a perspective sketch, will affect the looks of the resulting images.

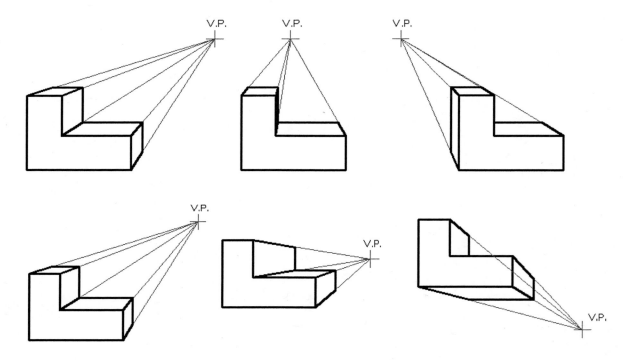

One-point Perspective

One-point perspective is commonly used because of its simplicity. The first step in creating a one-point perspective is to sketch the front face of the object just as in oblique sketching; followed by selecting the position for the vanishing point. For Mechanical designs, the vanishing point is usually placed above and to the right of the picture. The use of construction lines can be helpful in locating the edges of the object and to complete the sketch.

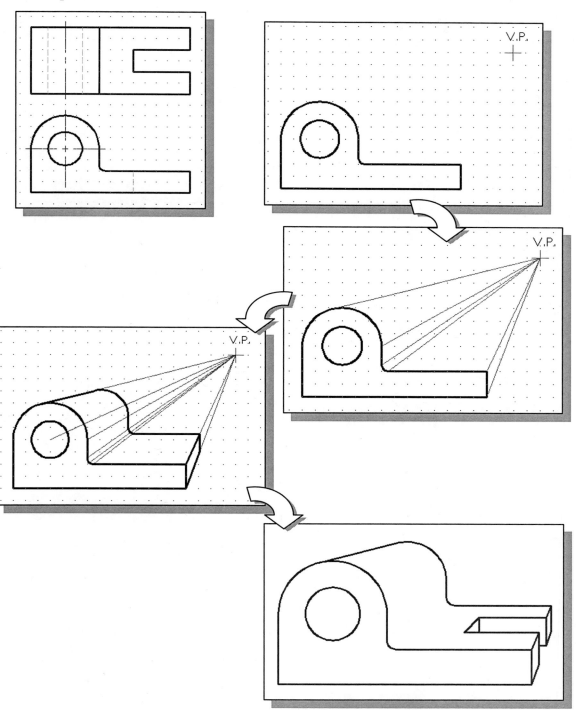

Two-point Perspective

Two-point perspective is perhaps the most popular of all perspective methods. The use of the two vanishing points gives very true to life images. The first step in creating a two-point perspective is to select the locations for the two vanishing points; followed by sketching an enclosing box to show the outline of the object. The use of construction lines can be very helpful in locating the edges of the object and to complete the sketch.

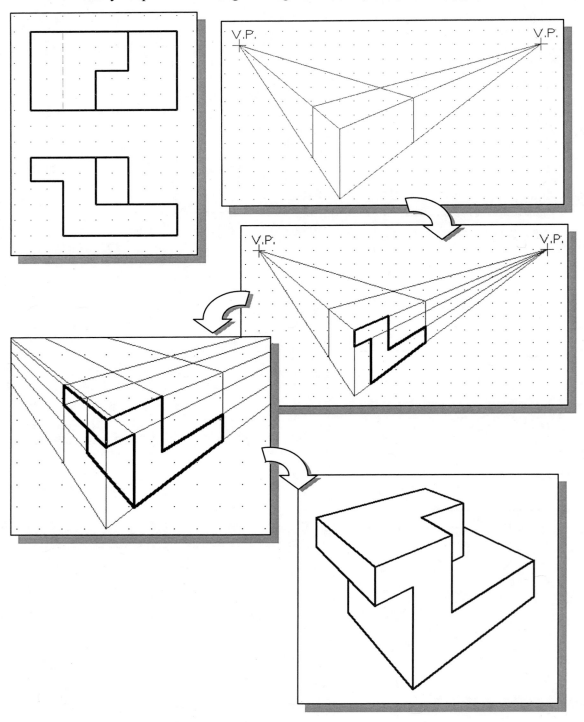

Perspective Sketching Exercises:

Given the Orthographic Top view and Front view, create one-point or two-point perspective views.

1.

2.

3.

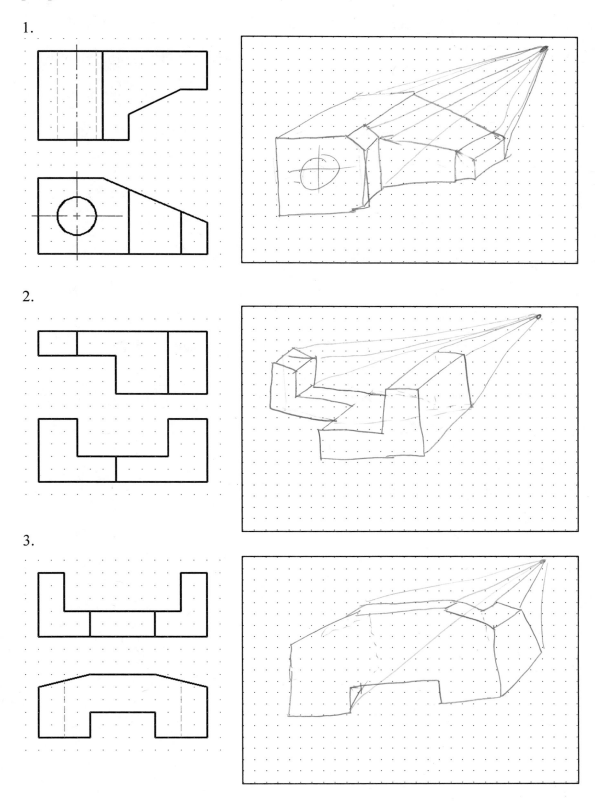

Questions:

1. What are the three types of Axonometric projection?

2. Describe the differences between an Isometric drawing and a Trimetric drawing.

3. What is the main advantage of Oblique projection over the isometric projection?

4. Describe the differences between a one-point perspective and a two-point perspective.

5. Which pictorial methods maintain true size and shape of geometry on the frontal plane?

6. What is a vanish point in a perspective drawing?

7. What is a Cabinet Oblique?

8. What is the angle between the three axes in an isometric drawing?

9. In an Axonometric drawing, are the projection lines perpendicular to the projection plane?

10. A cylindrical feature, in a frontal plane, will remain a circle in which pictorial methods?

11. In an Oblique drawing, are the projection lines perpendicular to the projection plane?

12. Create freehand pictorial sketches of:
    * Your desk
    * Your computer
    * One corner of your room
    * The tallest building in your area

Exercises:

1. Given the 2D views, construct the associated isometric views.

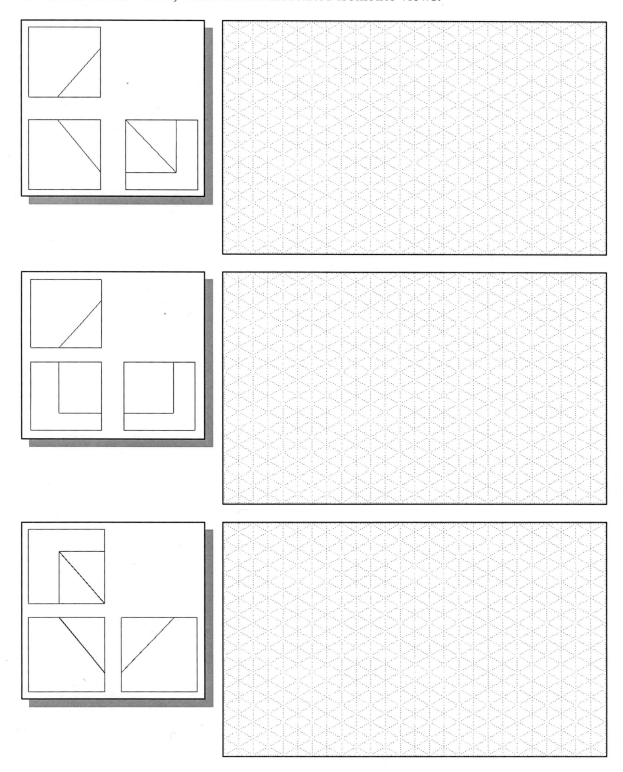

2. Given the 2D views, construct the associated two-point perspective views.

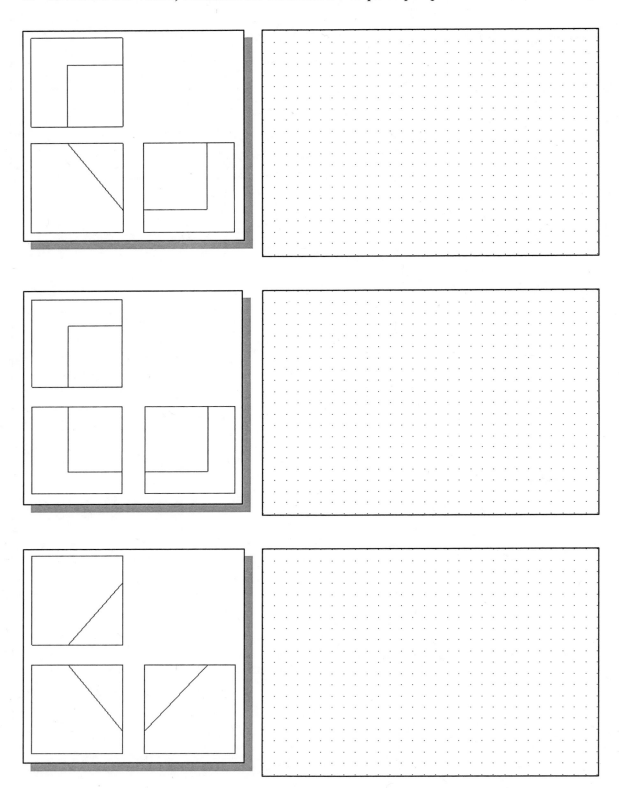

3.   Given the 2D views, construct the associated oblique views.

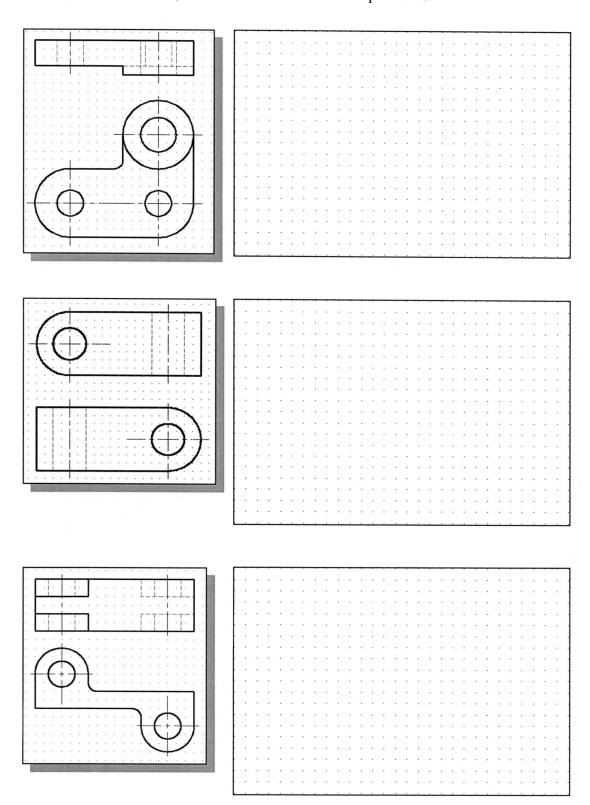

4.   Given the 2D views, construct the associated one-point perspective views.

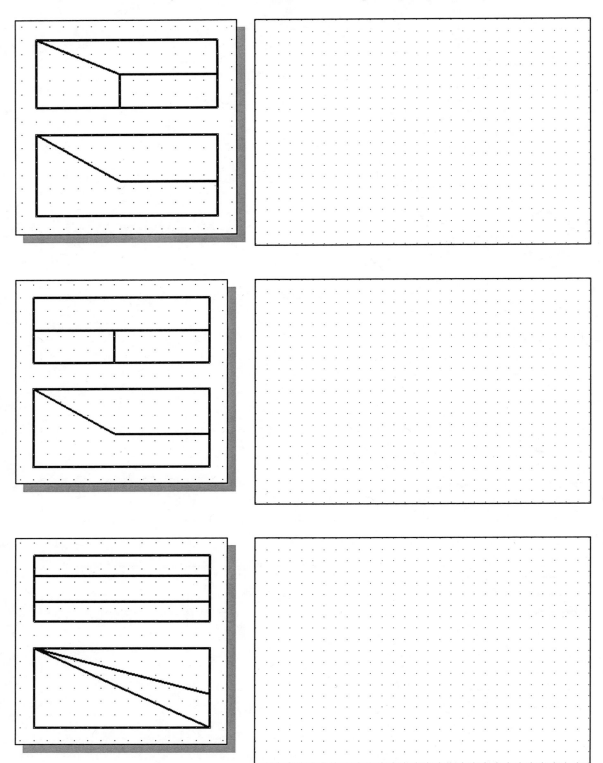

5. Complete the missing views. (Create a pictorial sketch as an aid in reading the views.)

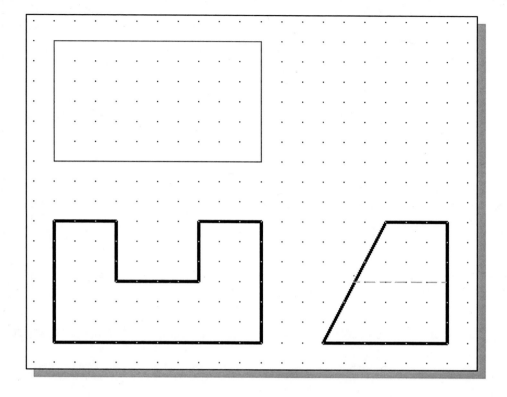

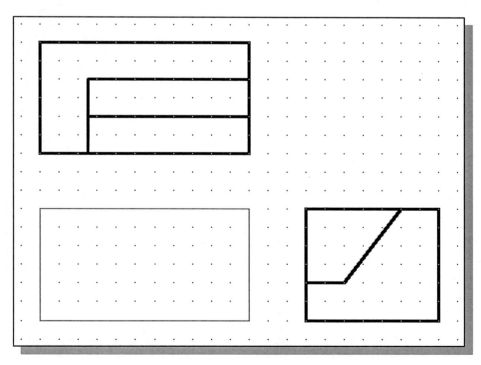

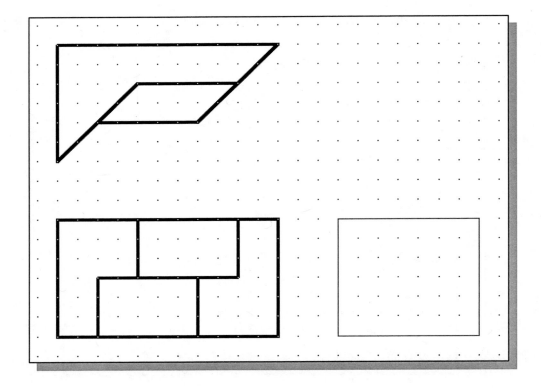

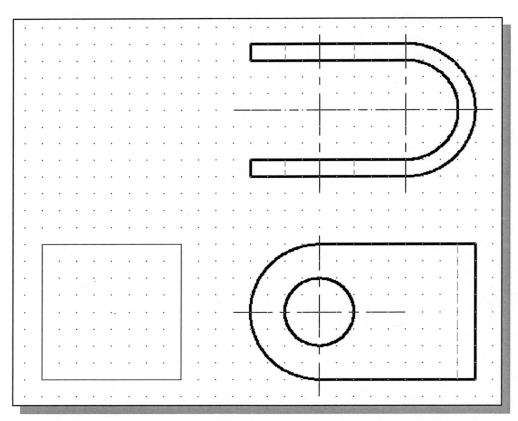

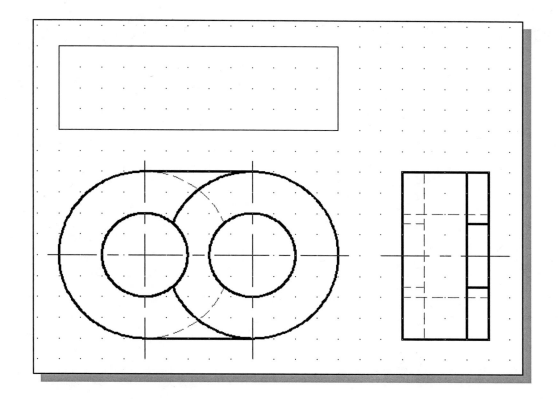

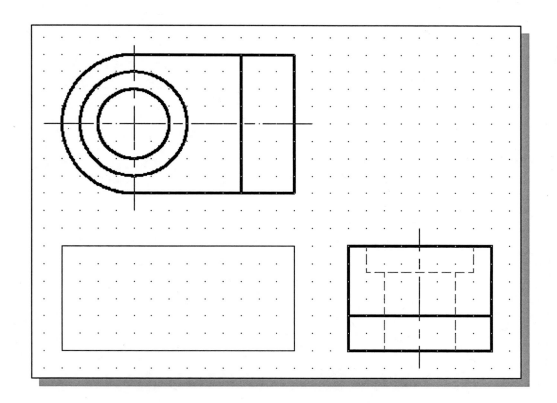

Notes:

Chapter 6
Dimensioning and Notes

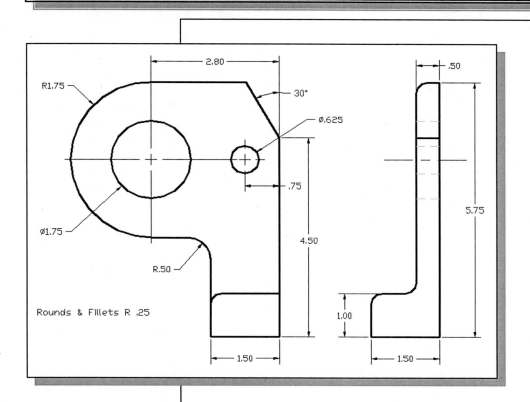

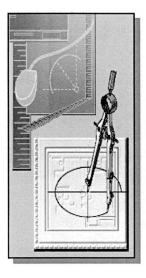

Learning Objectives

- ♦ **Understand Dimensioning Nomenclature and Basics**
- ♦ **Display and Use the Dimension Toolbar**
- ♦ **Use the DraftSight Dimension Style Manager**
- ♦ **Create Center Marks**
- ♦ **Add Linear and Angular Dimensions**
- ♦ **Use the Note Command**
- ♦ **Create SPECIAL CHARACTERS in Notes**

Introduction

In engineering graphics, a detailed drawing is a drawing consisting of the necessary orthographic projections, complete with all the necessary dimensions, notes, and specifications needed to manufacture the design. The dimensions put on the drawing are not necessarily the same ones used to create the drawing but are those required for the proper functioning of the part, as well as those needed to manufacture the design. It is therefore important, prior to dimensioning the drawing, to study and understand the design's functional requirements; then consider the manufacturing processes that are to be performed by the pattern-maker, die-maker, machinist, etc., in determining the dimensions that best give the information. In engineering graphics, a **detailed drawing** is a drawing consisting of the necessary orthographic projections, complete with all the necessary dimensions, notes, and specifications needed to manufacture the design.

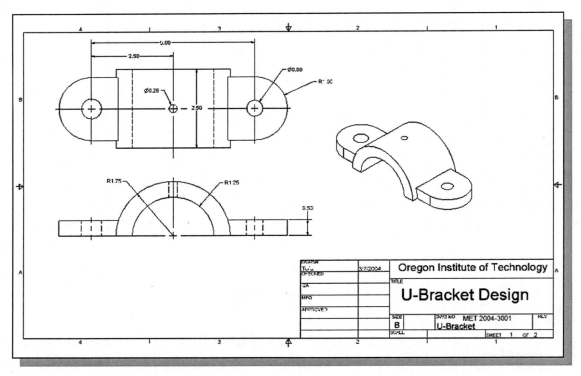

Considerable experience and judgment is required for accurate size and shape description. Dimensioning a design correctly requires conformance to many rules. For example, detail drawings should contain only those dimensions that are necessary to make the design. Dimensions for the same feature of the design should be given only once in the same drawing. Nothing should be left to chance or guesswork on a drawing. Drawings should be dimensioned to avoid any possibility of questions. Dimensions should be carefully positioned; preferably near the profile of the feature being dimensioned. The designer and the CAD operator should also be as familiar as possible with materials, methods of manufacturing and shop processes.

Dimensioning Standards and Basic Terminology

The first step to learning to dimension is a thorough knowledge of the terminology and elements required for dimensions and notes on engineering drawings. Various industrial standards exist for the different industrial sectors and countries; the appropriate standards must be used for the particular type of drawing that is being produced. Some commonly used standards include: **ANSI** (American National Standard Institute), **BSI** (British Standards Association), **DIN** (Deutsches Institut fur Normüng), **ISO** (International Standardization Organization), and **JIS** (Japanese Industry Standards). In this text, the discussions of dimensioning techniques are based primary on the standards of the *American National Standard Institute* (ANSI/ASME Y14.5); other common sense practices are also illustrated.

In engineering graphics, two basic methods are used to give a description of a measurement on a drawing: **Dimensions** and **Notes**.

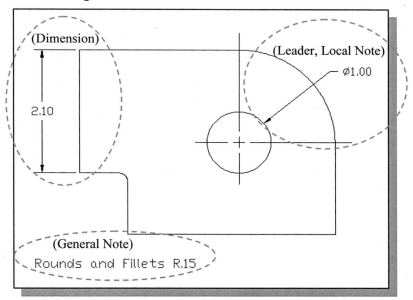

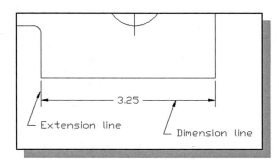

A dimension is used to give the measurement of an object or between two locations on a drawing. The **numerical value** gives the actual measurement, the **dimension lines** and the **arrowheads** indicate the direction in which the measurement applies. **Extension lines** are used to indicate the locations where the dimension is associated.

Two types of notes are generally used in engineering drawings: **Local Notes** and **General Notes**. A *Local Note* is done with a leader and an arrowhead referring the statement of the note to the proper place on the drawing. A *General Note* refers to descriptions applying to the design as a whole and it is given without a leader.

Selection and Placement of Dimensions and Notes

One of the most important considerations to assure proper manufacturing and functionality of a design is the selection of dimensions to be given in the drawing. The selection should always be based upon the **functionality of the part**, as well as the **production requirements in the shop**. The method of manufacturing can affect the type of detailed dimensions and notes given in the drawing. It would be very beneficial to have a good knowledge of the different shop practices to give concise information on an engineering drawing.

After the dimensions and notes to be given have been selected, the next step is the actual placement of the dimensions and notes on the drawing. In reading a drawing, it is natural to look for the dimensions of a given feature wherever that feature appears most characteristic. One of the views of an object will usually describe the shape of some detailed feature better than with other views. Placing the dimensions in those views will promote clarity and ease of reading. This practice is known as the **Contour Rule**.

The two methods of positioning dimension texts on a dimension line are the **aligned** system and the **unidirectional** system. The *unidirectional* system is more widely used as it is easier to apply, and easier to read, the texts horizontally. The texts are oriented to be read from the **bottom** of the drawing with the *unidirectional* system. The *unidirectional* system originated in the automotive and aircraft industries, and is also referred to as the "horizontal system."

For the *aligned* system, the texts are oriented to be aligned to the dimension line. The texts are oriented to be read from the **bottom or right side** of the drawing with the *aligned* system.

General Notes must be oriented horizontally and be read from the bottom of the drawing in both systems.

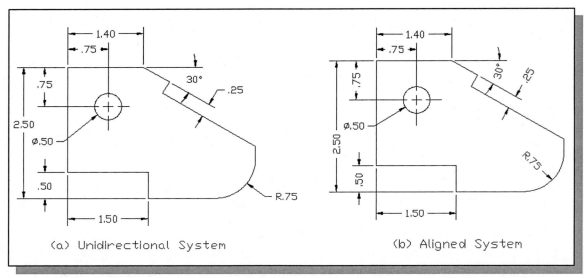

(a) Unidirectional System   (b) Aligned System

The following rules need to be followed for clearness and legibility when applying dimensions or notes to a design:

1. Always dimension **features**, not individual geometric entity. Consider the dimensions related to the **sizes** and **locations** of each feature.

2. Choose the view that best describes the feature to place the associated dimensions; this is known as the **Contour Rule**.

3. Place the dimensions next to the features being described; this is also known as the **Proximity Rule**.

4. Dimensions should be placed outside the view if possible; only place dimensions on the inside if they add clarity, simplicity, and ease of reading.

5. Dimensions common to two views are generally placed in between the views.

6. Dimensions should be applied to one view only. When dimensions are placed between views, the extension lines should be **drawn from one view**, not from both views.

7. Dimensions should be placed only on the view that shows the measurement in its **true length**.

8. Center lines may also be used as extension lines; therefore there should be **no gap** in between an extension line and a center line.

9. Center lines are also used to indicate the **symmetry** of shapes, and frequently eliminate the need for a positioning dimension. They should extend about 6 mm (0.25 in.) beyond the shape for which they indicate symmetry unless they are carried further to serve as extension lines. Center lines should not be continued between views.

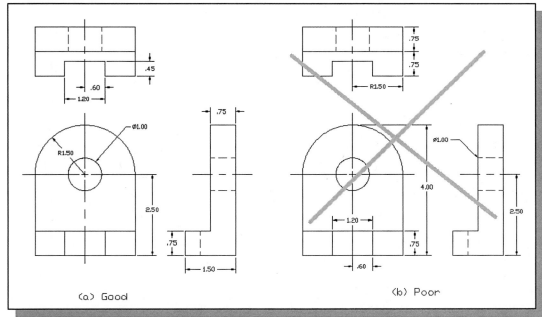

10. Always place a shorter dimension line inside a longer one to avoid crossing dimension lines with the extension lines of other dimensions. Thus an overall dimension, the maximum size of part in a given direction, will be placed outside all other dimensions.

11. Do not dimension to hidden lines, if necessary create sectional views to convert the hidden features into visible features.

12. The spacing of dimension lines should be uniform throughout the drawing. Dimension lines should be spaced, in general, **10 mm** (0.4 inches) away from the outlines of the view. This applies to a single dimension or to the first dimension of several in a series. The space between subsequent dimension lines should be at least **6 mm** (0.25 inches) and uniformly spaced.

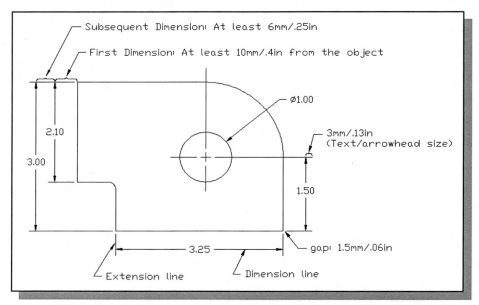

13. Dimension texts should be placed midway between the arrowheads, except when several parallel dimensions are present, where the texts should be staggered.

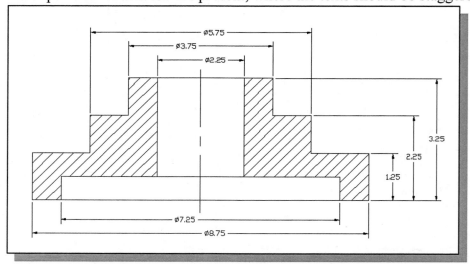

14. As a general rule, local notes (leaders) and general notes are created and placed after the regular dimensions.

15. A leader should always be placed to allow its extension to pass through the **center** of all round features.

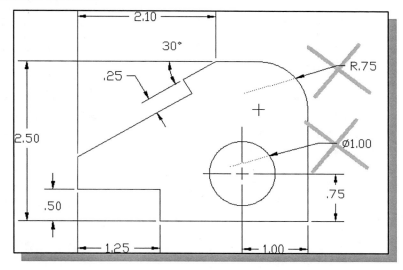

16. **Symbols** are preferred for features such as counter-bores, countersinks and spot faces; they should also be dimensioned using a leader. Each of these features has a special dimensioning symbol that can be used to show (a) Shape (b) Diameter and (c) Depth.

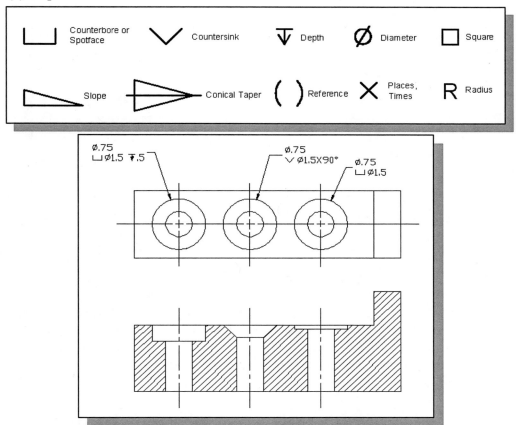

17. For leaders: avoid crossing leaders, avoid long leaders, avoid leaders in a horizontal or vertical direction, and avoid leaders parallel to adjacent dimension lines, extension lines, or section lines.

18. Dimensions should never be crowded. If the space is small and crowded, an enlarged view or a partial view may be used.

19. The **Overall Width**, **Height**, and **Depth** of the part should generally be shown in a drawing unless curved contours are present.

20. When dimensioning a circular feature, full cylinders (holes and bosses) must always be measured by their diameters. Arcs should always be shown by specifying a radius value. If a leader is used, the leader should meet the surface at an angle between 30° to 60° if possible.

21. Dual dimensions may be used, but they must be consistent and clearly noted. The dual-dimensioning can be shown by placing the alternate-units values below or next to the primary-units dimension, as shown in the figure.

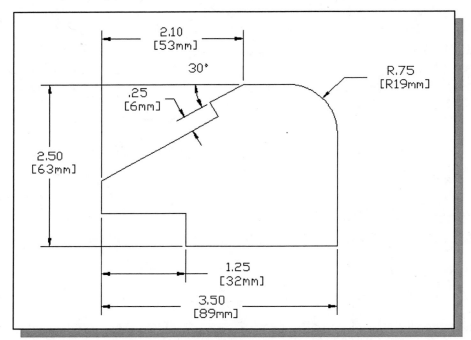

22. Never pass through a dimension text with any kind of line.

23. Never allow the crossing of dimension lines.

24. In general, Metric system is given in millimeters and they are generally rounded to the nearest whole number. English system is given in inches and they are typically shown with two decimal places. When a metric dimension is less than a millimeter, a zero is placed before the decimal point, but no zero is placed before a decimal point when inches are used.

Baseline and Chain Dimensioning

Frequently the need arises to dimension a feature which involves a series of dimensions. Two methods should be considered for this type of situation: **Baseline dimensioning** and **Chain dimensioning**. The baseline dimensioning method creates dimensions by measuring from a common baseline. The chain dimensioning method creates a series or a chain of dimensions that are placed one after another. It is important to always consider the functionality and the manufacturing process of the specific features to be dimensioned. Note that both methods can be used to different features within the same drawing as shown in the below figure.

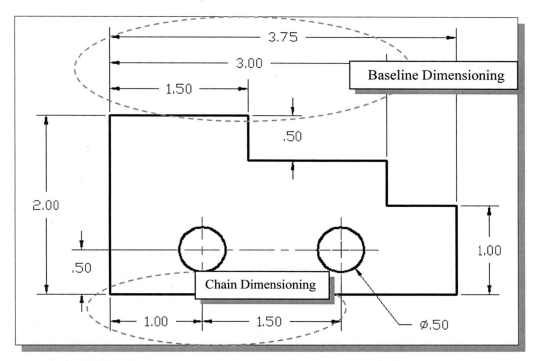

- **Baseline dimensioning:** used when the **location** of features must be controlled from a common reference point or plane.

- **Chain dimensioning:** Used when **tolerances** between adjacent features is more important than the overall tolerance of the feature. For example, dimensioning mating parts, hole patterns, slots, etc. Note that more in-depth discussions on tolerances are presented in the next section and also in the next chapter.

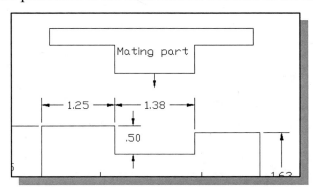

Dimensioning and Tolerancing

Drawings with dimensions and notes often serve as construction documents to ensure the proper functioning of a design. When dimensioning a drawing, it is therefore critical to consider the *precision* required for the part. *Precision* is the degree of accuracy required during manufacturing. Different machining methods will produce different degrees of precisions. However, one should realize it is nearly impossible to produce any dimension to an absolute, accurate measurement; some variation must be allowed in manufacturing. **Tolerance** is the allowable variation for any given size and provides a practical means to achieve the precision necessary in a design. With **tolerancing**, each dimension is allowed to vary within a specified zone. The general machining tolerances of some of the more commonly used manufacturing processes are listed in the figure below.

International Tolerance Grade (IT)							
4	5	6	7	8	9	10	11
Lapping or Honing							
	Cylindrical Grinding						
	Surface Grinding						
	Diamond Turning or Boring						
	Broaching						
	Powder Metal-sizes						
		Reaming					
			Turning				
			Powder Metal-sintered				
			Boring				
						Milling, Drilling	
						Planing & Shaping	
						Punching	
							Die Casting

As it was discussed in the previous sections, the selections and placements of dimensions and notes can have a drastic effect on the manufacturing of the designs. Further more, a poorly dimensioned drawing can create problems that may invalidate the design intent and/or become very costly to the company. One of the undesirable results in poorly dimensioned drawings is **Tolerance Accumulation**. *Tolerance Accumulation* is the effect of cumulative tolerances caused by the relationship of tolerances associated with relating dimensions. As an example, let's examine the *tolerance accumulation* that can occur with two mating parts, as shown in the below figure, using a standard tolerance of ± 0.01 for all dimensions.

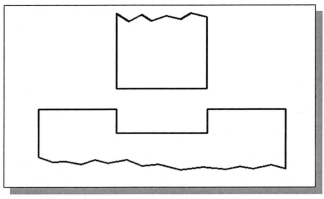

(1) Tolerance Accumulation - Baseline Dimensioning

Consider the use of the *Baseline dimensioning* approach, as described in the previous sections, to dimension the parts. First glance, it may appear that the tolerance of the overall size is maintained and thus this approach is a better approach in dimensioning the parts!?

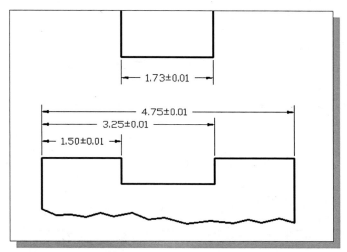

Now let's examine the size of the center slot, which is intended to fit the other part:

Upper limit of the slot size: 3.26-1.49= 1.77
Lower limit of the slot size: 3.24-1.51= 1.73

The tolerance of the center slot has a different range of tolerance than the standard ± 0.01. With this result, the two parts will not fit as good as the tolerance has been loosened.

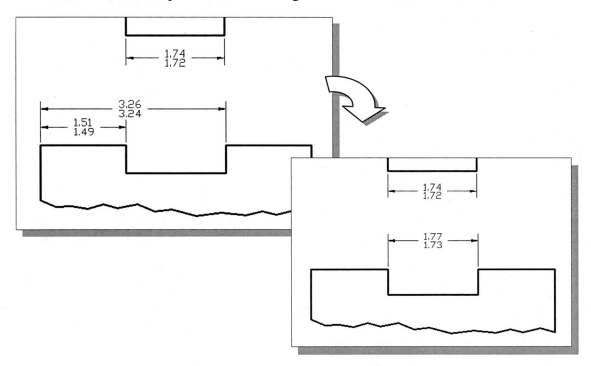

(2) Tolerance Accumulation - Chain Dimensioning

Now consider the use of the *chain dimensioning* approach, as described in the previous sections, to dimension the parts.

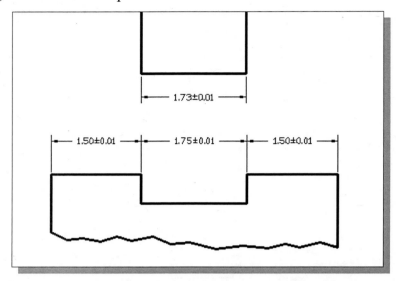

The *tolerance accumulation* occurred since the overall size is determined with the three dimensions that are chained together. Considering the upper and lower limits of the overall size of the bottom part:

> **Upper limit** of the overall size: 1.51+1.76+1.51= 4.78
> **Lower limit** of the overall size: 1.49+1.74+1.49= 4.72

With the chaining of the dimensions, the tolerance of the overall size has been changed, perhaps unintentionally, to a wider range.

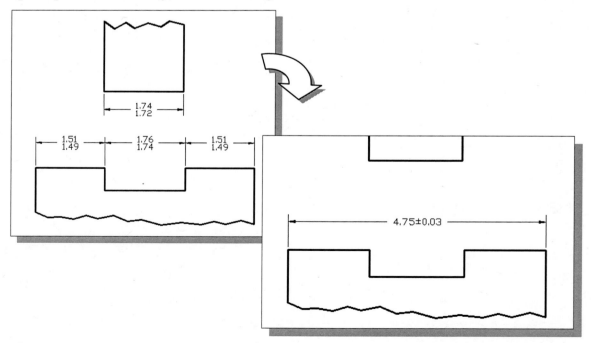

(3) Avoid Tolerance Accumulation – Dimensioning Features

The effect of the *tolerance accumulation* is usually undesirable. We could be using fairly precise and expensive manufacturing processes, but resulting in lower quality products simply due to the poor selections and placements of dimensions.

To avoid *tolerance accumulation,* proper dimensioning a drawing is critical. The first rule of dimensioning states that one should always dimension **features**, not individual geometric entity. Always consider the dimensions related to the **sizes** and **locations** of each feature. One should also consider the associated **design intent** of the **feature**, the **functionality** of the design and the related **manufacturing processes**.

For our example, one should consider the center slot as a feature, where the other part will be fit into, and therefore the **size** and **location** of the feature should be placed as shown in the figure below.

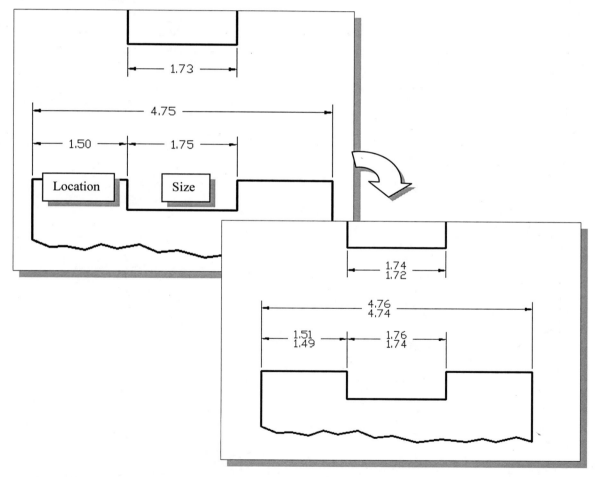

> More detailed discussions on tolerances are covered in the next chapter; however, the effects of *tolerance accumulation* should be avoided even during the initial selection and placement of dimensions. Note that there are also other options, generally covered under the topics of **Geometric Dimensioning and Tolerancing (GD&T)**, to assure the accuracy of designs through productions.

Dimensioning Tools in DraftSight

Thus far, the use of DraftSight to define the *shape* of designs has been illustrated. For the rest of the chapter, the general procedures to convey the *size* definitions of designs using DraftSight are discussed. The *tools of size description* are known as *dimensions* and *notes*.

Considerable experience and judgment is required for accurate size description. As it was outlined in the previous sections, detail drawings should contain only those dimensions that are necessary to make the design. Dimensions for the same feature of the design should be given only once in the same drawing. Nothing should be left to chance or guesswork on a drawing. Drawings should be dimensioned to avoid any possibility of questions. Dimensions should be carefully positioned; preferably near the profile of the feature being dimensioned. The designer and the CAD operator should be as familiar as possible with materials, methods of manufacturing, and shop processes.

Traditionally, detailing a drawing is the biggest bottleneck of the design process; and when doing board drafting, dimensioning is one of the most time consuming and tedious tasks. Today, most CAD systems provide what is known as an **auto-dimensioning feature**, where the CAD system automatically creates the extension lines, dimensional lines, arrowheads, and dimension values. Most CAD systems also provide an **associative dimensioning feature** so that the system automatically updates the dimensions when the drawing is modified.

The *P-Bracket* Design

Starting Up DraftSight

1. Select the **DraftSight** option on the *Program* menu or select the **DraftSight** icon on the *Desktop*.

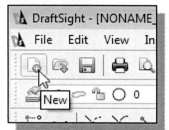

2. In the *Standard* toolbar, select the **New File** option with a single click of the left-mouse-button.

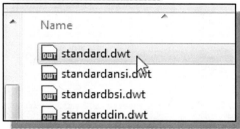

3. In the *Specify Template* dialog box, pick **Standard.dwt** as the template file to use.

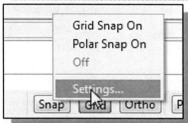

4. In the *Status* toolbar, right-mouse-click once on the *Snap* button to bring up the option menu.

5. Select **Settings** to bring up the setup dialog box as shown.

6. In the *Drafting Options* list, adjust the *Snap Spacing* to **0.5** for both *Horizontal* and *Vertical* directions.

7. Activate the **Match Grid spacing** option as shown.

8. Activate the *Snap* option by clicking on the **Enable Snap** box. Note function key **[F9]** can also be used to toggle *ON* and *OFF* the *Snap* option.

9. Pick **OK** to exit the *Drafting Settings* dialog box.

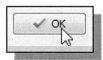

Layers setup

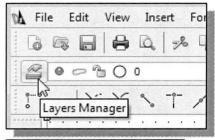

1. Pick **Layers Manager** in the *Layers* toolbar.

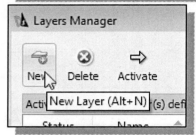

2. Click on the **New** icon to create new layers.

3. Create two **new** layers with the following settings:

Layer	Color	LineStyle	Lineweight
Construction	Gray(9)	Continuous	Default
Object_Lines	Blue	Continuous	0.6mm
Hidden_Lines	Cyan	Hidden	0.3mm
Center_Lines	Red	Center	Default
Dimensions	Magenta	Continuous	Default
Section_Lines	White	Continuous	Default
CuttingPlane_Lines	Dark Gray	Phantom	0.6mm
Title_Block	Green	Continuous	1.2mm
Viewport	White	Continuous	Default

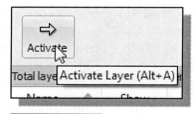

4. Highlight the layer *Construction* in the list of layers.

5. Click on the **Activate** button to set layer *Construction* as the *Active Layer*.

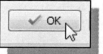

6. Click on the **OK** button to accept the settings and exit the *Layers Manager* dialog box.

7. In the *Status* toolbar area, reset the option buttons so that only *SNAP Mode* and *GRID Display* are switched **ON**.

The *P-Bracket* design

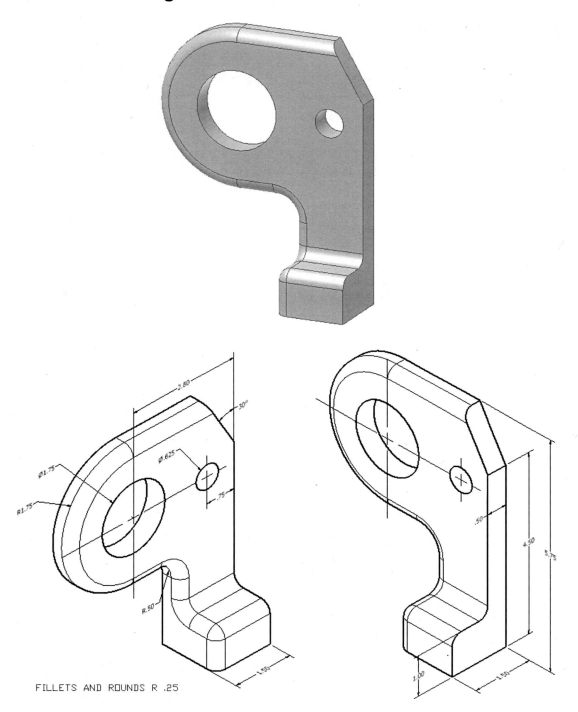

FILLETS AND ROUNDS R .25

> Before going through the tutorial, make a rough sketch of a multiview drawing of the part. How many 2D views will be necessary to fully describe the part? Based on your knowledge of **DraftSight** so far, how would you arrange and construct these 2D views? Take a few minutes to consider these questions and do preliminary planning by sketching on a piece of paper.

Drawing *Infinite Line*s

❖ We will place the *Infinite Lines* on the *Construction* layer so that the layer can later be frozen or turned off.

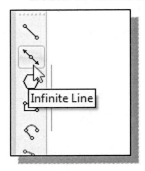

1. Select the **Infinite Line** icon in the *Draw* toolbar. In the command window, the message "*_Infiniteline Specify position:*" is displayed.

   ➤ To orient *Infinite Lines*, we generally specify two points, although other orientation options are also available.

2. Place the first point at world coordinate (**3,2**) on the screen.

3. Pick a location above the last point to create a **vertical line**.

4. Move the cursor toward the right of the first point and pick a location to create a **horizontal line**.

5. Inside the graphics window, right-mouse-click once to **end** the command.

6. In the *Status* toolbar area, turn *OFF* the *SNAP* option.

Using the *OFFSET* command

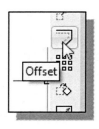

1. Select the **Offset** icon in the *Modify* toolbar. In the command window, the message "*Specify offset distance or [Through]:*" is displayed.

2. In the command window, enter: **2.8 [ENTER]**.

3. In the command window, the message "*Select source entity:*" is displayed. Pick the **vertical line** on the screen.

4. DraftSight next asks us to identify the direction of the offset. Pick a location that is to the **right** of the vertical line.

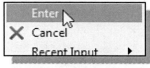

5. Inside the graphics window, **right-mouse-click** and choose **Enter** to end the Offset command.

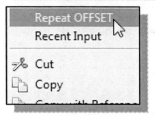

6. Inside the graphics window, **right-mouse-click** to bring up the option menu.

7. Select **Offset** in the popup list, to repeat the Offset command.

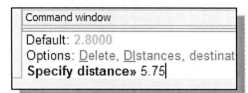

8. In the command window, enter: **5.75** [ENTER].

9. In the command window, the message *"Select source entity:"* is displayed. Pick the **horizontal line** on the screen.

10. DraftSight next asks us to identify the direction of the offset. Pick a location that is **above** the horizontal line.

11. Inside the graphics window, right-mouse-click once to bring up the option menu and select **Enter** to end the Offset command.

12. Repeat the **Offset** command and create the lines as shown.

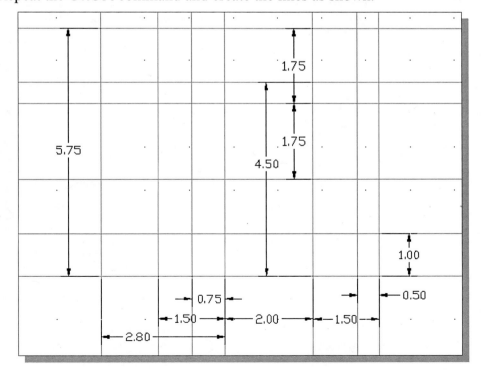

Set layer *Object_Lines* as the *Active Layer*

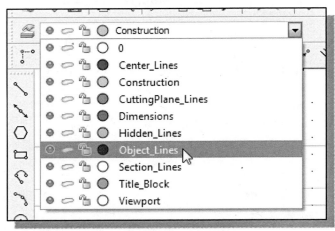

1. On the *Object Properties* toolbar, choose the **Layer Control** box with the left-mouse-button.

2. Move the cursor over the name of layer **Object_Lines** and the tool tip "*Object_Lines*" appears.

3. **Left-mouse-click once** and layer *Object_Lines* is set as the *Active Layer*.

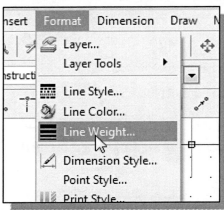

4. In the *Main Menu* area, select:
   [Format] → [Line Weight]

5. Switch *ON* the **Display weight in graphics area** option, and set the display *Scale* to **25** as shown.

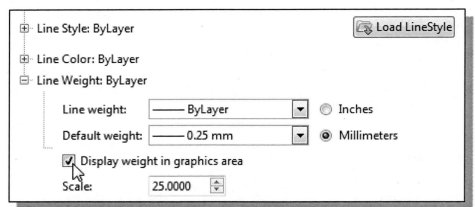

6. In the *Status* toolbar area, turn *ON* the *ESnap,* and *ETrack* options.

Creating *Object* lines

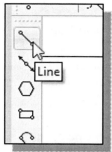

1. Select the **Line** command icon in the *Draw* toolbar. In the command window, the message "*Specify start point:*" is displayed.

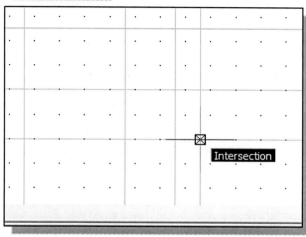

2. Move the cursor to the intersection of the construction lines at the lower right corner of the current sketch, and notice the visual aid automatically displayed at the intersection.

3. Create the object lines as shown below. (Hint: Use the *relative coordinate entry method* and the **Trim** command to construct the 30° line.)

4. Use the **Arc** and **Circle** commands to complete the object lines as shown.

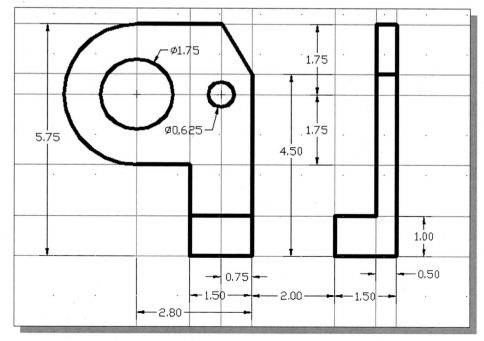

Creating *Hidden* lines

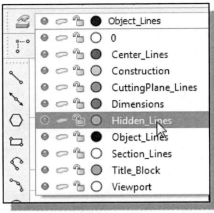

1. On the *Object Properties* toolbar, choose the *Layer Control* box with the left-mouse-button.

2. Move the cursor over the name of layer **Hidden_Lines**, **left-mouse-click once**, and set layer *Hidden_lines* as the *Active Layer*.

3. On your own, create the five hidden lines in the side view as shown.

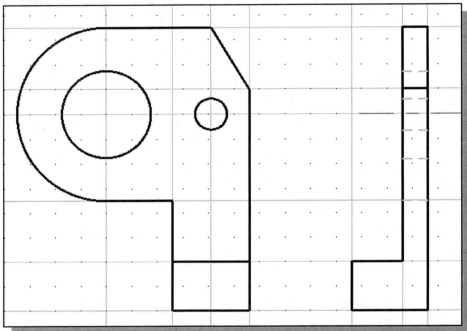

Creating *Center* lines

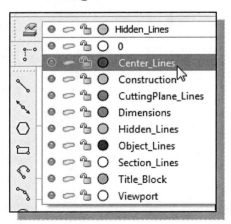

1. On the *Object Properties* toolbar, choose the *Layer Control* box to display the *Layer Control* list.

2. Move the cursor over the name of layer **Center_Lines**, **left-mouse-click once** to set the layer as the *Active Layer*.

3. On your own, create the center line in the *Side View* as shown in the figure. (The center lines in the *Front View* will be added using the *Center Mark* option.)

Turn *OFF* the Construction Lines

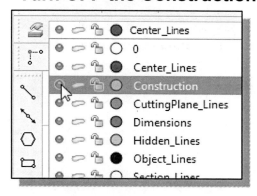

1. On the *Object Properties* toolbar, choose the *Layer Control* box with the left-mouse-button.

2. Move the cursor over the **Show** icon for layer *Construction_Lines*, **left-mouse-click once**, and notice the icon color is changed to a gray tone color, representing the layer (layer *Construction_Lines*) is turned *OFF*.

3. Move the cursor over the name of layer *Object_Lines*, **left-mouse-click once**, and set layer *Object_Lines* as the *Active Layer*.

Using the *FILLET* command

1. Select the **Fillet** command icon in the *Modify* toolbar. In the command window, the message *"Select first object or [Polyline/Radius/Trim]:"* is displayed.

2. Inside the graphics window, right-mouse-click to activate the option menu and select the **Radius** option with the left-mouse-button to specify the radius of the fillet.

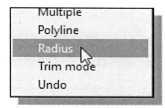

3. In the command window, the message *"Specify fillet radius:"* is displayed. *Specify fillet radius:* **0.5** [ENTER].

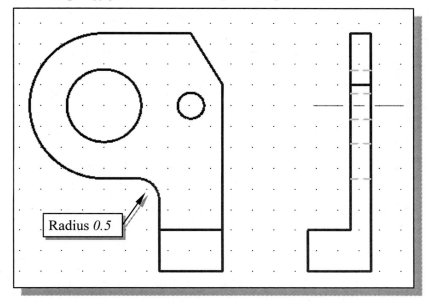

Radius *0.5*

4. Pick the **bottom horizontal line** of the *Front View* as the first object to fillet.

5. Pick the **adjacent vertical line** connected to the arc to create a rounded corner as shown.

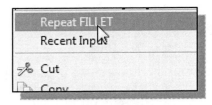

6. Repeat the **Fillet** command and create *four* additional rounded corners (radius **0.25**) as shown. (Hint: Use the **No Trim Mode** for the fillet in the *Front View*.)

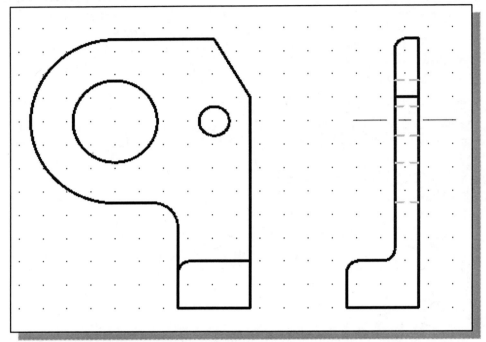

Saving the Completed CAD Design

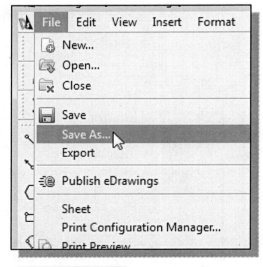

1. In the *Main Menu*, select:
    [File] → [Save As]

2. In the *Save Drawing As* dialog box, select the folder in which you want to store the CAD file and enter **P-Bracket** in the *File name* box.

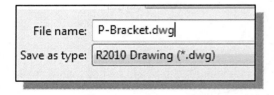

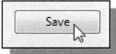

3. Click **Save** in the *Save Drawing As* dialog box to accept the selections and save the file.

Accessing the Dimensioning Commands

❖ The dimensioning commands in DraftSight can be accessed through several options.

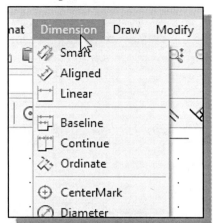

➢ The **Main Menu**: The majority of DraftSight commands can be found in the *Main Menu*. Specific task related commands are listed under the sub-items of the pull-down list. The commands listed under the *Main Menu* are more complete, but it might take several clicks to reach the desired command.

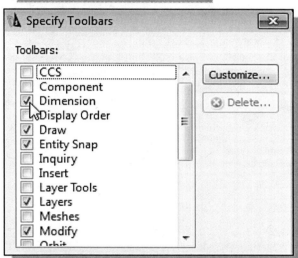

➢ The **Dimension toolbar panels**: The dimensioning commands are available in the *Dimension* toolbar as shown.

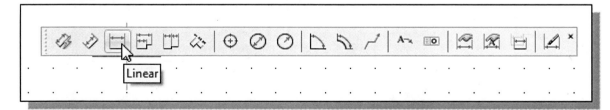

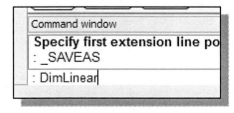

➢ The **command window**: We can also type the command at the command window. This option is always available, with or without displaying the toolbars.

The *Dimension* toolbar

➤ The *Dimension* toolbar offers the most flexible option to access the different dimensioning commands. The toolbar contains a complete list and can be repositioned anywhere on the screen.

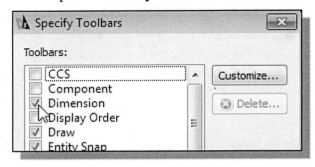

1. Move the cursor on top of any icon and right-mouse-click to bring up the option list. Select **Toolbar** in the list.

2. In the *Specify Toolbars* dialog box, switch on the **Dimension** toolbar as shown.

3. Move the cursor over the icons in the *Dimension* toolbar and read the brief description of each icon.

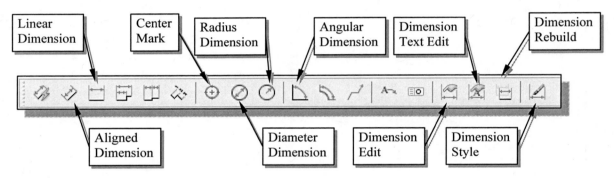

Using *Dimension Style Manager*

❖ The appearance of the dimensions is controlled by *dimension variables*, which we can set using the *Drafting Styles* dialog box.

1. In the *Dimension* toolbar, pick **Dimension Style**. The *Drafting Styles* dialog box appears on the screen.

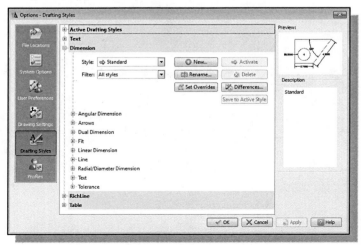

Dimensions nomenclature and basics

As it was stated in *Chapter 1*, the rule for creating CAD designs and drawings is that they should be created **full size** using real-world units. The importance of this practice is evident when we begin applying dimensions to the geometry. The features that we specify for dimensioning are measured and displayed automatically.

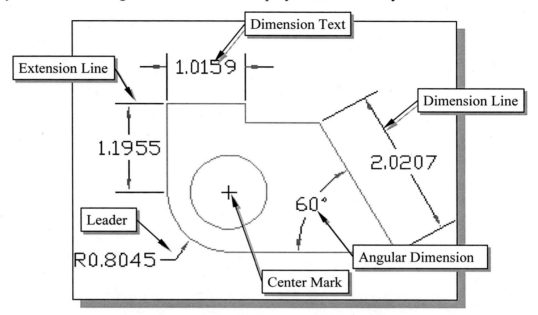

Selecting and placing dimensions can be confusing at times. The two main things to consider are: (1) the function of the part and (2) the manufacturing operations. Detail drawings should contain only those dimensions that are necessary to make the design. Dimensions for the same feature of the design should be given only once in the same drawing. Nothing should be left to chance or guesswork on a drawing. Drawings should be dimensioned to avoid any possibility of questions. Dimensions should be carefully positioned; preferably near the profile of the feature being dimensioned.

Notice in the *Dimension Style Manager* dialog box, the DraftSight default style name is *Standard*. We can create our own dimension style to fit the specific type of design we are working on, such as mechanical or architectual.

2. Click on the **New** button to create a new dimension style.

3. In the *Create New Dimension Style* dialog box, enter **Mechanical** as the dimension style name.

4. Click on the **OK** button to proceed.

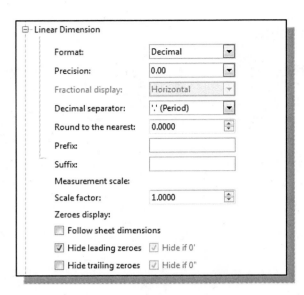

5. Click on the **Linear Dimension** list.

6. Select **Decimal** as the *Unit Format* and set the precision to 2 digits after the decimal point..

❖ On your own, examine the different options available; most of the settings are self-explanatory.

7. Select the **Fit** tab and notice the two options under *Scale for Dimension Features*.

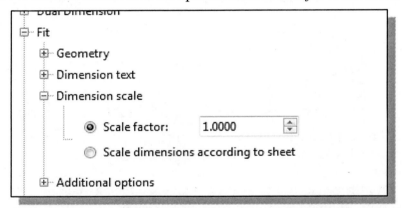

❖ We can manually adjust the dimension scale factor or let DraftSight automatically adjust the scale factor. For example, our current drawing will fit on A-size paper, and therefore we will use the scale factor of 1. If we decide to plot the same drawing on B-size paper, then we will need to set the dimension scale factor to 2.0. It is possible to let DraftSight determine the scale factor based on the *layout* settings; we will discuss more about the *layout* in the next chapter.

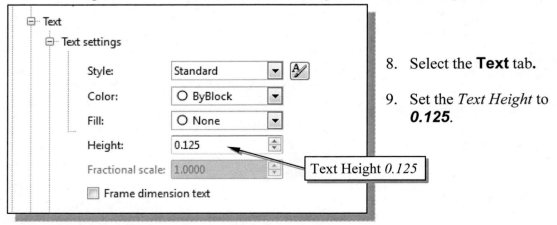

8. Select the **Text** tab.

9. Set the *Text Height* to **0.125**.

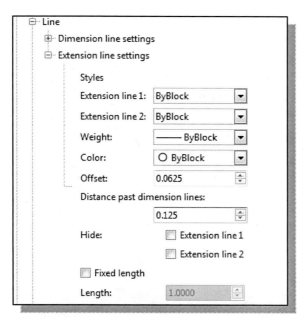

10. Select the **Extension line settings** under the **Lines** list and set *Distance past dimension lines* to **0.125**.

11. Select the **Arrows** list and set *Arrow Size* to **0.125**.

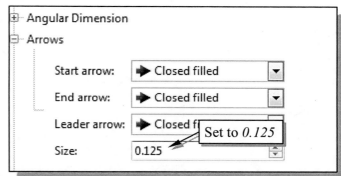

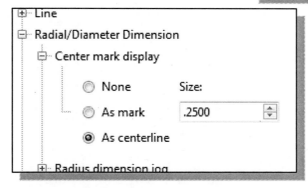

12. Select the **Radial/Diameter Dimension** list and set *Center mark size* to **0.25**. Also set the *Center mark type* to **As Centerline**.

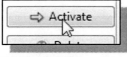

13. Pick the **Activate** button to make the *Mechanical* dimension style the current dimension style.

14. Click on the **OK** button to accept the settings and close the dialog box.

➤ The **Dimension Style Manager** allows us to easily control the appearance of the dimensions in the drawing.

Adding a *Radius Dimension*

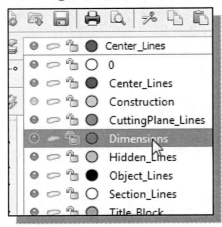

1. On the *Object Properties* toolbar, choose the **Layer Control** box with the left-mouse-button.

2. Move the cursor over the name of the layer **Center_Lines**, **left-mouse-click once**, and set layer *Center_lines* as the *Active Layer*.

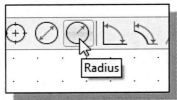

3. In the *Dimension* toolbar, click on the **Radius Dimension** icon.

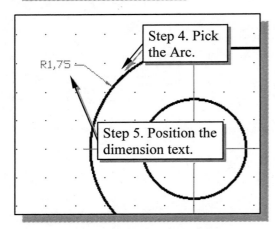

Step 4. Pick the Arc.

R1,75

Step 5. Position the dimension text.

4. Pick the **large arc** in the *Front View*.

5. Pick a point toward the left of the arc to place the dimension text.

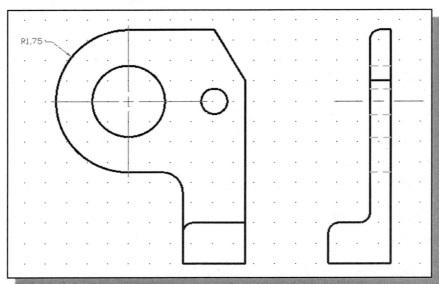

R1,75

Adding *Linear* dimensions

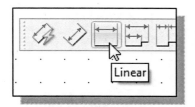

1. In the *Dimension* toolbar, click on the **Linear Dimension** icon.

➢ The Linear Dimension command measures and annotates a feature with a horizontal or vertical dimension.

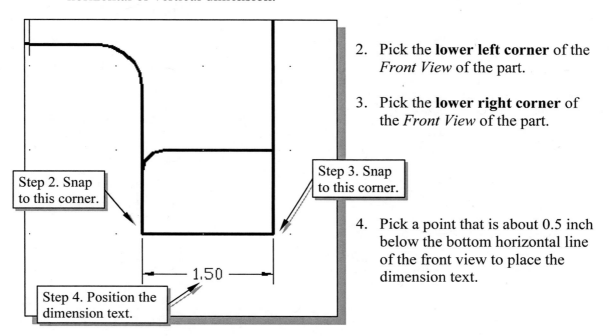

Step 2. Snap to this corner.

Step 3. Snap to this corner.

Step 4. Position the dimension text.

1,50

2. Pick the **lower left corner** of the *Front View* of the part.

3. Pick the **lower right corner** of the *Front View* of the part.

4. Pick a point that is about 0.5 inch below the bottom horizontal line of the front view to place the dimension text.

5. Repeat the **Linear Dimension** command and add the necessary linear dimensions as shown.

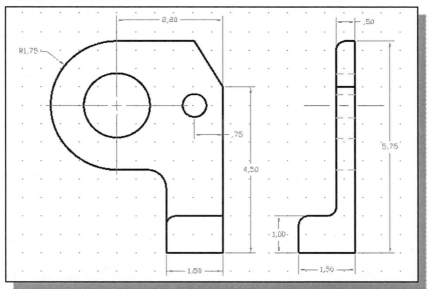

Adding an *Angular* dimension

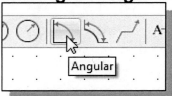

1. In the *Dimension* toolbar, click on the **Angular Dimension** icon.

- The Angular Dimension command measures and annotates a feature with an angle dimension.

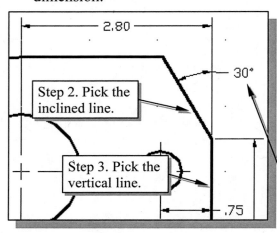

Step 2. Pick the inclined line.

Step 3. Pick the vertical line.

Step 4. Position the dimension text.

2. Pick the **inclined line** of the part in the *Front View*.

3. Pick the **right vertical line** of the part in the *Front View*.

4. Pick a point inside the desired quadrant and place the dimension text as shown.

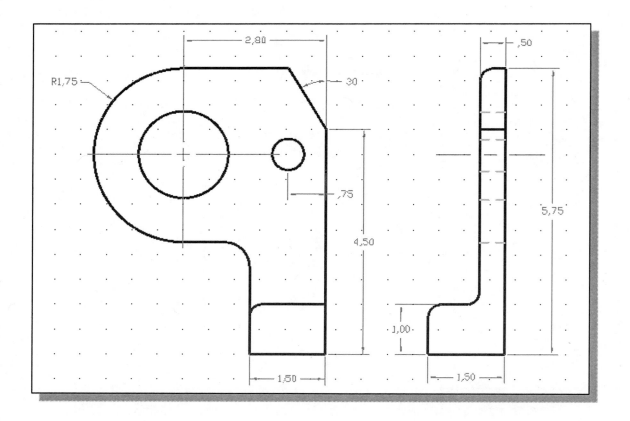

Adding *Diameter* dimensions

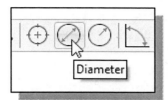

1. In the *Dimension* toolbar, click on the **Diameter Dimension** icon.

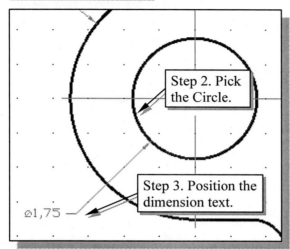

Step 2. Pick the Circle.

Step 3. Position the dimension text.

⌀1,75

2. Pick the **circle** in the *Front View*.

3. Pick a point toward the left of the circle to place the dimension text.

4. On your own, repeat the Dimension commands to add the necessary dimensions as shown.

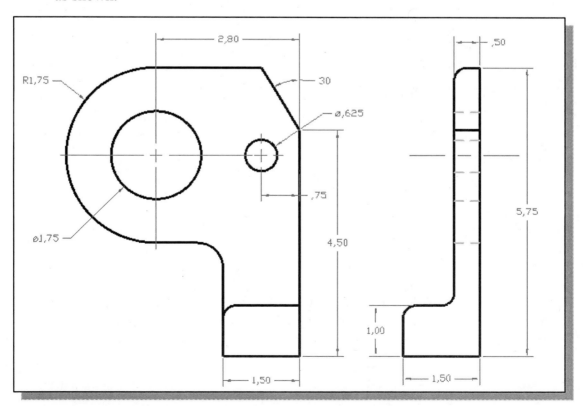

Using the *Note* command

❖ DraftSight provides two options to create notes. For simple entries, we can use the **Simple Note** command. For longer entries with internal formatting, we can use the **Note** command. The procedures for both of these commands are self-explanatory. The **Simple Note** command, also known as the **Text** command, can be used to enter several lines of text that can be rotated and resized. The text we are typing is displayed on the screen. Each line of text is treated as a separate object in DraftSight. To end a line and begin another, press the **[ENTER]** key after entering characters. To end the Text command, press the **[ENTER]** key without entering any characters.

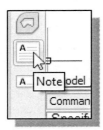

1. In the *Draw* toolbar, select **Note**.

2. In the command window, the message *"Specify first corner:"* is displayed. Pick a location near the world coordinate (**1,1.5**).

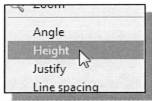

3. Right-mouse-click once to bring up the option list and chose **Height**. In the command window, the message *"Specify Height:"* is displayed.

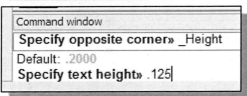

4. Enter **0.125** as the text height.

5. Click a position toward the right near the bottom corner of the *Front View*. The selected region will be used for the length of the added text.

6. In the *Edit Note* window, enter: **Rounds & Fillets R .25 [ENTER]**.

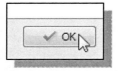

7. Note in the top section of the *Edit Note* window area, different command options are available to adjust the note entered. Click **OK** to end the command.

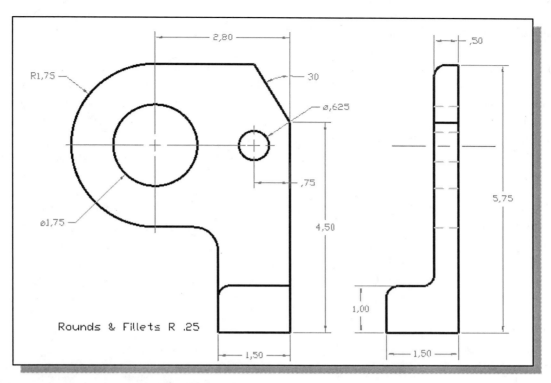

Adding special characters

- We can add special text characters to the dimensioning text and notes. We can type in special characters during any text command and when entering the dimension text. The most common special characters have been given letters to make them easy to remember.

Code	Character	Symbol
%%C	Diameter symbol	Ø
%%D	Degree symbol	°
%%P	Plus/Minus sign	±

➢ On your own, create notes containing some of the special characters listed.

➢ On your own, switch *ON* and *OFF* different layers to examine the information stored on each layer.

Saving the Completed Design

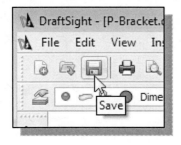

➢ In the *Main Menu* area, select the **Save** icon.

A special note on Layers containing Dimensions

DraftSight creates several hidden **BLOCKS** when we create associative dimensions and we will take a more in depth look at *blocks* in *Chapter 9*. DraftSight treats **blocks** as a special type of object called a *named object*. Each kind of *named object* has a *symbol table* or a *dictionary*, and each table or dictionary can store multiple *named objects*. For example, if we create five dimension styles, our drawing's dimension style *symbol table* will have five dimension style records. In general, we do not work with *symbol tables* or *dictionaries* directly.

When we create dimensions in DraftSight, most of the hidden blocks are placed in the same layer where the dimension was first defined. Some of the definitions are placed in the *DEFPOINTS* layer. When moving dimensions from one layer to another, DraftSight does not move these definitions. When deleting layers, we cannot delete the Active Layer, *Layer 0*, xref-dependent layers, or a layer that contains visible and/or invisible objects. Layers referenced by block definitions, along with the *DEFPOINTS* layer, cannot be deleted even if they do not contain visible objects.

To delete layers with hidden blocks, first use the **Clean** command **[File → Clean → Blocks]** to remove the invisible blocks. (We will have to remove all visible objects prior to using this command.) The empty layer can now be *deleted* or *cleaned*.

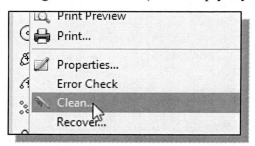

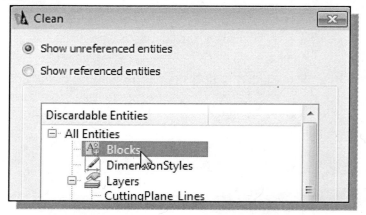

Review Questions:

1. Why are dimensions and notes important to a technical drawing?

2. List and describe some of the general dimensioning practices.

3. What is the effect of *Tolerance Accumulation*? How do we avoid it?

4. Describe the procedure in setting up a new *Dimension Style.*

5. What is the special way to create a diameter symbol when entering a dimension text?

6. What is the text code to create the Diameter symbol (Ø) in DraftSight?

7. Which command can be used to delete layers with hidden blocks? Can we delete *Layer 0*?

8. Which quick-key is used to display and hide the DraftSight *command window*?

9. What is the length and angle of the inclined line, highlighted in the figure below, in the *Front View* of the **P-Bracket** design?

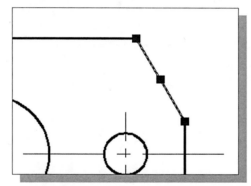

10. Construct the following drawing and measure the **angle α**.

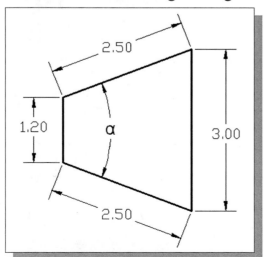

Exercises:

1. Shaft Guide (Design is symmetrical and dimensions are in inches.)

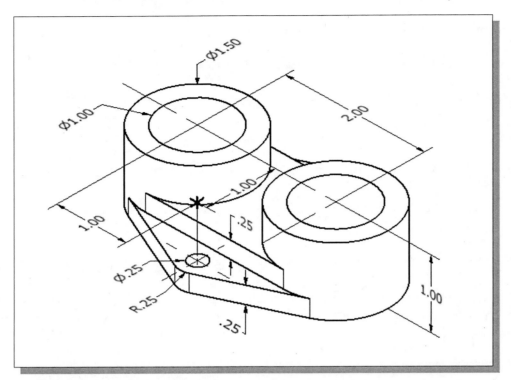

2. Fixture Cap (Dimensions are in millimeters.).

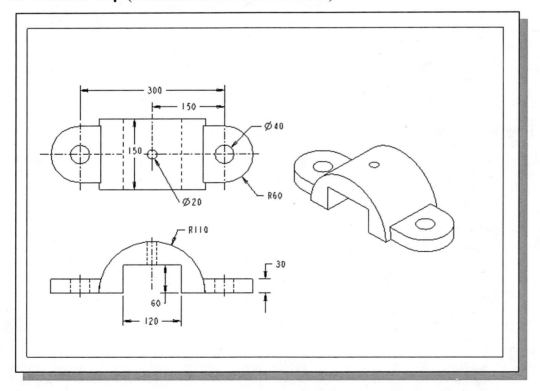

3. Cylinder Support (Dimensions are in inches.)

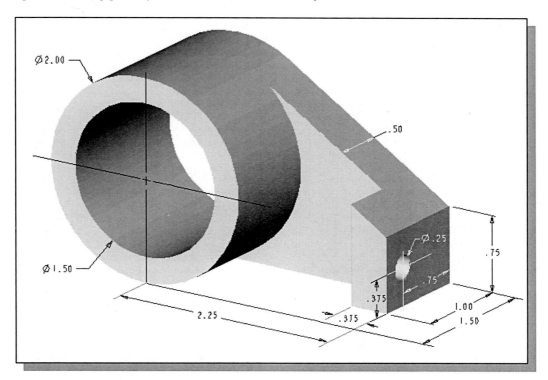

4. Swivel Base (Dimensions are in inches.)

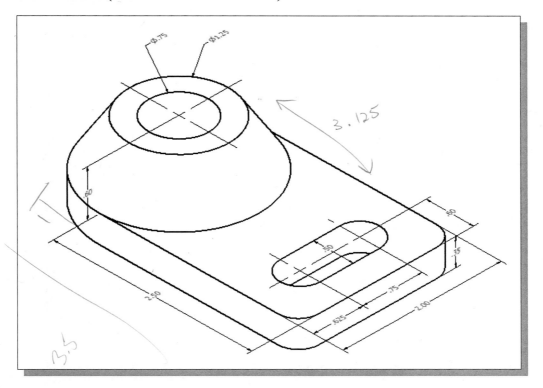

Notes:

Chapter 7
Tolerancing and Fits

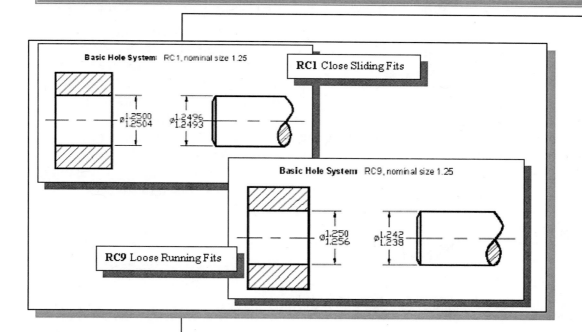

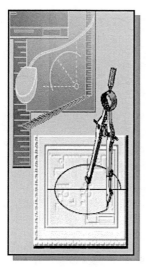

Learning Objectives

♦ **Understand Tolerancing Nomenclature**
♦ **The Tolerancing Designation Method**
♦ **Understand the Basics of ANSI Standard Fits**
♦ **Use of the ISO Metric Standard Fits**
♦ **Use the Open Files DraftSight Option**
♦ **Setup the Tolerancing Option in DraftSight**

Precision and Tolerance

In the manufacturing of any product, quality and cost are always the two primary considerations. Drawings with dimensions and notes often serve as construction documents and legal contracts to ensure the proper functioning of a design. When dimensioning a drawing, it is therefore critical to consider the *precision* required for the part. *Precision* is the degree of accuracy required during manufacturing. However, it is impossible to produce any dimension to an absolute, accurate measurement; some variation must be allowed in manufacturing. Specifying higher precision on a drawing may ensure better quality of a product, but doing so may also raise the costs of the product. And requiring unnecessary high precision of a design, resulting in high production costs, may cause the inability of the design to compete with similar products in the market. As an example, consider a design that contains cast parts. A cast part usually has two types of surfaces: mating surfaces and non-mating surfaces. The mating surfaces, as they will interact with other parts, are typically machined to a proper smoothness and require higher precision on all corresponding dimensions. The non-mating surfaces are usually left in the original rough-cast form as they have no important relationship with the other parts. The dimensions on a drawing must clearly indicate which surfaces are to be finished and provide the degree of precision needed for the finishing.

The method of specifying the degree of precision is called **Tolerancing. Tolerance** is the allowable variation for any given size and provides a practical means to achieve the precision necessary in a design. Tolerancing also ensure interchangeability in manufacturing, parts can be made by different companies in different locations and still maintain the proper functioning of the design. With tolerancing, each dimension is allowed to vary within a specified zone. By assigning as large a tolerance as possible, without interfering with the functionality of a design, the production costs can be reduced. The smaller the tolerance zone specified, the more expensive it is to manufacture.

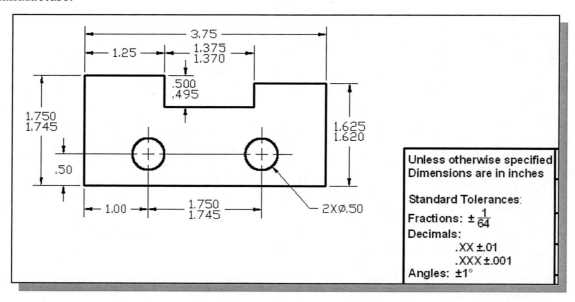

Methods of Specifying Tolerances – English System

Three methods are commonly used in specifying tolerances; **Limits**, **Unilateral tolerances** and **Bilateral tolerances**. Note that the unilateral and bilateral methods employ the use of a **Base Dimension** in specifying the variation range.

- Limits – Specifies the range of size that a part may be.
  This is the preferred method as approved by ANSI/ASME Y14.5M; the maximum and minimum limits of size and locations are specified. The maximum value is placed above the minimum value. In single-line form, a dash is used to separate the two values.

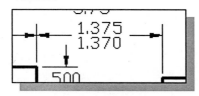 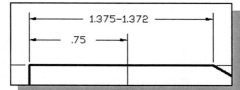

- Bilateral – Variation of size is in both directions.
  This method uses a basic size and is followed by a plus-and-minus expression of tolerance. The bilateral tolerances method allows variations in both directions from the basic size. If an equal variation in both directions is desired, the combined plus-and minus symbol is used with a single value.

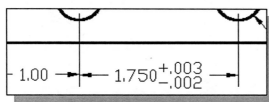 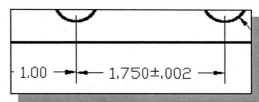

- Unilateral – Variation of size is in only one direction.
  This method uses a basic size and is followed by a plus-or-minus expression of tolerance. The unilateral tolerances method allows variations only in one direction from the basic size.

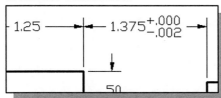 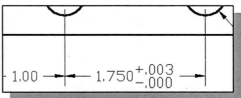

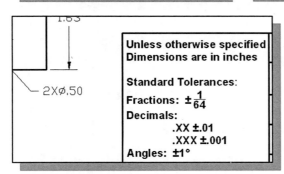

- General tolerances – General tolerances are typically covered in the title block; the general tolerances are applied to the dimensions in which tolerances are not given.

Nomenclature

The terms used in tolerancing and dimensioning should be clearly understood before more detailed discussion are studied. The following are definitions as defined in the ANSI/ASME Y 14.5M standard.

- **Nominal size** is the designation used for the purpose of general identification.
- **Basic size, or basic dimension,** is the theoretical size from which limits of size are derived. It is the size from which limits are determined for the size or location of a feature in a design.
- **Actual size** is the measured size of the manufactured part.
- **Fit** is the general term used to signify the range of tightness in the design of mating parts.
- **Allowance** is the minimum clearance space or maximum interference intended between two mating parts under the maximum material condition.
- **Tolerance** is the total permissible variation of a size. The tolerance is the difference between the limits of size.
- **Maximum Material Condition (MMC)** is the size of the part when it consists of the most material.
- **Least Material Condition (LMC)** is the size of the part when it consists of the least material.

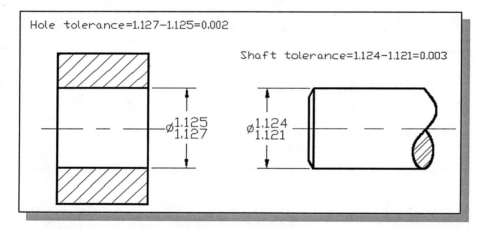

In the figure above, the tightest fit between the two parts will be when the largest shaft is fit inside the smallest hole. The allowance between the two parts can be calculated as:

Allowance = (MMC Hole)-(MMC Shaft)=1.125-1.124 = 0.001

The loosest fit between the above two parts will be when the smallest shaft is fit inside the largest hole. The maximum clearance between the two parts can be calculated as:

Max. Clearance = (LMC Hole)-(LMC Shaft)=1.127-1.121 = 0.006

➤ Note that the above dimensions will assure there is always a space between the two mating parts.

Example 7.1

The size limits of two mating parts are as shown in the below figure. Determine the following items, as described in the previous page: nominal size, tolerance of the shaft, tolerance of the hole, allowance and maximum clearance between the parts.

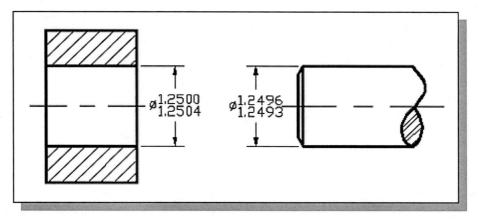

Solution:

Nominal size = 1.25

Tolerance of the shaft = Max. Shaft - Min. Shaft
= 1.2496-1.2493 = 0.0003

Tolerance of the hole = Max. Hole - Min. Hole
= 1.2504-1.2500 = 0.0004

Allowance = Min. Hole (MMC Hole) - Max. Shaft (MMC Shaft)
= 1.2500-1.2496 = 0.0004

Max. Clearance = Max. Hole (LMC Hole) - Min. Shaft (LMC Shaft)
=1.2504-1.2493 = 0.0011

Exercise: Given the size limits of two mating parts, determine the following items: nominal size, tolerance of the shaft, tolerance of the hole, allowance and maximum clearance between the parts.

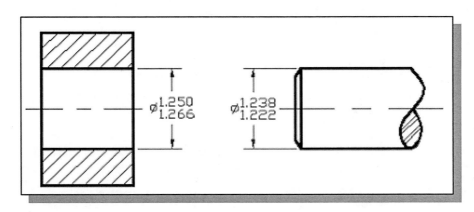

Fits between Mating Parts

Fit is the general term used to signify the range of tightness in the design of mating parts. In ANSI/ASME Y 14.5M, four general types of fits are designated for mating parts.

- **Clearance Fit:** A clearance fit is the condition in which the internal part is smaller than the external part; and always leaves a space or clearance between the parts.

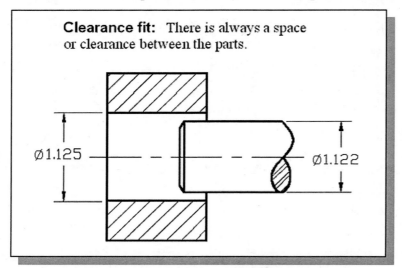

Clearance fit: There is always a space or clearance between the parts.

- **Interference Fit:** An interference fit is the condition in which the internal part is larger than the external part; and there is always an interference between the parts.

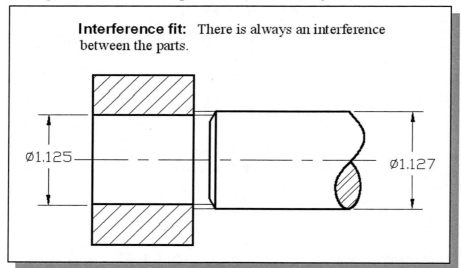

Interference fit: There is always an interference between the parts.

- **Transition Fit:** A transition fit is the condition in which there is either a *clearance* or *interference* between the parts.

- **Line Fit:** A line fit is the condition in which the limits of size are such that a clearance or surface contact may result between the mating parts.

Selective Assembly

By specifying the proper allowances and tolerances, mating parts can be completely interchangeable. But sometimes the fit desired may require very small allowances and tolerances, and the production cost may become very high. In such cases, either manual or computer-controlled selective assembly is often used. The manufactured parts are then graded as small, medium and large based on the actual sizes. In this way, very satisfactory fits may be achieved at much lower cost than to manufacturing all parts to very accurate dimensions. Interference and transition fits often require the use of selective assembly to get the desirable interference or clearance.

Basic Hole and Basic Shaft Systems

In manufacturing, standard tools (such as reamers, drills) are often used to produce holes. In the **basic hole system**, the **minimum size of the hole** is taken as a base, and an allowance is assigned to derive the necessary size limits for both parts. The hole can often be made with a standard size tool and the shaft can easily be machined to any size desired.

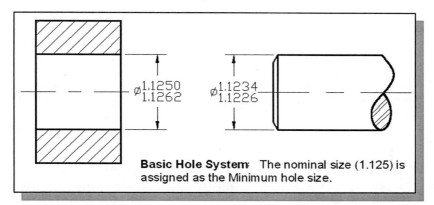

Basic Hole System The nominal size (1.125) is assigned as the Minimum hole size.

On the other hand, in some branches of manufacturing industry, where it is necessary to manufacture the shafts using standard sizes, the **basic shaft system** is often used. This system should only be used when there is a special need for it. For example, if a shaft is to be assembled with several other parts using different fits. In the **basic shaft system**, the **maximum shaft** is taken as the basic size, and all size limits are derived from this basic size.

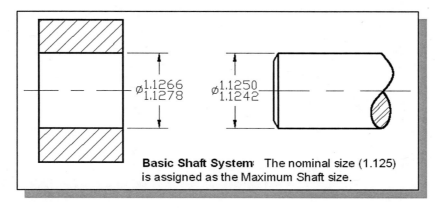

Basic Shaft System The nominal size (1.125) is assigned as the Maximum Shaft size.

American National Standard Limits and Fits – Inches

The standard fits designated by the American National Standards Institute are as follows:

- **RC** Running or Sliding Clearance Fits (See appendix A for the complete table.)
- **LC** Locational Clearance Fits
- **LT** Transition Clearance or Interference Fits
- **LN** Locational Interference Fits
- **FN** Force or Shrink Fits

These letter symbols are used in conjunction with numbers for the class of fit. For example, **RC5** represents a class 5 Running or Sliding Clearance Fits. The limits of size for both of the mating parts are given in the standard.

1. **Running or Sliding Clearance Fits :** RC1 through RC9
   These fits provide limits of size for mating parts that require sliding and running performance, with suitable lubrication allowance.
   RC1, **close sliding fits,** are for mating parts to be assembled without much play in between.
   RC2, **sliding fits,** are for mating parts that need to move and turn easily but not run freely.
   RC3, **precision running fits,** are for precision work running at low speed and light journal pressure. This class provides the closest running fits.
   RC4, **close running fits,** are for moderate running speed and journal pressure in accurate machinery.
   RC5, RC6 and RC7, **medium running fits,** are for running at higher speed and/or higher journal pressure.
   RC8 and RC9, **loose running fits,** are for general purpose running condition where wide commercial tolerances are sufficient; typically used for standard stock parts.

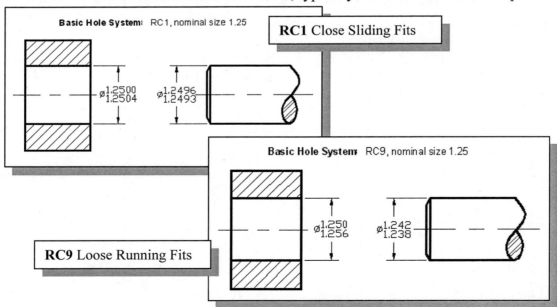

2. **Locational Clearance Fits :** LC1 through LC11
   These fits provide limits of size for mating parts that are normally stationary
   and can be freely assembled and disassembled. They run from snug fits for parts
   requiring accuracy location, through the medium clearance fits for parts (such as
   spigots,) to the looser fastener fits where freedom of assembly is of prime
   importance.

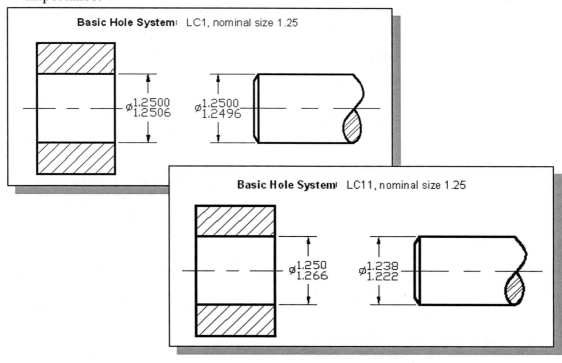

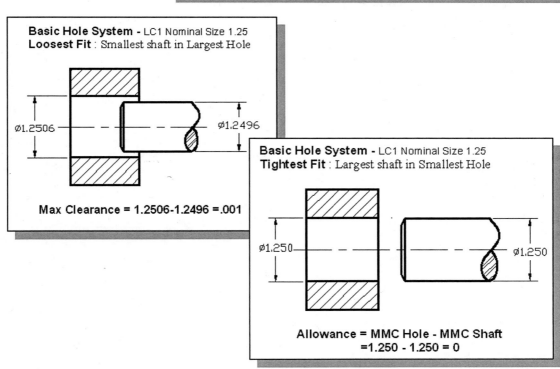

3. Transition Clearance or Interference Fits : LT1 through LT6

These fits provide limits of size for mating parts requiring accuracy location, but either a small amount of clearance or interference is permissible.

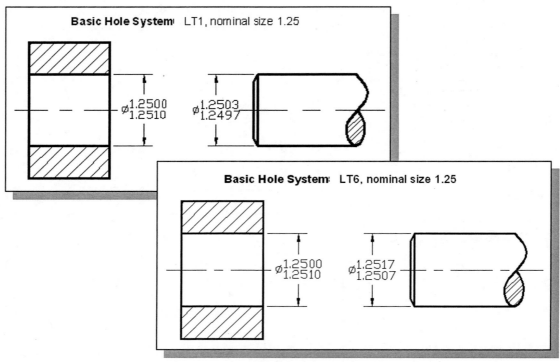

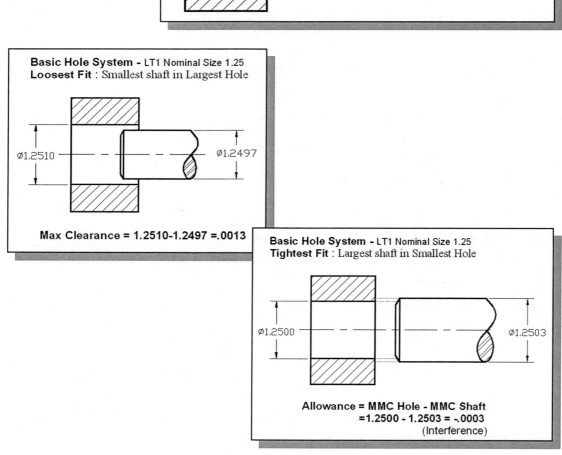

4. **Locational Interference Fits :** LN1 through LN3
   These fits provide limits of size for mating parts requiring accuracy location, and for parts needing rigidity and alignment. Such fits are not for parts that transmit frictional loads from one part to another by the tightness of the fit.

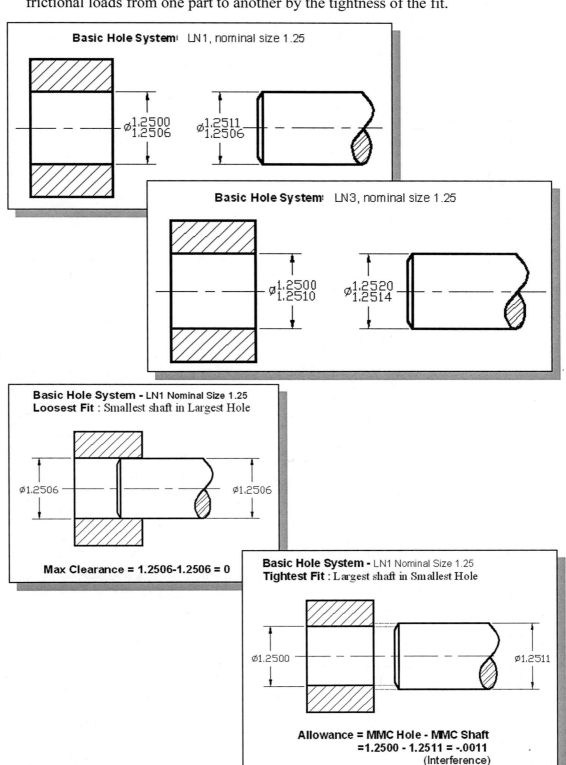

Basic Hole System LN1, nominal size 1.25

$\phi^{1.2500}_{1.2506}$ $\phi^{1.2511}_{1.2506}$

Basic Hole System LN3, nominal size 1.25

$\phi^{1.2500}_{1.2510}$ $\phi^{1.2520}_{1.2514}$

Basic Hole System - LN1 Nominal Size 1.25
Loosest Fit : Smallest shaft in Largest Hole

$\phi 1.2506$ $\phi 1.2506$

Max Clearance = 1.2506-1.2506 = 0

Basic Hole System - LN1 Nominal Size 1.25
Tightest Fit : Largest shaft in Smallest Hole

$\phi 1.2500$ $\phi 1.2511$

Allowance = MMC Hole - MMC Shaft
=1.2500 - 1.2511 = -.0011
(Interference)

5. **Force or Shrink Fits :** FN1 through FN5

These fits provide limits of size for mating parts requiring constant bore pressure in between the parts. The interference amount varies almost directly with the size of parts.

FN1, **light drive fits,** are for mating parts that requiring light assembly pressures, and produce more or less permanent assemblies. They are suitable for thin sections or long fits, or in cast-iron external members.

FN2, **medium drive fits,** are suitable for ordinary steel parts or for shrink fits in light sections.

FN3, **heavy drive fits,** are suitable for ordinary steel parts or for shrink fits in medium sections.

FN4, **force fits,** are for parts that can be highly stressed or for shrink fits where heavy pressing forces are impractical.

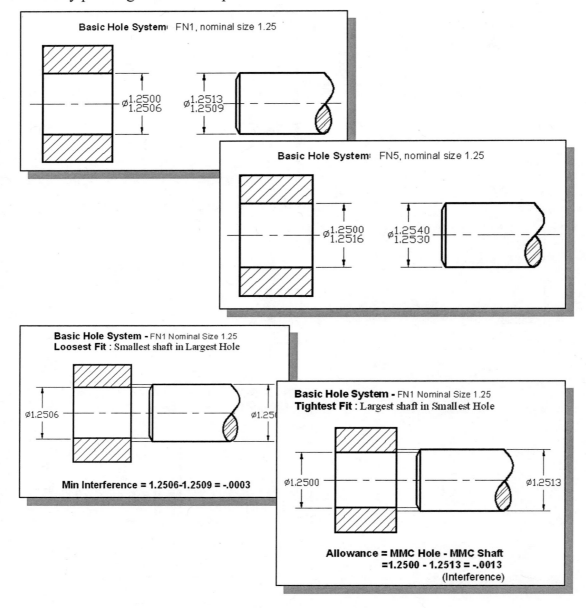

Example 7.2 Basic Hole System

A design requires the use of two mating parts with a nominal size of **0.75** inches. The shaft is to run with moderate speed but with a fairly heavy journal pressure. The fit class chosen is **Basic Hole System RC6**. Determine the size limits of the two mating parts.

From Appendix A, the RC6 fit for 0.75 inch nominal size:

Nominal size Range	Limits of Clearance	RC6 Standard Limits – Basic Hole	
		Hole	Shaft
0.71 - 1.19	1.6	+2.0	-1.6
	4.8	-0.0	-2.8

Using the *Basic Hole System*, the *BASIC* size 0.75 is designated as the minimum hole size. And the maximum hole size is 0.75+0.002 = 0.752 inches.

The maximum shaft size is 0.75-0.0016 = 0.7484 inches
The minimum shaft size is 0.75-0.0028 = 0.7472 inches

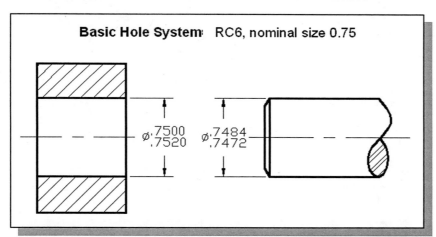

Basic Hole System RC6, nominal size 0.75

> Note the important tolerances and allowance can also be obtained from the table:

Tolerance of the shaft = Max. Shaft – Min. Shaft = 0.7484 – 0.7472 = 0.0012
This can also be calculated from the table above = 2.8 – 2.6 = **1.2 (thousandths)**

Tolerance of the hole = Max. Hole – Min. Hole = 1.2520 – 1.2500 = 0.002
This can also be calculated from the table above = 2.0 – 0.0 = **2.0 (thousandths)**

Allowance = Min. Hole (MMC Hole) – Max. Shaft (MMC Shaft)
        = 0.7500 – 0.7484 = 0.0016
This is listed as the minimum clearance in the table above: **+1.6 (thousandths)**

Max. Clearance = Max. Hole (LMC Hole) – Min. Shaft (LMC Shaft)
        = 0.7520 – 0.7472 = 0.0048
This is listed as the maximum clearance in the table above: **+4.8 (thousandths)**

Example 7.3 Basic Hole System

A design requires the use of two mating parts with a nominal size of **1.25** inches.
The shaft and hub is to be fastened permanently using a drive fit. The fit class chosen
is **Basic Hole System FN4**. Determine the size limits of the two mating parts.

From ANSI/ASME B4.1 Standard, the FN4 fit for 1.25 inches nominal size:

Nominal size Range	Limits of Interference	FN4 Standard Limits – Basic Hole	
		Hole	Shaft
1.19 - 1.97	1.5 3.1	+1.0 -0.0	+3.1 +2.5

Using the *Basic Hole System*, the *BASIC* size 1.25 is designated as the minimum hole
size. And the maximum hole size is 1.25+0.001 = 1.251 inches.

The maximum shaft size is 1.25+0.0031 = 1.2531 inches
The minimum shaft size is 1.25+0.0025 = 1.2525 inches

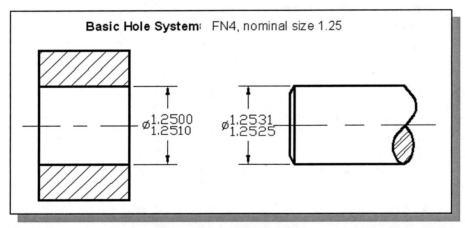

Basic Hole System: FN4, nominal size 1.25

> Note the important tolerances and allowance can also be obtained from the table:

Tolerance of the shaft = Max. Shaft – Min. Shaft = 1.2531 – 1.2525 = 0.0006
This can also be calculated from the table above = 3.1 – 2.5 = 0.6 (thousandths)

Tolerance of the hole = Max. Hole – Min. Hole = 1.2510 – 1.2500 = 0.001
This can also be calculated from the table above = 1.0 – 0.0 = 1.0 (thousandths)

Allowance = Min. Hole (MMC Hole) – Max. Shaft (MMC Shaft)
**   = 1.2500 – 1.2531 = -0.0031**
This is listed as the maximum interference in the table above: **3.1 (thousandths)**

Min. interference = Max. Hole (LMC Hole) – Min. Shaft (LMC Shaft)
**   = 1.2510 – 1.2525 = -0.0015**
This is listed as the minimum interference in the table above: **1.5 (thousandths)**

Example 7.4 Basic Shaft System

Use the **Basic Shaft System** from example 7.2. A design requires the use of two mating parts with a nominal size of **0.75** inches. The shaft is to run with moderate speed but with a fairly heavy journal pressure. The fit class chosen is **Basic Shaft System RC6**. Determine the size limits of the two mating parts.

From Appendix A, the Basic Hole System RC6 fit for 0.75 inch nominal size:

Nominal size Range	Limits of Clearance	RC6 Standard Limits – Basic Hole	
		Hole	Shaft
0.71 - 1.19	1.6	+2.0	-1.6
	4.8	-0.0	-2.8

Using the Basic Shaft System, the BASIC size 0.75 is designated as the MMC of the shaft, the maximum shaft size. The conversion of limits to the Basic shaft System is performed by adding 1.6 (thousandths) to the four size limits as shown:

Nominal size Range	Limits of Clearance	RC6 Standard Limits – Basic Shaft	
		Hole	Shaft
0.71 - 1.19	1.6	+3.6	-0.0
	4.8	+1.6	-1.2

Therefore, the maximum shaft size is 0.75
The minimum shaft size is 0.75-0.0012 = 0.7488 inches.
The maximum hole size is 0.75+0.0036 = 0.7536 inches
The minimum hole size is 0.75+0.0016 = 0.7516 inches

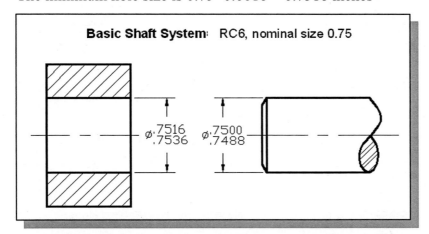

Basic Shaft System: RC6, nominal size 0.75

> Note that all the tolerances and allowance are maintained in the conversion.

Allowance = Min. Hole – Max. Shaft = 0.7517 – 0.7500 = 0.0016
This is listed as the minimum clearance in the table above: **1.6 (thousandths)**

Max. Clearance = Max. Hole – Min. Shaft = 0.7537 – 0.7488 = 0.0048
This is listed as the maximum clearance in the table above: **4.8 (thousandths)**

Example 7.5 Basic Shaft System

Use the **Basic Shaft System** from example 7.3. A design requires the use of two mating parts with a nominal size of **1.25** inches. The shaft and hub is to be fastened permanently using a drive fit. The fit class chosen is **Basic Shaft System FN4**. Determine the size limits of the two mating parts.

From ANSI/ASME B4.1 Standard, the FN4 fit for 1.25 inches nominal size:

Nominal size Range	Limits of Interference	FN4 Standard Limits – Basic Hole	
		Hole	Shaft
1.19 - 1.97	1.5	+1.0	+3.1
	3.1	-0.0	+2.5

With the *Basic Shaft System*, the *BASIC* size 1.25 is designated as the MMC of the shaft, the maximum shaft size. The conversion of limits to the Basic shaft System is performed by subtracting 3.1 (thousandths) to the four size limits as shown:

Nominal size Range	Limits of Interference	FN4 Standard Limits – Basic Shaft	
		Hole	Shaft
1.19 - 1.97	1.5	-2.1	-0.0
	3.1	-3.1	-0.6

Therefore, the maximum shaft size is 1.25
The minimum shaft size is 1.25-0.0006 = 1.2494 inches.
The maximum hole size is 1.25-0.0021 = 1.2479 inches
The minimum hole size is 1.25-0.0031 = 1.2469 inches

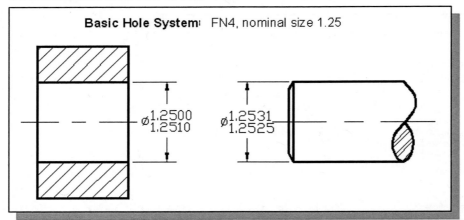

> Note that all the tolerances and allowance are maintained in the conversion.

Allowance = Min. Hole – Max. Shaft = 1.2469 – 1.2500 = -0.0031
This is listed as the maximum interference in the table above: **3.1 (thousandths)**

Min. Interference = Max. Hole – Min. Shaft = 1.2479 – 1.2494 = -0.0015
This is listed as the minimum interference in the table above: **1.5 (thousandths)**

Tolerancing – Metric System

The concepts described in previous sections on the English tolerancing system are also applicable to the Metric System. The commonly used system of preferred metric tolerancing and fits are outlined by the International Organization for Standardization (ISO). The system is specified for holes and shafts, but it is also adaptable to fits between features of parallel surfaces.

- **Basic size** is the theoretical size from which limits or deviations of size are derived.

- **Deviation** is the difference between the basic size and the hole or shaft size. This is equivalent to the word "Tolerance" in the English system.

- **Upper Deviation** is the difference between the basic size and the permitted maximum size. This is equivalent to "Maximum Tolerance" in the English system.

- **Lower Deviation** is the difference between the basic size and the permitted minimum size. This is equivalent to "Minimum Tolerance" in the English system.

- **Fundamental Deviation** is the deviation closest to the basic size. This is equivalent to "Minimum Allowance" in the English system.

- **Tolerance** is the difference between the permissible variations of a size. The tolerance is the difference between the limits of size.

- **International tolerance grade (IT)** is a set of tolerances that varies according to the basic size and provides a uniform level of accuracy within the grade. There are 18 IT grades- IT01, IT0, and IT1 through IT16.

  ❖ IT01 through IT7 is typically used for measuring tools; IT5 through IT11 are used for Fits and IT12 through IT16 for large manufacturing tolerances.

  ❖ The following is a list of IT grade related to machining processes:

	International Tolerance Grade (IT)						
4	5	6	7	8	9	10	11
Lapping or Honing							
	Cylindrical Grinding						
	Surface Grinding						
	Diamond Turning or Boring						
	Broaching						
	Powder Metal-sizes						
		Reaming					
			Turning				
			Powder Metal-sintered				
			Boring				
						Milling, Drilling	
						Planing & Shaping	
						Punching	
							Die Casting

Metric Tolerances and Fits Designation

Metric tolerances and fits are specified by using the fundamental deviation symbol along with the IT grade number. An upper case **H** is used for the fundamental deviation for the hole tolerance using the **Hole Basis system**, where a lower case **h** is used to specify the use of the **Shaft Basis System**.

1. **Hole: 30H8**

    Basic size = 30 mm
    Hole size is based on hole basis system using IT8 for tolerance.

2. **Shaft: 30f7**

    Basic size = 30 mm
    Shaft size is based on hole basis system using IT7 for tolerance.

3. **Fit: 30H8/f7**

    Basic size = 30 mm
    Hole basis system with IT8 hole tolerance and IT7 for shaft tolerance.

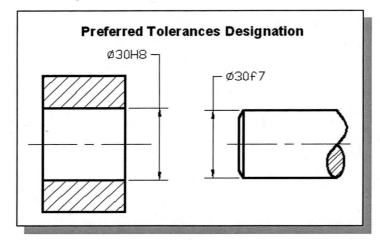

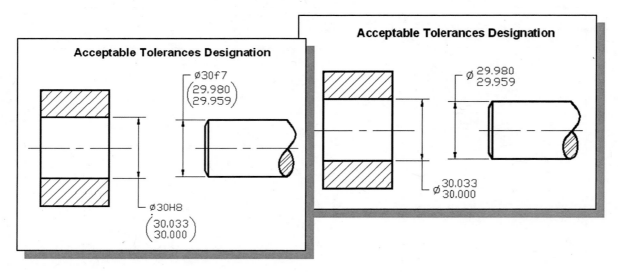

Preferred ISO Metric Fits

The symbols for either the hole-basis or shaft-basis preferred fits are given in the table below. These are the preferred fits; select the fits from the table whenever possible. See **Appendix B** for the complete *ISO Metric Fits* tables.

- The **Hole-Basis** system is a system in which the basic size is the minimum size of the hole. The *hole-basis* system is the preferred method; the fundamental deviation is specified by the uppercase **H**.

- The **Shaft-Basis** system is a system in which the basic size is the maximum size of the shaft. The fundamental deviation of the *shaft-basis* system is specified by the lowercase **h**.

	Hole Basis	Shaft Basis	Description
	ISO Preferred Metric Fits		
Clearance Fits	H11/c11	C11/h11	*Loose running* fit for wide commercial tolerance or allowances.
	H9/d9	D9/h9	*Free running* fit not for use when accuracy is essential, but good for large temperature variation, high running speed, or heavy jpurnal pressure.
	H8/f7	F8/h7	*Close running* fit for running on accurate machines running at moderate speeds and journal pressure.
	H7/g6	G7/h6	*Sliding* fit not intended to run freely, but to move and turn frely and locate accurately.
Transition Fits	H7/h6	H7/h6	*Locational clearance* fit provides snug fit for locating stationary parts; but can be freely assembled and disassembled.
	H7/k6	K7/h6	*Locational transition* fit for accurate location, a compromise between clearance and interference.
	H7/n6	N7/h6	*Locational transition* fit for accurate location where interference is permissible.
	H7/p6	P7/h6	*Locational interference* fit for parts requiring rigidity and alignment with prime accuracy but without special bore pressure.
Interference Fits	H7/s6	S7/h6	*Medium drive* fit for ordinary steel parts or shrink fits on light sections, the tightest fit usable with cast iron.
	H7/u6	U7/h6	*Force* fit suitable for parts which can be highly stressed or for shrink fits where the heavy pressing forces required are impractical.

Example 7.6 Metric Hole Basis System

A design requires the use of two mating parts with a nominal size of **25** millimeters. The shaft and hub is to be fastened permanently using a drive fit. The fit class chosen is **Hole-Basis System H7/s6**. Determine the size limits of the two mating parts.

From Appendix B, the H7/s6 fit for 25 millimeters size:

Basic size	H7/s6 Medium Drive –Hole Basis		
	Hole H7	Shaft s6	Fit
25	25.021	25.048	-0.014
	25.000	25.035	-0.048

Using the *Hole Basis System*, the *BASIC* size 25 is designated as the minimum hole size. And the maximum hole size is 25.021 millimeters
The maximum shaft size is 25.048 millimeters
The minimum shaft size is 25.035 millimeters

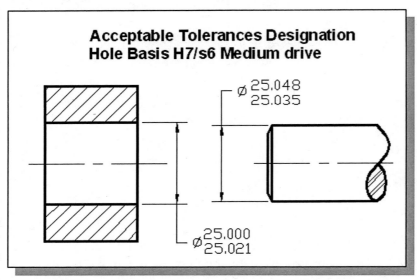

Tolerance of the shaft = Max. Shaft – Min. Shaft = 25.048 – 25.035 = 0.013

Tolerance of the hole = Max. Hole – Min. Hole = 25.021 – 25.000 = 0.021

Allowance = Min. Hole (MMC Hole) – Max. Shaft (MMC Shaft)
         = 25.000 – 25.048 = -0.0048
This is listed as the maximum interference in the table above: **-0.048**

Min. interference = Max. Hole (LMC Hole) – Min. Shaft (LMC Shaft)
         = 25.021 – 25.035 = -0.0014
This is listed as the minimum interference in the table above: **-0.0014**

Example 7.7 Shaft Basis System

A design requires the use of two mating parts with a nominal size of **25** millimeters. The shaft is to run with moderate speed but with a fairly heavy journal pressure. The fit class chosen is **Shaft Basis System F8/h7**. Determine the size limits of the two mating parts.

From Appendix B, the Shaft Basis System F8/h7 fit for 25 millimeters size:

Basic size	F8/h7 Medium Drive –Shaft Basis		
	Hole F8	**Shaft h7**	**Fit**
25	25.053 25.020	25.000 24.979	0.074 0.020

Therefore, the maximum shaft size is 25
The minimum shaft size is 24.979
The maximum hole size is 25.053
The minimum hole size is 25.020

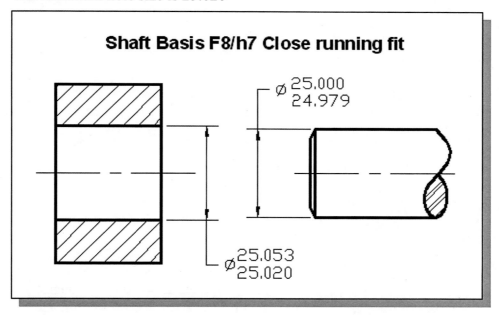

Shaft Basis F8/h7 Close running fit

Tolerance of the shaft = Max. Shaft – Min. Shaft = 25.000 – 24.979 = 0.021

Tolerance of the hole = Max. Hole – Min. Hole = 25.053 – 25.020 = 0.023

Allowance = Min. Hole – Max. Shaft = 25.020 – 25.000 = 0.020
This is listed as the minimum clearance in the table above: **0.020**

Max. Clearance = Max. Hole – Min. Shaft = 25.053 – 24.979 = 0.074
This is listed as the maximum clearance in the table above: **0.074**

Updating the *P-Bracket* Drawing

1. Select the **DraftSight** option on the *Program* menu or select the **DraftSight** icon on the *Desktop*.

2. In the DraftSight *Standard* toolbar, select **Open a Drawing** with a single click of the left-mouse-button.

3. In the *File* list section, pick ***P-Bracket.dwg***, the drawing from the last chapter, as the drawing to be loaded.

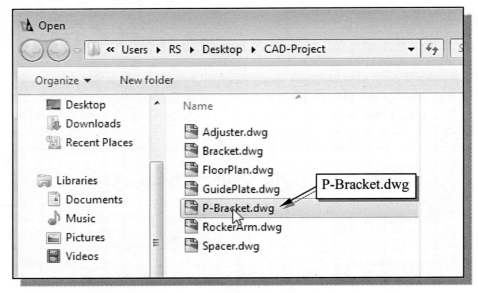

4. Click on the **OK** button to open the selected file.

The *Dimension Style* Manager

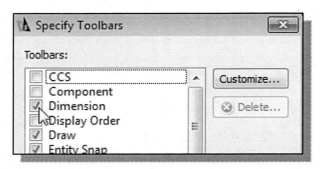

1. On your own, bring up the **Dimension** toolbar through the **Specify Toolbars** command as shown.

2. In the *Dimension* toolbar, pick **Dimension Style**. The *Dimension Style Manager* dialog box appears on the screen.

Tolerances Settings in the *Dimension Style* Manager

1. Confirm the **Mechanical** *Dimension Style* is the *active style*.

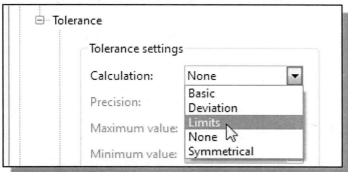

2. Click on the **Tolerances** list and set the *Tolerance format* to **Limits** as shown in the figure.

3. Set the *Precision* to **three digits** after the decimal point as shown.

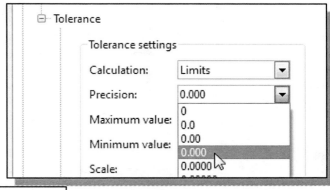

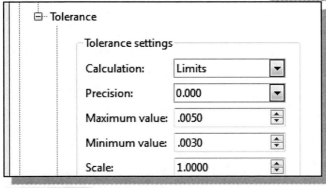

4. Enter **0.005** for the *upper value* as shown.

5. Enter **0.003** for the *Lower value* as shown.

6. Click on the **OK** button to accept the settings.

- Note that the tolerances settings affected all of the dimensions. The actual dimension values were used as the base dimensions and the limits are calculated using the upper and lower values we entered in the *Dimension Style Manager*.

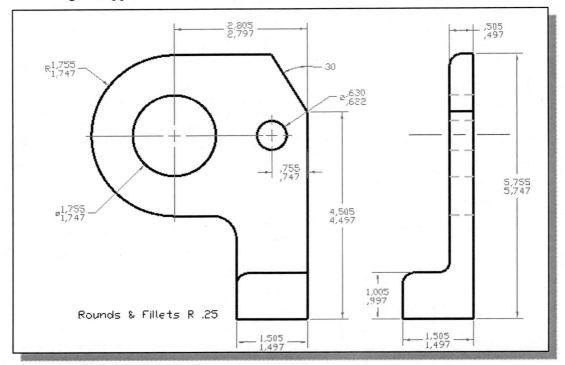

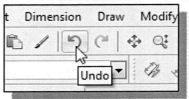

7. Click on the **Undo** button to remove the tolerances settings we made.

Determining the Tolerances Required

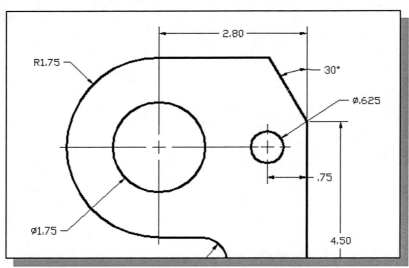

The *P-Bracket* design requires two sets of tolerances: (1) The nominal size of a **1.75** inch hole and (2) the nominal size of a **0.625** inch hole.

(1) The Nominal size of 1.75

A shaft is to run with moderate speed but with a fairly heavy journal pressure through the larger hole. The fit class chosen is **Basic Hole System RC6**. We will first determine the size limits of the two mating parts.

From Appendix A, the RC6 fit for 1.75 inch nominal size:

Nominal size Range	Limits of Clearance	RC6 Standard Limits – Basic Hole	
		Hole	Shaft
1.19 - 1.97	2.0	+2.5	-2.0
	6.1	-0.0	-3.6

Using the *Basic Hole System*, the *BASIC* size 1.75 is designated as the minimum hole size.

The maximum hole size is 1.75+0.0025 = 1.7525 inches
The minimum hole size is 1.75-0.00= 1.7500 inches

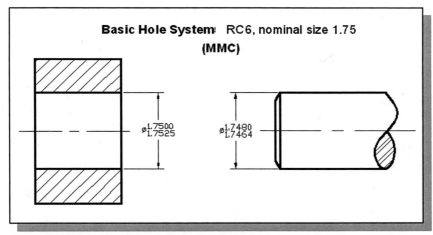

Basic Hole System RC6, nominal size 1.75
(MMC)

⌀1.7500 / 1.7525

⌀1.7480 / 1.7464

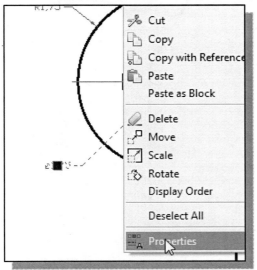

1. Pre-select the diameter *1.75* dimension as shown.

2. **Right-mouse-click** to bring up the option menu and select **Properties** as shown.

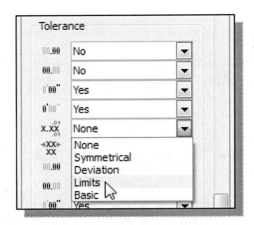

3. Set the *Tolerance display* option to **Limits** as shown.

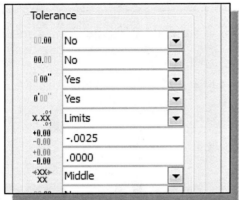

- In order to display the minimum hole size on top, we will **reverse** the tolerance values in the option boxes.

4. Enter **-0.0025** in the *Tolerance upper limit* box as shown.

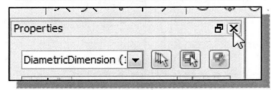

5. Exit the *Properties* palette by clicking on the upper [X] as shown. The toleranced dimension is as shown.

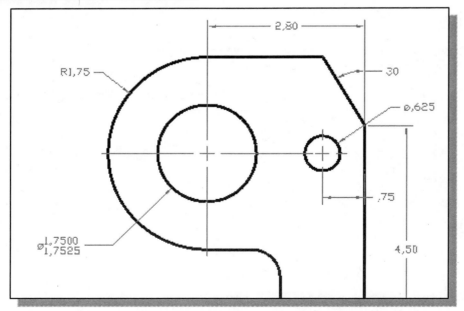

(2) The Nominal size of 0.625

A pin is to be placed through the diameter 0.625 hole. The fit class chosen is **Basic Hole System RC2**. We will first determine the size limits of the two mating parts.

From Appendix A, the RC2 fit for 0.625 inch nominal size:

Nominal size Range	Limits of Clearance	RC2 Standard Limits – Basic Hole	
		Hole	Shaft
0.40 - 0.71	0.25	+0.4	-0.25
	0.95	-0.0	-0.55

Using the *Basic Hole System*, the *BASIC* size 0.625 is designated as the minimum hole size.

The maximum hole size is 0.625+0.0004 = 0.6254 inches
The minimum hole size is 0.625-0.00= 0.62500 inches

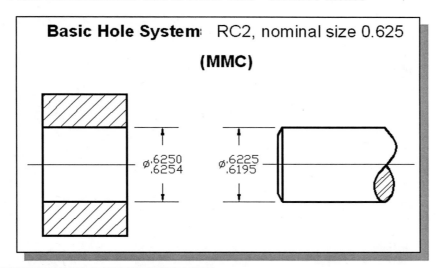

On your own, set the tolerances using the above values.

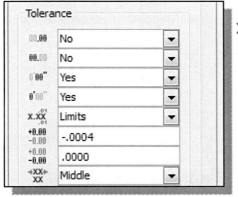

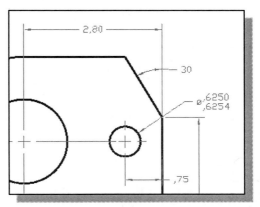

Review Questions:

1. Why are **Tolerances** important to a technical drawing?

2. Using the **Basic Shaft system**, calculate the size limits of a nominal size of 1.5 inches.

   Use the following FN4 fit table for 1.5 inches nominal size: (Numbers are in thousandth of an inch.)

Nominal size Range	Limits of Interference	FN4 Standard Limits – Basic Hole	
		Hole	Shaft
1.19 - 1.97	1.5	+1.0	+3.1
	3.1	-0.0	+2.5

3. Using the **Shaft Basis D9/h9** fits, calculate the size limits of a nominal size of 30 mm.

4. What is the procedure to set tolerances in DraftSight?

5. Explain the following terms:

   (a) Limits

   (b) MMC

   (c) Tolerances

   (d) Basic Hole System

   (e) Basic Shaft System

6. Given the dimensions as shown in the figure below, determine the tolerances of the two parts, and the allowance between the parts.

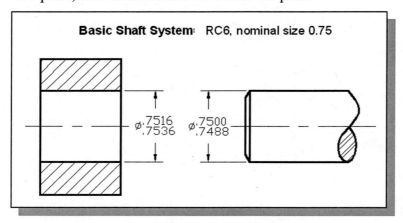

Exercises: (Create the drawings with the following Tolerances.)

1. Shaft Guide (Dimensions are in inches.)
   Fits: Diameter 0.25, Basic Hole system RC1, Diameter 1.00, Basic Hole system RC6

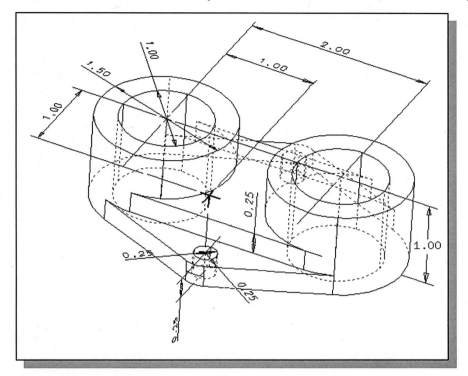

2. Pivot Lock (Dimensions are in inches.)
   Fits: Diameter 0.5, Basic Hole system RC2, Diameter 1.00, Basic Hole system RC5

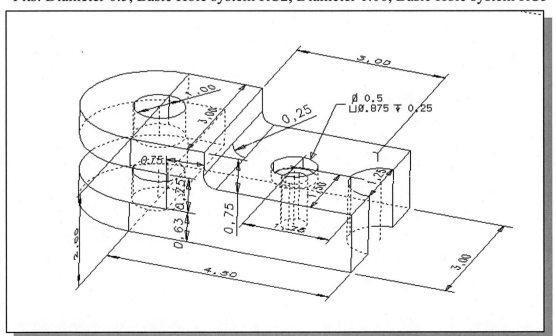

3. **Fixture Cap** (Dimensions are in millimeters.) Fits: Diameter 40, H7/g6.

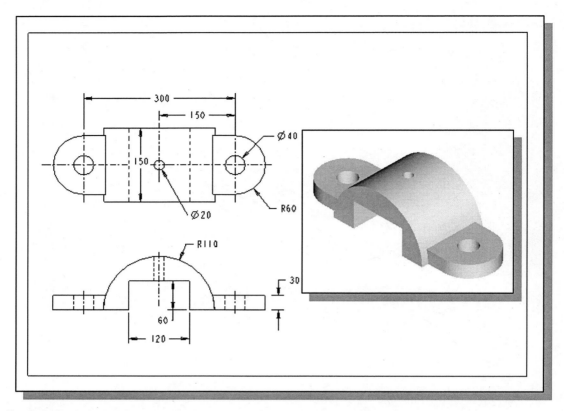

4. **Cylinder Support** (Inches.) Fits: Diameter 1.50, Basic Hole system RC8.

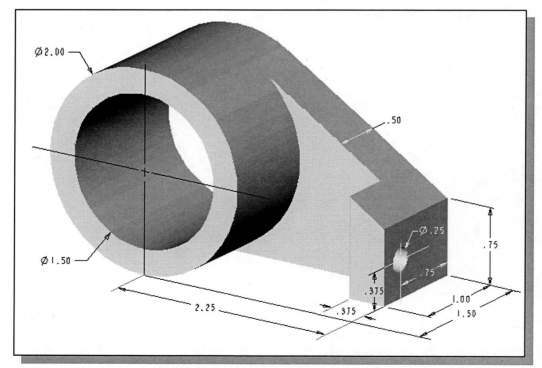

Chapter 8
Symmetrical Features in Designs

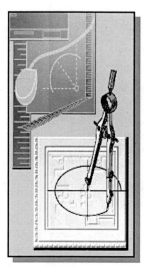

Learning Objectives

- ◆ **Set up the DraftSight Plot Style Option**
- ◆ **Create a Template File**
- ◆ **Use the MIRROR Command**
- ◆ **Create Multiple Copies of Objects**
- ◆ **Set Up Layouts in Paper Space**
- ◆ **Create Viewports in Paper Space**
- ◆ **Use the PROPERTIES Command**
- ◆ **Adjust the Text Scale for Plotting**

Introduction

One of the main advantages of using CAD systems is that we can easily reuse information that is already in the system. For example, many of the system settings, such as setting up layers, colors, linetypes and grids, are typically performed in all DraftSight files. In DraftSight, we can set up **template files** to eliminate these repetitive steps and make our work much more efficient. Using template files also helps us maintain consistent design and drafting standards. In this chapter, we will illustrate the procedure to set up template files that can contain specific plotting settings, system units, environment settings and other drafting standard settings.

We can also reuse any of the geometry information that is already in the system. For example, we can easily create multiple identical copies of geometry with the **Array** command, or create mirror images of objects using the **Mirror** command. In this chapter, we will examine the use of these more advanced construction features and techniques in DraftSight.

Also in this chapter, we will demonstrate the printing/plotting procedure to create a hardcopy of our design. DraftSight provides plotting features that are very easy to use. The DraftSight plotting features include: WYSIWYG (What You See Is What You Get) layouts; onscreen lineweights; Print Style tables; device-accurate paper sizes; and creating custom paper sizes.

The *GenevaCam* Design

Starting Up DraftSight

1. Select the **DraftSight** option on the *Program* menu or select the **DraftSight** icon on the *Desktop*.

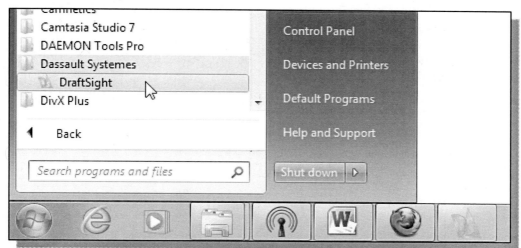

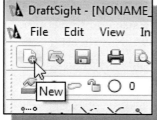

2. In the *Standard* toolbar, select the **New File** option with a single click of the left-mouse-button.

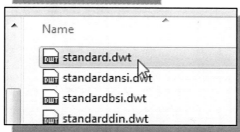

3. In the *Specify Template* dialog box, pick **Standard.dwt** as the template file to use.

4. In the *Specify Template* dialog box, click **Open**.

❖ One of the important rules for creating CAD designs and drawings is that they should be created **<u>full size</u>**. The importance of this practice is evident when we are ready to create hardcopies of the design, or transfer the designs electronically to manufacturing equipment, such as a CNC machine. Internally, CAD systems do not distinguish whether the one unit of measurement is one inch or one millimeter. DraftSight provides several options to control the unit settings.

Setting up the *Print Style Mode*

❖ Using DraftSight *Print Styles* and *Print Style tables* allows us to control the way drawings look at plot time. We can reassign object properties, such as color, linetype, and lineweight, and plot the same drawing differently. The default DraftSight *Print Style Mode* is set to use the *Color-Dependent Print Style*, which controls the plotting of objects based on the object colors and is the *basic* method of adjusting the plotted hardcopy in DraftSight. The other plot method in DraftSight is to use the *Named Print Style table* that works independently of color. In this chapter, we will learn to plot with the new DraftSight *Named Print Style*, which provides a more flexible and fast way to control the plotting of our designs.

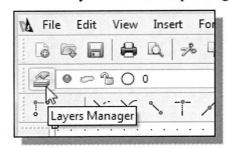

1. Pick **Layers Manager** in the *Layers* toolbar.

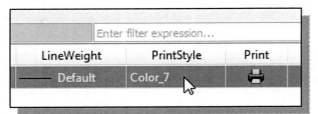

➢ Notice the *PrintStyle* option, in the *Layers Properties* list, displays the setting based on the *Color* of the layer. Note the *PrintStyle* cannot be edited.

2. On your own, change the color of *Layer 0* to **Red**, and confirm the **PrintStyle** for the layer is also updated.

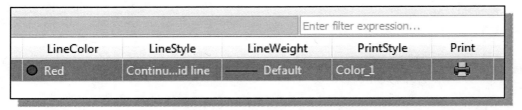

- The default **Print Style** is set to the *Color-Dependent Print Style*, and therefore the object color is also used for printing.

3. Click **Cancel** to exit the *Layers Manager*.

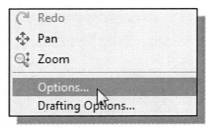

4. Inside the graphics area, **right-mouse-click** to bring up the option menu.

5. Select **Options** as shown in the figure.

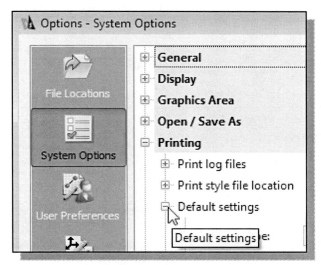

6. Switch to the *System Options* group as shown.

7. Click on the **Printing → Default Settings** to expand the list as shown.

8. In the default settings list, switch to **Use named print styles** as shown.

9. In the *Default PrintStyle* table, select ***default.stb*** from the list of *PrintStyle* tables.

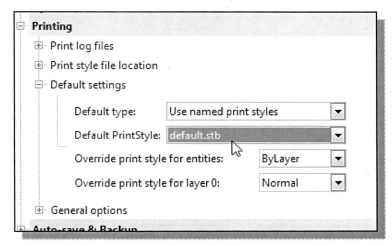

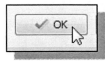

10. Pick **OK** to accept the selected settings and close the ***Options*** dialog box.

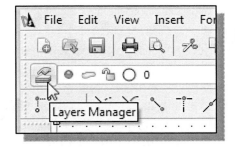

11. On your own, open the *Layers Manager* dialog box, and examine the *PrintStyle* setting.

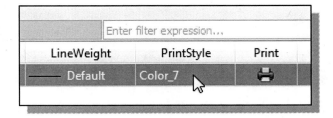

❖ Note the *PrintStyle* still displays the same setting, which is *By Color* and still cannot be adjusted. This is because the plotting settings are stored in each file. We will need to start a new file to have the new settings take effect.

Starting a new file

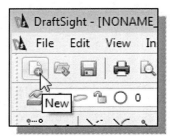

1. Click the **New** icon in the *Standard* toolbar.

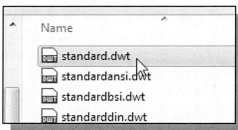

2. In the *Specify Template* dialog box, pick **Standard.dwt** as the template file to be used.

3. In the *Specify Template* dialog box, click **Open**.

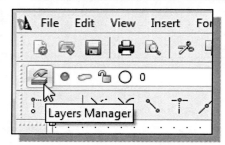

4. Pick **Layers Manager** in the *Layers* toolbar.

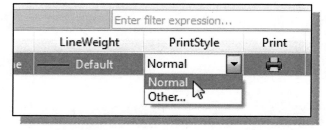

❖ Notice the *PrintStyle* setting now displays the setting of **Normal** and can also be edited. This indicates we are now using the *Named Print Style*, with different options to control plotting of the design.

➤ In the following sections, we will go over the procedure to use the **Named Print Style** in creating a hardcopy of the *Geneva Cam* design. The steps described in the above sections are required to switch from using the default *Print Style* to using the *Named Print Style*. Note that the switch needs to be done prior to creating the design. A similar procedure can be used to switch back to using the *By Color Print Style*.

Layers setup

1. In the *Layers Manager* dialog box, click on the **New** button (or the key combination [**Alt+N**]) to create a new layer.

2. Create **layers** with the following settings:

Layer	Color	LineStyle	Lineweight	PlotStyle
Construction	Gray(9)	Continuous	Default	Normal
Object_Lines	Blue	Continuous	0.6mm	Normal
Hidden_Lines	Cyan	Hidden	0.3mm	Normal
Center_Lines	Red	Center	Default	Normal
Dimensions	Magenta	Continuous	Default	Normal
Section_Lines	White	Continuous	Default	Normal
CuttingPlane_Lines	Dark Gray	Phantom	0.6mm	Normal
Title_Block	Green	Continuous	1.2mm	Normal
TitleBlockLettering	Green	Continuous	Default	Normal
Viewport	White	Continuous	Default	Normal

➢ Using the *Normal PlotStyle* enables plotting of *lineweights* defined in the specific layer. Note that the *Lineweight* settings are set for proper printing of different line types.

3. Highlight the layer *Construction* in the list of layers.

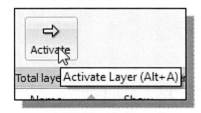

4. Click on the **Current** button to set layer *Construction* as the *Current Layer*.

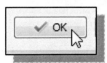

5. Click on the **OK** button to accept the settings and exit the *Layers Manager* dialog box.

6. In the *Status* toolbar area, reset the option buttons so that only *SNAP Mode* and *GRID Display* are switched *ON*.

Adding borders and title block in the Sheet layout

DraftSight allows us to create plots to any exact scale on the paper. Until now, we have been working in **model space** to create our design in <u>full size</u>. When we are ready to plot, we can arrange our design on a two-dimensional sheet of paper so that the plotted hardcopy is exactly what we wanted. This two-dimensional sheet of paper is known as the **paper space** in DraftSight. We can place borders and title blocks on *paper space*, the objects that are less critical to our design.

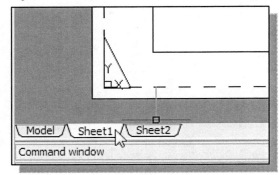

1. Click the **Sheet1** icon to switch to the two-dimensional paper space.

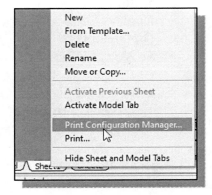

2. To adjust any *Printing Setup* options, right-mouse-click once on the tab and select **Print Configuration Manager**.

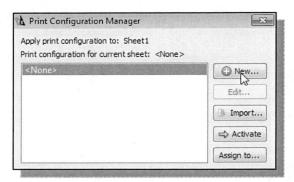

3. In the *Print Configuration Manager* click **New** to start a new configuration.

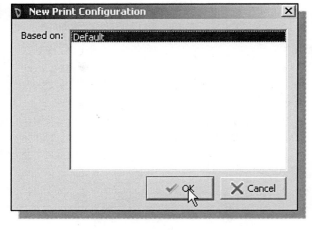

4. In the *New Print Configuration* dialog box, click **OK** to accept using the default configuration.

- Note that multiple configurations can be set up for different printers and paper sizes.

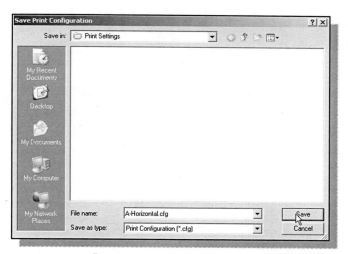

5. In the *Save Print Configuration* dialog box, name and save the new configuration as **A-Horizontal.cfg**.

6. In the *Page Setup* dialog box, select a plotter/printer that is available to plot/print your design. Consult with your instructor or technical support personnel if you have difficulty identifying the hardware.

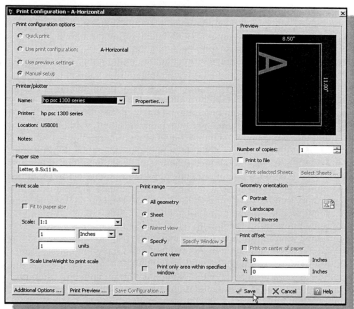

❖ Here we will set up the plotting for an A-size plot on a LaserJet printer. You should select settings that are applicable to your printers and plotters.

➢ Also note the *Printable area* is typically smaller than the paper size listed in the *Paper size* section, due to the limitations of the hardware.

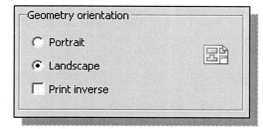

7. Confirm the *Paper size* is set to **Letter** or equivalent (8.5″ by 11″) and the *Geometry orientation* is set to **Landscape**.

8. Click on the **Save** button to accept the settings and exit the Page Setup command.

❖ In the graphics window, a rectangular outline on a gray background indicates the paper size. The dashed lines displayed within the paper indicate the *printable area*.

9. Select the rectangle inside the dashed lines.

10. Hit the [**Delete**] key once to remove it.

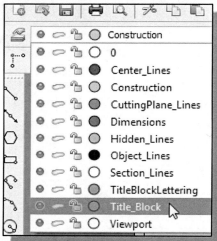

11. In the *Object Properties* toolbar area, select the **Layer Control** box and set layer **Title_Block** as the *Current Layer*.

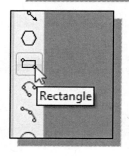

12. Select the **Rectangle** icon in the *Draw* toolbar. In the command window area, the message "*Specify start corner:*" is displayed.

13. Pick a location that is on the inside and near the lower left corner of the dashed rectangle.

14. In the command window area, use the *relative coordinate entry method* and create a 10.25″ × 7.75″ rectangle as the outline of the title block.

15. On your own, complete the title block as shown.

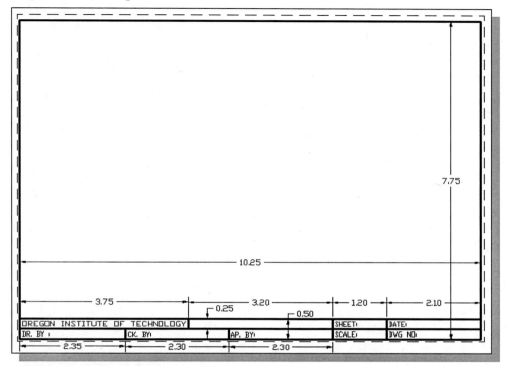

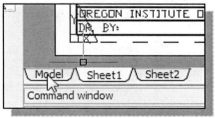

16. Click the **Model** tab to switch back to *model space*.

➤ Notice the title block we created is shown only in *paper space*.

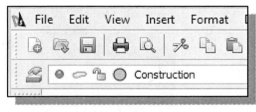

17. Select the *Layer Control* box and set layer *Construction Lines* as the *Current Layer*.

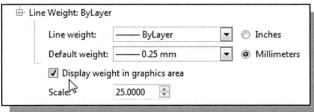

18. On your own, set up the **Line Weight** display options as shown.

19. Switch *ON* the following options in the *Status* toolbar: *SNAP* and *GRID*.

Create a Template file

The heart of any CAD system is the ability to reuse information that is already in the system. In the preceding sections, we spent a lot of time setting up system variables, such as layers, colors, linetypes and plotting settings. We will make a **template file** containing all of the settings and the title block we have created so far.

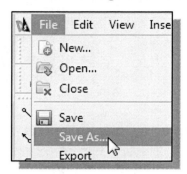

1. In the *Main Menu*, click **Save As** under *File*.

2. In the *Save As* dialog box, select the *template file* type and switch to the default template folder (or select the folder in which you want to store the *template file)*. Enter **Standard-A-H-Title** in the *File name* box.

3. Click **Save** in the *Save Drawing As* dialog box to close the dialog box.

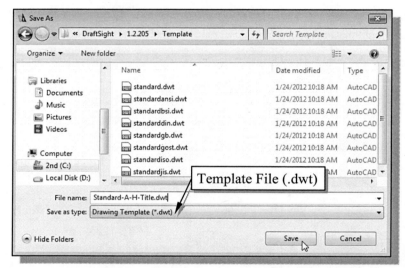

Template File (.dwt)

➤ The only difference between a DraftSight template file and a regular DraftSight drawing file is the filename extension, (.dwt) versus (.dwg). We can convert any DraftSight drawing into a DraftSight template file by simply changing the filename extension to *.dwt*. It is recommended that you keep a second copy of any template files on a separate disk as a backup.

Exit DraftSight

❖ To demonstrate the effects of using the new template file, we will exit and restart **DraftSight**.

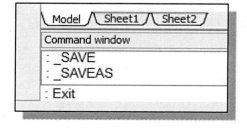

➤ In the command window, type **Exit** as shown.

Starting Up DraftSight

1. Select the **DraftSight** option on the *Program* menu or select the **DraftSight** icon on the *Desktop*.

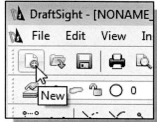

2. In the *Standard* toolbar, select the **New File** option with a single click of the left-mouse-button.

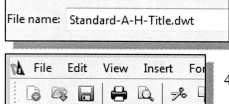

3. Select the ***Standard-A-H-Title*** template file from the list of template files.

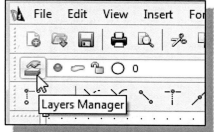

4. Pick **Layers Manager** in the *Object Properties* toolbar.

5. Examine the layer property settings in the *Layers Manager* dialog box.

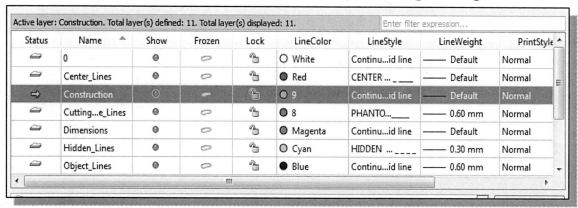

6. Confirm layer ***Construction*** is set as the *Current Layer*.

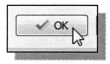

7. Click on the **Close** button to exit the *Layers Manager* dialog box.

The *Geneva Cam* Design

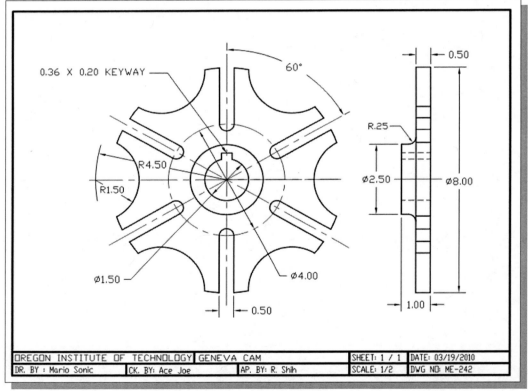

- Before going through the tutorial, how would you proceed to create a multiview drawing of the part. Since symmetrical features are present in the design, would this affect your decision in the construction steps of the design. You are also encouraged to construct the orthographic views on your own prior to following through the tutorial.

Drawing Construction lines

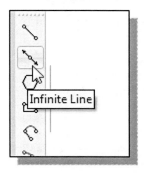

1. Select the **Infinite Line** icon in the *Draw* toolbar. In the command window area, the message *"Specify position:"* is displayed.

2. Place the first point at world coordinate (**5,4.5**) on the screen.

3. Pick a location above the last point to create a **vertical line**.

4. Move the cursor toward the right of the first point, and then pick a location to create a **horizontal line**.

5. Next, to create a construction line that is rotated 30 degrees from horizontal, enter **@2<30** [ENTER].

6. Inside the graphics window, **right-mouse-click** to end the Infinite Line command.

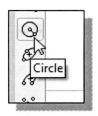

7. Select the **Circle** icon in the *Draw* toolbar. In the command window area, the message *"Specify center point:"* is displayed.

8. Pick the intersection of the lines as the center point of the circle.

9. In the command window area, the message *"Specify radius:"* is displayed. Enter **0.75** [ENTER].

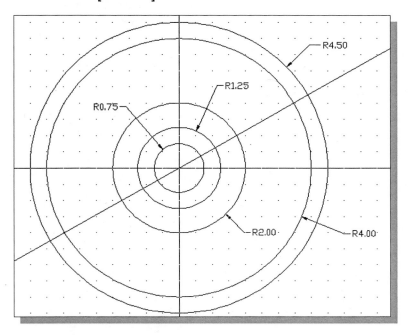

10. Repeat the Circle command and create four additional circles of radii **1.25**, **2.0**, **4.0** and **4.5** as shown.

Creating object lines

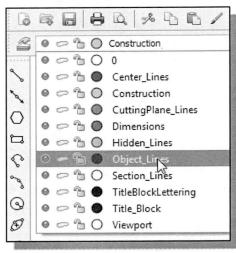

1. On the *Object Properties* toolbar, choose the **Layer Control** box with the left-mouse-button.

2. Move the cursor over the name of layer **Object_Lines**; the tooltip "*Object_Lines*" appears.

3. **Left-mouse-click once** and layer *Object_Lines* is set as the *Current Layer*.

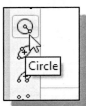

4. Select the **Circle** icon in the *Draw* toolbar. In the command window area, the message "*Specify center point:*" is displayed.

5. Move the cursor to the center of the circles, then left-click once to select the intersection as the center of the new circle.

6. In the *Status* toolbar, turn *ON* the *ESnap* option as shown.

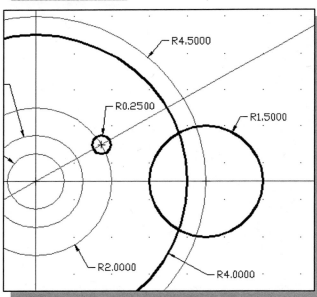

7. In the command window area, the message "*Specify radius of circle or [Diameter]:*" is displayed. Pick the **right intersection** of the *horizontal line* and the *radius 4.0 circle*.

8. Repeat the Circle command and pick the **right intersection** of the *horizontal line* and the *radius 4.5 circle* as the center point of the circle.

9. In the command window area, the message "*Specify radius:*" is displayed. Enter **1.5 [ENTER]**.

10. Repeat the **Circle** command and create a circle of radius **0.25** centered at the intersection of the inclined line and the radius **2.0** circle as shown.

Using the *OFFSET* command

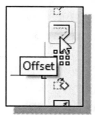

1. Select the **Offset** icon in the *Modify* toolbar. In the command window area, the message "*Specify distance:*" is displayed.

2. In the command window area, enter: **0.25** [ENTER].

3. In the *Status* toolbar, turn *OFF* the *Snap* option as shown.

4. In the command window area, the message "*Select source entity:*" is displayed. Pick the **inclined line** on the screen.

5. DraftSight next expects us to identify the direction of the offset. Pick a location that is **below** the inclined line.

6. Inside the graphics window, **right-mouse-click** and pick **Enter** to end the Offset command.

❖ Notice that the new line created by the Offset command is placed on the same layer as the line we selected to offset. Which layer is current does not matter; the offset object will always be on the same layer as the original object.

7. On your own, using the **Dynamic Viewing** commands, zoom in on the 30 degrees region as shown.

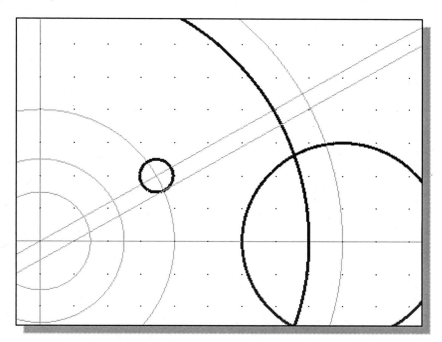

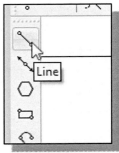

8. Select the **Line** command icon in the *Draw* toolbar. In the command window area, the message "*Specify start point:*" is displayed.

9. Move the cursor to the **intersection** of the *small circle* and the lower *inclined line* and notice the visual aid that automatically displays at the intersection. **Left-click** once to select the point.

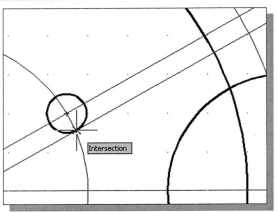
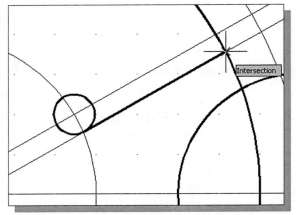

10. Pick the next **intersection point**, toward the right side, along the inclined line.

➢ On your own, use the **Trim** and **Erase** commands to remove the unwanted portions of the objects until your drawing contains only the objects shown below.

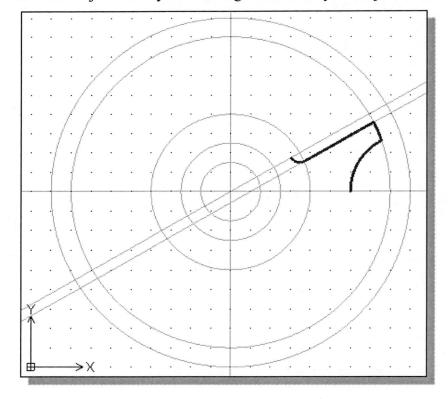

Using the *MIRROR* command

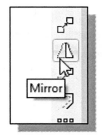

1. Select the **Mirror** command icon in the *Modify* toolbar. In the command window area, the message "*Select entities:*" is displayed.

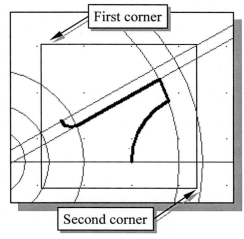

2. Create a *selection* window by selecting the two corners as shown.

➢ Note that, in DraftSight, creating the selection window from **left to right** will select only objects entirely within the selection area. Going from **right to left** (*crossing selection*) selects objects within and objects crossing the selection area. Objects must be at least partially visible to be selected.

3. Inside the graphics window, **right-mouse-click** to accept the selection and continue with the Mirror command.

4. In the command window area, the message "*Specify start point of the mirror line:*" is displayed. Pick any **intersection point along the horizontal line** on the screen.

5. In the command window area, the message "*Specify the end point:*" is displayed. Pick any other intersection point along the **horizontal line** on the screen.

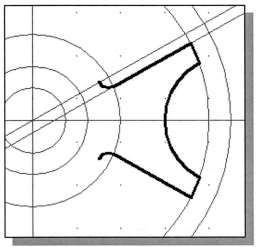

6. In the command window area, the message "*Delete source entities? Specify Yes or No:*" is displayed. Inside the graphics window, **right-mouse-click** and select **No** to retain the original objects.

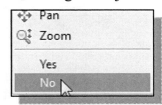

Using the *PATTERN* command

❖ We can make multiple copies of objects in polar, rectangular or path arrays (patterns). For polar arrays, we control the number of copies of the object and whether the copies are rotated. For rectangular arrays, we control the number of rows and columns and the distance between them.

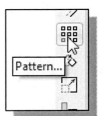

1. Select the **Pattern** command icon in the *Modify* toolbar.

   • Note that both the circular and linear patterns are available in DraftSight.

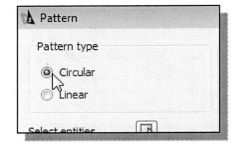

2. In the *Pattern* dialog box, set the *Pattern type* to **Circular** as shown.

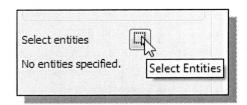

3. Click the **Select entities** icon as shown.

4. Using a *selection* window, enclose the objects we mirrored and the mirrored copies as shown.

5. In the command window area, the message "*Select entities:*" is displayed. Inside the graphics window, **right-mouse-click** to accept the selection.

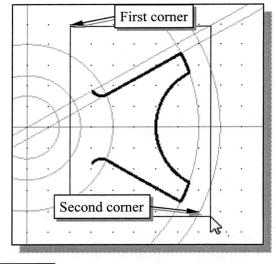

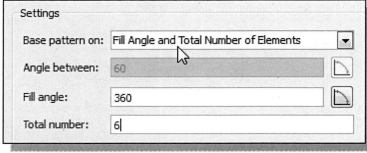

6. In the *Settings* section, set the *Base pattern on* option to **Fill Angle and Total Number of Elements**, and enter values **360** and **6** as shown.

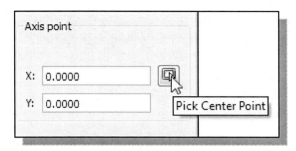

7. In the *Axis point* section, click the **Pick Center Point** icon as shown.

8. In the command window area, the message "*Specify pattern center point:*" is displayed. Pick the ***Center point* location** of the design as shown.

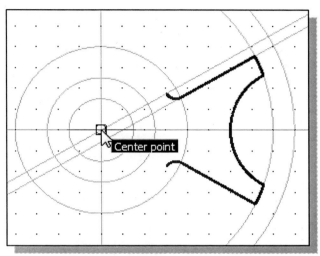

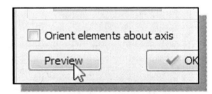

9. Uncheck the *Orient elements about axis* option as shown.

10. Click **Preview** to examine the pattern with the current settings.

- Note the current setting set the orientation of the elements to be same as the original set.

11. Press **[Esc]** once to return to the *Pattern* dialog box.

12. Set the *Orient elements about axis option* as shown.

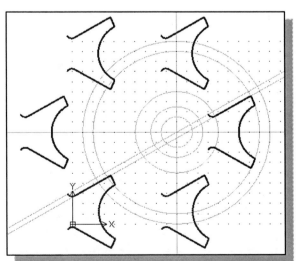

13. Click **OK** to create the circular pattern.

14. On your own, construct the **two inner circles** with the *0.36 × 0.20* keyway. (Hint: First create parallel lines at 0.95 and 0.18 distance of the horizontal and vertical construction lines.)

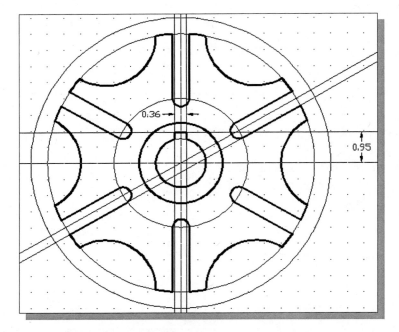

➤ On your own, complete the two views with dimensions. (In the *Dimension Style Manager*, set options under the **Fit** list to control the appearance of radius and diameter dimensions.)

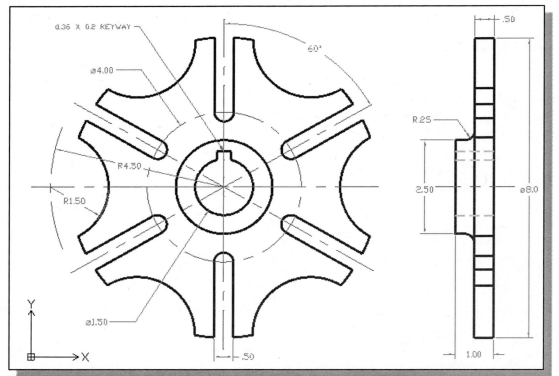

Creating a *Viewport* inside the title block

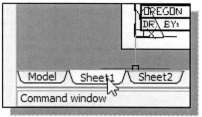

1. Click the **Sheet1** tab to switch to the two-dimensional paper space containing the title block.

2. If a view is displayed inside the title block, use the **Delete** command and delete the view by selecting any edge of the viewport.

3. Set the *Viewport* layer as the *Current Layer*.

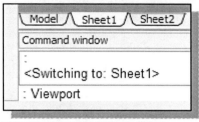

4. In the command window, enter *Viewport* to activate the command.

• The **Viewport** command creates and controls multiple tiled views on sheets.

5. In the *Status* toolbar area, turn *OFF* the *ESnap* and *ETrack* options as shown.

6. Create a viewport inside the title block area as shown.

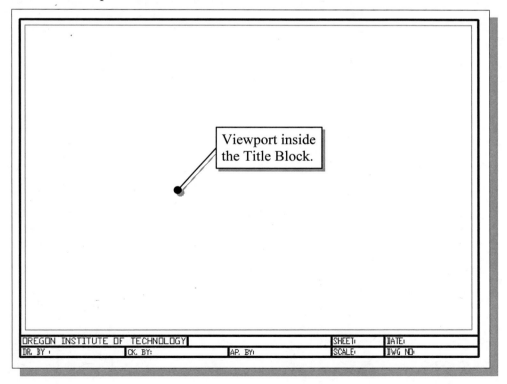

Viewport inside the Title Block.

Viewport properties

1. Pre-select the viewport by left-clicking once on any edge of the viewport.

2. In the *Standard* toolbar, click the **Properties** icon.

3. In the *Properties* dialog box, scroll down near the bottom of the list. Notice the current scale is set to *Custom scale, 0.7457*. (The number on your screen might be different.)

4. Below the *Custom scale*, the *Standard scale* list is available.

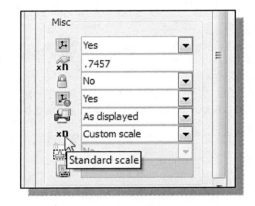

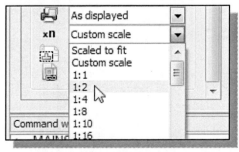

5. Select *1:2* in the standard scale list. This will set the plotting scale factor to half scale.

6. Click on the [**X**] button to close the *Properties* dialog box.

Hide the *Viewport borders*

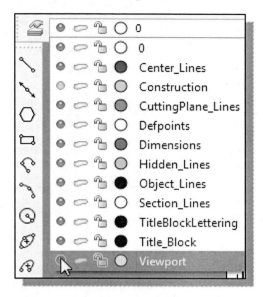

❖ We will **turn off** the *viewport borders* so that the lines will not be plotted.

1. Choose the **Layer Control** box, and select *Layer 0* as the active layer.

2. On your own, turn **OFF** layer *Viewport* in the *Layer Control* box.

Adjusting the dimension scale

1. In the *Main Menu* area, select **Dimension Style** in the *Format* tab.

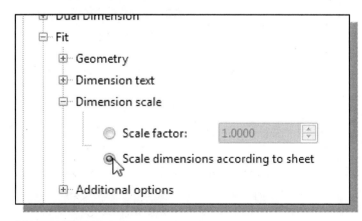

2. In the *Dimension* list, expand the **Fit** list.

3. Set the *Dimension scale* to using the **Scale dimensions according to sheet** option.

4. Click **OK** to accept the settings and exit the Dimension Style command.

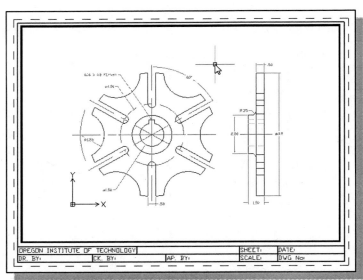

5. Inside the *Sheet1* layout, double-click once to switch to the **Model Mode**.

• The darker border inside the viewport indicates the Model Mode is active.

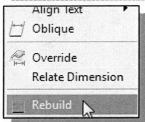

6. In the *Main Menu* area, select **Rebuild** in the *Dimension* tab as shown.

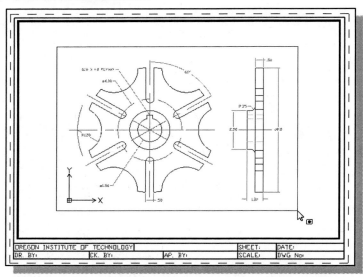

7. Using a *selection* window, enclose all of the dimensions in the *Model* mode as shown.

8. **Right-mouse-click** once to accept the selection.

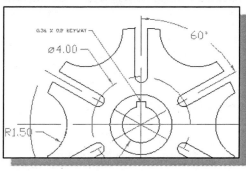

• The text height of the dimensions has been updated. Notice the local note did not update, as it is created as a *Note*.

9. On your own, readjust the locations of dimensions that got shifted due to the update.

Plot/Print the drawing

1. Move the cursor outside the *Sheet1* layout; double-click to switch back to the *Layout* mode.

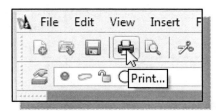

2. In the *Standard* toolbar, select the **Print** icon.

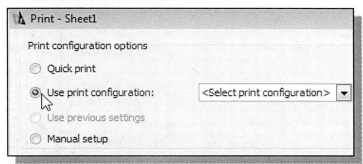

3. In the *Print Configuration* options section, choose **Use print Configuration** as shown.

4. On your own, choose the *print configuration* we created from the drop-down section.

- All settings stored in the *print configuration* are applied and some items can still be adjusted.

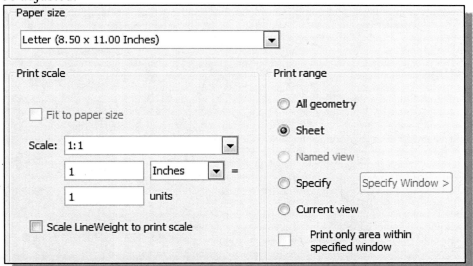

5. In the *Plot Scale* section, confirm it is set to *1:1*. Our *paper space* is set to the correct paper size.

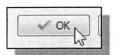

6. Click on the **OK** button to proceed with plotting the drawing.

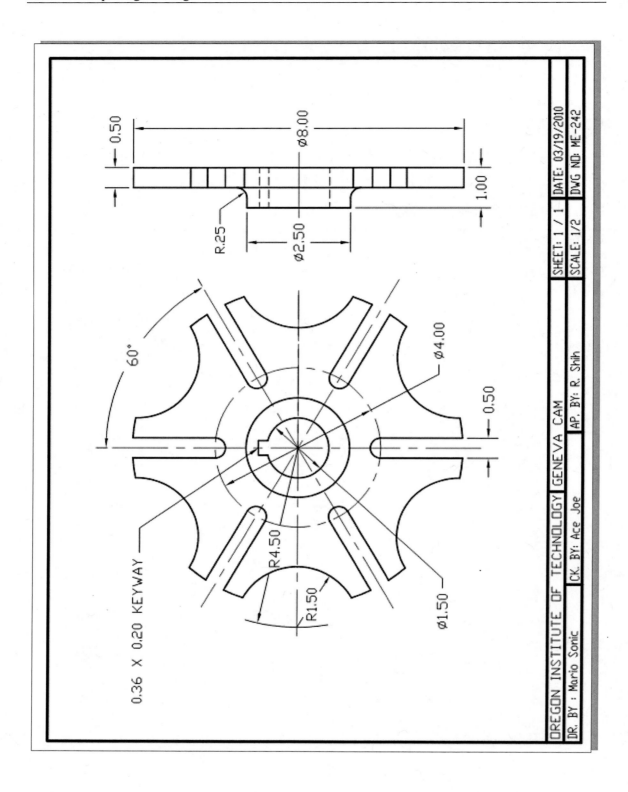

0.50

Ø8.00

R.25

Ø2.50

1.00

60°

Ø4.00

0.50

0.36 X 0.20 KEYWAY

R4.50

R1.50

Ø1.50

SHEET: 1 / 1   DATE: 03/19/2010

SCALE: 1/2   DWG NO: ME-242

OREGON INSTITUTE OF TECHNOLOGY GENEVA CAM

DR. BY : Mario Sonic   CK. BY: Ace Joe   AP. BY: R. Shih

Review Questions:

1. List and describe three advantages of using *template* files.

2. Describe the items that were included in the *Standard-A-H-Title* template file.

3. List and describe two methods of creating copies of existing objects in DraftSight.

4. Describe the procedure in determining the scale factor for plotting a DraftSight layout.

5. What is the difference between the DraftSight's *Model Space* and the *Paper Space*?

6. Why should we use the DraftSight *Paper Space*?

7. What does the *ORTHO* option allow us to do?

8. Which DraftSight command allows us to view and change properties of constructed geometric objects?

9. What is the main difference between a DraftSight drawing file (.dwg) and a DraftSight template file (.dwt)?

10. What does the **Dimension Rebuild** command allow us to do?

Exercises: (Unless otherwise specified, dimensions are in inches.)

1. Ratchet Plate (Thickness: 0.125 inch)

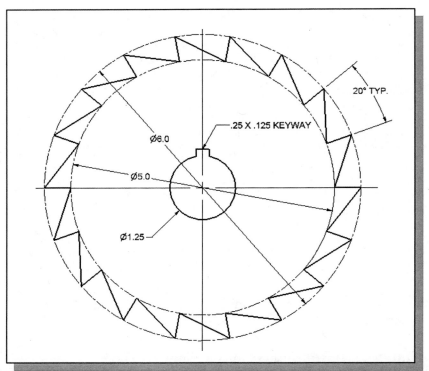

2. Shaft Support

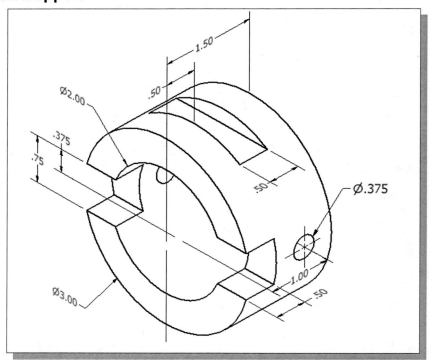

3. Auxiliary Support

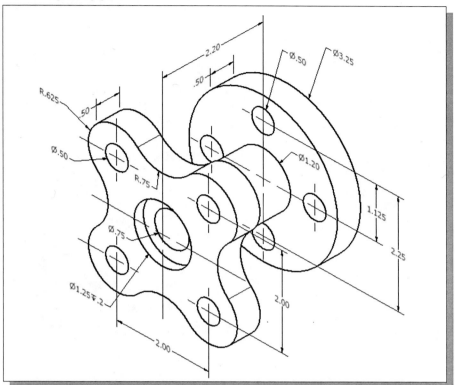

4. Indexing Guide

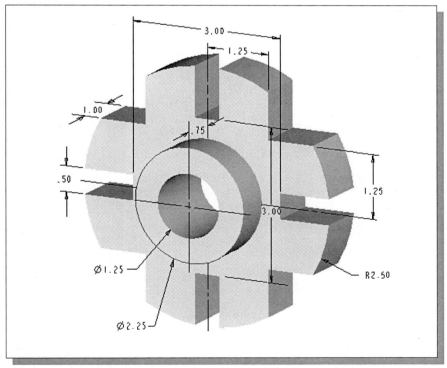

5. Coupling Base

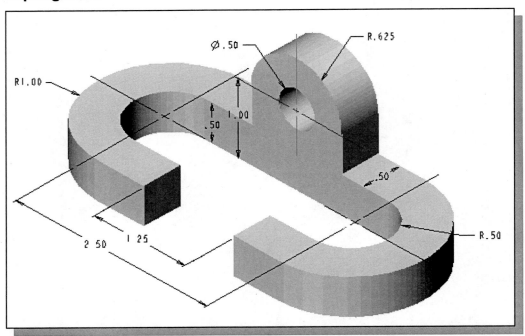

Lesson 9
Auxiliary Views

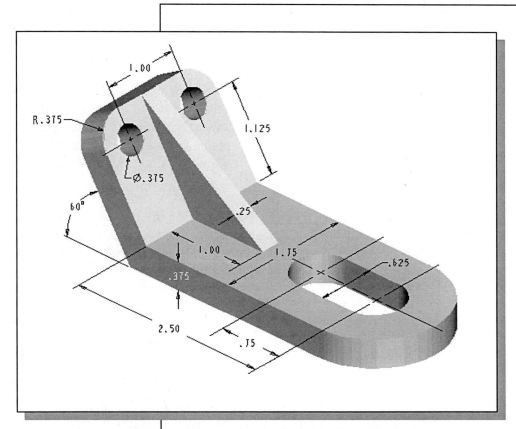

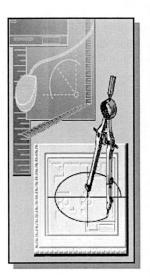

Learning Objectives

- **Understand the Principles of Creating Auxiliary Views**
- **Use 2D Projection Method to Draw Auxiliary Views**
- **Create Rectangles**
- **Use the basic Editing Commands**
- **Set up and use the Polar Tracking Option**
- **Create Viewports in Paper Space**

Introduction

An important rule concerning multiview drawings is to draw enough views to accurately describe the design. This usually requires two or three of the regular views, such as a front view, a top view and/or a side view.

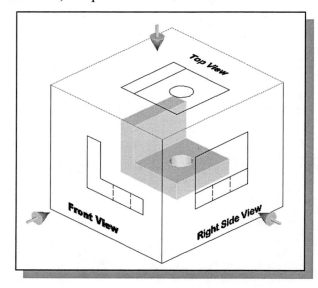

In the left figure, the L-shape object is placed with the surfaces parallel to the principal planes of projection. The top, front and right side views show the true shape of the different surfaces of the object. Note especially that planes of projection are parallel to the top, front and right side of object.

Based on the principle of orthographic projection, it is clear that a plane surface is shown in true shape when the direction of view is perpendicular to the surface.

Many designs have features located on inclined surfaces that are not parallel to the regular planes of projection. To truly describe the feature, the true shape of the feature must be shown using an **auxiliary view**. An *auxiliary view* has a line of sight that is perpendicular to the inclined surface, as viewed looking directly at the inclined surface. An *auxiliary view* is a supplementary view that can be constructed from any of the regular views. A primary *auxiliary view* is projected onto a plane that is perpendicular to one of the principal planes of projection and is inclined to the other two. A secondary *auxiliary view* is projected onto a plane that is inclined to all three principal planes of projection. In the figures below, the use of the standard views does not show the true shape of the upper feature of the design; the use of an auxiliary view provided the true shape of the feature and also eliminated the need of front and the right side views.

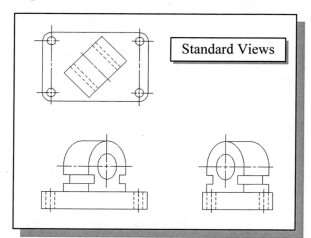

Standard Views

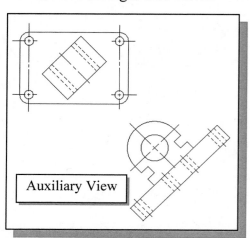

Auxiliary View

Normal View of an Inclined Surface

No matter what the position of a surface may be, the fundamentals of projecting a normal view of the surface remain the same: **The projection plane is placed parallel to the surface to be projected. The line of sight is set to be perpendicular to the projection plane and therefore perpendicular to the surface to be projected.** This type of view is known as **normal view**. In geometry, the word "*normal*" means "*perpendicular*".

In the figure below, the design has an inclined face that is inclined to the horizontal and profile planes and **perpendicular to the frontal plane**.

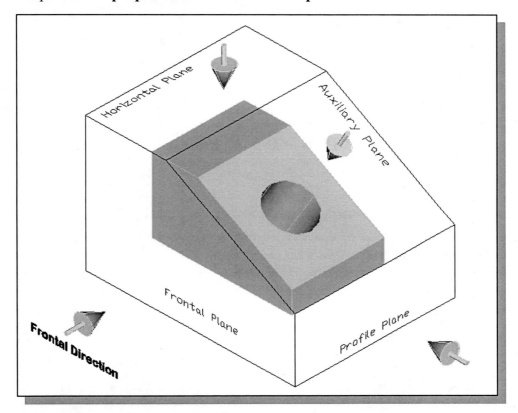

The principal views (*Top*, *Front* and *Right Side Views*) do not show the **true size and shape** of the inclined surface. Note the inclined surface does appear as an edge in the *Front View*. To show the true size and shape of the inclined surface, a *normal* view is needed.

To get the normal view of the inclined surface, a projection is made perpendicular to the surface. This projection is made from the view where the surface shows as an edge, in this case, the *Front View*. The perpendicularity between the surface and the line of sight is seen in true relationship in the 2D views. These types of extra normal views are known as **auxiliary views** to distinguish them from the principal views. However, since an auxiliary is made for the purpose of showing the true shape of a surface, the terms *normal view* and *edge view* are also used to describe the relations of the views.

An auxiliary is constructed following the rules of orthographic projection. An auxiliary view is aligned to the associated views, in this case, the front view. The line of sight is perpendicular to the edge view of the surface, as shown in the below figures.

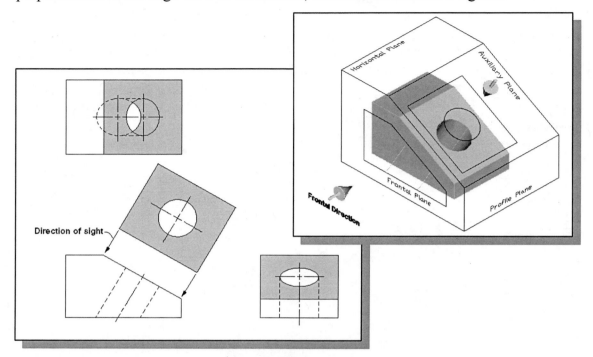

The orientation of the inclined surface may be different, but the direction of the normal view remains the same as shown in the figures below.

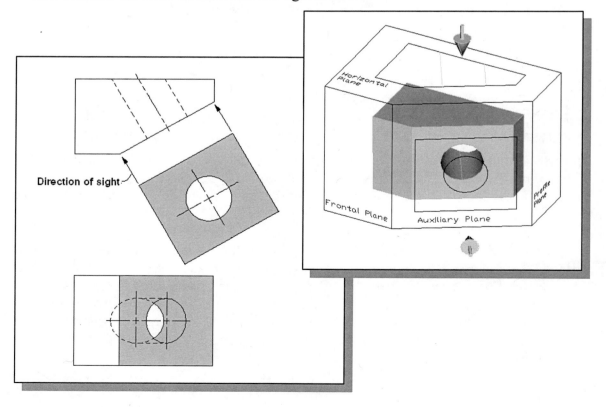

Construction Method I – Folding Line Method

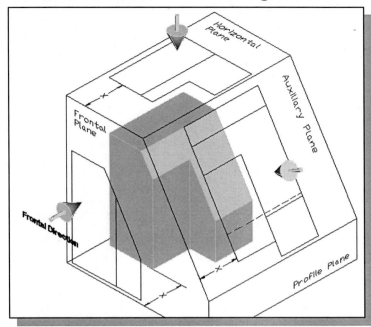

Two methods are commonly used to construct auxiliary views: The **folding-line** method and the **reference plane** method. The folding-line method uses the concept of placing the object inside a glass-box, the distances of the object to the different projection planes are used as measurements to construct the necessary views, including the auxiliary views.

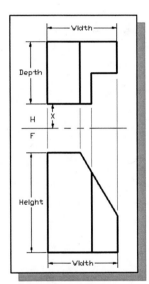

The following steps outline the general procedure to create an auxiliary view:

1. Construct the necessary principal views; in this case, the front and top views.

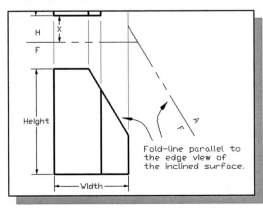

2. Construct a folding line parallel to the edge view of the inclined surface.

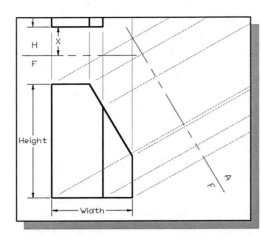

3. Construct the projection lines perpendicular to the edge view of the inclined surface, and also perpendicular to the folding line.

4. Use the corresponding distances, X, and the depth of the object from the principal views to construct the inclined surface.

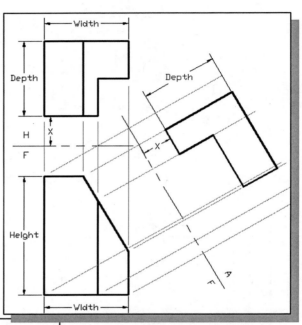

5. Complete the auxiliary view by following the principles of orthographic projection.

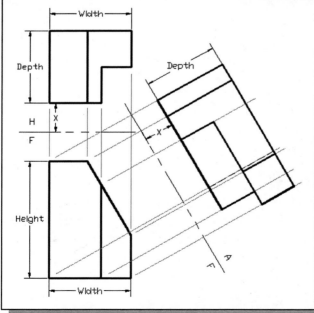

Construction Method II – Reference Plane Method

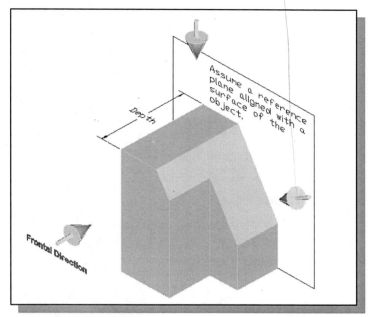

The **reference plane method** uses the concept of placing a reference plane aligned with a surface of the object that is perpendicular to the inclined surface. The reference plane is, typically a flat surface or a plane which runs through the center of the object. The distances of the individual corner to the reference plane is then used as measurements to construct the auxiliary view.

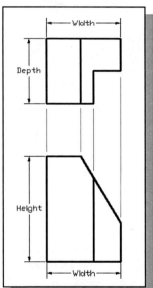

The following steps outline the general procedure to create an auxiliary view:

1. Construct the necessary principal views; in this case, the front and top views.

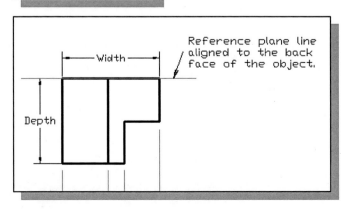

2. Construct a reference plane line aligned to a flat face and perpendicular to the inclined surface of the object, in this case, the back face of the object.

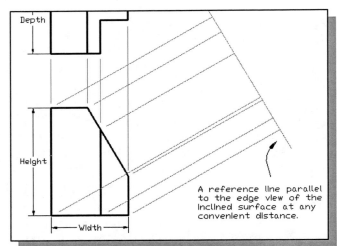

A reference line parallel to the edge view of the inclined surface at any convenient distance.

3. Construct a reference line parallel to the edge view of the inclined surface and construct the projection lines perpendicular to the edge view of the inclined surface.

4. Using the corresponding distances, such as the depth of the object, and construct the inclined surface.

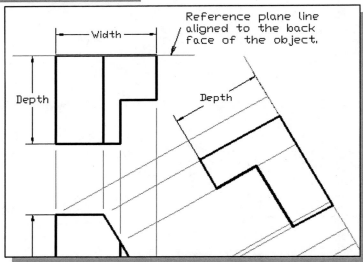

Reference plane line aligned to the back face of the object.

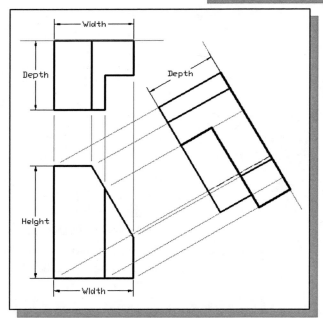

5. Complete the auxiliary view by following the principles of orthographic projection.

Partial Views

The primary purpose of using auxiliary views is to provide detailed descriptions of features that are on inclined surfaces. The use of an auxiliary view often makes it possible to omit one or more standard views. But it may not be necessary to draw complete auxiliary views, as the completeness of detail may be time consuming to construct and add nothing to the clearness of the drawing.

 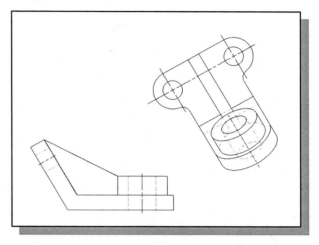

In these cases, partial views are often sufficient, and the resulting drawings are much simplified and easier to read.

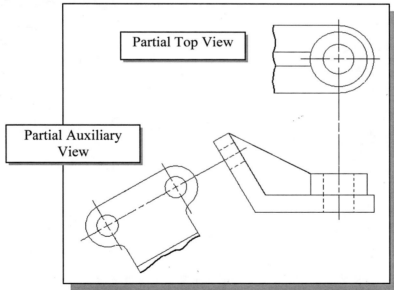

- To clarify the relationship of partial auxiliary views and the standard views, a center line or a few projection lines should be used. This is especially important when the partial views are small.

- In practice, hidden lines are generally omitted in auxiliary views, unless they provide clearness to the drawings.

Creating Auxiliary Views in DraftSight

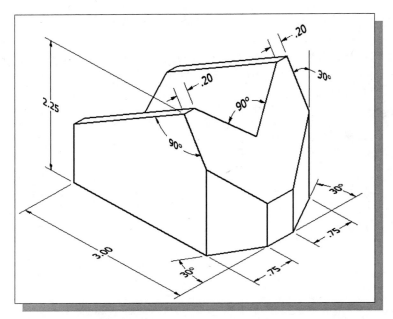

> ➢ Before going through the tutorial, make a rough sketch of a multiview drawing of the part. How many 2D views will be necessary to fully describe the part? Based on your knowledge of *DraftSight* so far, how would you arrange and construct these 2D views? Take a few minutes to consider these questions and do preliminary planning by sketching on a piece of paper. You are also encouraged to construct the orthographic views on your own prior to going through the tutorial.

Starting Up DraftSight

1. Select the **DraftSight** option on the *Program* menu or select the **DraftSight** icon on the *Desktop*.

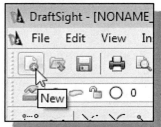

2. In the *Standard* toolbar, select the **New File** option with a single click of the left-mouse-button.

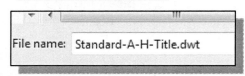

3. Select the ***Standard-A-H-Title*** template file from the list of template files.

4. Click **Open** to start a new DraftSight drawing file.

Setting up the Principal Views

- We will first create some of the related construction geometry for the front view.

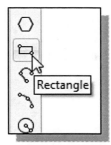

1. Select the **Rectangle** icon in the *Draw* toolbar. In the command prompt area, the message "*Specify start corner:*" is displayed.

2. Place the first corner point of the rectangle near the lower left corner of the screen. Do not be overly concerned about the actual coordinates of the location; the CAD drawing space is a very flexible virtual space.

3. Create a 3″ × 2.25″ rectangle. Using the *relative input* option, enter **@3,2.25 [ENTER]**.

❖ The Rectangle command creates rectangles as *polyline* features, which means all segments of a rectangle, are created as a single object.

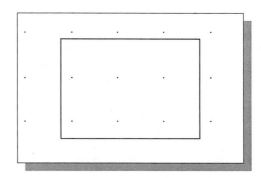

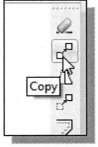

4. Next, we will make a copy of the rectangle. Click on the **Copy** icon in the *Modify* toolbar as shown.

5. In the *Status* toolbar area, reset the options as shown.

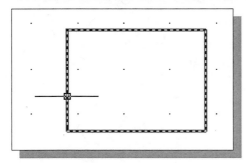

6. Pick any edge of the rectangle we just created.

7. Inside the graphics window, **right-mouse-click** to accept the selection.

8. In the command prompt area, the message "*Specify from:*" is displayed. Pick the **lower right corner** as the base point. A copy of the rectangle is attached to the cursor at the base point.

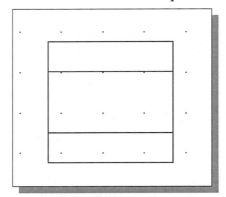

9. In the command prompt area, the message "*Specify second point of displacement, or <use first point as displacement>:*" is displayed. Enter: **@0,0.75** [ENTER].

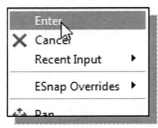

10. Inside the graphics window, **right-mouse-click** to bring up the option menu and select **Enter** to end the Copy command.

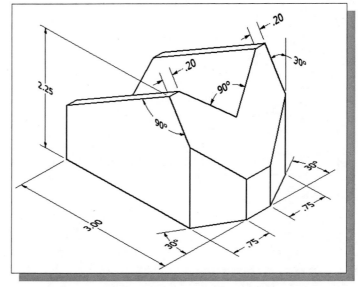

❖ This second rectangle will be used to construct the inclined face located at 30-degree to the vertical right surface.

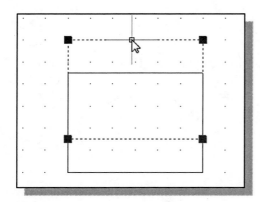

11. **Pre-select** the **copy** by picking the top horizontal line on the screen. The second rectangle, the copy we just created, is selected.

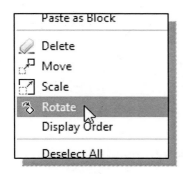

12. Inside the graphics window, **right-mouse-click** to bring up the popup option menu and select the **Rotate** option.

- Besides using commands in the *Modify* toolbar, some of the more commonly used editing tools are also available in the popup option menu.

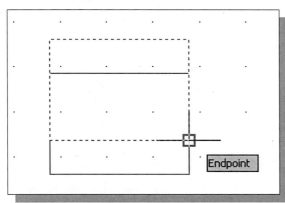

13. In the command prompt area, the message *"Specify pivot point:"* is displayed. Pick the **lower right corner** of the **selected rectangle** as the base point.

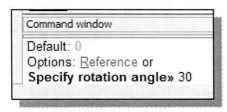

14. In the command prompt area, the message *"Specify the rotation angle:"* is displayed. Enter: **30** [ENTER].

15. Inside the graphics window, **right-mouse-click** once to bring up the option menu and choose **Enter** to exit the Rotate option.

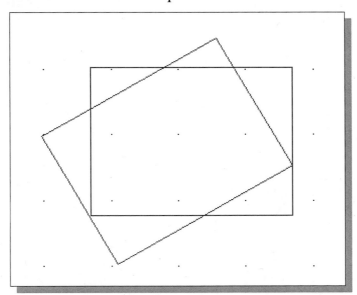

Setting up the Top View

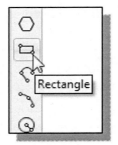

1. Select the **Rectangle** icon in the *Draw* toolbar. In the command prompt area, the message "*Specify first corner point or [Chamfer/ Elevation/Fillet/Thickness/Width]:*" is displayed.

2. Move the cursor over the top left corner of the first rectangle we created. This will activate the ***object tracking*** alignment feature to the corner.

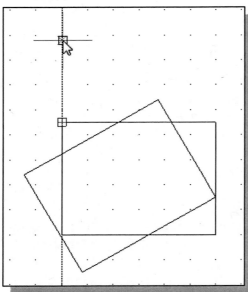

3. Move the cursor upward to a location that is about 1.5″ away from the reference point. (Hint: Use the *ETrack* option to assure the alignment.) Left-click once to place the first corner point of the rectangle.

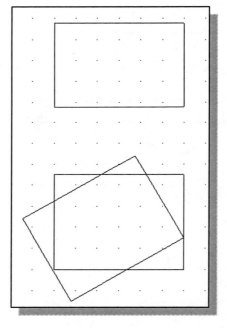

4. We will create a 3″ × 2″ rectangle. Enter: **@3,2 [ENTER]**.

- We have created the outline of the *Top View* of the *V-block* design.

5. Pre-select the **rectangle** we just created by left-clicking any edge of the rectangle.

6. Select the **Explode** icon in the *Modify* toolbar.

- The top rectangle now consists of four separate line segments.

Using the *OFFSET* Command

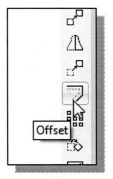

1. Click the **Offset** icon in the *Modify* toolbar. In the command prompt area, the message "*Specify distance:*" is displayed.

2. In the command prompt area, enter: **0.2** [ENTER].

3. In the command prompt area, the message "*Select source entity:*" is displayed. Pick the **top horizontal line** of the *Top View* on the screen.

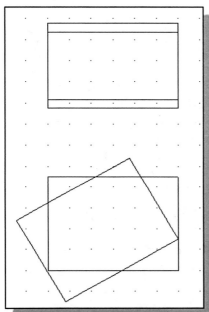

4. DraftSight next asks us to identify the direction of the offset. Pick a location that is **below** the selected line.

5. In the command prompt area, the message "*Select source entity:*" is displayed. Pick the **bottom horizontal line** of the top view on the screen.

6. DraftSight next asks us to identify the direction of the offset. Pick a location that is **above** the selected line.

7. Inside the graphics window, **right-mouse-click** and select **Enter** to end the Offset command.

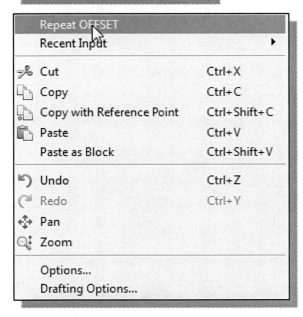

8. Inside the graphics window, right-mouse-click to bring up the popup option menu and select the **Repeat Offset** option.

- Notice in the popup menu, none of the extra editing commands is displayed; those editing commands are displayed only if objects are pre-selected.

9. In the command prompt area, the message *"Specify distance:"* is displayed. Enter: **0.75** [ENTER].

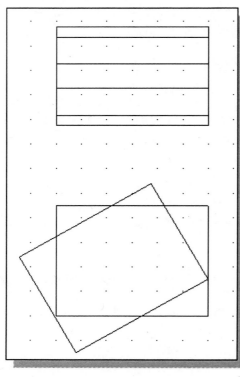

10. In the command prompt area, the message *"Select source entity:"* is displayed. Pick the **top horizontal line** of the *Top View* on the screen.

11. DraftSight next asks us to identify the direction of the offset. Pick a location that is **below** the selected line.

12. In the command prompt area, the message *"Select source entity:"* is displayed. Pick the **bottom horizontal line** of the *Top View* on the screen.

13. *DraftSight* next asks us to identify the direction of the offset. Pick a location that is **above** the selected line.

14. Inside the graphics window, **right-mouse-click** and choose **Enter** to end the Offset command.

• The four parallel lines will be used to construct the top v-cut feature and the two 0.75″ × 30° cut features at the base of the *V-block* in the *Top View*.

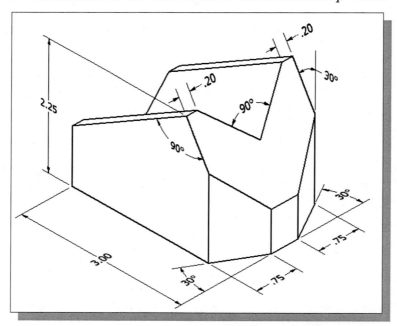

Creating Object Lines in the Front View

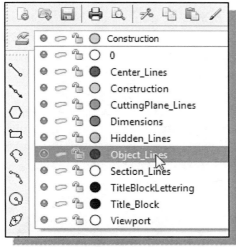

1. On the *Object Properties* toolbar, choose the *Layer Control* box with the left-mouse-button.

2. Move the cursor over the name of layer **Object_Lines**; the tool tip "*Object_Lines*" appears.

3. **Left-mouse-click once** and layer *Object_Lines* is set as the *Current Layer*.

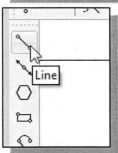

4. Select the **Line** command icon in the *Draw* toolbar. In the command prompt area, the message "*_line Specify first point:*" is displayed.

5. Pick the **lower left corner** of the bottom horizontal line in the *Front View* as the starting point of the line segments.

6. Pick the **lower right corner** of the bottom horizontal line in the *Front View* as the second point.

7. Select the **third** and **fourth** points as shown in the figure below.

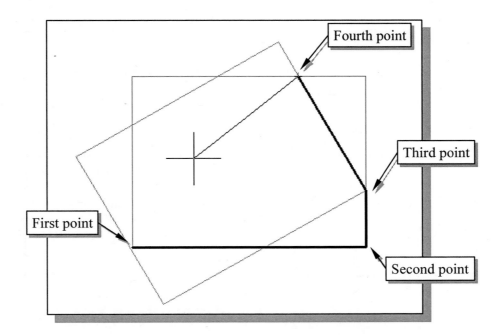

Setting the *POLAR TRACKING* Option

1. In the *Status* toolbar area, turn *ON* the *Polar Tracking* option.

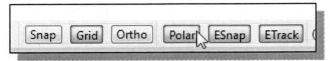

*   Note that the *Polar Tracking* option is one of the DraftSight *ETrack* features. The *ETrack* features include two tracking options: polar tracking and entity snap tracking. When the *Polar Tracking* option is turned *ON*, alignment markers are displayed to help us create objects at precise positions and angles. A quick way to change the settings of the *ETrack* feature is to use the option menu.

2. Move the cursor on top of the *Polar Tracking* option in the *Status* toolbar area.

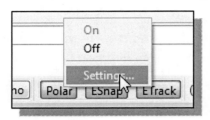

3. Click once with the right-mouse-button to bring up the option menu.

4. Select **Settings** in the option menu as shown in the figure.

5. In the *Drafting Options* list, set the *Increment angle* to *30* as shown in the figure.

6. Click **OK** to accept the modified settings.

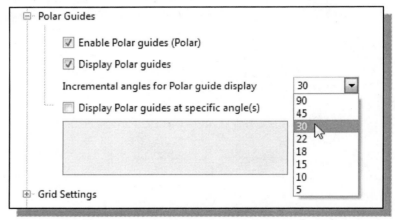

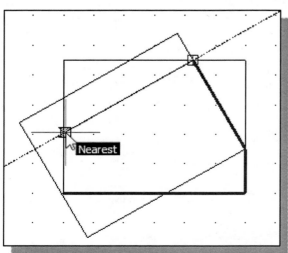

7. Move the cursor near the left vertical line as shown and notice that DraftSight *ETrack* automatically snaps the cursor to the intersection point and displays the alignment marker as shown.

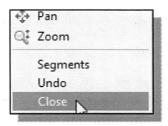

8. Inside the graphics area, right-mouse-click to bring up the option menu.

9. Select the **Close** option in the option list. DraftSight will create a line connecting the last point to the first point of the line sequence.

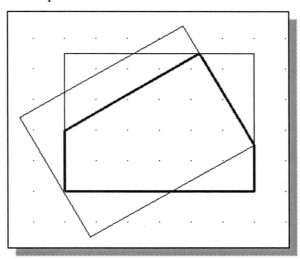

Setting up an Auxiliary View

1. Click on the **Copy** icon in the *Modify* toolbar as shown.

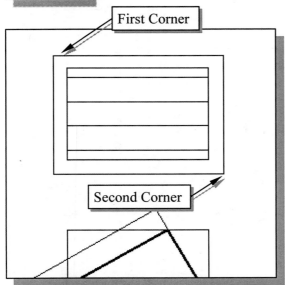

2. Select all objects in the *Top View* by enclosing the objects inside a **selection** window.

3. Inside the graphics window, **right-mouse-click** once to accept the selection.

4. In the command prompt area, the message *"Specify from point:"* is displayed. Pick the **lower left corner** of the *Top View* as the base point.

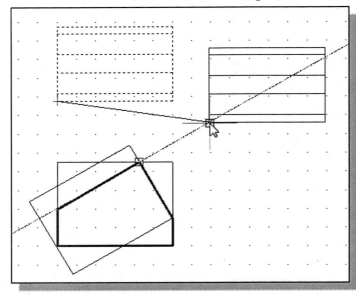

5. Using the *Entity Track* features, place the copy of the *Top View* by aligning it to the inclined object line we just created. **Left-click** once to position the copy about 2″ away from the top corner of the *Front View*.

6. Inside the graphics window, **right-mouse-click** and choose **Enter** to end the Copy command

Aligning the Auxiliary View to the Front View

1. **Pre-select** all objects in the auxiliary view by enclosing the objects inside a *selection* window.

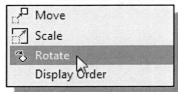

2. Inside the graphics window, right-mouse-click to bring up the popup option menu and select the **Rotate** option.

3. In the command prompt area, the message *"Specify base point:"* is displayed. Pick the **bottom left corner** of the auxiliary view as the base point.

4. In the command prompt area, the message *"Specify the rotation angle or [Reference]:"* is displayed. Enter: **-60 [ENTER]**.

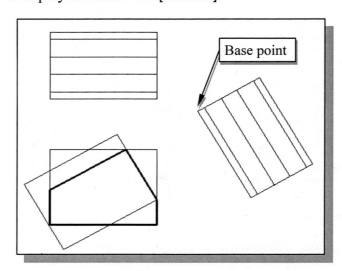

Creating the V-cut in the Auxiliary View

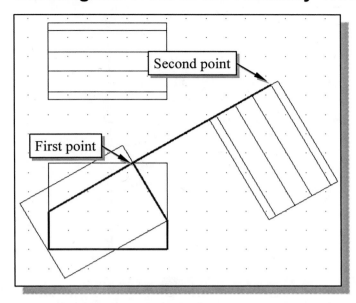

1. Select the **Line** icon in the *Draw* toolbar. In the command prompt area, the message *"Specify start point:"* is displayed.

2. Pick the **top corner** of the inclined object line in the *Front View* as the starting point of the line segments.

3. Pick the **second top end point** in the auxiliary view as the second point.

4. Inside the graphics window, right-mouse-click and select **Enter** to end the Line command.

5. Pre-select the line we just created.

6. Inside the graphics window, right-mouse-click to bring up the popup option menu and select the **Rotate** option.

7. In the command prompt area, the message *"Specify base point:"* is displayed. Pick the top right endpoint of the line as the base point.

8. In the command prompt area, the message *"Specify rotation angle* is displayed. Enter: **45 [ENTER]**.

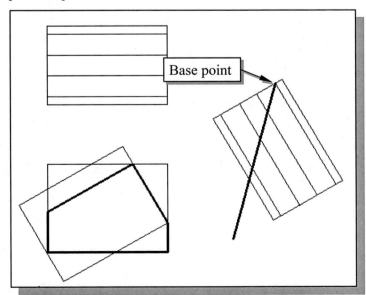

9. On your own, repeat the above steps and create the other line as shown.

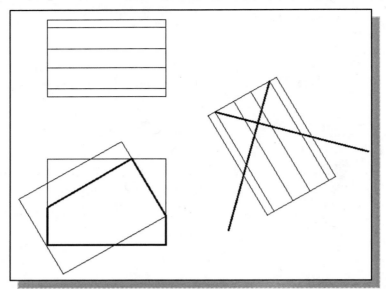

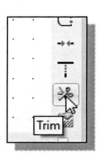

10. Select the **Trim** command icon in the *Modify* toolbar. In the command prompt area, the message "*Specify cutting edges:*" is displayed.

11. Pick the two inclined lines we just created in the auxiliary view as the *cutting edges*.

12. Inside the graphics window, **right-mouse-click** to proceed with the Trim command.

13. On your own, trim the two inclined lines as shown in the figure.

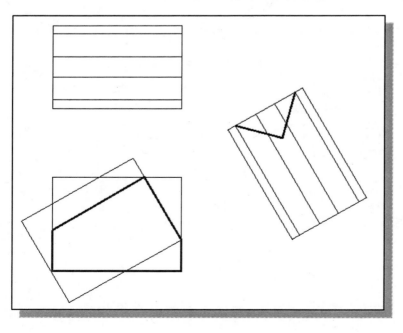

➢ The V-cut is shown at its true size and shape only in the auxiliary view. It is therefore necessary to create the V-cut in the auxiliary view. Now that we have constructed the feature in the auxiliary view, we can use projection lines to transfer the feature to the *Front View* and *Top View*.

Creating the V-cut in the Front View and Top View

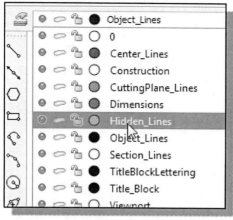

1. On the *Object Properties* toolbar, choose the *Layer Control* box with the left-mouse-button.

2. Move the cursor over the name of layer **Hidden_Lines**; the tooltip *"Hidden_Lines"* appears.

3. **Left-mouse-click once** and layer *Hidden_Lines* is set as the *Current Layer*.

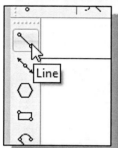

4. Select the **Line** command icon in the *Draw* toolbar. In the command prompt area, the message *"Specify start point:"* is displayed.

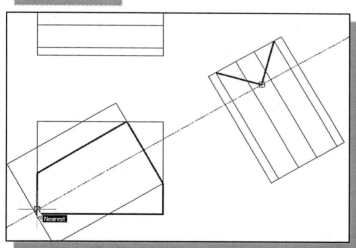

5. Move the cursor on top of the **vertex** of the V-cut in the *auxiliary view* to activate the *ETrack* function.

6. Move the cursor to the *Front View* and select the intersection point on the left edge as shown in the figure below.

7. On your own, create a line that is perpendicular to the inclined line as shown.

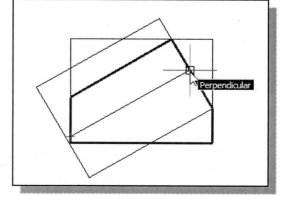

> ➢ On your own, first create the two construction lines and then construct the V-cut feature in the *Top View*. Use the **Trim** and **Extend** commands to assist the construction.

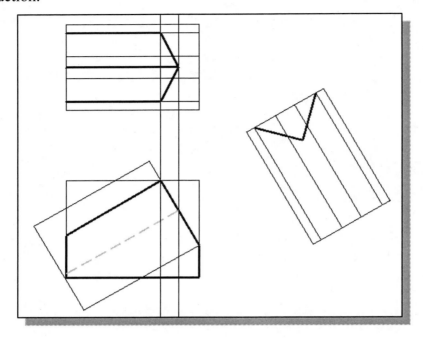

Completing the Top View

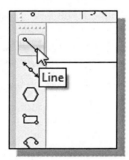

1. Select the **Line** icon in the *Draw* toolbar.

2. In the command prompt area, the message "*Specify start point:*" is displayed. Pick the **right endpoint** of the third horizontal line in the *Top View* as the starting point of the line segments.

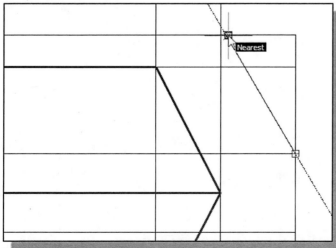

3. **Left-click** at the intersection of the polar tracking and the top horizontal line as shown. Do not select the intersection between the top horizontal line and the vertical line. (Use the Zoom Realtime command to zoom in further, if necessary.)

4. Inside the graphics window, right-mouse-click and select **Enter** to end the Line command.

➢ On your own, complete the *Top View* by adding all the necessary object lines in the *Top View*. Use the **Trim** and **Extend** commands to assist the construction.

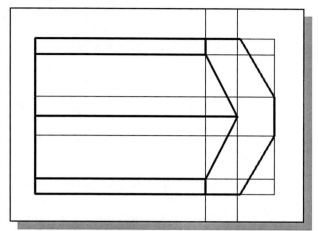

• Notice that the two 30° cut features are shown as **true size and shape** only in the *Top View* and therefore it is necessary for us to construct the features in the *Top View*.

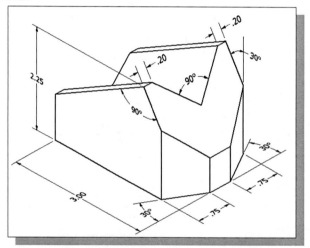

➢ On your own, create the **vertical construction line** through the front corner of the 30° cut as shown.

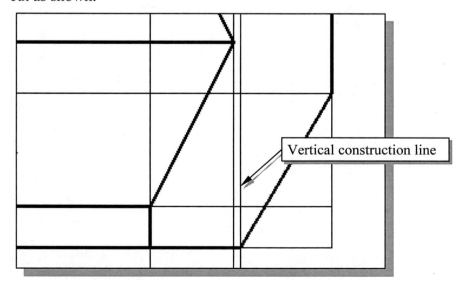

Vertical construction line

➤ On your own, complete the views by adding all the necessary object lines in the views.

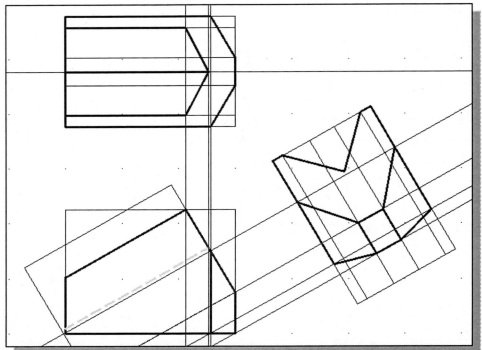

➤ Complete the drawing by adding the proper dimensions.

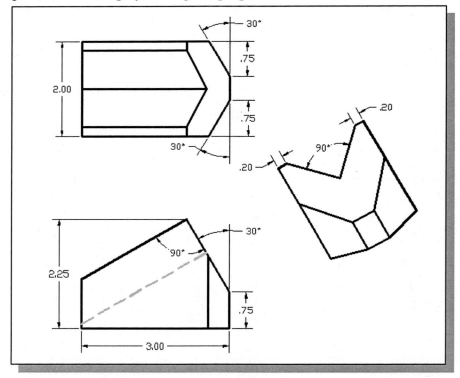

➤ On your own, print out a copy of the *V-block* drawing using the modified plot style table.

Using the Area Inquiry Tool to Measure Area and Perimeter

DraftSight also provides several tools that will allow us to measure distance, area, and perimeter.

1. In the *Main Menu* area, select the **Get Area** command in the *Tools* tab as shown.

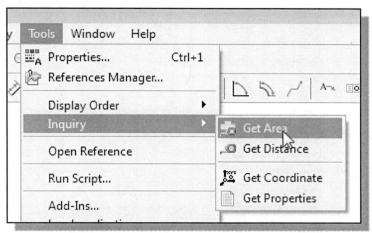

*   Note the other **Inquiry** options that are also available.

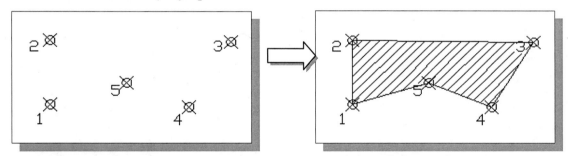

2. In the command prompt area, the message "*Specify first corner point*" is displayed. By default, DraftSight expects us to select points that will form a polygon. The area and perimeter of the polygon will then be calculated.

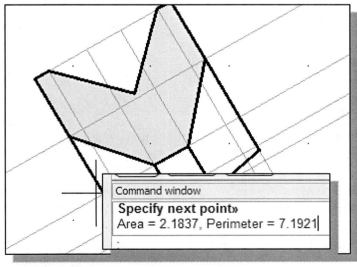

3. Select the **points** defining the **inclined surface** in the *auxiliary view* as shown. (See the above example and select the corresponding corners.)

4. **Right-mouse-click** once to bring up the option list and select **Enter** to accept the selection. Note the area and perimeter of the selected region are displayed.

❖ DraftSight can also calculate the area and perimeter of objects that define closed regions. For example, a circle or a rectangle can be selected as both of these objects define closed regions. We can also select a region defined by a *polyline*.

5. On your own, create a diameter 1″ circle and a 2″ by 2″ square as shown.

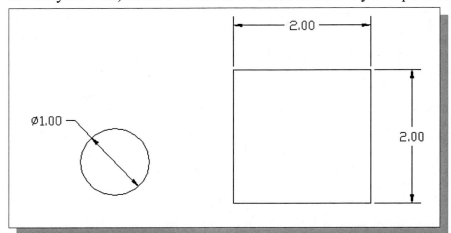

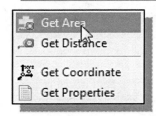

6. On your own, activate the **Get Area** command.

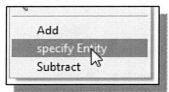

7. To activate this option, **right-mouse-click** once inside the graphics window and select **Entity** as shown.

❖ Also note the available **Add** and **Subtract** options.

8. In the command prompt area, the message "*Select Objects:*" is displayed. Pick the **circle** and note the associated area and perimeter information are shown in the prompt area.

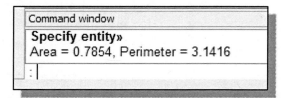

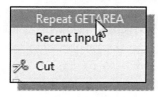

9. Inside the graphics window, **right-mouse-click** once and select **Repeat GETAREA** as shown.

10. On your own, confirm the area and perimeter of the sketched **square** calculated by DraftSight is accurate.

❖ A *polyline* in DraftSight is a 2D line of adjustable width composed of line and arc segments. A *polyline* is treated as a single object with definable options.

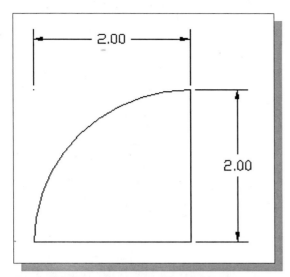

11. On your own, create a radius 2″ arc inside the 2″ by 2″ square as shown.

12. Trim the square so that the arc and the remaining two edges of the square form a closed region.

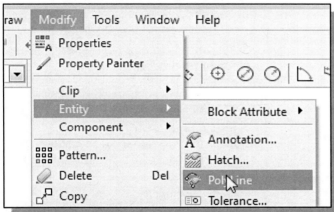

13. In the *Modify* toolbar, select: **[Edit Polyline]**

14. The message "*Select polyline:*" is displayed in the command prompt area. Select the **arc** we just created.

15. The message "*Object selected is not a polyline, Do you want to turn it into one?*" is displayed in the command prompt area. **Right-mouse-click** and select *Yes*.

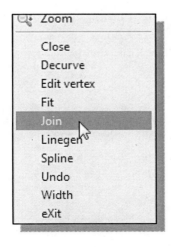

16. Inside the graphics window, right-mouse-click to activate the option menu and select the **Join** option with the left-mouse-button to add objects to the polyline.

17. Pick the two **adjacent edges** to form a closed region.

18. Inside the graphics window, **right-mouse-click** to accept the selected objects.

19. Inside the graphics window, right-mouse-click to activate the option menu and select **Enter** to end the Edit Polyline command.

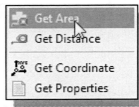

20. On your own, activate the **Get Area** command.

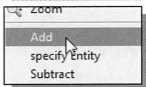

21. We can also select a region defined by multiple *objects*. To activate this option, **right-mouse-click** once inside the graphics window and select **Add** as shown.

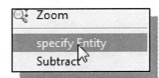

22. To activate also selection of regions defined by *polylines*, **right-mouse-click** once inside the graphics window and select **Entity** as shown.

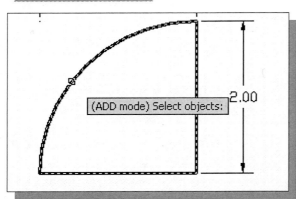

23. In the command prompt area, the message "*Select Entity:*" is displayed. Pick the newly created polyline. The associated area and perimeter information are shown in the command window area.

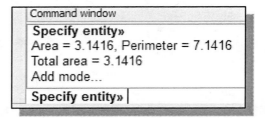

24. In the command prompt area, the message *Select Entity:*" is displayed. Pick the **circle**.

❖ Note the area and perimeter of the circle is displayed first, while the total area of the *polyline* plus the circle is shown directly below it.

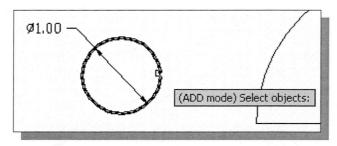

Review Questions:

1. What is an auxiliary view and why would it be important?

2. When is a line viewed as a point? How can a line be shown in true length?

3. List three entity editing commands you have used in the tutorial.

4. What does the *Polar Tracking* option allow us to do?

5. Find the area A defined by the two arcs, as described in the figure below.

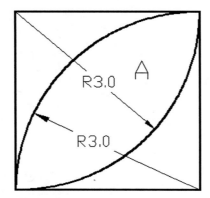

6. Find the area A defined by the three arcs, as described in the figure below.

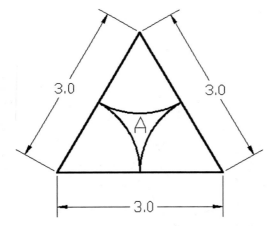

Exercises:

1. Angle Base (Dimensions are in inches.)

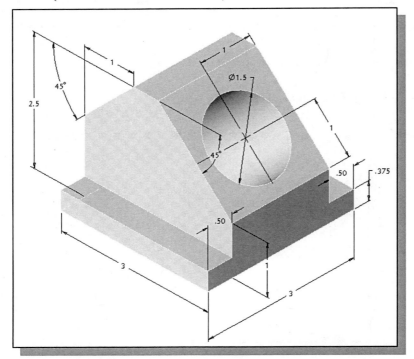

2. Indexing Guide (Dimensions are in inches.)

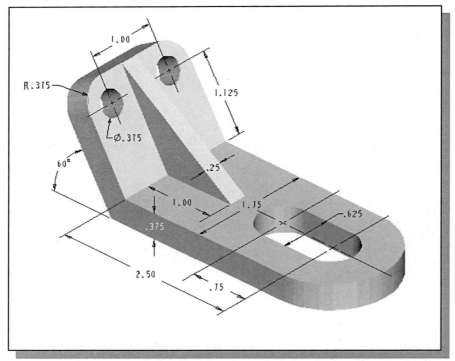

3. Spindle Base (Dimensions are in millimeters.)

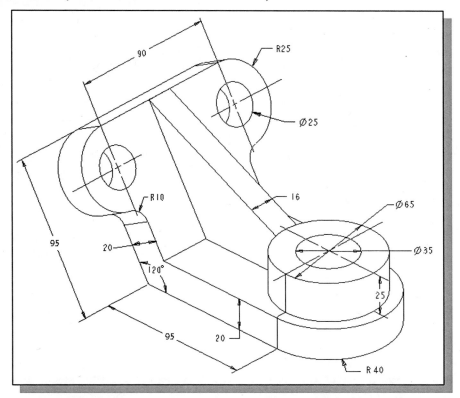

4. Transition Support (Dimensions are in inches.)

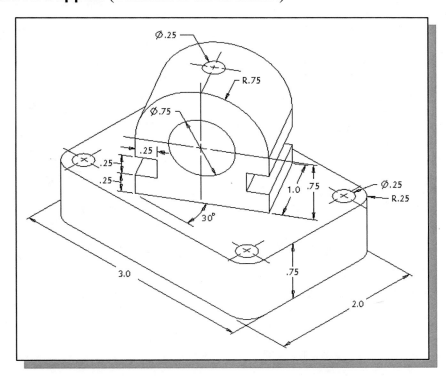

5. Support Hanger (Dimensions are in inches.)

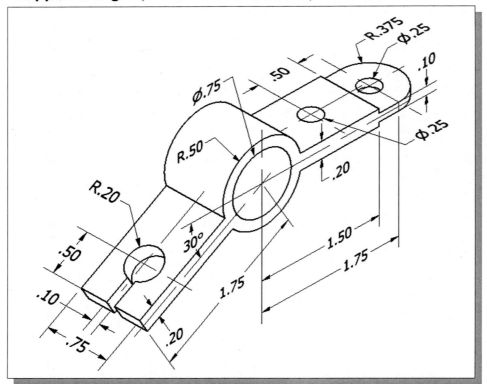

6. Automatic Stop (Dimensions are in inches.)

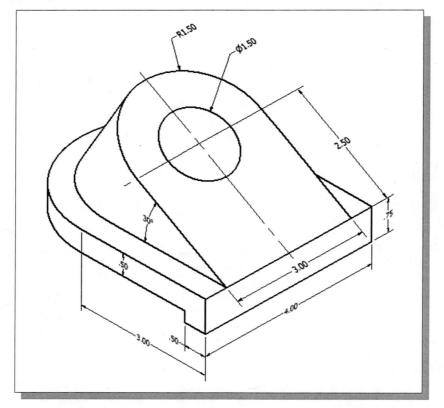

Lesson 10
Section Views

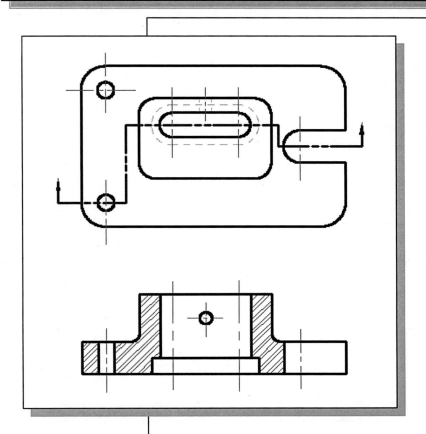

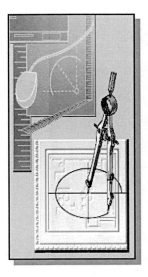

Learning Objectives

- ♦ **Understand the Basic Principles of Section Views**
- ♦ **Use the Proper Types of Section Views**
- ♦ **Use CAD Methods to Create Section Views**
- ♦ **Use the Object Snap Shortcut Options**
- ♦ **Change the Line Scale Property**
- ♦ **Stretch and Move Objects with GRIPS**
- ♦ **Use the HATCH command**

Introduction

In the previous chapters, we have explored the basic CAD methods of creating orthographic views. By carefully selecting a limited number of views, the external features of most complicated designs can be fully described. However, we are frequently confronted with the necessity of showing the interiors of parts, or when parts are assembled, that cannot be shown clearly by means of hidden lines.

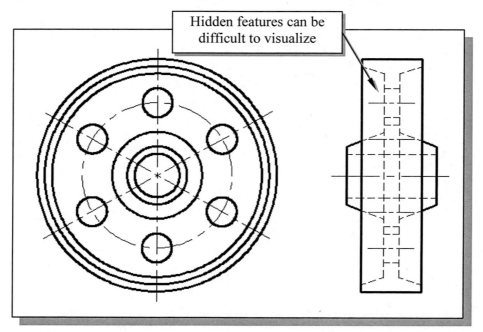

Hidden features can be difficult to visualize

In cases of this kind, to aid in describing the object, one or more views are drawn to show the object as if a portion of the object had been cut away to reveal the interior.

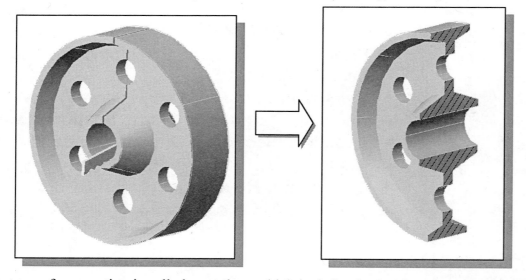

This type of convention is called a **section**, which is defined as an imaginary cut made through an object to expose the interior of a part. Such kind of cutaway view is known as a **section view**.

In a *section view*, the place from which the section is taken must be identifiable on the drawing. If the place from which the section is taken is obvious, as it is for the below figure, no further description is needed.

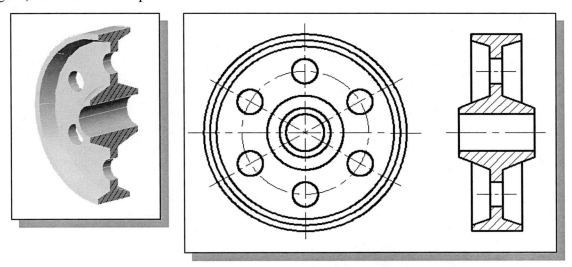

If the place from which the section is taken is not obvious, as it is for the below figure, a **cutting plane** is needed to identify the section. Two arrows are also used to indicate the viewing direction. A *cutting plane line* is drawn with the *phantom* or *hidden* line.

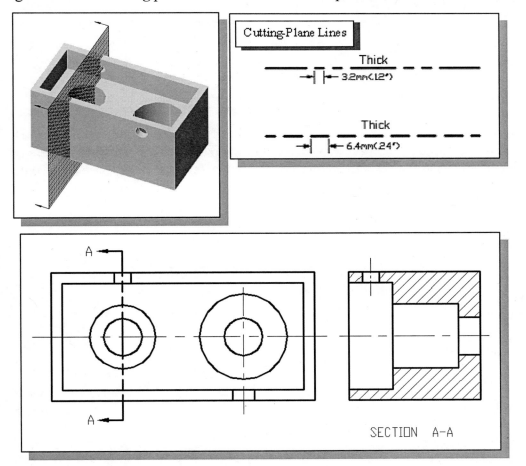

General Rules of Section Views

Section views are used to make a part drawing more understandable, showing the internal details of the part. Since the sectioned drawing is showing the internal features there is generally no need to show hidden lines.

A section view still follows the general rules of any view in a multiview drawing. Cutting planes may be labeled at their endpoints to clarify the association of the cut and the section views, especially when multiple cutting plane lines are used. When using multiple cutting planes, each sectioned drawing is drawn as if the other cutting plane lines do not exist. The cutting plane line takes precedence over center lines and, remember, cutting plane lines may be omitted when their location is obvious.

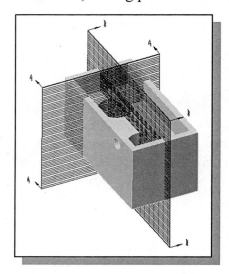
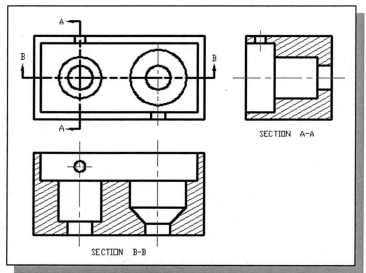

Section lines or **cross-hatch lines** are drawn where the cutting plane passes through the object. This is done as if a saw was used to cut the part and then section lines are used to represent the cutting marks left by the saw blade. Different materials are represented by the use of different section line types. The line type for iron may be used as the general section line type for any material.

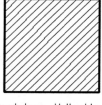

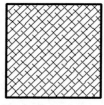

Cast iron, Malleable iron and general use for all materials   Steel   Bronze, Brass and composition Materials   Magnesium, aluminum and aluminum alloys

Section lines should not be parallel or perpendicular to object lines. Section lines are generally drawn at 45°, 30° or 60°, unless there are conflicts with other rules. Section lines should be oriented at different angles for different parts.

Section Drawing Types

- **Full Section:** The cutting plane passes completely through the part as a single flat plane.

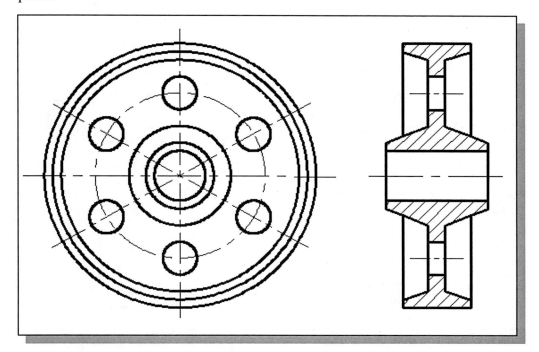

- **Half Section:** The cutting plane only passes half way through the part and the other half is drawn as usual. Hidden lines are generally not shown on either half of the part. However, hidden lines may be used in the un-sectioned half if necessary for dimensioning. Half section is mostly used on cylindrical parts, and a center line is used to separate the two halves.

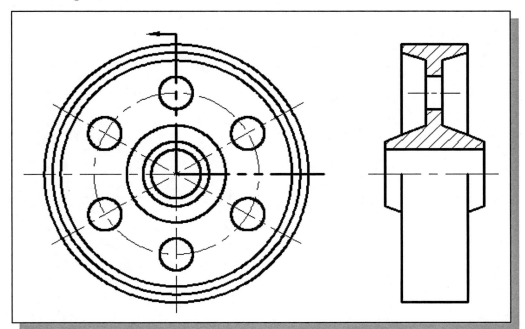

- **Offset Section:** It is often difficult to interpret a multiview drawing when there are multiple features on the object. An **offset section** allows the cutting plane to pass through several places by "**offsetting**" or **bending** the cutting plane. The offsets or bends in the cutting plane are all 90° and are *not* shown in the section view.

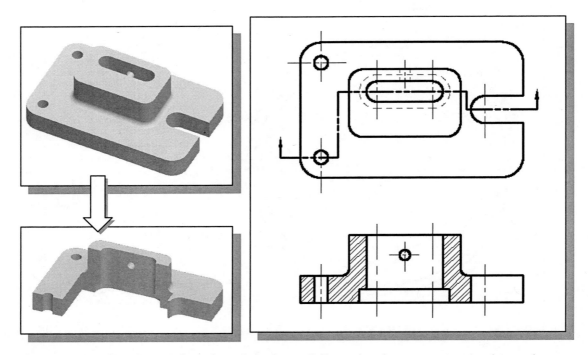

- **Broken-Out Section:** It is quite often that a full section is not necessary, but only a partial section is needed to show the interior details of a part. In a **broken-out section**, only a portion of the view is sectioned and a jagged break-line is used to divide the sectioned and un-sectioned portion of the view.

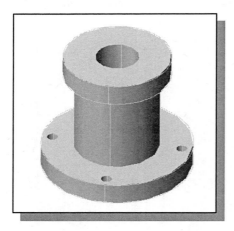
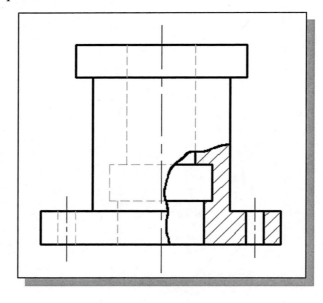

- **Aligned Section:** To include certain angled features in a section view, the cutting plane may be bent to pass through those features to their true radial position.

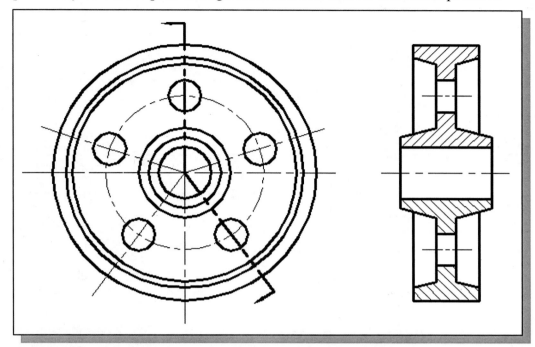

- **Half Views:** When space is limited, a symmetrical part can be shown as a half view.

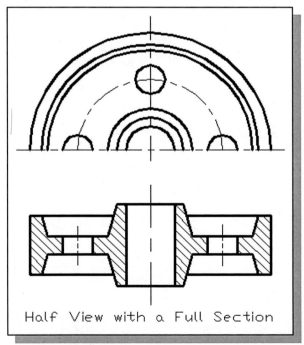

Half View with a Full Section

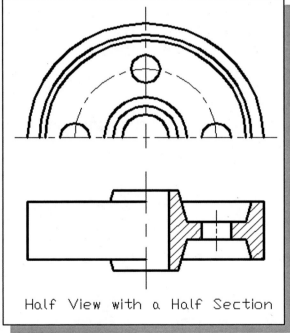

Half View with a Half Section

- **Thin Sections:** For thin parts, typically parts that are less than 3mm thickness such as sheet metal parts and gaskets, section lines are ineffective and therefore should be omitted. Thin sections are generally shown in solid black without section lines.

- **Revolved Section:** A cross section of the part is revolved 90° and superimposed on the drawing.

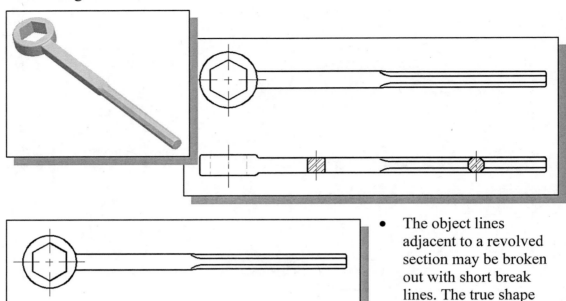

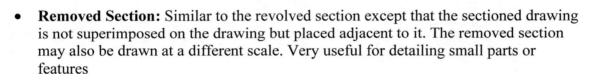

- The object lines adjacent to a revolved section may be broken out with short break lines. The true shape of a revolved section is retained regardless of the object lines in the view.

- **Removed Section:** Similar to the revolved section except that the sectioned drawing is not superimposed on the drawing but placed adjacent to it. The removed section may also be drawn at a different scale. Very useful for detailing small parts or features

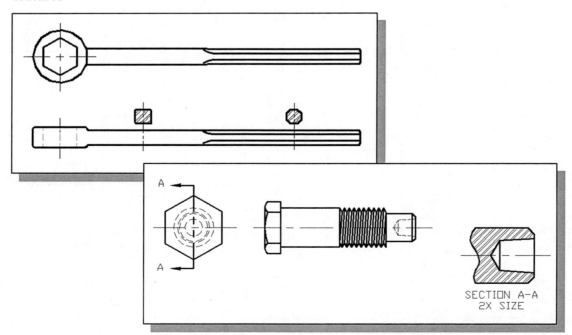

- **Conventional Breaks:** In making the details of parts that are long and with a uniform cross section, it is rarely necessary to draw its whole length. Using the Conventional Breaks to shorten such an object will allow the part to be drawn with a larger scale. S-Breaks are preferred for cylindrical objects and jagged lines are used to break non-circular objects.

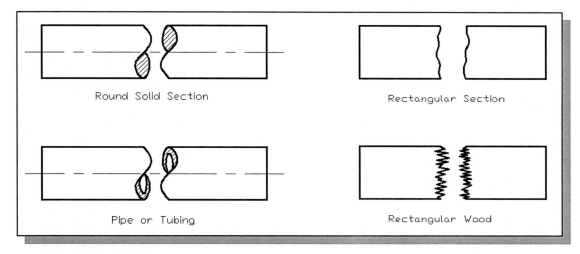

- **Ribs and Webs in Sections:** To avoid a misleading effect of thickness and solidity, ribs, webs, spokes, gear teeth and other similar are drawn without crosshatching when the cutting plane passes through them lengthwise. Ribs are sectioned if the cutting plane passes through them at other orientations.

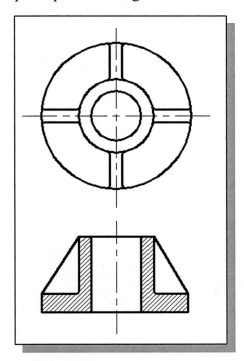 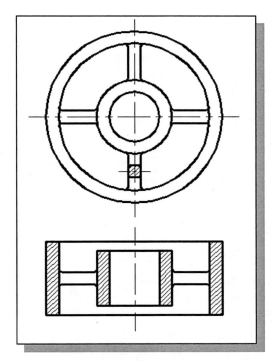

- **Parts Not Sectioned:** Many machine elements, such as fasteners, pins, bearings and shafts, have no internal features, and are generally more easily recognized by their exterior views. Do not section these parts.

Section Views in DraftSight

In the following sections, we will demonstrate the procedure to construct a section view using DraftSight.

In DraftSight, a **_GRIP_** is a small square displayed on a pre-selected object. Grips are key control locations such as the endpoints and midpoints of lines and arcs. Different types of objects display different numbers of grips. Using grips, we can _stretch_, _move_, _mirror_, _scale_, _rotate_, and _copy_ objects without entering commands or clicking toolbars. Grips reduce the keystrokes and object selection required in performing common editing commands. To edit with grips, we select the objects <u>before</u> issuing any commands. To remove a specific object from a selection set that displays grips, we hold down the **[SHIFT]** key as we select the object. To exit the _grips mode_ and return to the _command prompt_, press the **[Esc]** key.

In a section view, section lines, or cross-hatch lines, are added to indicate the surfaces that are cut by the imaginary cutting plane. The type of section line used to represent a surface varies according to the type of material. DraftSight's **Hatch** command can be used to fill a pattern inside an area. We define a boundary that consists of an object or objects that completely enclose the area. DraftSight comes with a solid fill and more than 50 industry-standard hatch patterns that we can use to differentiate the components of objects or represent object materials.

Starting Up DraftSight

1. Select the **DraftSight** option on the _Program_ menu or select the **DraftSight** icon on the _Desktop_.

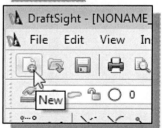

2. In the _Standard_ toolbar, select the **New File** option with a single click of the left-mouse-button.

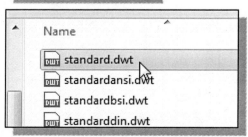

3. Select the **_Standard-A-H-Title_** template file from the list of template files.

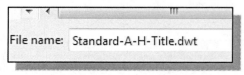

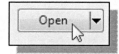

4. Click **Open** to start a new DraftSight drawing file.

The *Bearing* Design

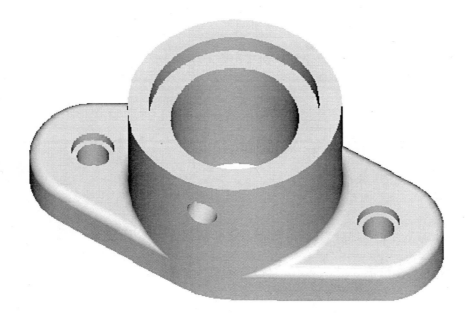

The *Bearing* Drawing

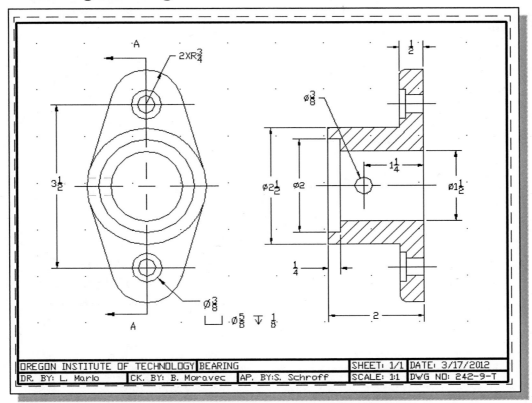

Setting up the Principal Views

- We will first create construction lines for the *Front View*.

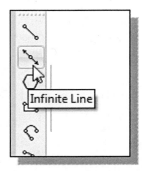

1. Click the **Infinite Line** icon in the *Draw* toolbar to activate the **Infinite Line** command.

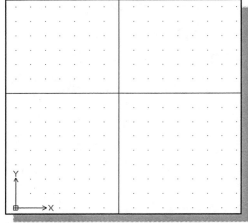

2. On your own, create a vertical line and a horizontal line, to the left side of the screen. These lines will be used as the references for the circular features of the design.

3. Click on the **Offset** icon in the *Modify* toolbar. In the command window area, the message "*Specify offset distance or [Through]:*" is displayed.

4. In the command window area, enter: **1.75** [**ENTER**].

5. In the command window area, the message "*Select object to offset or <exit>:*" is displayed. Pick the **horizontal line** on the screen.

6. DraftSight next expects us to identify the direction of the offset. Pick a location that is **above** the selected line.

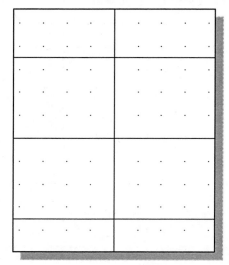

7. We will also create a line that is below the original horizontal line at 1.75. Pick the original **horizontal line** on the screen.

8. Pick a location that is **below** the selected line.

9. Inside the graphics window, **right-mouse-click** and select **Enter** to end the Offset command.

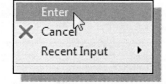

Creating Object Lines in the Front View

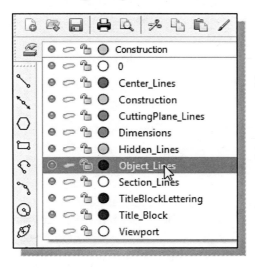

1. On the *Object Properties* toolbar, choose the **Layer Control** box with the left-mouse-button.

2. Move the cursor over the name of layer **Object_Lines**; the tooltip "*Object_Lines*" appears.

3. **Left-mouse-click once** and layer *Object_Lines* is set as the *Active Layer*.

4. In the *Status* toolbar, reset the options as shown.

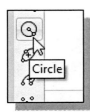

5. Click on the **Circle** icon in the *Draw* toolbar. In the command window area, the message "*Specify center point for circle or [3P/2P/Ttr (tan tan radius)]:*" is displayed.

6. Pick the center intersection point as the center of the circle.

7. In the command window area, the message "*Specify radius of circle or [Diameter]:*" is displayed. Enter: **1.25 [ENTER]**.

8. Repeat the **Circle** command and create the two **diameter 1.5** circles as shown.

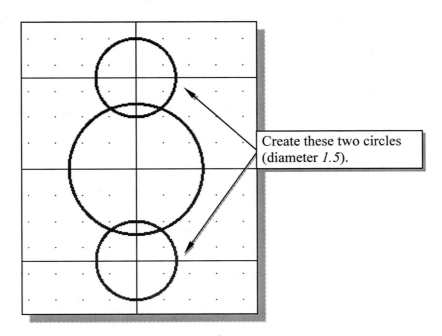

Create these two circles (diameter *1.5*).

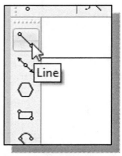

9. Select the **Line** command icon in the *Draw* toolbar. In the command window area, the message "*Specify start point:*" is displayed.

10. Inside the graphics window, hold down the [**SHIFT**] key and **right-mouse-click** once to bring up the *Object Snap* shortcut menu.

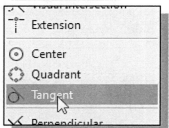

11. Select the **Tangent** option in the popup window. Move the cursor near the circles and notice the *Tangent* marker appears at different locations.

- The Tangent option enables us to create tangent lines; **select objects by clicking near the expected tangency locations**.

12. Pick the top circle by clicking on the upper right section of the circle.

13. In the command window area, the message "*Specify the next point or [Undo]:*" is displayed. Inside the graphics window, **right-mouse-click** once and select **Snap Overrides**.

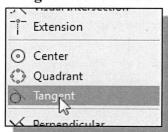

14. Select the **Tangent** option in the popup menu.

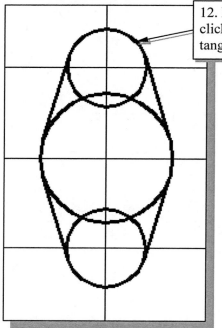

12. Pick the top circle by clicking near the expected tangency location.

15. Pick the center circle by clicking on the right side of the circle. A line tangent to the two circles appears on the screen.

16. Inside the graphics window, right-mouse-click and select **Enter** to end the Line command.

17. Repeat the **Line** command and create the four tangent lines as shown.

Editing the Circles

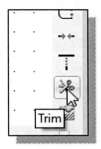

1. Select the **Trim** icon in the *Modify* toolbar. In the command window area, the message *"Specify cutting edges:"* is displayed.

2. Pick the four lines we just created as the *boundary edges*.

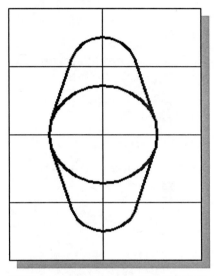

3. Inside the graphics window, **right-mouse-click** to proceed with the Trim command. The message *"Specify entity to trim:"* is displayed in the command window area.

4. Trim the unwanted portions of the top and bottom circles and complete the outline of the front view as shown.

5. Inside the graphics window, right-mouse-click to activate the option menu and select **Enter** with the left-mouse-button to end the Trim command.

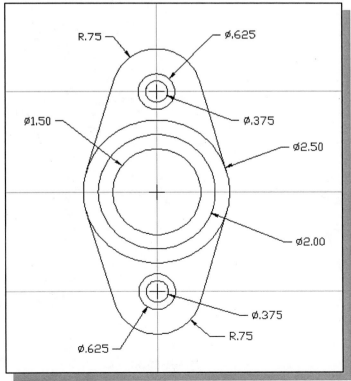

➢ On your own, create the additional circles as shown.

Setting up the Side-View

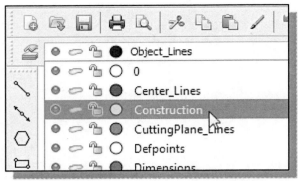

1. In the *Layer Control* box, set layer *Construction* as the *Active Layer*.

2. Select the **Offset** icon in the *Modify* toolbar. In the command window area, the message "*Specify offset distance:*" is displayed.

3. In the command window area, enter: **5.0** [**ENTER**].

4. In the command window area, the message "*Specify source entity:*" is displayed. Pick the **vertical line** on the screen.

5. DraftSight next expects us to identify the direction of the offset. Pick a location that is toward the right side of the selected line.

6. Inside the graphics window, right-mouse-click to end the **Offset** command.

7. On your own, repeat the **Offset** command and create two additional lines parallel to the line we just created as shown (distances of **0.5** and **2.0**).

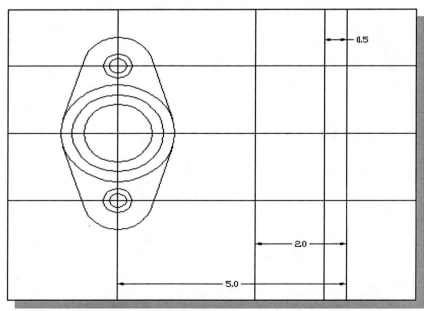

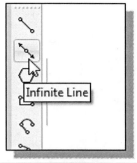

8. Select the **Infinite Line** icon in the *Draw* toolbar. In the command window area, the message "*Specify position:*" is displayed.

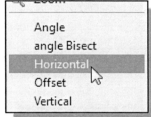

9. Select the **Horizontal** option in the option menu as shown.

➢ The **Horizontal** option enables us to create a horizontal line by specifying one point in the graphics window.

10. Create **projection lines** by clicking at the intersections between the vertical line and the circles (and arcs) in the *Front View*.

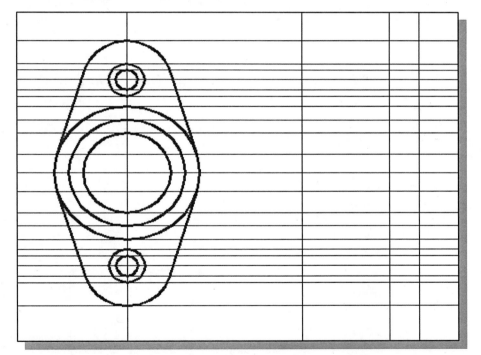

11. Also create two horizontal projection lines that pass through the two tangency-points on the Ø2.5 circle.

12. Inside the graphics window, right-mouse-click to end the **Infinite Line** command.

➢ On your own, create object lines to show the outline of the side view.

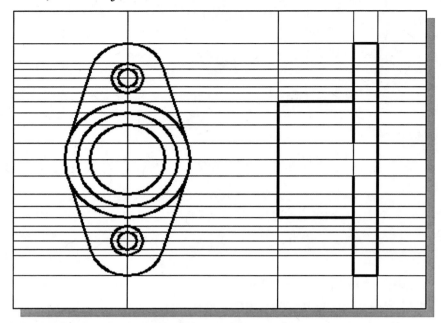

Adding Hidden Lines in the Side-View

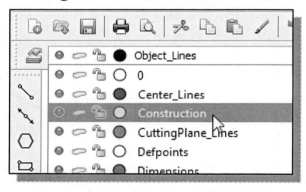

1. In the *Layer Control* box, set layer *Construction_Lines* as the *Active Layer*.

2. Use the **Offset** command and create the two additional vertical lines, for the counter-bore features, as shown.

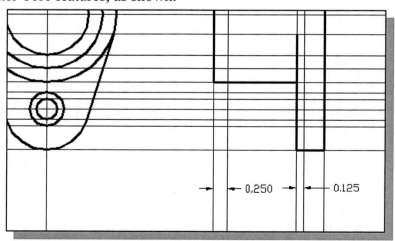

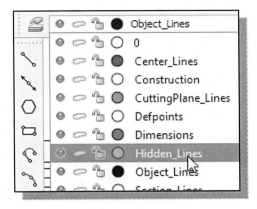

3. Set layer **Hidden_Lines** as the *Active Layer* in the *Layer Control* box.

4. Use the **Line** command and create the hidden lines as shown.

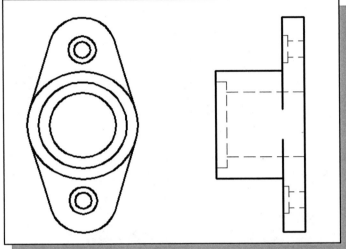

➢ On your own, complete the views by adding the side-drill, the centerlines, and the rounded corners as shown in the figure below.

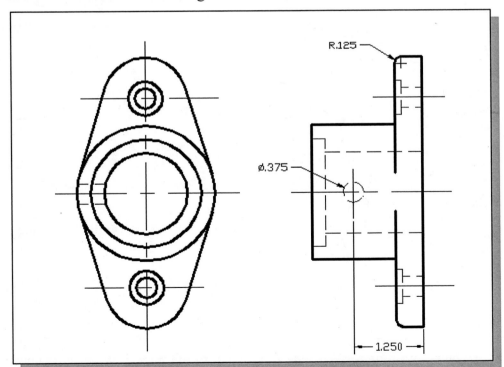

Changing the *Line scale* Property

❖ Looking at the centerlines we just created in the side view, not all of the lengths of the dash-dot linestyle appear properly on the screen. The appearances of the dash-dot linestyle can be adjusted by modifying the ***Line scale*** setting, which can be found under the *Entity Property* option.

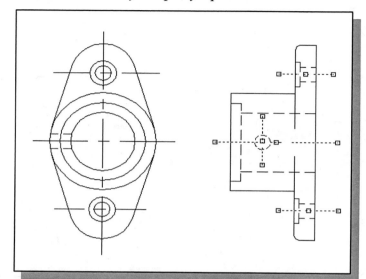

1. **Pre-select** the four lines in the side view as shown.

2. In the *Standard* toolbar, select the **Properties** icon.

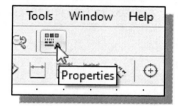

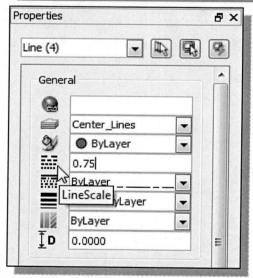

3. In the *Properties* dialog box, notice the default *Line scale* is 1.00.

4. Left-click on ***Line scale*** in the list and enter a new value: ***0.75*** **[ENTER]**.

5. Click on the **[X]** button to exit the *Properties* dialog box.

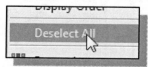

6. Inside the graphics window, **right-mouse-click** and select **Deselect All**.

➢ The appearance of the dash-dot linestyles of the selected objects is adjusted to half the size of the other objects. Keep in mind that the dash-dot linestyles may appear differently on paper, depending on the type of printer/plotter being used. You may want to do more adjustments after examining a printed/plotted copy of the drawing. It is also more common to adjust the *Line scale* for all objects of the same linestyle to maintain a consistent presentation of the drawing.

Stretching and Moving Objects with *GRIPS*

We can usually *stretch* an object by moving selected grips to new locations. Some grips will not stretch the object but will move the object. This is true of grips on text objects, blocks, midpoints of lines, centers of circles, centers of ellipses, and point objects.

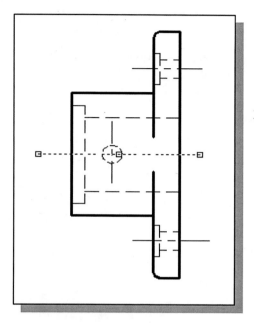

1. **Pre-select** the horizontal centerline that goes through the center of the part as shown.

2. Select the **right grip** by left-clicking once on the grip. Notice the grip is highlighted.

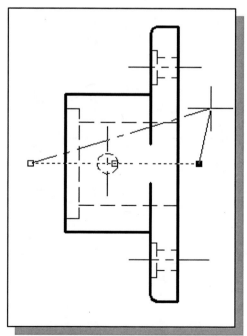

3. Move the cursor inside the graphics window and notice the center line is being stretched; the base point is attached to the cursor.

4. Pick a location on the screen to stretch the centerline.

5. Click on the **Undo** icon in the *Standard* toolbar area to undo the stretch we just did.

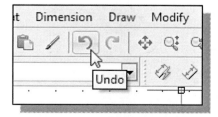

> On your own, experiment with moving the center grip of the centerline.

Drawing a Cutting Plane Line

- Most section views require a cutting plane line to indicate the location on which the object is cut.

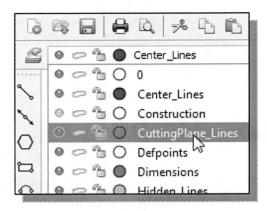

1. In the *Layer Control* box, turn **OFF** the *Construction* layer and set layer ***CuttingPlane_Lines*** as the *Active Layer*.

2. Use the **Line** command and create the vertical cutting plane line aligned to the vertical centerline of the *Front View*.

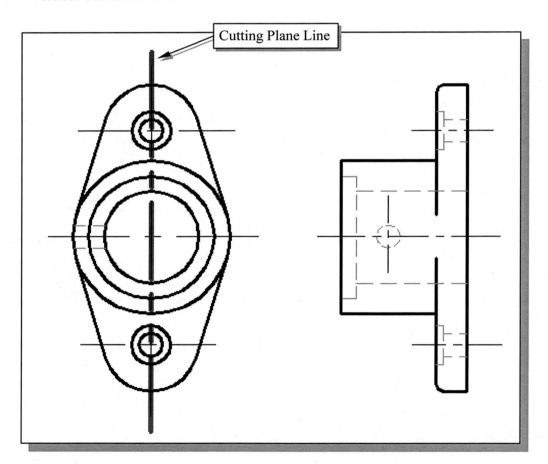

Cutting Plane Line

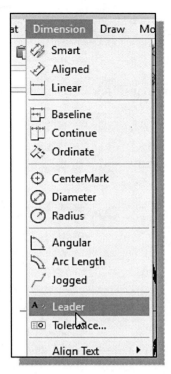

3. In the Main Menu, select:
   [Dimension] → [Leader]

4. Inside the *graphics window*, **right-mouse-click** to bring up the option menu and select **Settings** as shown.

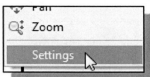

5. Notice the different options available to adjust the appearance of leaders.

6. On your own, set the *leader alignment* as shown.

7. Select **OK** to end the settings options.

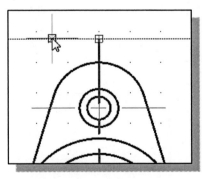

8. Using the object tracking option and set the endpoint of the leader about **0.75** to set the starting point of the leader of the cutting plane line.

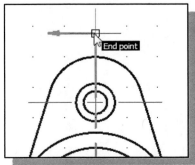

9. Pick the top endpoint of the cutting plane line to create a horizontal leader as shown.

➢ Note that DraftSight expects us to type in the text that will be associated with the leader.

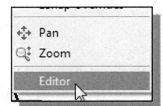

10. Inside the graphics window, **right-mouse-click** and select **Editor**.

- In DraftSight, the *Leader* is an entity which consists of an arrow and a note. The Note Editor is also available for the Leader command.

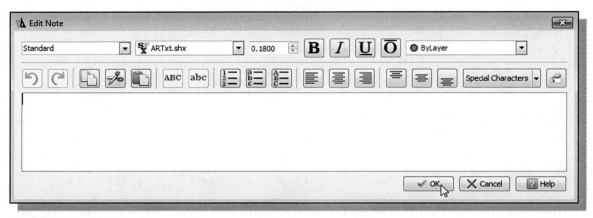

11. In the *Edit Note* dialog box, click **OK** to close the dialog box without entering any text.

12. Repeat the **Leader** command and create the other arrow as shown.

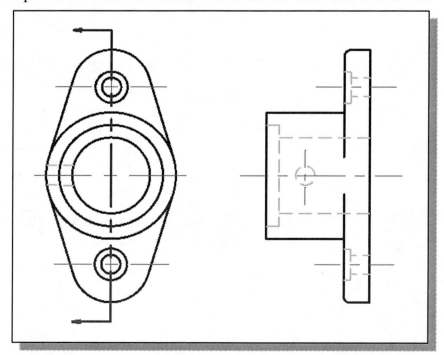

Converting the Side View into a Section View

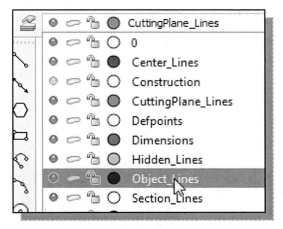

1. In the *Layer Control* box, set layer **Object_Lines** as the *Active Layer*.

2. In the *Layer Control* box, turn **OFF** the *Center_Lines* layer.

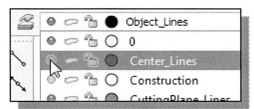

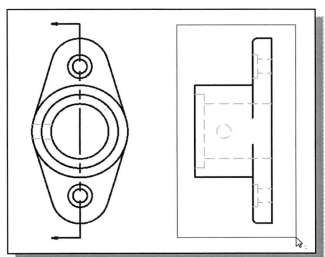

3. **Pre-select** all the objects in the *Side View* by using a selection window.

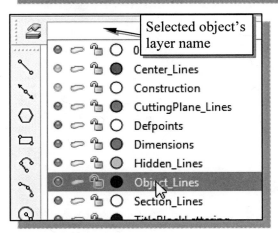

4. On the *Object Properties* toolbar, choose the **Layer Control** box with the left-mouse-button.

❖   Notice the layer name displayed in the *Layer Control* box is left blank, as the selected objects are assigned to different layers.

5. In the *Layer Control* box, click on the **Object_Lines** layer name to move all the selected entities to this layer.

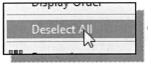

6. Inside the graphics window, **right-mouse-click** and select **Deselect All**.

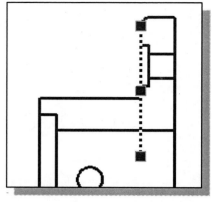

7. On your own, use the **grip editing options** and modify the *Side View* as shown.

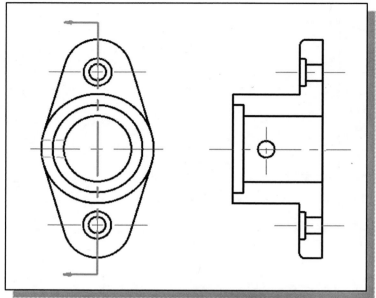

Adding Section Lines

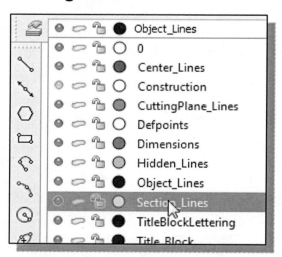

1. In the *Layer Control* box, set layer **Section_Lines** as the *Active Layer*.

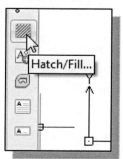

2. Select the **Hatch** icon in the *Draw* toolbar. The *Hatch/Fill* dialog box appears on the screen.

- We will use the *ANSI31* standard hatch pattern and create an associative hatch, which means the hatch is updated automatically if the boundaries are modified.

❖ We can define a boundary by *Specify Entities* or *Specify Points*. The *Specify Points* option is usually the easier and faster way to define boundaries. We specify locations inside the regions to be crosshatched and DraftSight will automatically derive the boundary definition from the location of the specified point.

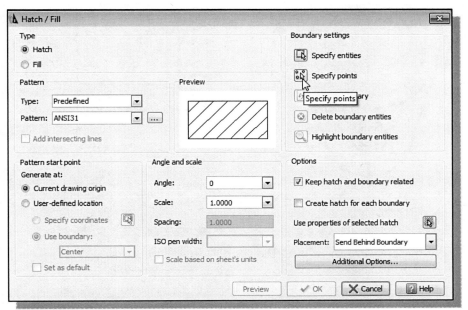

3. Click on the **Specify points** icon in the *Boundary settings*.

4. **Left-click** inside the four regions as shown.

5. Inside the graphics window, **right-mouse-click** to bring up the popup menu and select **ENTER** to continue with the Hatch command.

6. Click on the **OK** button to close the *Hatch/Fill* dialog box.

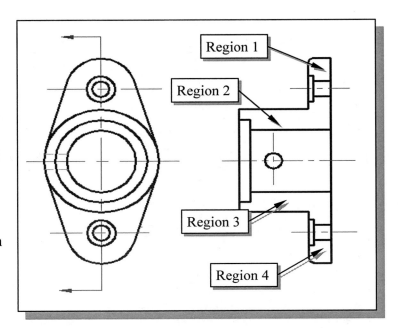

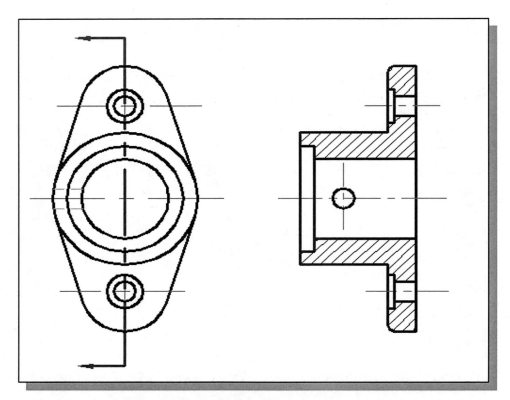

➤ Complete the drawing by adding the proper dimensions.

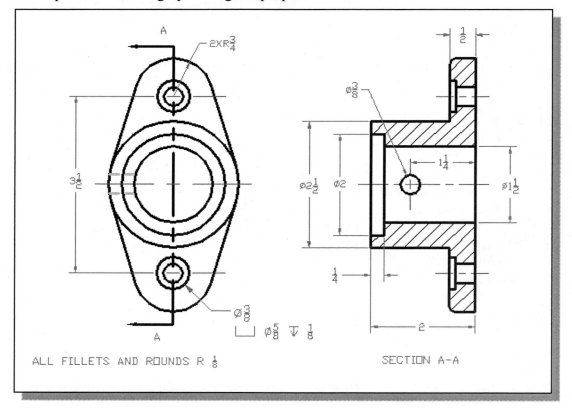

➤ On your own, create a drawing layout and print out the drawing.

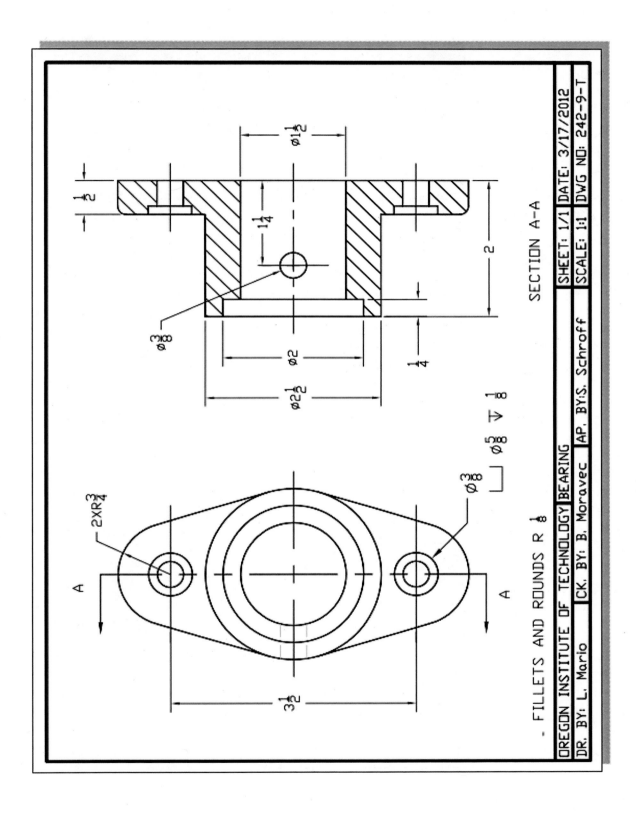

SECTION A-A

FILLETS AND ROUNDS R $\frac{1}{8}$

OREGON INSTITUTE OF TECHNOLOGY	BEARING		SHEET: 1/1	DATE: 3/17/2012
DR. BY: L. Mario	CK. BY: B. Moravec	AP. BY: S. Schroff	SCALE: 1:1	DWG NO: 242-9-T

Review Questions:

1. When and why is a *section view* necessary?

2. Describe the general procedure to create a *section view* in DraftSight.

3. In DraftSight, can the angle and spacing of hatch patterns be altered?

4. Explain the concept of using a cutting plane line in a section view?

5. Can we mirror text in DraftSight?

6. Using the **Trim** command, what would happen if we do not specify a boundary and just press [**ENTER**] at the "*Specify Cutting Entities*" prompt?

7. Which command do we use to define the region of the grid display in the current DraftSight screen?

8. Construct the drawing shown and measure the area A. (Units: mm.)

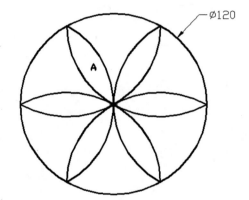

9. Construct the drawing shown and measure the length L. Show the length with two digits after the decimal point. (Units: inches.)

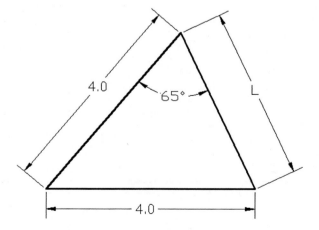

Exercises: (All Dimensions are in inches.)

1. Center Support

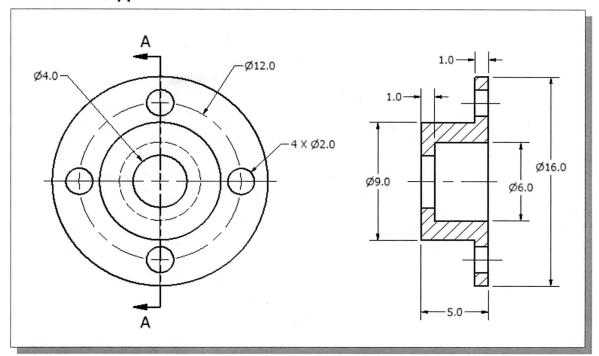

2. Ratchet Wheel

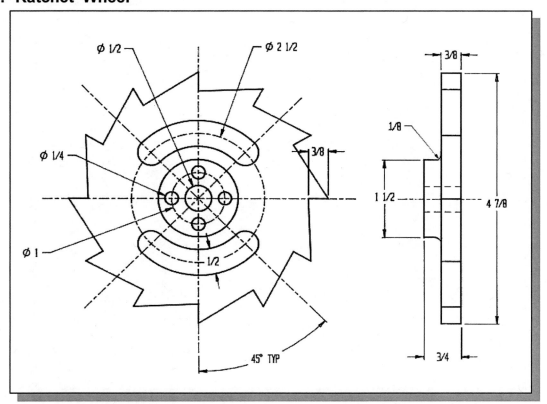

3. Mounting Bracket

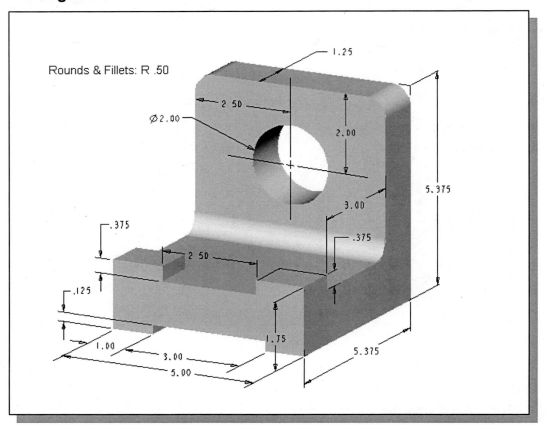

4. Position Guide

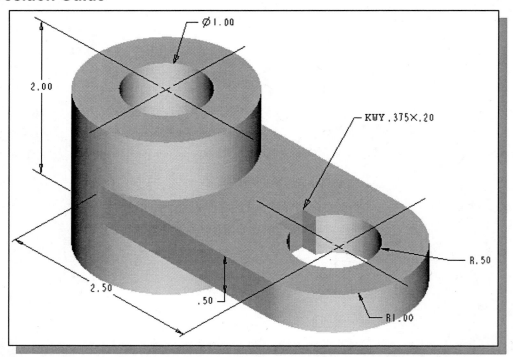

5. Yoke Support

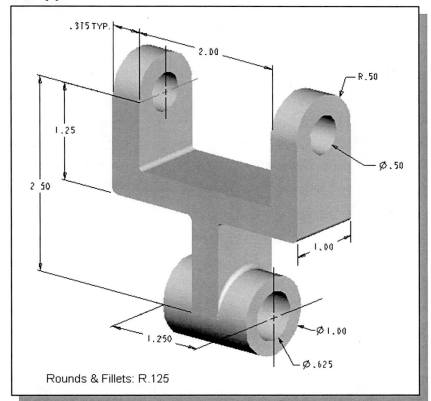

.375 TYP.
2.00
R.50
1.25
Ø.50
2.50
1.00
1.250
Ø1.00
Ø.625

Rounds & Fillets: R.125

6. Lock Cap

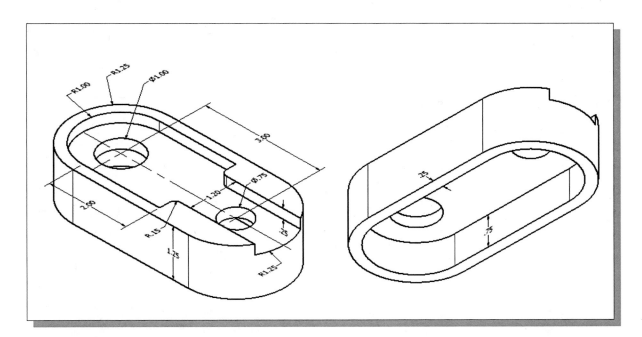

R1.00
R1.25
Ø1.00
3.00
2.00
Ø.75
1.20
.25
R.15
1.25
R1.25
.75
.75

Notes:

Chapter 11
Threads and Fasteners

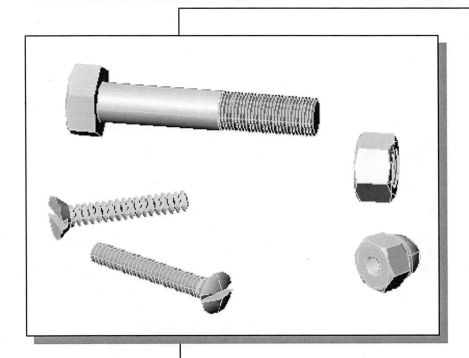

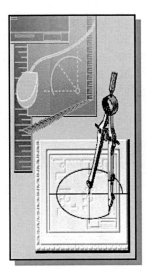

Learning Objectives

- **Understand Screw-Threads Terminology**
- **Define and Label the Different Parts of a Screw Thread**
- **Draw Detailed, Schematic and Simplified Threads in Section and Standard Views**
- **Use the Fastener Clearance Fits**
- **Identify Various Fasteners and Describe Their Use**

Introduction

Threads and fasteners are the principal means of assembling parts. Screw threads occur in one form or another on practically all engineering products. Screw threads are designed for many different purposes; the three basic functionalities are to hold parts together, to transmit power and for use as adjustment of locations of parts.

The earliest records of the screw threads are found in the writings of Archimedes (278 to 212 B.C.), the mathematician who described several designs applying the screw principle. Screw thread was a commonly used element in the first century B.C., but was crudely made during that period of time. Machine production of screws started in England during the Industrial Revolution and the standardization of the screw threads was first proposed by Sir Joseph Whitworth in 1841. His system was generally adopted in England but not in the United States during the 1800s. The initial attempt to standardize screw threads in the United States came in 1864 with the adoption of the thread system designed by William Sellers. The "Sellers thread" fulfilled the need for a general-purpose thread; but it became inadequate with the coming of the modern devices, such as the automobiles and the airplanes. Through the efforts of various engineering societies, the National Screw Thread Commission was authorized in 1918. The Unified Screw Thread, a compromise between the American and British systems, was established on November 18, 1948.

The Metric fastener standard was established in 1946, through the cooperative efforts of several organizations: The International Organization for Standardization (ISO), the Industrial Fasteners Institute (IFI) and the American National Standards Institute.

The following sections describe the general thread definitions, for a more complete description refers to the ANSI/ASME standards: B1.1, B1.7M, B1.13M, Y14.6 and Y14.6aM. (The letter M is for metric system.)

Screw-Thread Terminology

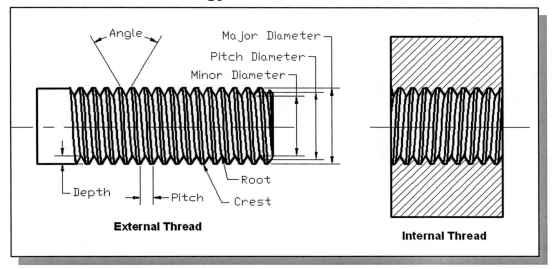

External Thread

Internal Thread

Screw Thread (Thread): A ridge of a uniform section in the form of a helix on the external or internal surface of a cylinder or cone.

External Thread: A thread on the external surface of a cylinder or cone.

Internal Thread: A thread on the internal surface of a cylinder or cone.

Major Diameter: The largest diameter of a screw thread.

Minor Diameter: The smallest diameter of a screw thread.

Pitch Diameter: The diameter of an imaginary cylinder, the surface of which cuts the thread where the width of the thread and groove are equal.

Crest: The outer edge or surface that joins the two sides of a thread.

Root: The bottom edge or surface that joins the sides of two adjacent threads.

Depth of Thread: The distance between crest and root measured normal to the axis.

Angle of Thread: The angle included between the two adjacent sides of the threads.

Pitch: The distance between corresponding points on adjacent thread forms measured parallel to the axis. This distance is a measure of the size of the thread form used, which is equal to 1 divided by the number of threads per inch.

Threads per Inch: The reciprocal of the pitch and the value specified to govern the size of the thread form.

Form of Thread: The profile (cross section) of a thread. The next section shows various forms.

Right-hand Thread (RH): A thread which advances into a nut when turned in a clockwise direction. Threads are always considered to be right-handed unless otherwise specified.

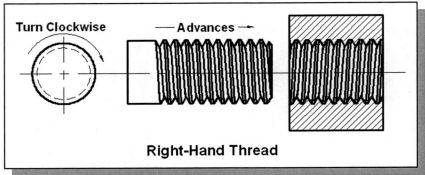

Left-hand Thread (LH): A thread which advances into a nut when turned in a counter-clockwise and receding direction. All left-hand threads are labeled **LH**.

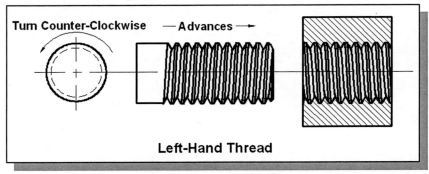

Lead: The distance a threaded part moves axially, with respect to a fixed mating part, in one complete revolution. See the definition and examples of multiple thread in the below figures.

Multiple Threads: A thread having two or more helical curves of the cylinder running side by side. For a single thread, lead and pitch are identical values; for a double thread, lead is twice the pitch; and for a triple thread, lead is three times the pitch. A multiple thread permits a more rapid advance without a larger thread form. The *slope line* can be used to aid the construction of multiple threads; it is the hypotenuse of a right triangle with the short side equals .5P for single threads, P for double threads and so on.

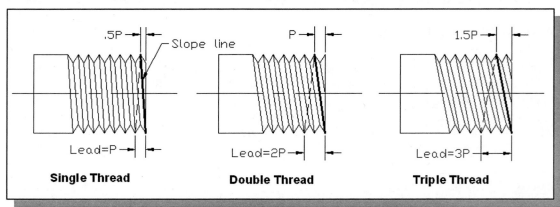

Thread Forms

Screw threads are used on fasteners to fasten parts together, on devices for making adjustments, and for the transmission of power and motion. For these different purposes, a number of thread forms are in use. In practical usage, clearance must be provided between the external and internal threads.

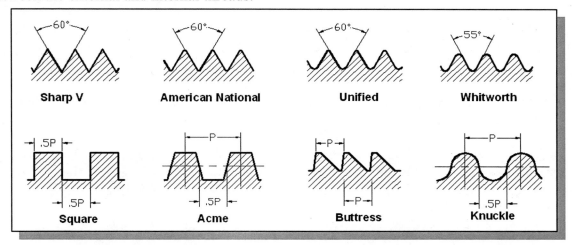

The most common screw thread form is the one with a symmetrical V-Profile. The **Sharp V** is rarely used now, because it is difficult to maintain the sharp roots in production. The form is of interest, however, as the basis of more practical V-type threads; also, because of its simplicity, it is used on drawings as a conventional representation for other (V-profile) threads. The modified V-profile standard thread form in the United States is the **American National**, which is commonly used in fasteners. The V-profile form is prevalent in the **Unified** Screw Thread (UN, UNC, UNF, UNEF) form as well as the ISO/Metric thread. The advantage of symmetrical threads is that they are easier to manufacture and inspect compared to non-symmetrical threads.

The **Unified Screw Thread** is the standard of the United States, Canada, and Great Britain and as such is known as the **Unified** thread. Note that while the crest may be flat or rounded, the root is rounded by design. These are typically used in general purpose fasteners.

The former British standard was the **Whitworth**, which has an angle of 55° with crests and roots rounded. The British Association Standard that uses an angle of 47°, measured in the metric system, is generally used for small threads. The French and the International Metric Standards have a form similar to the American National but are in the metric system.

The V shapes are not desirable for transmitting power since part of the thrust tends to be transmitted to the side direction. **Square thread** is used for this purpose as it transmits all the forces nearly parallel to the axis. The square thread form, while strong, is harder to manufacture. It also cannot be compensated for wear unlike an **Acme** thread. Because of manufacturing difficulties, the square thread form is generally modified by providing a slight taper (5°) to the sides.

The **Acme** is generally used in place of the square thread. It is stronger, more easily produced, and permits the use of a disengaging or split nut that cannot be used on a square thread.

The **buttress**, for transmitting power in one direction, has the efficiency of the square and the strength of the V thread.

The **knuckle** thread is especially suitable when threads are to be molded or rolled in sheet metal. It is commonly used on glass jars and in a shallow form on bases of ordinary light bulbs.

Internal threads are produced by cutting, while external threads are made by cutting or rolling. For internal threads, a hole is first drilled and then the threads are cut using a tap. The tap drill hole is a little bigger than the minor diameter of the mating external thread. The depth of the tap drill is generally deeper than the length of the threads. There are a few useless threads at the end of a normal tap. For external threads, a shaft that is the same size of the major diameter is cut using a die or on a lathe. Chamfers are generally cut to allow easy assembly.

Thread Representations

The true representation of a screw thread is almost never used in making working drawings. In true representation, the crest and root lines appear as the projections of helical curves, which are extremely tedious to draw.

On practical working drawings, three representation methods are generally used: **detailed**, **schematic** and **simplified**.

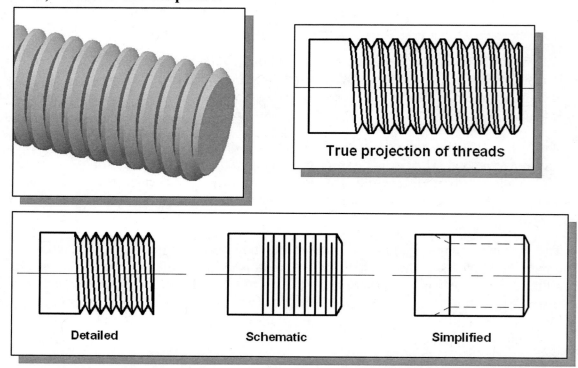

True projection of threads

Detailed   Schematic   Simplified

Detailed Representation

The detailed representation simplifies the drawing of the thread principally by constructing the projections of the helical curves into straight lines. And where applicable, further simplifications are made. For example, the 29° angle of the Acme is generally drawn as 30°, and the *American National* and *Unified* threads are represented by the sharp V. In general, true pitch should be shown, although a small increase or decrease in pitch is permissible so as to have even measurements in making the drawing. For example, seven threads per inch may be decreased to six. Remember this is only to simplify the drawing, the actual threads per inch must be specified in the drawing.

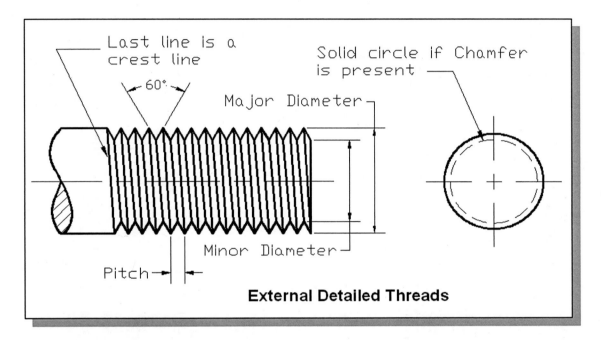

External Detailed Threads

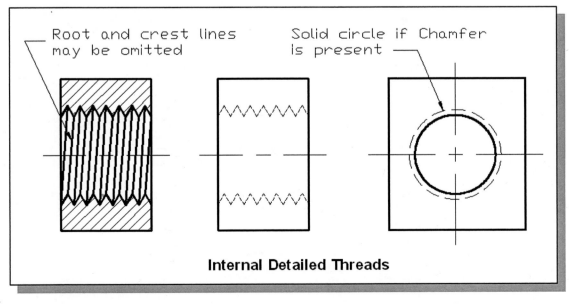

Internal Detailed Threads

Schematic Representation

The schematic representation simplifies the drawing of the thread even further. This method omits the true forms and indicates the crests and roots by lines perpendicular to the main axis. And the schematic representation is nearly as effective as the detailed representation, but is much easier to construct. This representation should not be used for section views of external threads or when internal threads are shown as hidden lines; the simplified representation is used instead. Also, to avoid too dense of line pattern, do not use this method when the pitch is less than 1/8 inch or 3 mm.

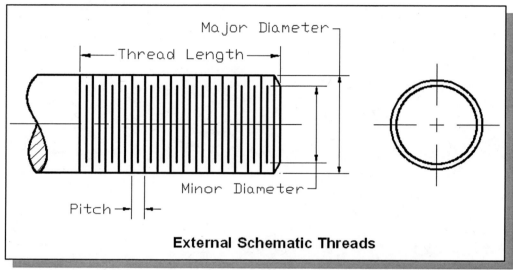

External Schematic Threads

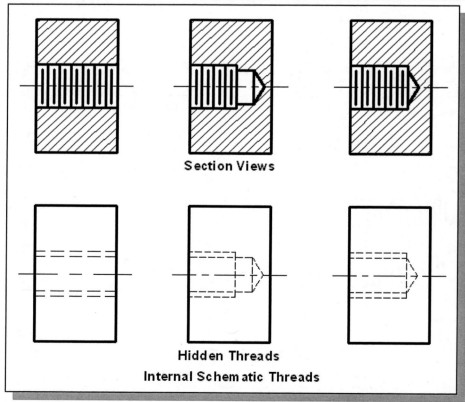

Section Views

Hidden Threads

Internal Schematic Threads

Simplified Representation

The simplified representation omits both form and crest-lines and indicates the threaded portion by dashed lines parallel to the axis at the approximate depth of thread. The simplified representation is less descriptive than the schematic representation, but they are quicker to draw and for this reason are preferred whenever feasible.

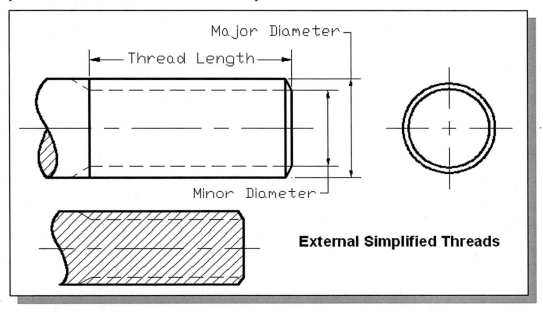

External Simplified Threads

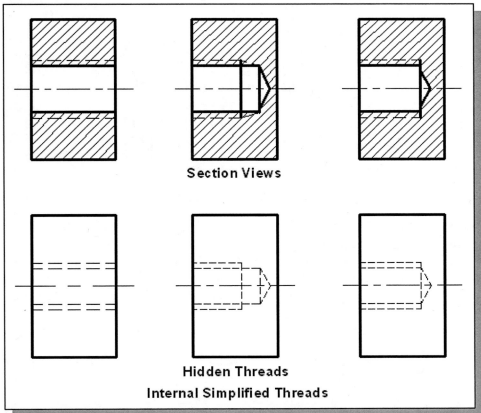

Section Views

Hidden Threads
Internal Simplified Threads

Thread Specification – English Units

The orthographic views of a thread are necessary in order to locate the position of the thread on the part. In addition, the complete thread specification is normally conveyed by means of a local note or dimensions and a local note. The essential information needed for manufacturing are **form**, **nominal (major) diameter**, **threads per inch**, and **thread class** or **toleranced dimensions**. In addition, if the thread is left-hand, the letters **LH** must be included in the specification; also, if the thread is other than single, its multiplicity must be indicated. In general, threads other than the Unified and Metric threads, Acme and buttress require tolerances.

Unified and Metric threads can be specified completely by note. The form of the specification always follows the same order: The first is the nominal size, then the number of threads per inch and the series designation (UNC, NC, etc.), and then the thread fits class. If the thread is left-hand, the letters **LH** are placed after the class. Also, when the Unified-thread classes are used, the letter **A** indicates the thread is external and letter **B** indicates the thread is internal.

For example, a thread specification of **3/4-10UNC-3A**

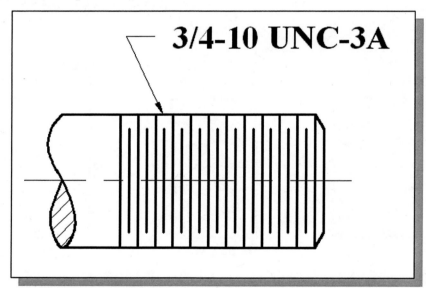

Major diameter: **3/4** in. diameter
Number of threads per inch: **10** threads per inch
Thread form and Series: **UNC** stands for **Unified National Coarse** series thread
Thread Fits: Class **3** is for high accuracy
External or Internal thread: Letter **A** indicates **external thread**

The descriptions of **thread series** and **thread fits class** are illustrated in the following sections.

Unified Thread Series

Threads are classified in "series" according to the number of threads per inch used with a specific diameter. The above Unified thread example having 20 threads per inch applied to a 1/4-in. diameter results in a thread belonging to the coarse-thread series; note that one with 28 threads per inch on the same diameter describes a thread belonging to the fine-thread series. In the United States, the Unified and Metric threads, the Acme, pipe threads, buttress, and the knuckle thread all have standardized series designations. Note that only the Unified system has more than one series of standardized forms. The Unified and Metric threads standard covers eleven series of screw threads. In the descriptions of the series which follow, the letters "U" and "N" used in the series designations stand for the words "Unified" and "National," respectively. The three standard series include the **coarse-thread series**, the **fine-thread series** and the **extra fine-thread series**.

- The coarse-thread series, designated "**UNC**" or "**NC**," is recommended for general use where conditions do not require a fine thread.

- The fine-thread series, designated "**UNF**" or "**NF**," is recommended for general use in automotive and aircraft work and where special conditions require a fine thread.

- The extra fine-thread series, designated "**UNEF**" or "**NEF**," is used particularly in aircraft and aeronautical equipments, where an extremely shallow thread or a maximum number of threads within a given length is required.

There are also the eight **constant pitch series**: **4, 6, 8, 12, 16, 20, 28** and **32 threads** with constant pitch. The **8, 12** and **16** series are the more commonly used series.

- The 8-thread series, designated **8UN** or **8N**, is a uniform-pitch series using eight threads per inch for any diameters. This series is commonly used for high-pressure conditions. The constant pitch allows excessive torque be applied and maintain a proper initial tension during assembly. Accordingly, the 8-thread series has become the general series used in many types of engineering work and as a substitute for the coarse-thread series.

- The 12-thread series, designated **12UN** or **12N**, is a uniform-pitch series using 12 threads per inch for any diameters. Sizes of 12-pitch threads range from 1/2 to 13/4 in. in diameter. This series is commonly used for machine construction, where fine threads are needed for strength. It also provides continuation of the extra fine-thread series for diameters larger than 11/2 in.

- The 16-thread series, designated **16UN** or **16N**, is a uniform-pitch series using 16 threads per inch for any diameters. This series is intended for applications requiring a very fine thread, such as threaded adjusting collars and bearing retaining nuts. It also provides continuation of the extra-fine-thread series for diameters larger than 2 in.

In addition, there are three special thread series, designated **UNS**, **NS** and **UN**, as covered in the standards include special combinations of diameter, pitch, and length of engagement.

Thread Fits

The classes provided by the American Standard (ANSI) are classes 1, 2 and 3. These classes are achieved through toleranced thread dimensions given in the standards.

- **Classes 1 fit**: This class of fit is intended for rapid assembly and easy production. Tolerances and allowance are largest with this class.

- **Classes 2 fit**: This class of fit is a quality standard for the bulk of screws, bolts, and nuts produced and is suitable for a wide variety of applications. A moderate allowance provides a minimum clearance between mating threads to minimize galling and seizure. A thread fit class of **2** is used as the normal production fit, this fit is assumed if none is specified.

- **Classes 3 fit**: This class of fit provides a class where accuracy and closeness of fit are important. No allowance is provided. This class of fit is only recommended where precision tools are used.

Thread Specification – Metric

Metric threads, similar to the Unified threads, can also be specified completely by note. The form of the specification always follows the same order: The first is the letter M for metric thread, and then the nominal size, then the pitch and then the tolerance class. If the thread is left-hand, the letters **LH** is placed after the class.

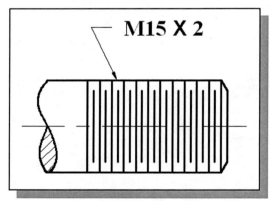

For example, the basic thread note **M15 x 2** is an adequate description for general commercial products.

Letter M: **Metric** thread
Major Diameter: **15** mm.
Pitch: **2** mm.

- **Tolerance Class**: This is used to indicate the tightness or looseness fit between the internal and external threads. In a thread note, the minor or pitch diameter tolerance is stated first followed by the major diameter tolerance if it is different. For general purpose threads, the fit 6H/6g should be used; this fit is assumed if none is specified. For a closer fit, use 6H/5g6g. Note that the number 6 in metric threads is equivalent to the Unified threads class 2 fit. Also, the letter g and G are used for small allowances, where h and H are used for no allowance.

Thread Notes Examples

(a) Metric

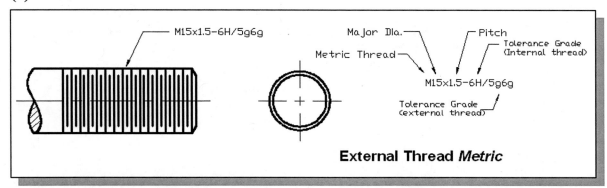

External Thread *Metric*

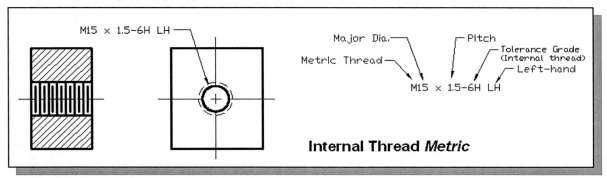

Internal Thread *Metric*

(b) Unified

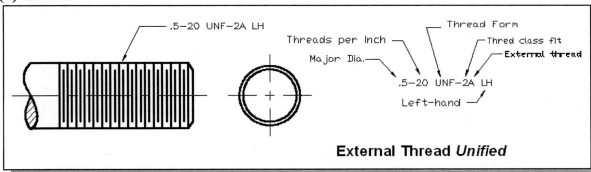

External Thread *Unified*

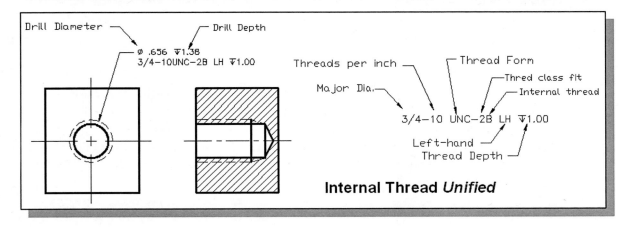

Internal Thread *Unified*

Specifying Fasteners

Fastener is a generic term that is used to describe a fairly large class of parts used to connect, fasten, or join parts together. Fasteners are generally identified by the following attributes: **Type**, **Material**, **Size**, and **Thread information**.

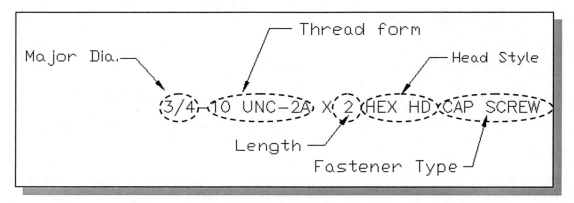

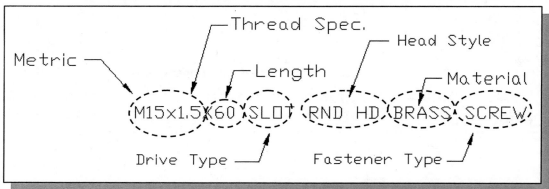

- **Type**
  Fasteners are divided into categories based on their function or design; for example, Wood Screw, Sheet Metal Screw, Hex Bolt, Washer, etc. Within the same category, some variations may exist, such as **Drive Type** and **Head Style**.

  (a) Drive Type
  Fasteners in some categories are available with different drive types such as *Philips* or *Slotted*; for example, Philips, Slotted, Allen/Socket etc.

  (b) Head Style
  Many categories are also available with different head shapes or styles; for example, Flat head, Pan head, Truss head, etc.

  For some types of fasteners, there is either only one drive type or the head style is implied to be of a standard type; for example, Socket screws have the implied Allen drive.

- **Material**
  Fastener material describes the material from which the fastener was made as well as any material grade; for example, Stainless Steel, Bronze, etc

- **Size**
  Descriptions of a fastener's size typically include its **diameter** and **length**. The fastener diameter is measured either as a size number or as a direct measurement. How fastener length is measured varies based on the type of head. As a general rule, the length of fasteners is measured from the surface of the material, to the end of the fastener. For fasteners where the head usually sits above the surface such as hex bolts and pan head screws, the measurement is from directly under the head to the end of the fastener. For fasteners that are designed to be counter sunk such as flat head screws, the fastener is measured from the point on the head where the surface of the material will be, to the end of the fastener.

- **Thread Information**
  Thread pitch or thread count is used only on machine thread fasteners. The thread pitch or count describes how fine the threads are.

Commonly used Fasteners

Hex bolts

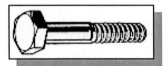

A bolt is a fastener having a head on one end and a thread on the other end. A bolt is used to hold two parts together, by means of passed through aligned clearance holes with a nut screwed on the threaded end. (See Appendix E for specs.)

Studs

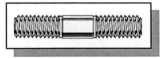

A stud is a rod with threaded ends.

Cap Screws

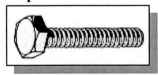

A hexagon cap screw is similar to a bolt except it is used without a nut, and generally has a longer thread. Cap screws are available in a variety of head styles and materials. (See Appendix E for specs.)

Machine screws

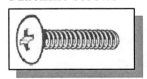

A machine screw is similar to the slot-head cap screw but smaller, available in many styles and materials. A machine screw is also commonly referred to as a stove bolt. (See Appendix E for specs.)

Wood screws

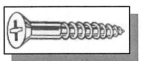

A tapered shank screw is for use exclusively in wood. Wood screws are available in a variety of head styles and materials.

Sheet metal screws

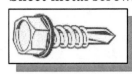

Highly versatile fasteners designed for thin materials. Sheet metal screws can be used in wood, fiberglass and metal, also called self-tapping screws, available in steel and stainless steel.

Carriage bolts

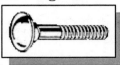

A carriage bolt is mostly used in wood with a domed shape top and a square under the head, which is pulled into the wood as the nut is tightened.

Socket screws

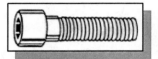

Socket screws, also known as **Allen head** are fastened with a hexagon Allen wrench, available in several head styles and materials. (See Appendix E for specs.)

Set Screws

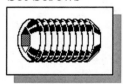

Set screws are used to prevent relative motion between two parts. A set screw is screwed into one part so that its point is pushed firmly against the other part, available in a variety of point styles and materials.

Nuts

Nuts are used to attach machine thread fasteners. (See Appendix E for specs.)

Washers

Washers provide a greater contact surface under the fastener. This helps prevent a nut, bolt or screw from breaking through the material. (See Appendix E for specs.)

Keys

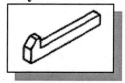

Keys are used to prevent relative motion between shafts and wheels, couplings and similar parts attached to shafts.

Rivets

Rivets are generally used to hold sheet metal parts together. Rivets are generally considered as permanent fasteners and are available in a variety of head styles and materials.

Drawing Standard Bolts

As a general rule, standard bolts and nuts are not drawn in the detail drawings unless they are non-standard sizes. The standard bolts and nuts do appear frequently in assembly drawings, and they may be drawn from the exact dimensions from the ANSI/ASME B18.2.1- 1996 standard (see Appendix E) if accuracy is important. Note that for small or unspecified chamfers, fillets, or rounds, the dimension of 1/16 in. (2mm) is generally used in creating the drawing. A simplified version of a bolt is illustrated in the following figure. Note that many companies now offer free thousands of standard fasteners and part drawings in DraftSight DWG or DXF formats. You are encouraged to do a search on the internet and compare the downloaded drawings to the specs as listed in the appendix.

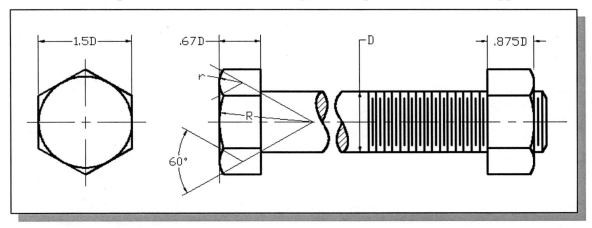

Bolt and Screw Clearances

Bolts and screws are generally used to hold parts together; and it is frequently necessary to have a clearance hole for the bolt or screw to pass through. The size of the clearance hole depends on the major diameter of the fastener and the type of fit that is desired. For bolts and screws, three standard fits are available: **normal fit**, **close fit** or **loose fit**. See Appendix for the counter-bore and countersink clearances also. (See Appendix G for more details.)

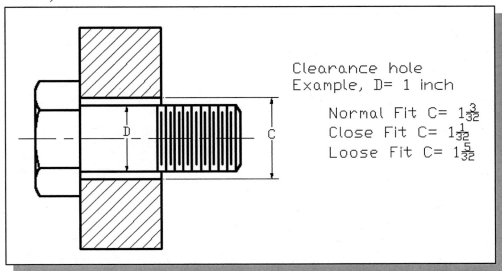

Clearance hole
Example, D= 1 inch

Normal Fit C= $1\frac{3}{32}$
Close Fit C= $1\frac{1}{32}$
Loose Fit C= $1\frac{5}{32}$

Review Questions:

1. Describe the thread specification of **3/4-16 UNF -3A**.

2. Describe the thread specification of **M25X3**.

3. List and describe four different types of commonly used fasteners.

4. Determine the sizes of a clearance hole for a **0.75** bolt using the *Close fit* option.

5. Perform an internet search and find information on the different type of **set-screws**, create freehand sketches of four point styles of set screws you have found.

6. Perform an internet search and examine the different types of **machine screws** available, create freehand sketches of four different styles of machine screws you have found.

7. Perform an Internet search and find information on **locknuts**, create freehand sketches of four different styles of locknuts you have found.

Exercises:

1. Using DraftSight, construct a simplified representation of a **#10-24 (TPI) 0.5″ long Socket Head Cap Screw**. (See Appendix for detail dimensions.)

2. Using DraftSight, construct a schematic representation of a **1/4-24 (TPI) x 3/4″, Round head slotted machine screw**. (See Appendix for detail dimensions.)

3. Using DraftSight, construct a detailed representation of a **5/8-11 (TPI) X 1″ Standard Bolt**. (See Appendix for detail dimensions.)

4. Using the simplified method shown below, construct a **7/8 –14 (TPI) X 1.5″ Hex. HD. bolt and nut**.

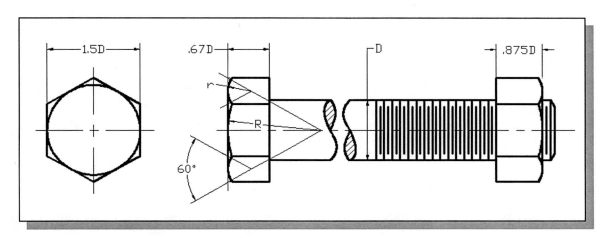

Notes:

Lesson 12
Working Drawings

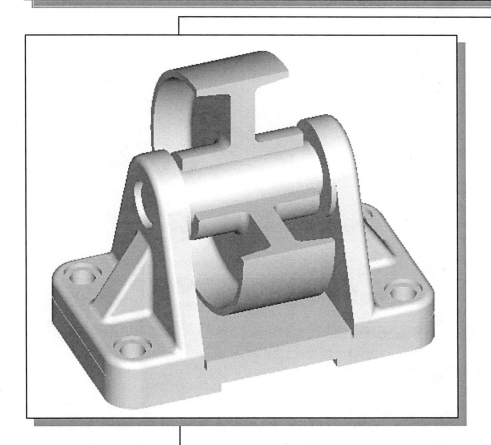

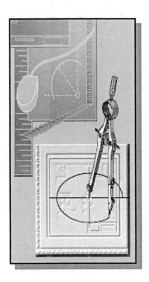

Learning Objectives

- ♦ **Understand the Terminology Related to Working Drawings**
- ♦ **Create an Assembly Drawing from Part Files**
- ♦ **Use DraftSight with the Internet**
- ♦ **Load Multiple Drawings into a Single DraftSight Session**
- ♦ **Define a Block**
- ♦ **Create Multiple Copies Using BLOCKS**

General Engineering Design Process

Engineering design is the ability to create and transform ideas and concepts into a product definition that meets the desired objective.

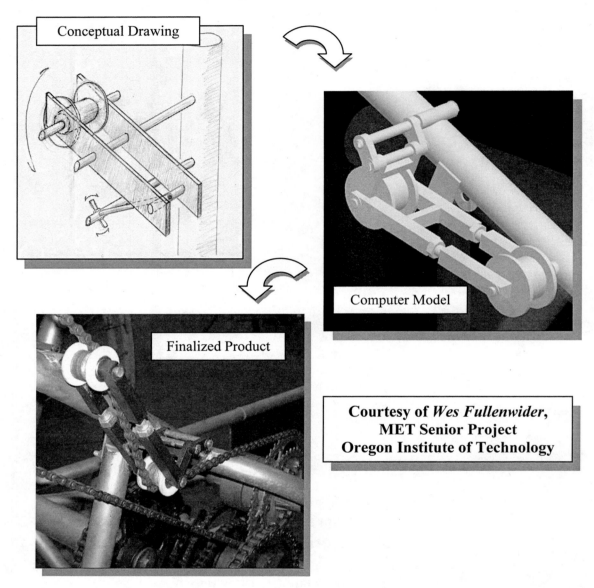

Conceptual Drawing

Computer Model

Finalized Product

**Courtesy of *Wes Fullenwider*,
MET Senior Project
Oregon Institute of Technology**

The general procedure for the design of a new product or improving an existing product involves the following six stages:

1. **Develop and identify the desired objectives.**
2. **Conceptual design stage – concepts and ideas of possible solutions.**
3. **Engineering analysis of components**
4. **Computer Modeling and/or prototypes.**
5. **Refine and finalize the design.**
6. **Working drawings of the finalized design.**

It is during the **conceptual design** stage, the first drawings, known as **conceptual drawings**, are usually created. The conceptual drawings are typically done in the form of freehand sketches showing the original ideas and concepts of possible solutions to the set objectives. From these conceptual drawings, engineering analyses are performed to improve and confirm the suitability of the proposed design is created. Working from the sketches and the results of the analyses, the design department then creates prototypes or performs computer simulations to further refine the design. Once the design is finalized, a set of detailed drawings of the proposed design is created. It is accurately made and shows the shapes and sizes of the various parts; this is known as the **detail drawing**. On a detail drawing, all the views necessary for complete shape description of a part are provided, and all the necessary dimensions and manufacturing directions are given. The set of drawings is completed with the addition of an **assembly drawing** and a parts list or bill of material. The assembly drawing is necessary as it provides the location and relationship of the parts. The completed drawing set is known as **working drawings**.

Working Drawings

Working drawings are the set of drawings used to give information for the manufacturing of a design.

The description given by a set of working drawings generally includes the followings:
1. The **assembly** description of the design, which provides an overall view of what the design is and also shows the location and relationship of the parts required.
2. A **parts list** or **bill of material** provides a detailed material description of the parts used in the design.
3. The **shape description** of the individual parts, which provides the full graphical representation of the shape of each part.
4. The **size description** of the individual parts, which provides the necessary dimensions of the parts used in the design.
5. **Explanatory notes** are the general and local notes on the individual drawings, giving the specific information, such as material, heat-treatment, finish, and etc.

A set of drawings will include, in general, two classes of drawings: **detail drawings** giving details of individual parts; and an **assembly drawing** giving the location and relationship of the parts.

Detail Drawings

A detail drawing is the drawing of the individual parts, giving a complete and exact description of its form, dimensions, and related construction information. A successful detail drawing will provide the manufacturing department all the necessary information to produce the parts. This is done by providing adequate orthographic views together with dimensions, notes, and a descriptive title. Information on a detail drawing usually include the shape, size, material and finish of a part; specific information of shop operations, such as the limits of accuracy and the number of parts needed are also provided. The detail drawing should be complete and also exact in description, so that a satisfactory part can be produced. The drawings created in the previous chapters are all detail drawings.

Assembly Drawings

An assembly drawing is, as its name implies, a drawing of the design put together, showing the relative positions of the different parts. The assembly drawing of a finalized design is generally done after the detail drawings are completed. The assembly drawing can be made by tracing from the detail drawings. The assembly drawing can also be drawn from the dimensions of the detail drawings; this provides a valuable check on the correctness of the detail drawings.

The assembly drawing sometimes gives the overall dimensions and dimensions that can be used to aid the assembly of the design. However, many assembly drawings need no dimensions. An assembly drawing should not be overloaded with detail, particularly hidden detail. Unnecessary dashed lines (hidden lines) should not be used on any drawing, this is even more critical on assembly drawings.

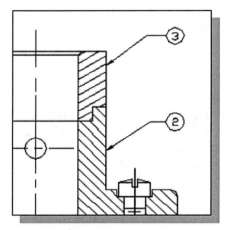

Assembly drawings usually have reference letters or numbers designating the different parts. These "numbers" are typically enclosed in circles ("balloons") with a leader pointing to the part; these numbers are used in connection with the parts list and bill of material.

For complicated designs, besides the assembly drawing, subassembly drawings are generally used. A subassembly is a drawing showing the details of a related group of parts, as it would not be practical to include all the features on a single assembly drawing. Thus, a subassembly is used to aid in clarifying the relations of a subset of an assembly.

Bill of Materials (BOM) and Parts List

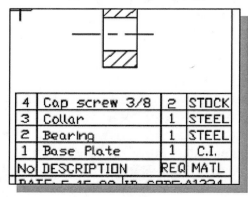

A bill of materials (BOM) is a table that contains information about the parts within an assembly. The BOM can include information such as part names, quantities, costs, vendors, and all of the other information related to building the part. The *parts list*, which is used in an assembly drawing, is usually a partial list of the associated BOM.

Drawing Sizes

The standard drawing paper sizes are as shown in the below tables.

American National Standard	International Standard
A – 8.5" X 11.0"	A4 – 210 mm X 297 mm
B – 11.0" X 17.0"	A3 – 297 mm X 420 mm
C – 17.0" X 22.0"	A2 – 420 mm X 594 mm
D – 22.0" X 34.0"	A1 – 594 mm X 841 mm
E – 34.0" X 44.0"	A0 – 841 mm X 1189 mm

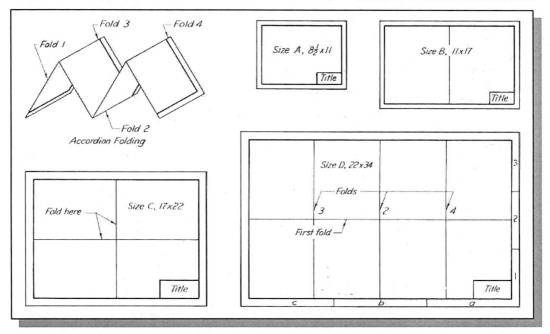

Drawing Sheet Borders and Revisions Block

The drawing sheet borders are generally drawn at a distance parallel to the edges of the sheet, typically with distance varying from 0.25″ to 0.5″ or 5 mm to 10 mm.

Once a drawing has been released to the shop, any alterations or changes should be recorded on the drawing and new prints be issued to the production facilities. In general, the upper right corner of a working drawing sheet is the designated area for such records, this is known as the **revisions** block.

REVISIONS				
ZONE	REV	DESCRIPTION	DATE	APPROVED

Title Blocks

The title of a working drawing is usually placed in the lower right corner of the sheet. The spacing and arrangement of the space depend on the information to be given. In general, the title of a working drawing should contain the following information:

1. **Name of the company and its location.**
2. **Name of the part represented.**
3. **Signature of the person who made the drawing and the date of completion.**
4. **Signature of the checker and the date of completion.**
5. **Signature of the approving personnel and the date of approval.**
6. **Scale of the drawing.**
7. **Drawing number.**

Other information may also be given in the title blocks area, such as material, heat treatment, finish, hardness, general tolerances, depends on the company and the peculiarities of the design.

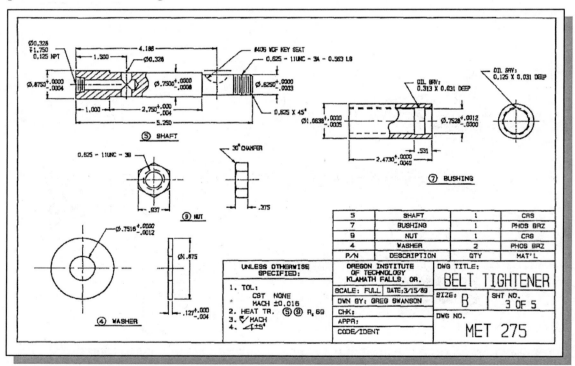

Working Drawings with DraftSight

The term **assembly drawing** refers to the type of drawing in which the various parts of a design are shown in their relative positions in the finished product. Assembly drawings are used to represent the function of each part and the proper working relationships of the mating parts. Sectioning is used more extensively on assembly drawings than on detail drawings to show the relationship of various parts. Assembly drawings should not be overly detailed since precise information is provided on the detail drawings. In most cases dimensions are omitted on assembly drawings except for assembly dimensions such as important center distances, overall dimensions, and dimensions showing relationships between the parts. For the purpose of clarity, *subassembly drawings* are often made to give the information needed for the smaller units of a larger assembly. Several options are available in DraftSight to assist us in creating assembly drawings.

In DraftSight, a **block** is a collection of objects that is identified by a unique name and essentially behaves as if it is a single object. Using blocks can help us organize our design by associating the related objects into smaller units. We can insert, scale, and rotate multiple objects that belong to the same block with a single selection. We can insert the same block numerous times instead of re-creating the individual geometric objects each time. We can also import a block from a CAD file outside the current drawing. We can use blocks to build a standard library of frequently used symbols, components, or standard parts; the blocks can then be inserted into other drawings. Using blocks also helps us save disk space by storing all references to the same block as one block definition in the database. We can *explode* a block to separate its component objects, modify them, and redefine the block. DraftSight updates all instances of that block based on the *block definition*. Blocks can also be nested, so that one block is a part of another block. Using blocks greatly reduces repetitive work.

In DraftSight, we can load multiple drawings into a single DraftSight session. This feature enables us to work with multiple drawings at the same time, and we can easily copy objects from one drawing to another by using the *Windows Clipboard*. The *Windows Clipboard* options, *copying-to* and *pasting-from,* can be used to quickly assemble objects in different files and thus increase our productivity.

DraftSight also allows us to create a collaborative design environment, where files and resources can be shared through the Internet. We can open and save DraftSight drawings to an Internet location, insert blocks by dragging drawings from a web site, and insert hyperlinks in drawings so that others can access related documents. An Internet connection is required in order to utilize the DraftSight internet features.

In this lesson, we will demonstrate using the DraftSight Internet features to access drawings through the Internet, as well as using blocks and the *Windows Clipboard* to create a subassembly drawing. We will use the bearing part that was created in the previous lesson.

The *Shaft Support* Subassembly

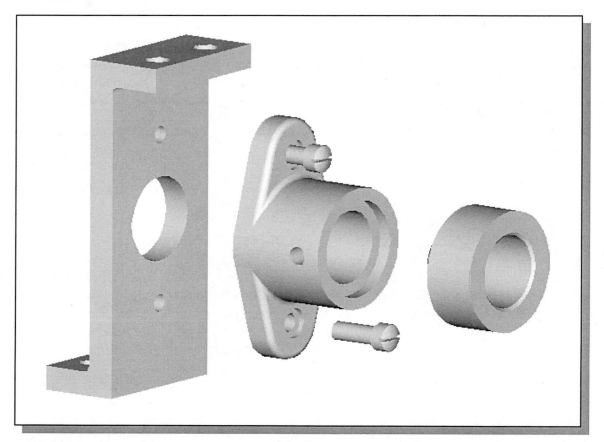

Additional Parts

Besides the ***Bearing*** part, we will need three additional parts: (1) ***Cap-Screw***, (2) ***Collar*** and (3) ***Base-Plate***. Create the *Collar* and *Base-Plate* drawings as shown below; save the drawings as separate part files (*Collar*, *Base-Plate*). (Exit **DraftSight** after you have created the files.)

(1) ***Cap-Screw***
(We will open this drawing through the Internet.)

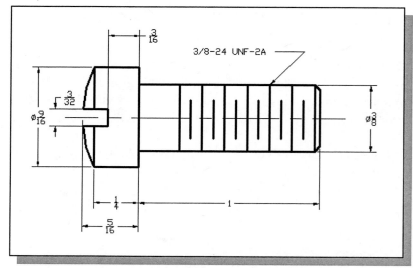

(2) *Collar*

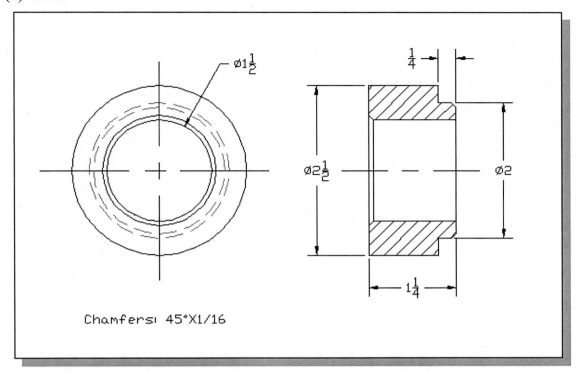

Chamfers: 45°X1/16

(3) *Base-Plate*

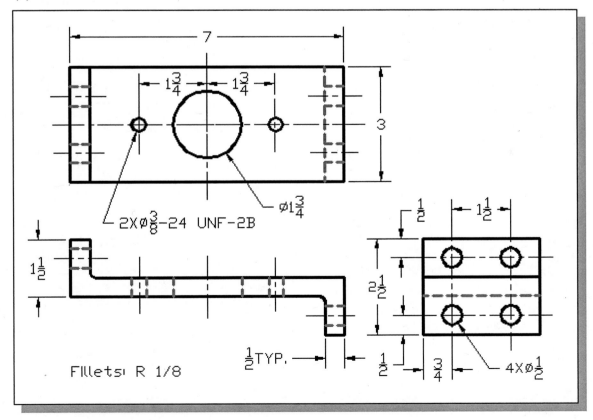

Fillets: R 1/8

Starting Up DraftSight and Loading Multiple Drawings

1. Select the **DraftSight** option on the *Program* menu or select the **DraftSight** icon on the *Desktop*.

2. On your own, close the *NoName_0.dwg* file.

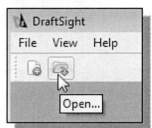

3. In the DraftSight *Startup* dialog box, select **Open a Drawing** with a single click of the left-mouse-button.

4. In the *File* list section, pick **Bearing.dwg** as the first drawing to be loaded.

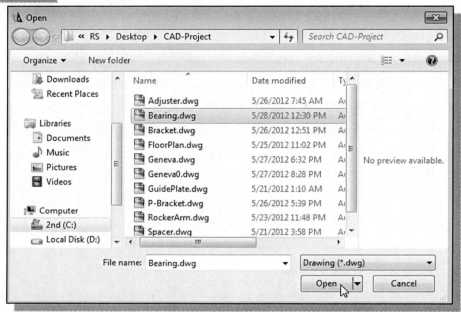

5. Click on the **Open** button to open the selected design.

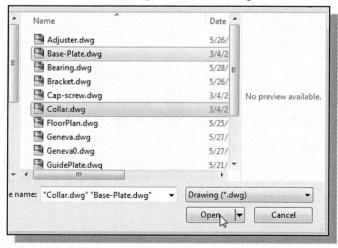

6. On your own, repeat the above steps and open the **Base-Plate.dwg** and the **Collar.dwg** designs.

Using DraftSight with the Internet

- DraftSight allows us to share files and resources through the Internet. Drawings can be placed and opened to an Internet location, insert blocks by dragging drawings from a web site, and insert hyperlinks in drawings so that others can access related documents. Note that to use the DraftSight Internet features an Internet connection is required.

We will illustrate the procedure to open a DraftSight file from the Internet by *Uniform Resource Locator* (URL).

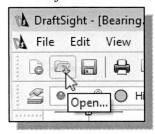

1. Click the **Open** icon in the *Standard* toolbar area as shown.

2. In the *Select File* dialog box, enter
   http://www.schroff.com/DraftSight/Cap-screw.dwg
   as shown in the figure below.

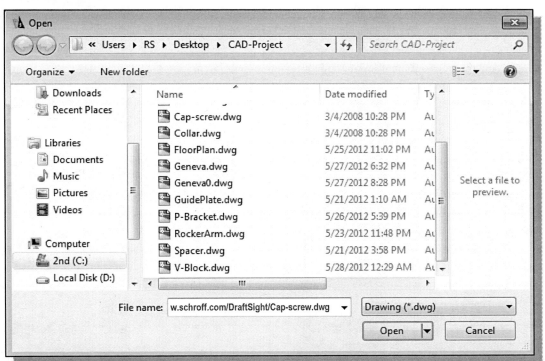

3. Click the **Open** icon and the *Cap-screw* file is downloaded from the www.schroff.com web site to the local computer.

- The URL entered must be of the *Hypertext Transfer Protocol* (http://) and the complete filename must be entered including the filename extension (.dwg or .dwt).

Rearrange the Displayed Windows

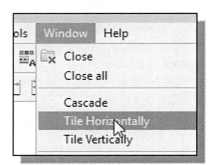

1. In the pull-down menus, select:

   ### [Window] → [Tile Horizontally]

   ➢ Note that the highlighted window and the shape of the graphics cursor indicate the **active window** in the current DraftSight session. We can switch to any window by clicking inside the desired window.

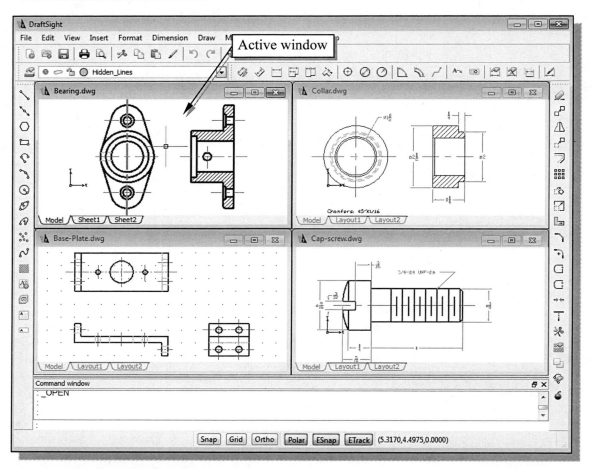

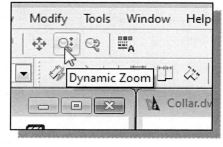

➢ On your own, adjust the display of each window by left-clicking inside each window and using the **Dynamic Zoom** command.

Defining a *Block*

1. Set the ***Cap-Screw*** window as the *active window* by left-mouse-clicking inside the window.

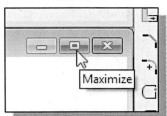

2. Click on the **Maximize** icon at the top right corner of the ***Cap-Screw*** window to enlarge the window.

3. In the *Layer Control* box, switch ***OFF*** the ***Dimension* layer** and leave only the ***Object_Lines*** and ***Center_Lines*** layers visible.

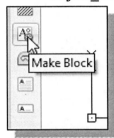

4. Pick the **Make Block** command icon in the *Draw* toolbar. The *Block Definition* dialog box appears on the screen.

5. In the *Block Definition* dialog box, enter ***Cap Screw*** as the block *Name*.

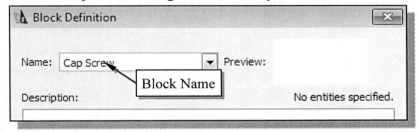

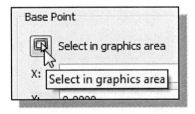

6. Click on the **Pick Base Point** button to define a reference point of the block.

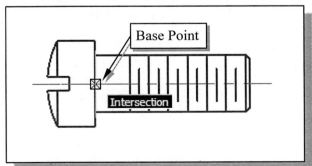

7. Pick the intersection of the centerline and the base of the *Cap-Screw* head as the base point.

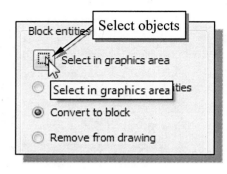

8. Click on the **Select Objects** icon to select the objects to be placed in the block.

9. Select all *objects* by using a selection window on the screen.

10. Inside the graphics window, **right-mouse-click** once to accept the selected objects.

- The selected objects will be included in the new block, and several options are available regarding the selected objects after the block is created. We can retain or delete the selected objects or convert them to a block instance.

  ➢ *Reserve as separate entities*: Keep the selected objects as regular objects in the drawing after creating the block.

  ➢ *Convert to Block*: Convert the selected objects to a block instance in the drawing after creating the block.

  ➢ **Delete**: Remove the selected objects from the drawing after creating the block.

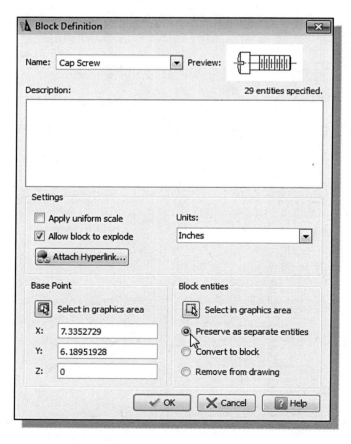

11. Pick the *Reserve as separate entities* option to keep the objects as regular lines and arcs.

➢ Notice in the upper right corner, the *Preview* area, a small icon of the selected objects is displayed.

12. Click the **OK** button to accept the settings and proceed to create the new block.

Inserting a *Block*

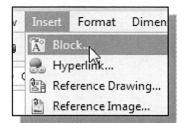

1. In the *Main Menu* area, select **[Insert]** → **[Block]**. The *Block Definition* dialog box appears on the screen.

2. In the *Insert* dialog box, notice the block name ***Cap Screw*** appears in the block *Name* box. (Note: In this example, we created only one block; DraftSight allows us to define multiple blocks in the same drawing.)

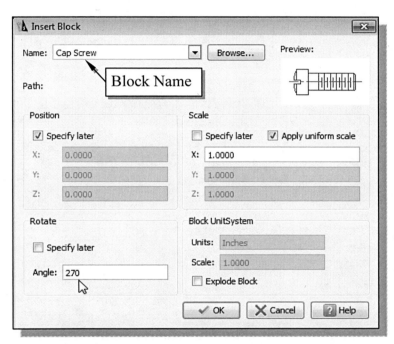

3. Set the *Position* option to **Specify later**, which allows us to position the block on the screen.

4. Set the *Scale* option to **Apply uniform scale** as shown.

5. In the *Rotate* section, we will enter a ***270*** angle to orient the *Cap-screw* in a vertical direction.

6. Click on the **OK** button to accept the settings and proceed to insert the block into the drawing.

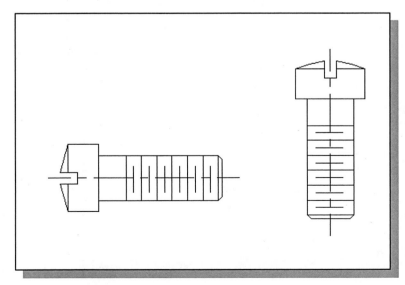

7. Move the cursor toward the right side of the original copy of the *Cap-Screw*. Left-click to place a copy of the block.

➢ On your own, place additional copies of the block on the screen while experimenting with the *Block Scale* and *Rotate* options.

Starting the *Assembly Drawing*

1. Switch back to the four tiled-windows display by left-clicking on the **Restore Down** icon near the upper right corner of the graphics window.

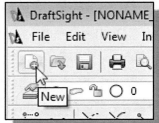

2. Select the **New** icon in the *Standard* toolbar area.

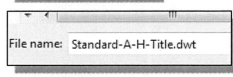

3. Select the ***Standard-A-H-Title*** template file from the list of template files.

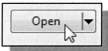

4. Click the **OK** button to open the selected template file.

5. On your own, resize the new window as shown.

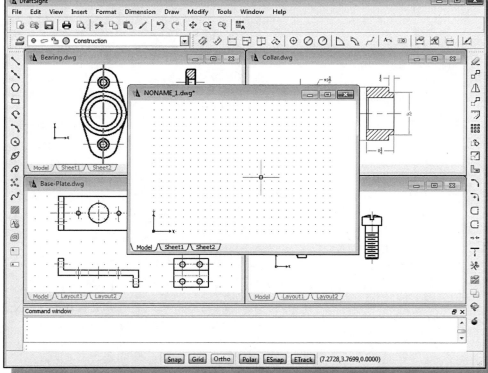

Copying and Pasting with the *Windows Clipboard*

1. Set the *Base-Plate* window as the *current window* by left-mouse-clicking inside the window.

2. In the *Layer Control* box, switch off all layers except the *Object_Lines*, *Hidden_Lines*, and *Center_Lines* layers.

3. Select the *Front View* of the **Base-Plate** by enclosing the *Front View* using a selection window.

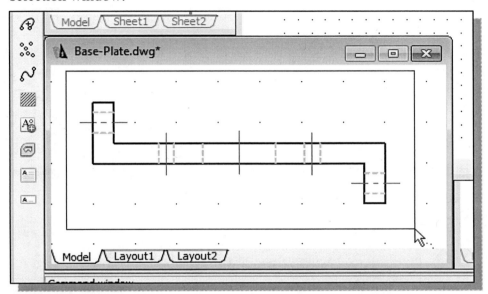

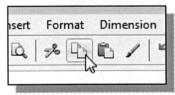

4. Select the **Copy to Clipboard** icon in the *Standard* toolbar area.

5. Set the **New Drawing** window as the *current window* by left-mouse-clicking inside the window.

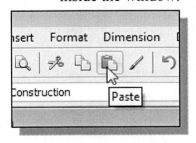

6. Select the **Paste from Clipboard** icon in the *Standard* toolbar area.

7. Position the *Front View* of the **Base-Plate** near the center of the graphics window as shown on the next page.

❖ Note that we are using the *Windows Clipboard* options; the selected items are copied into the new drawing and all of the layer settings are retained.

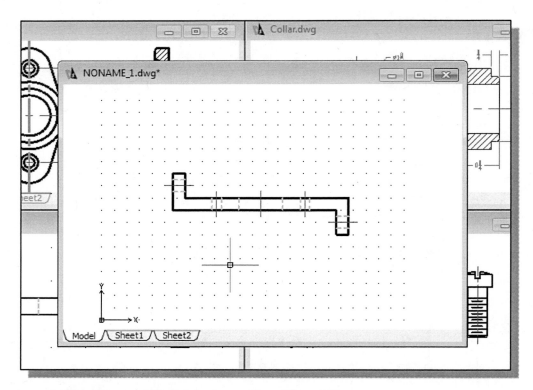

Convert the Base Plate into a Section View

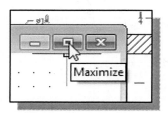

1. Click on the **Maximize** icon at the top right corner of the *NoName_1* window to enlarge the window.

2. On your own, convert the hidden lines to object lines and add the hatch pattern as shown.

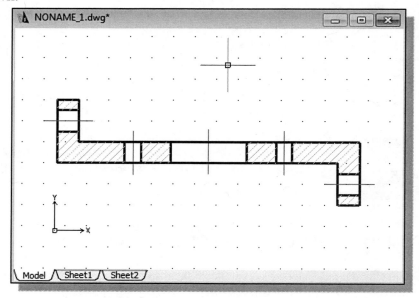

Adding the *Bearing* to the Assembly

1. Switch back to the tiled-windows display and set the ***Bearing*** window as the *current window* by a left-mouse-click inside the window.

2. In the *Layer Control* box, switch *OFF* all layers except the *Object_Lines, Hidden_Lines, Center_Lines*, and *Section_Lines* layers.

3. Select the *Side View* of the **Bearing** by enclosing the *Side View* using a selection window.

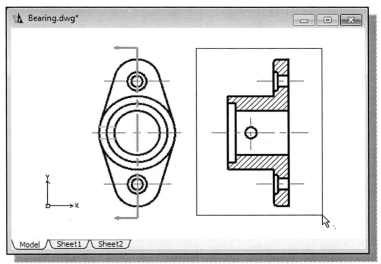

4. Inside the graphics window, **right-mouse-click** and select the **Copy with Reference Point** option under *Clipboard* as shown.

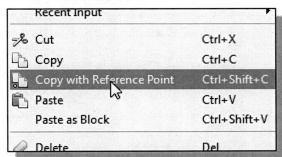

5. Pick the **center intersection** on the right vertical line of the *Side View* as the base point.

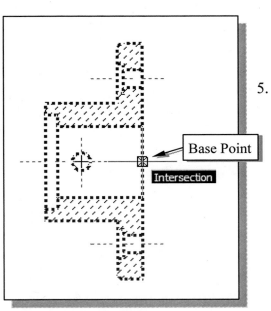

6. Set the *NoName_1* window as the *current window* by left-mouse-clicking inside the window.

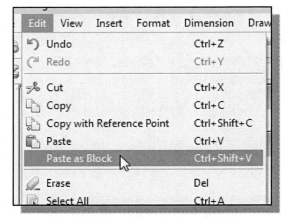

7. In the *Main Menu*, select

    [Edit] → [Paste as Block]

8. Align the *Side View* of the *Bearing* to the top center intersection of the *Base-Plate* as shown.

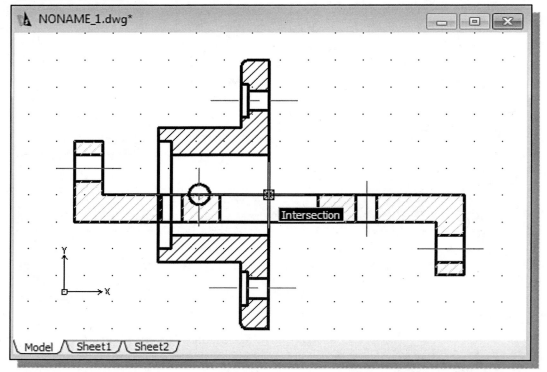

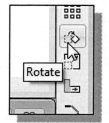

9. Click on the **Rotate** icon in the *Modify* toolbar.

10. Pick the pasted view of the *Bearing* we just placed into the assembly drawing. Notice the entire view is treated as a block object.

11. Inside the graphics window, **right-mouse-click** to accept the selection and proceed with the Rotate command.

12. Pick the base point as the rotation reference point.

13. Rotate the *Bearing* part to the top of the *Base-Plate*.

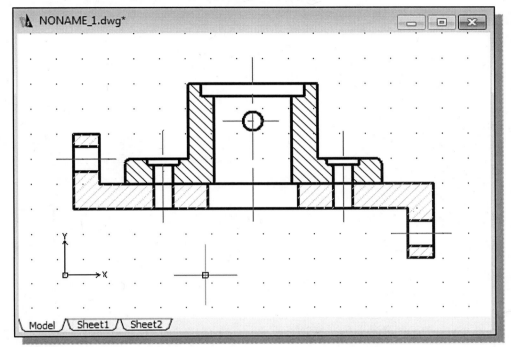

14. Select the **Explode** icon in the *Modify* toolbar.

15. Pick the *Bearing* to break the block into its component objects.

➢ On your own, copy and paste the *Collar* to the top of the *Bearing*.

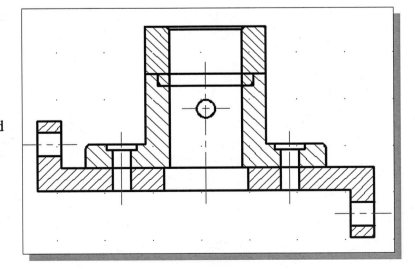

16. Use the **Explode**, **Trim**, **Erase** and **Properties** commands and modify the assembly as shown.

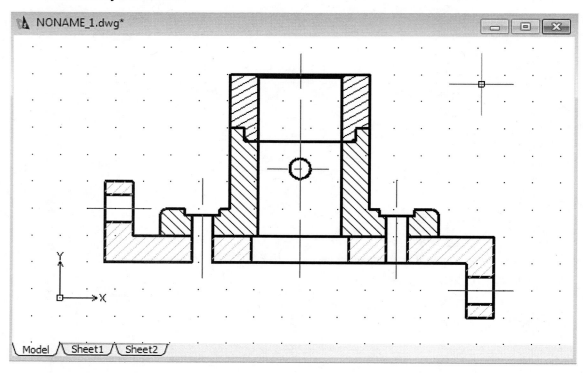

Adding the *Cap-Screws* to the Assembly

1. Set the **Cap-Screw** window as the *current window* by a left-mouse-click inside the window.

2. Pre-select the vertical *Cap-Screw*. Since all objects belong to a block we can quickly select the block.

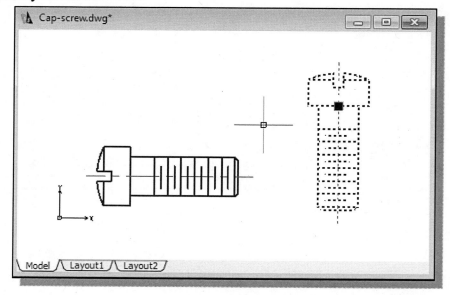

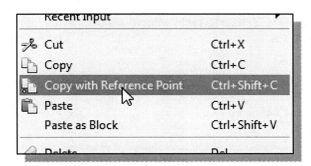

3. Inside the graphics window, **right-mouse-click** and select the **Copy with Reference Point** option.

4. Pick the *GRIP* point as the copy base point.

5. Set the *NoName_1* window as the *current window* by left-mouse-clicking inside the window.

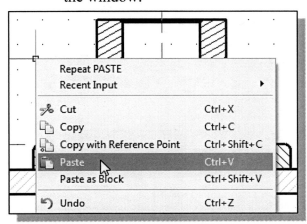

6. Inside the graphics window, **right-mouse-click** and select the **Paste** option.

7. Align the *Cap-Screw* to the *Bearing* part as shown.

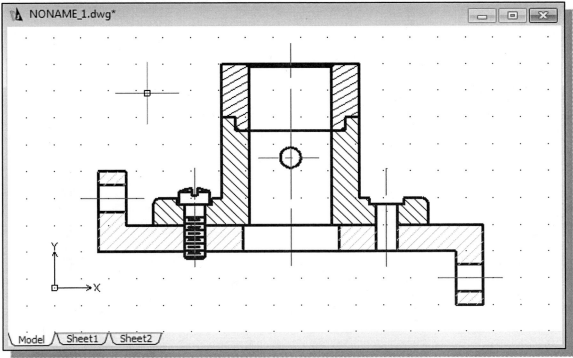

➤ On your own, repeat the **Paste** command and place the other *Cap-Screw* in place.

Creating *Callouts* with the *LEADER* Command

1. In the *Main Menu* area, select:

    [Dimension] → [Leader]

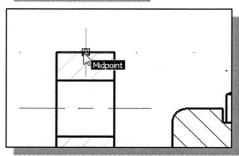

2. Place the arrowhead near the midpoint of the right vertical edge of the *Base Plate* part as shown.

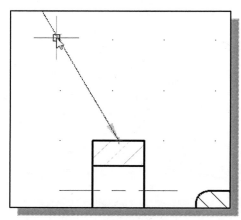

3. Select a location that is toward the left side of the **Base Plate** part as shown in the figure.

4. Right-click twice to accept the default for the text height.

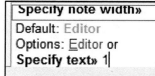

5. Enter *1* as the *tag number* as shown in the figure.

6. On your own, create a circle around the text.

7. On your own, repeat the above process and create the four callouts as shown in the figure below.

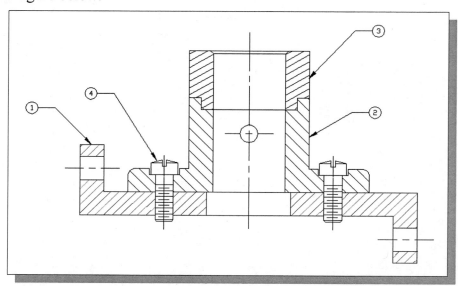

Creating a *Viewport* in the A-size Layout

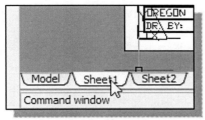

1. Click the **Sheet1** tab to switch to the two-dimensional paper space containing the title block.

2. If a view·is displayed inside the title block, use the **Delete** command and delete the view by selecting any edge of the viewport.

3. Set the *Viewport* layer as the *Current Layer*.

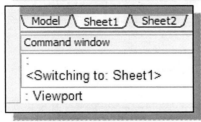

4. In the command window, enter **Viewport** to activate the command.

- The **Viewport** command creates and controls multiple tiled views on Sheets.

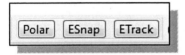

5. In the *Status* toolbar area, turn *OFF* the *ESnap* and *ETrack* options as shown.

6. Create a viewport inside the title block area as shown.

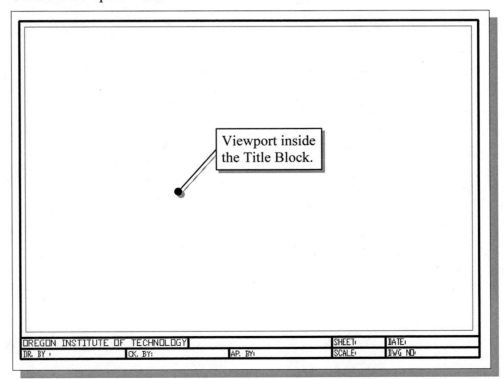

Viewport inside the Title Block.

Viewport properties

1. Pre-select the viewport by left-clicking once on any edge of the viewport.

2. In the *Standard* toolbar, click the **Properties** icon.

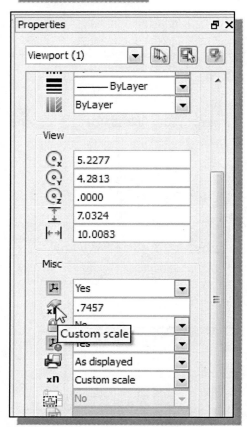

3. In the *Properties* dialog box, scroll down near the bottom of the list. Notice the current scale is set to *Custom scale, 0.7457.* (The number on your screen might be different.)

4. Below the *Custom scale*, the *Standard scale* list is available.

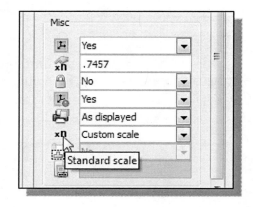

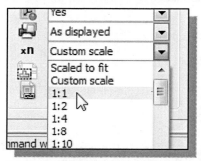

5. Select *1:1* in the standard scale list. This will set the plotting scale factor to *full scale.*

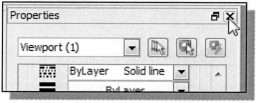

6. Click on the [**X**] button to close the *Properties* dialog box.

7. On your own, turn **OFF** the display of the *Viewport* layer.

Adding a *PARTS LIST* to the Assembly Drawing

    1.   Set the ***Titleblock_lettering*** layer as the *Current Layer*.

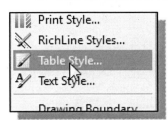

    2.   In the *Main Menu* area, select:

         [Format] → [Table Style]

    3.   Click the **New** icon to start a new **Table Style**.

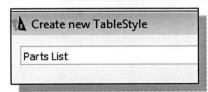

    4.   Enter **Parts List** as the *New style name* as shown.

    5.   Click **OK** to proceed with the new style setup.

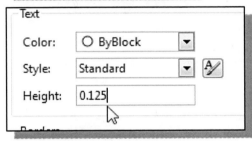

    6.   Set the *Text Height* to ***0.125*** as shown.

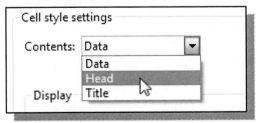

    7.   Select **Head** in the *Cell style settings* section as shown.

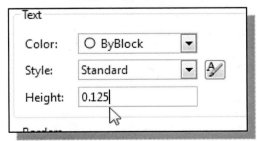

    8.   Set the *Text Height* to ***0.125*** as shown.

9. Set the *Table header orientation* to **Up** by selecting in the *Table direction* option list as shown.

10. Click on the **Activate** button to make the new style the active style.

11. Click on the **OK** button to close the *Table Style* dialog box

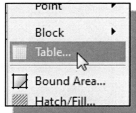

12. In the *Main Menu* area, select:

    [Draw] → [Table]

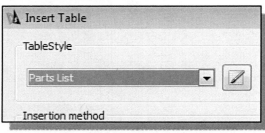

13. Confirm the ***Parts_List*** is the *active TableStyle* as shown.

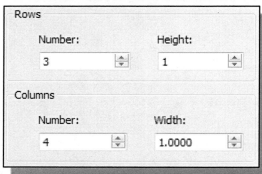

14. Set the number of *Rows* to **3** and height to **1**.

15. Set the number of *Columns* to **4** and width to **1.0**.

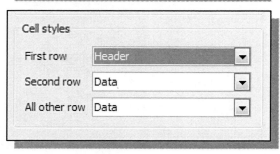

16. In the *Cell styles* section, set the *First row* cell style to **Header**.

17. Set the *Second row* cell style to **Data**.

18. Click the **OK** button to accept the settings as shown.

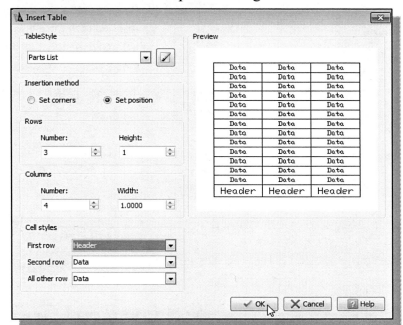

19. Place the table near the lower left corner of the title block as shown.

20. Set text height to *0.125* and enter "*No.*", "*Description*", "*REQ*" and "*MATL*" as the four headers of the *Parts_List* table as shown. Hit the [**Tab**] key to go to the next cell and click **OK** to end the text input option.)

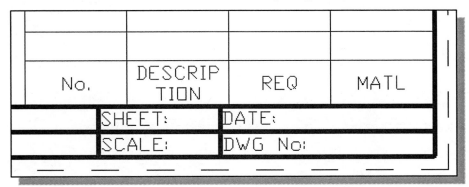

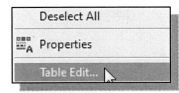

21. Select the ***Parts_List*** table by clicking on any one of the edges.

22. Inside the graphics window, **right-mouse-click** and select the **Table Edit** option.

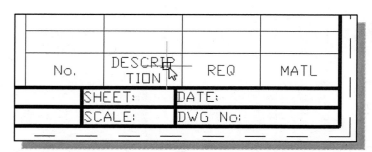

23. Click inside the second header box and notice the text editor reappeared on screen.

- Note the [**Tab**] key can still be used to go to the next cell.

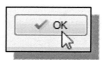

24. Click **OK** to end the text input option.

25. Select the *Parts_List* table by clicking on any one of the edges.

➤ Notice the different control GRIPS that are available to resize and reposition the table.

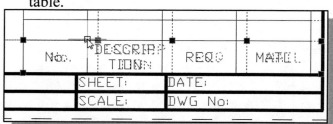

26. Drag the second square GRIP point toward the left to adjust the width of the first column.

27. Enter the following information into the *Parts_List*.

4	Cap Screw 3/8	2	Stock
3	Collar	1	Steel
2	Bearing	1	Steel
1	Base Plate	1	C.I.
No.	DESCRIPTION	REQ	MATL

28. On your own, complete the drawing and create a hard copy of it.

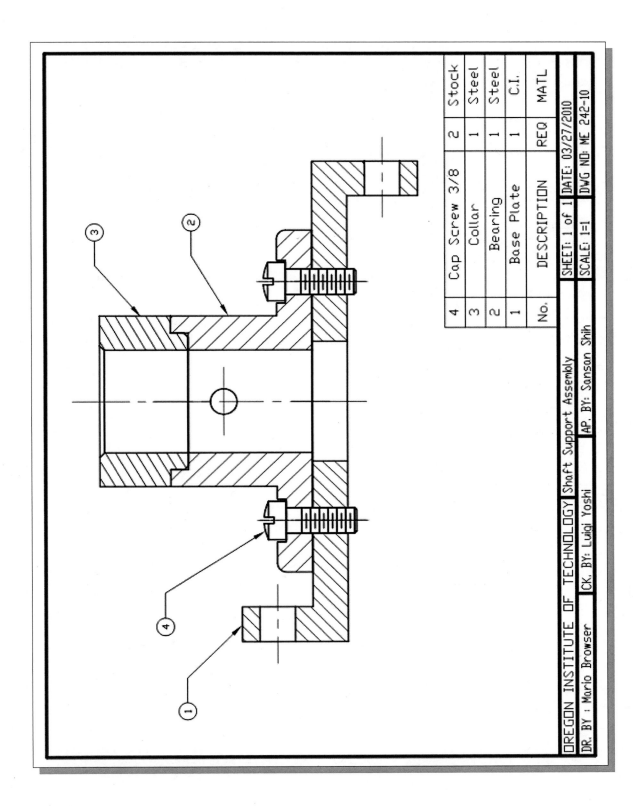

No.	DESCRIPTION	REQ	MATL
4	Cap Screw 3/8	2	Stock
3	Collar	1	Steel
2	Bearing	1	Steel
1	Base Plate	1	C.I.

SHEET: 1 of 1 | DATE: 03/27/2010

DWG N0: ME 242-10

SCALE: 1=1

OREGON INSTITUTE OF TECHNOLOGY | Shaft Support Assembly

DR. BY : Mario Browser | CK. BY: Luigi Yoshi | AP. BY: Sanson Shih

Review Questions:

1. What is an *assembly drawing*? What are the basic differences between an assembly drawing and a detail drawing?

2. What is a *block*? List some the advantages of using blocks in DraftSight.

3. Which command allows us to separate a block into its component objects?

4. Describe the differences between *PASTE* and *PASTE AS BLOCK*.

5. Which command did we use to set up the style of the *Parts_List* for the *Shaft Support* assembly?

6. Construct the drawing shown and measure the length **L**. Show the length with three digits after the decimal point. (Units: inches.)

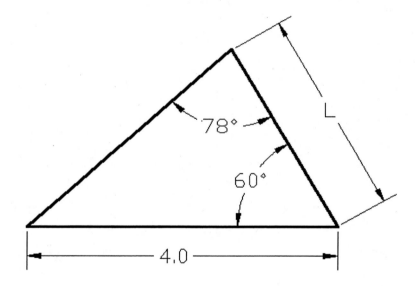

Exercises:

1. Wheel Assembly (Create a set of detail and assembly drawings. All dimensions are in mm.)

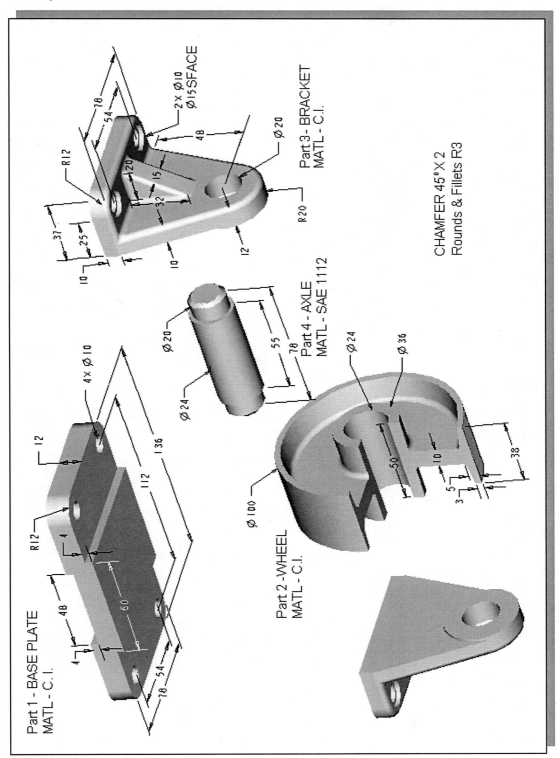

2. Leveling Device Assembly (Create a set of detail and assembly drawings. All dimensions are in mm.)

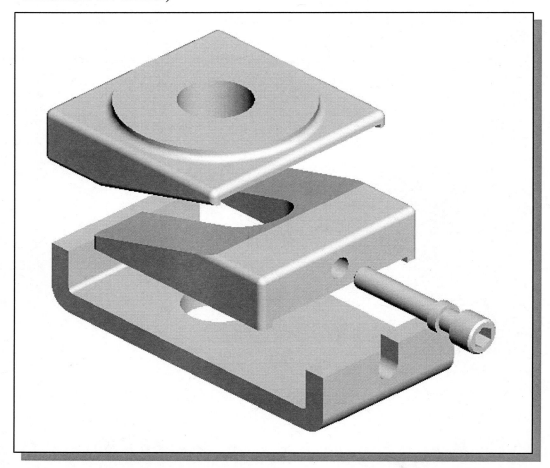

(a) Base Plate

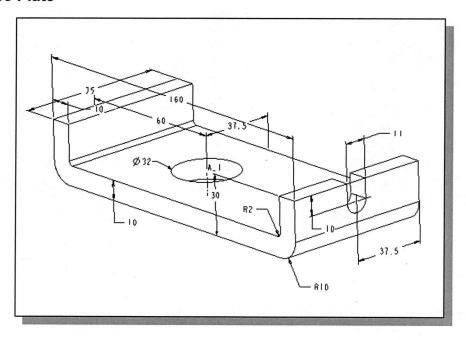

(b) Sliding Block (Rounds & Fillets: R3)

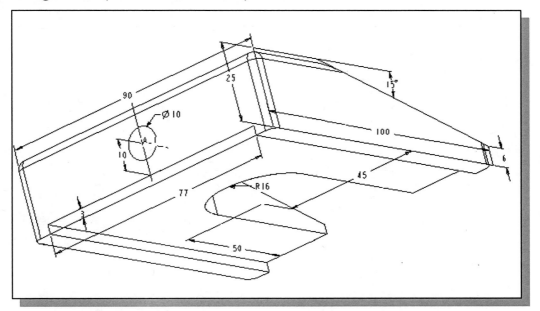

(c) Lifting Block (Rounds & Fillets: R3)

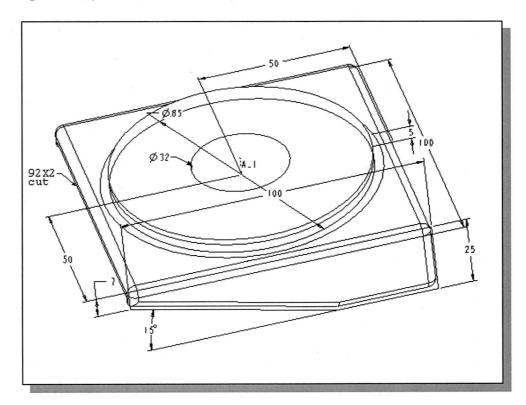

(d) Adjusting Screw (M10 X 1.5)

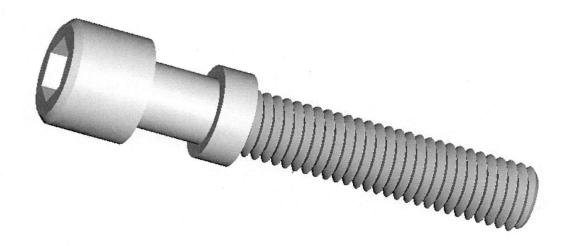

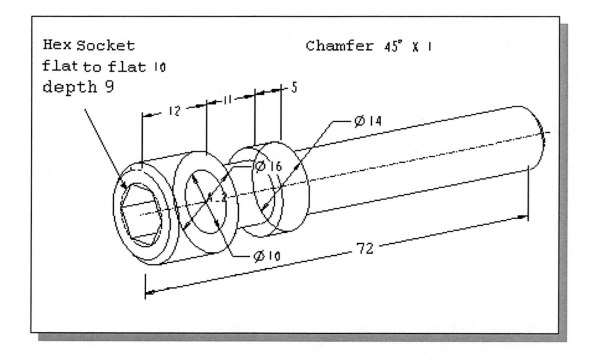

3. Vise Assembly (Create a set of detail and assembly drawings. All dimensions are in inches.)

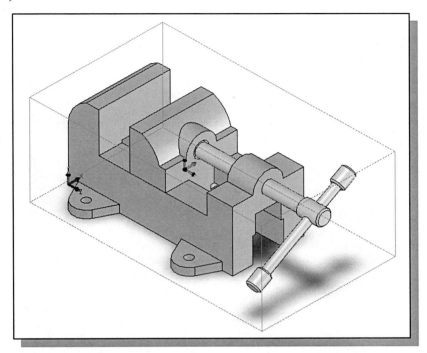

(a) Base: The 1.5 inch wide and 1.25 inch wide slots are cut through the entire Base. Material: Gray Cast Iron.

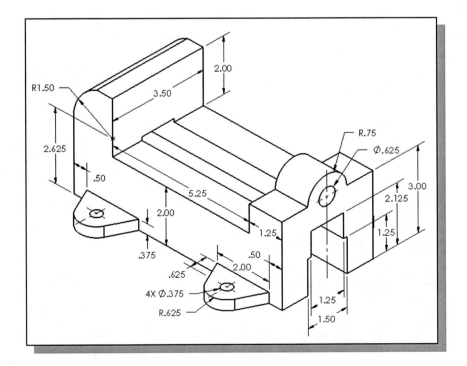

(b) Jaw: The shoulder of the Jaw rests on the flat surface of the Base and the Jaw opening is set to 1.5 inches. Material: Gray Cast Iron.

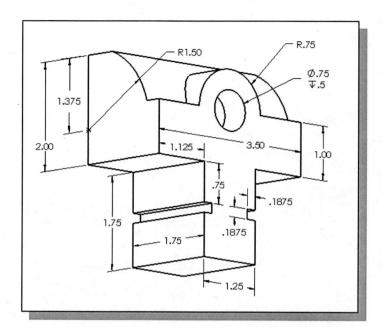

(c) Key: 0.1875 inch H x 0.375 inch W x 1.75 inch L. The keys fit into the slots on the jaw with the edge faces flush as shown in the sub-assembly to the right. Material: Alloy Steel.

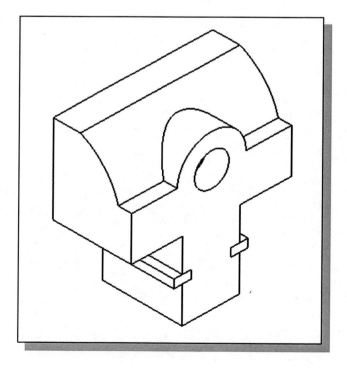

(d) Screw: There is one chamfered edge (0.0625 inch x 45°). The flat ⌀ 0.75″ edge of the screw is flush with the corresponding recessed ⌀ 0.75 face on the jaw. Material: Alloy Steel.

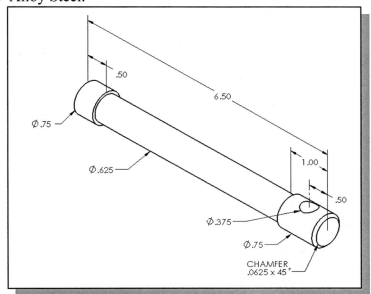

(e) Handle Rod: ⌀ 0.375″ x 5.0″ L. The handle rod passes through the hole in the screw and is rotated to an angle of 30° with the horizontal as shown in the assembly view. The flat ⌀ 0.375″ edges of the handle rod are flush with the corresponding recessed ⌀ 0.735 faces on the handle knobs. Material: Alloy Steel.

(f) Handle Knob: There are two chamfered edges (0.0625 inch x 45°). The handle knobs are attached to each end of the handle rod. The resulting overall length of the handle with knobs is 5.50″. The handle is aligned with the screw so that the outer edge of the upper knob is 2.0″ from the central axis of the screw. Material: Alloy Steel.

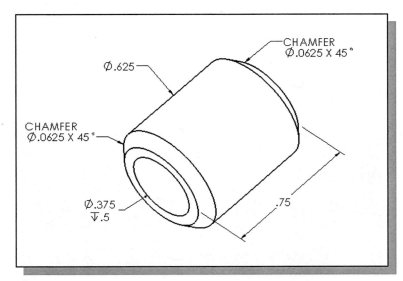

Notes:

APPENDIX A

Running and Sliding Fits – American National Standard

Basic Hole System, Limits are in thousandths of an inch.
Limits for hole and shaft are applied to the basic size to obtain
the limits of sizes for the parts.

Nominal Size Range, Inches Over To	Class RC1			Class RC2			Class RC3			Class RC4		
	Limits of Clearance	Standard Limits		Limits of Clearance	Standard Limits		Limits of Clearance	Standard Limits		Limits of Clearance	Standard Limits	
		Hole H5	Shaft g4		Hole H6	Shaft g5		Hole H7	Shaft f6		Hole H8	Shaft f7
0 – 0.12	0.1 0.45	+0.2 +0	-0.1 -0.25	0.1 0.55	+0.25 0	-0.1 -0.3	0.3 0.95	+0.4 0	-0.3 -0.55	0.3 1.3	+0.6 0	-0.3 -0.7
0.12 – 0.24	0.15 0.5	+0.2 0	-0.15 -0.3	0.15 0.65	+0.3 0	-0.15 -0.35	0.4 1.12	+0.5 0	-0.4 -0.7	0.4 1.6	+0.7 0	-0.4 -0.9
0.24 – 0.40	0.2 0.6	+0.25 0	-0.2 -0.35	0.2 0.85	+0.4 0	-0.2 -0.45	0.5 1.5	+0.6 0	-0.5 -0.9	0.5 2.0	+0.9 0	-0.5 -1.1
0.40 – 0.71	0.25 0.75	+0.3 +0	-0.25 -0.45	0.25 0.95	+0.4 0	-0.25 -0.55	0.6 1.7	+0.7 0	-0.6 -1.0	0.6 2.3	+1.0 0	-0.6 -1.3
0.71 – 1.19	0.3 0.95	+0.4 0	-0.3 -0.55	0.3 1.2	+0.5 0	-0.3 -0.7	0.8 2.1	+0.8 0	-0.8 -1.3	0.8 2.8	+1.2 0	-0.8 -1.6
1.19 – 1.97	0.4 1.1	+0.4 0	-0.4 -0.7	0.4 1.4	+0.6 0	-0.4 -0.8	1.0 2.6	+1.0 0	-1.0 -1.6	1.0 3.6	+1.6 0	-1.0 -2.0
1.97 – 3.15	0.4 1.2	+0.5 0	-0.4 -0.7	0.4 1.6	+0.7 0	-0.4 -0.9	1.2 3.1	+1.2 0	-1.2 -1.9	1.2 4.2	+1.8 0	-1.2 -2.4
3.15 – 4.73	0.5 1.5	+0.6 0	-0.5 -0.9	0.5 2.0	+0.9 0	-0.5 -1.1	1.4 3.7	+1.4 0	-1.4 -2.3	1.4 5.0	+2.2 0	-1.4 -2.8
4.73 – 7.09	0.6 1.8	+0.7 0	-0.6 -1.1	0.6 2.3	+1.0 0	-0.6 -1.3	1.6 4.2	+1.6 0	-1.6 -2.6	1.6 5.7	+2.5 0	-1.6 -3.2
7.09 – 9.85	0.6 2.0	+0.8 0	-0.6 -1.2	0.6 2.6	+1.2 0	-0.6 -1.4	2.0 5.0	+1.8 0	-2.0 -3.2	2.0 6.6	+2.8 0	-2.0 -3.8
9.85 – 12.41	0.8 2.3	+0.9 0	-0.8 -1.4	0.8 2.9	+1.2 0	-0.7 -1.6	2.5 5.7	+2.0 0	-2.5 -3.7	2.5 7.5	+3.0 0	-2.2 -4.2
12.41– 15.75	1.0 2.7	+1.0 0	-1.0 -1.7	1.0 3.4	+1.4 0	-0.7 -1.7	3.0 6.6	+2.2 0	-3.0 -4.4	3.0 8.7	+3.5 0	-2.5 -4.7
15.75– 19.69	1.2 3.0	+1.0 0	-1.2 -2.0	0.8 3.4	+1.6 0	-0.8 -1.8	4.0 8.1	+2.5 0	-4.0 -5.6	2.8 9.3	+4.0 0	-2.8 -5.3

USAS/ASME B4.1 – 1967 (R2004) Standard. For larger diameters, see the standard. ASME/ANSI
B18.3.5M – 1986 (R2002) Standard. Reprinted from the standard listed by permission of the American
Society of Mechanical Engineers. All rights reserved.

APPENDIX A (Continued)

Running and Sliding Fits – American National Standard

Basic Hole System, Limits are in thousandths of an inch.
Limits for hole and shaft are applied to the basic size to obtain
the limits of sizes for the parts.

Nominal size Range, Inches Over To	Class RC5			Class RC6			Class RC7			Class RC8			Class RC9		
	Limits of Clearance	Standard Limits		Limits of Clearance	Standard Limits		Limits of Clearance	Standard Limits		Limits of Clearance	Standard Limits		Limits of Clearance	Standard Limits	
		Hole H8	Shaft e7		Hole H9	Shaft e8		Hole H9	Shaft d8		Hole H10	Shaft C9		Hole H11	Shaft
0 – 0.12	0.6 1.6	+0.6 0	-0.6 -1.0	0.6 2.2	+1.0 0	+0.6 -1.2	1.0 2.6	+1.0 0	-1.0 -1.6	2.5 5.1	+1.6 0	-2.5 -3.5	4.0 8.1	+2.5 0	-4.0 -5.6
0.12 – 0.24	0.8 2.0	+0.7 0	-0.8 -1.3	0.8 2.7	+1.2 0	-0.8 -1.5	1.2 3.1	+1.2 0	-1.2 -1.9	2.8 5.8	+1.8 0	-2.8 -4.0	4.5 9.0	+3.0 0	-4.5 -6.0
0.24 – 0.40	1.0 2.5	+0.9 0	-1.0 -1.6	1.0 3.3	+1.4 0	-1.0 -1.9	1.6 3.9	+1.4 0	-1.6 -2.5	3.0 6.6	+2.2 0	-3.0 -4.4	5.0 10.7	+3.5 0	-5.0 -7.2
0.40 – 0.71	1.2 2.9	+1.0 0	-1.2 -1.9	1.2 3.8	+1.6 0	-1.2 -2.2	2.0 4.6	+1.6 0	-2.0 -3.0	3.5 7.9	+2.8 0	-3.5 -5.1	6.0 12.8	+4.0 0	-6.0 -8.8
0.71 – 1.19	1.6 3.6	+1.2 0	-1.6 -2.4	1.6 4.8	+2.0 0	-1.6 -2.8	2.5 5.7	+2.0 0	-2.5 -3.7	4.5 10.0	+3.5 0	-4.5 -6.5	7.0 15.5	+5.0 0	-7.0 -10.5
1.19 – 1.97	2.0 4.6	+1.6 0	-2.0 -3.0	2.0 6.1	+2.5 0	-2.0 -3.6	3.0 7.1	+2.5 0	-3.0 -4.6	5.0 11.5	+4.0 0	-5.0 -7.5	8.0 18.0	+6.0 0	-8.0 12.0
1.97 – 3.15	2.5 5.5	+1.8 0	-2.5 -3.7	2.5 7.3	+3.0 0	-2.5 -4.3	4.0 8.8	+3.0 0	-4.0 -5.8	6.0 13.5	+4.5 0	-6.0 -9.0	9.0 20.5	+7.0 0	-9.0 -13.5
3.15 – 4.73	3.0 6.6	+2.2 0	-3.0 -4.4	3.0 8.7	+3.5 0	-3.0 -5.2	5.0 10.7	+3.5 0	-5.0 -7.2	7.0 15.5	+5.0 0	-7.0 -10.5	10.0 24.0	+9.0 0	-10.0 -15.0
4.73 – 7.09	3.5 7.6	+2.5 0	-3.5 -5.1	3.5 10.0	+4.0 0	-3.5 -6.0	6.0 12.5	+4.0 0	-6.0 -8.5	8.0 18.0	+6.0 0	-8.0 -12.0	12.0 28.0	+10.0 0	-12.0 -18.0
7.09 – 9.85	4.0 8.6	+2.8 0	-4.0 -5.8	4.0 11.3	+4.5 0	-4.0 -6.8	7.0 14.3	+4.5 0	-7.0 -9.8	10.0 21.5	+7.0 0	-10.0 -14.5	15.0 34.0	+12.0 0	-15.0 -22.0
9.85–12.41	5.0 10.0	+3.0 0	-5.0 -7.0	5.0 13.0	+5.0 0	-5.0 -8.0	8.0 16.0	+5.0 0	-8.0 -11	12.0 25.0	+8.0 0	-12.0 -17.0	18.0 38.0	+12.0 0	-18.0 -26.0
12.41– 15.75	6.0 11.7	+3.5 0	-6.0 -8.2	6.0 15.5	+6.0 0	-6.0 -9.5	10.0 19.5	+6.0 0	-10 -13.5	14.0 29.0	+9.0 0	-14.0 -20.0	22.0 45.0	+14.0 0	-22.0 -31.0
15.75– 19.69	8.0 14.5	+4.0 0	-8.0 -10.5	8.0 18.0	+6.0 0	-8.0 -12.0	12.0 22.0	+6.0 0	-12.0 -16.0	16.0 32.0	+10.0 0	-16.0 -22.0	25.0 51.0	+16.0 0	-25.0 -35.0

APPENDIX B – METRIC LIMITS AND FITS

Hole Basis Clearance Fits

Preferred Hole Basis Clearance Fits. Dimensions in mm.

Basic Size		Loose Running		Free Running		Close Running		Sliding		Locational Clearance	
		Hole H11	Shaft c11	Hole H9	Shaft d9	Hole H8	Shaft f7	Hole H7	Shaft g6	Hole H7	Shaft h6
1	max	1.060	0.940	1.025	0.980	1.014	0.994	1.010	0.998	1.010	1.000
	min	1.000	0.880	1.000	0.955	1.000	0.984	1.000	0.992	1.000	0.994
1.2	max	1.260	0.940	1.225	1.180	1.214	1.194	1.210	1.198	1.210	1.200
	min	1.200	0.880	1.200	1.155	1.200	1.184	1.200	1.192	1.200	1.194
1.6	max	1.660	1.540	1.625	1.580	1.614	1.594	1.610	1.598	1.610	1.600
	min	1.600	1.480	1.600	1.555	1.600	1.584	1.600	1.592	1.600	1.594
2	max	2.060	1.940	2.025	1.980	2.014	1.994	2.010	1.998	2.010	2.000
	min	2.000	1.880	2.000	1.955	2.000	1.984	2.000	1.992	2.000	1.994
2.5	max	2.560	2.440	2.525	2.480	2.514	2.494	2.510	2.498	2.510	2.500
	min	2.500	2.380	2.500	2.455	2.500	2.484	2.500	2.492	2.500	2.494
3	max	3.060	2.940	3.025	2.980	3.014	2.994	3.010	2.998	3.010	3.000
	min	3.000	2.880	3.000	2.955	3.000	2.984	3.000	2.992	3.000	2.994
4	max	4.075	3.930	4.030	3.970	4.018	3.990	4.012	3.996	4.012	4.000
	min	4.000	3.855	4.000	3.940	4.000	3.987	4.000	3.988	4.000	3.992
5	max	5.075	4.930	5.030	4.970	5.018	4.990	5.012	4.998	5.012	5.000
	min	5.000	4.855	5.000	4.940	5.000	4.978	5.000	4.988	5.000	4.992
6	max	6.075	5.930	6.030	5.970	6.018	5.990	6.012	5.996	6.012	6.000
	min	6.000	5.855	6.000	5.940	6.000	5.978	6.000	5.988	6.000	5.992
8	max	8.090	7.920	8.036	7.960	8.022	7.987	8.015	7.995	8.015	8.000
	min	8.000	7.830	8.000	7.924	8.000	7.972	8.000	7.986	8.000	7.991
10	max	10.090	9.920	10.036	9.960	10.022	9.987	10.015	9.995	10.015	10.000
	min	10.000	9.830	10.000	9.924	10.000	9.972	10.000	9.986	10.000	9.991
12	max	12.110	11.905	12.043	11.950	12.027	11.984	12.018	11.994	12.018	12.000
	min	12.000	11.795	12.000	11.907	12.000	11.966	12.000	11.983	12.000	11.989
16	max	16.110	15.905	16.043	15.950	16.027	15.984	16.018	15.994	16.018	16.000
	min	16.000	15.795	16.000	15.907	16.000	15.966	16.000	15.983	16.000	15.989
20	max	20.130	19.890	20.052	19.935	20.033	19.980	20.021	19.993	20.021	20.000
	min	20.000	19.760	20.000	19.883	20.000	19.959	20.000	19.980	20.000	19.987
25	max	25.130	24.890	25.052	24.935	25.033	24.980	24.993	25.021	25.021	25.000
	min	25.000	24.760	25.000	24.883	25.000	24.959	24.980	25.000	25.000	24.987
30	max	30.130	29.890	30.052	29.935	30.033	29.980	30.021	29.993	30.021	30.000
	min	30.000	29.760	30.000	29.883	30.000	29.959	30.000	29.980	30.000	29.987
40	max	40.160	39.880	40.062	39.920	40.039	39.975	40.025	39.991	40.025	40.000
	min	40.000	39.720	40.000	39.858	40.000	39.950	40.000	39.975	40.000	39.984

APPENDIX B – METRIC LIMITS AND FITS (Continued)

Hole Basis Transition and Interference Fits

Preferred Hole Basis Clearance Fits. Dimensions in mm.

Basic Size		Locational Transition		Locational Transition		Locational Transition		Medium Drive		Force	
		Hole H7	Shaft k6	Hole H7	Shaft n6	Hole H7	Shaft p6	Hole H7	Shaft s6	Hole H7	Shaft u6
1	max	1.010	1.006	1.010	1.010	1.010	1.012	1.010	1.020	1.010	1.024
	min	1.000	1.000	1.000	1.004	1.000	1.006	1.000	1.014	1.000	1.018
1.2	max	1.210	1.206	1.210	1.210	1.210	1.212	1.210	1.220	1.210	1.224
	min	1.200	1.200	1.200	1.204	1.200	1.206	1.200	1.214	1.200	1.218
1.6	max	1.610	1.606	1.610	1.610	1.610	1.612	1.610	1.620	1.610	1.624
	min	1.600	1.600	1.600	1.604	1.600	1.606	1.600	1.614	1.600	1.618
2	max	2.010	2.006	2.010	2.020	2.010	2.012	2.010	2.020	2.010	2.024
	min	2.000	2.000	2.000	2.004	2.000	2.006	2.000	1.014	2.000	2.018
2.5	max	2.510	2.510	2.510	2.510	2.510	2.512	2.510	2.520	2.510	2.524
	min	2.500	2.500	2.500	2.504	2.500	2.506	2.500	2.514	2.500	2.518
3	max	3.010	3.010	3.010	3.010	3.010	3.012	3.010	3.020	3.010	3.024
	min	3.000	3.000	3.000	3.004	3.000	3.006	3.000	3.014	3.000	3.018
4	max	4.012	4.012	4.012	4.016	4.012	4.020	4.012	4.027	4.012	4.031
	min	4.000	4.000	4.000	4.008	4.000	4.012	4.000	4.019	4.000	4.023
5	max	5.012	5.009	5.012	5.016	5.012	5.020	5.012	5.027	5.012	5.031
	min	5.000	5.001	5.000	5.008	5.000	5.012	5.000	5.019	5.000	5.023
6	max	6.012	6.009	6.012	6.016	6.012	6.020	6.012	6.027	6.012	6.031
	min	6.000	6.001	6.000	6.008	6.000	6.012	6.000	6.019	6.000	6.023
8	max	8.015	8.010	8.015	8.019	8.015	8.024	8.015	8.032	8.015	8.037
	min	8.000	8.001	8.000	8.010	8.000	8.015	8.000	8.023	8.000	8.028
10	max	10.015	10.010	10.015	10.019	10.015	10.024	10.015	10.032	10.015	10.037
	min	10.000	10.001	10.000	10.010	10.000	10.015	10.000	10.023	10.000	10.028
12	max	12.018	12.012	12.018	12.023	12.018	12.029	12.018	12.039	12.018	12.044
	min	12.000	12.001	12.000	12.012	12.000	12.018	12.000	12.028	12.000	12.033
16	max	16.018	16.012	16.018	16.023	16.018	16.029	16.018	16.039	16.018	16.044
	min	16.000	16.001	16.000	16.012	16.000	16.018	16.000	16.028	16.000	16.033
20	max	20.021	20.015	20.021	20.028	20.021	20.035	20.021	20.048	20.021	20.054
	min	20.000	20.002	20.000	20.015	20.000	20.022	20.000	20.035	20.000	20.041
25	max	25.021	25.015	25.021	25.028	25.021	25.035	25.021	25.048	25.021	25.061
	min	25.000	25.002	25.000	25.015	25.000	25.022	25.000	25.035	25.000	25.048
30	max	30.021	30.015	30.021	30.028	30.021	30.035	30.021	30.048	30.021	30.061
	min	30.000	30.002	30.000	30.015	30.000	30.022	30.000	30.035	30.000	30.048
40	max	40.025	40.018	40.025	40.033	40.025	40.042	40.025	40.059	40.025	40.076
	min	40.000	40.002	40.000	40.017	40.000	40.026	40.000	40.043	40.000	40.060

APPENDIX B – METRIC LIMITS AND FITS (Continued)

Shaft Basis Clearance Fits

Preferred Shaft Basis Clearance Fits. Dimensions in mm.

Basic Size	Loose Running		Free Running		Close Running		Sliding		Locational Clearance	
	Hole C11	Shaft h11	Hole D9	Shaft h9	Hole F8	Shaft h7	Hole G7	Shaft h6	Hole H7	Shaft h6
1 max	1.120	1.000	1.045	1.000	1.020	1.000	1.012	1.000	1.010	1.000
min	1.060	0.940	1.020	0.975	1.006	0.990	1.002	0.994	1.000	0.994
1.2 max	1.320	1.200	1.245	1.200	1.220	1.200	1.212	1.200	1.210	1.200
min	1.260	1.140	1.220	1.175	1.206	1.190	1.202	1.194	1.200	1.194
1.6 max	1.720	1.600	1.645	1.600	1.620	1.600	1.612	1.600	1.610	1.600
min	1.660	1.540	1.620	1.575	1.606	1.590	1.602	1.594	1.600	1.594
2 max	2.120	2.000	2.045	2.000	2.020	2.000	2.012	2.000	2.010	2.000
min	2.060	1.940	2.020	1.975	2.006	1.990	2.002	1.994	2.000	1.994
2.5 max	2.620	2.500	2.545	2.500	2.520	2.500	2.512	2.500	2.510	2.500
min	2.560	2.440	2.520	2.475	2.506	2.490	2.502	2.494	2.500	2.494
3 max	3.120	3.000	3.045	3.000	3.020	3.000	3.012	3.000	3.010	3.000
min	3.060	2.940	3.020	2.975	3.006	2.990	3.002	2.994	3.000	2.994
4 max	4.145	4.000	4.060	4.000	4.028	4.000	4.016	4.000	4.012	4.000
min	4.070	3.925	4.030	3.970	4.010	3.988	4.004	3.992	4.000	3.992
5 max	5.145	5.000	5.060	5.000	5.028	5.000	5.016	5.000	5.012	5.000
min	5.070	4.925	5.030	4.970	5.010	4.988	5.004	4.992	5.000	4.992
6 max	6.145	6.000	6.060	6.000	6.028	6.000	6.016	6.000	6.012	6.000
min	6.070	5.925	6.030	5.970	6.010	5.988	6.004	5.992	6.000	5.992
8 max	8.170	8.000	8.076	8.000	8.035	8.000	8.020	8.000	8.015	8.000
min	8.080	7.910	8.040	7.964	8.013	7.985	8.005	7.991	8.000	7.991
10 max	10.170	10.000	10.076	10.000	10.035	10.000	10.020	10.000	10.015	10.000
min	10.080	9.910	10.040	9.964	10.013	9.985	10.005	9.991	10.000	9.991
12 max	12.205	12.000	12.093	12.000	12.043	12.000	12.024	12.000	12.018	12.000
min	12.095	11.890	12.050	11.957	12.016	11.982	12.006	11.989	12.000	11.989
16 max	16.205	16.000	16.093	16.000	16.043	16.000	16.024	16.000	16.018	16.000
min	16.095	15.890	16.050	15.957	16.016	15.982	16.006	15.989	16.000	15.989
20 max	20.240	20.000	20.117	20.000	20.053	20.000	20.028	20.000	20.021	20.000
min	20.110	19.870	20.065	19.948	20.020	19.979	20.007	19.987	20.000	19.987
25 max	25.240	25.000	25.117	25.000	25.053	25.000	25.028	25.000	25.021	25.000
min	25.110	24.870	25.065	24.948	25.020	24.979	25.007	24.987	25.000	24.987
30 max	30.240	30.000	30.117	30.000	30.053	30.000	30.028	30.000	30.021	30.000
min	30.110	29.870	30.065	29.948	30.020	29.979	30.007	29.987	30.000	29.987
40 max	40.280	40.000	40.142	40.000	40.064	40.000	40.034	40.000	40.025	40.000
min	40.120	39.840	40.080	39.938	40.025	39.975	40.009	39.984	40.000	39.984

APPENDIX B - METRIC LIMITS AND FITS (Continued)

Shaft Basis Transition and Interference Fits

Preferred Shaft Basis Transition and Interference Fits. Dimensions in mm.

Basic Size	Locational Transition		Locational Transition		Locational Interference		Medium Drive		Force	
	Hole K7	Shaft h6	Hole N7	Shaft h6	Hole P7	Shaft h6	Hole S7	Shaft h6	Hole U7	Shaft h6
1 max	1.000	1.000	0.996	1.000	0.994	1.000	0.986	1.000	0.982	1.000
min	0.990	0.994	0.986	0.994	0.984	0.994	0.976	0.994	0.972	0.994
1.2 max	1.200	1.200	1.196	1.200	1.194	1.200	1.186	1.200	1.182	1.200
min	1.190	1.194	1.186	1.194	1.184	1.194	1.176	1.194	1.172	1.194
1.6 max	1.600	1.600	1.596	1.600	1.594	1.600	1.586	1.600	1.582	1.600
min	1.590	1.594	1.586	1.594	1.584	1.594	1.576	1.594	1.572	1.594
2 max	2.000	2.000	1.996	2.000	1.994	2.000	1.986	2.000	1.982	2.000
min	1.990	1.994	1.986	1.994	1.984	1.994	1.976	1.994	1.972	1.994
2.5 max	2.500	2.500	2.496	2.500	2.494	2.500	2.486	2.500	2.482	2.500
min	2.490	2.494	2.486	2.494	2.484	2.494	2.476	2.494	2.472	2.494
3 max	3.000	3.000	2.996	3.000	2.994	3.000	2.986	3.000	2.982	3.000
min	2.990	2.994	2.986	2.994	2.984	2.994	2.976	2.994	2.972	2.994
4 max	4.003	4.000	3.996	4.000	3.992	4.000	3.985	4.000	3.981	4.000
min	3.991	5.992	3.984	5.992	3.980	5.992	3.973	5.992	3.969	5.992
5 max	5.003	5.000	4.996	5.000	4.992	5.000	4.985	5.000	4.981	5.000
min	4.991	4.992	4.984	4.992	4.980	4.992	4.973	4.992	4.969	4.992
6 max	6.003	6.000	5.996	6.000	5.992	6.000	5.985	6.000	5.981	6.000
min	5.991	5.992	5.984	5.992	5.980	5.992	5.973	5.992	5.969	5.992
8 max	8.005	8.000	7.996	8.000	7.991	8.000	7.983	8.000	7.978	8.000
min	7.990	7.991	7.981	7.991	7.976	7.991	7.968	7.991	7.963	7.991
10 max	10.005	10.000	9.996	10.000	9.991	10.000	9.983	10.000	9.978	10.000
min	9.990	9.991	9.981	9.991	9.976	9.991	9.968	9.991	9.963	9.991
12 max	12.006	12.000	11.995	12.000	11.989	12.000	11.979	12.000	11.974	12.000
min	11.988	11.989	11.977	11.989	11.971	11.989	11.961	11.989	11.956	11.989
16 max	16.006	16.000	15.995	16.000	15.989	16.000	15.979	16.000	15.974	16.000
min	15.988	15.989	15.977	15.989	15.971	15.989	15.961	15.989	15.956	15.989
20 max	20.006	20.000	19.993	20.000	19.986	20.000	19.973	20.000	19.967	20.000
min	19.985	19.987	19.972	19.987	19.965	19.987	19.952	19.987	19.946	19.987
25 max	25.006	25.000	24.993	25.000	24.986	25.000	24.973	25.000	24.960	25.000
min	24.985	24.987	24.972	24.987	24.965	24.987	24.952	24.987	24.939	24.987
30 max	30.006	30.000	29.993	30.000	29.986	30.000	29.973	30.000	29.960	30.000
min	29.985	29.987	29.972	29.987	29.965	29.987	29.952	29.987	29.939	29.987
40 max	40.007	40.000	39.992	40.000	39.983	40.000	39.966	40.000	39.949	40.000
min	39.982	39.984	39.967	39.984	39.958	39.984	39.941	39.984	39.924	39.984

APPENDIX C – UNIFIED NATIONAL THREAD FORM

(External Threads) Approximate Minor diameter = D – 1.0825P   P = Pitch

Nominal Size, in.	Basic Major Diameter (D)	Coarse UNC		Fine UNF		Extra Fine UNEF	
		Thds. Per in.	Tap Drill Dia.	Thds Per in.	Tap Drill. Dia.	Thds. Per in.	Tap Drill Dia.
#0	0.060	...	...	80	3/64	...	...
#1	0.0730	64	0.0595	72	0.0595	...	...
#2	0.0860	56	0.0700	64	0.0700	...	...
#3	0.0990	48	0.0785	56	0.0820	...	...
#4	0.1120	40	0.0890	48	0.0935	...	...
#5	0.1250	40	0.1015	44	0.1040	...	...
#6	0.1380	32	0.1065	40	0.1130	...	...
#8	0.1640	32	0.1360	36	0.1360	...	...
#10	0.1900	24	0.1495	32	0.1590	...	...
#12	0.2160	24	0.1770	28	0.1820	32	0.1850
1/4	0.2500	20	0.2010	28	0.2130	32	7/32
5/16	0.3125	18	0.257	24	0.272	32	9/32
3/8	0.3750	16	5/16	24	0.332	32	11/32
7/16	0.4375	14	0.368	20	25/64	28	13/32
1/2	0.5000	13	27/64	20	29/64	28	15/32
9/16	0.5625	12	31/64	18	33/64	24	33/64
5/8	0.6250	11	17/32	18	37/64	24	37/64
11/16	0.675	...	...	...	...	24	41/64
3/4	0.7500	10	21/32	16	11/16	20	45/64
13/16	0.8125	...	...	...	...	20	49/64
7/8	0.8750	9	49/64	14	13/16	20	53/64
15/16	0.9375	...	...	...	...	20	57/64
1	1.0000	8	7/8	12	59/64	20	61/64
1 1/8	1.1250	7	63/64	12	1 3/64	18	1 5/64
1 1/4	1.2500	7	1 7/64	12	1 11/64	18	1 3/16
1 3/8	1.3750	6	1 7/32	12	1 19/64	18	1 5/16
1 1/2	1.5000	6	1 11/32	12	1 27/64	18	1 7/16
1 5/8	1.6250	...	...	...	...	18	1 9/16
1 3/4	1.7500	5	1 9/16	...	...	...	...
1 7/8	1.8750	...	...	...	...	...	...
2	2.0000	4 1/2	1 25/32	...	...	...	...
2 1/4	2.2500	4 1/2	2 1/32	...	...	...	...
2 1/2	2.5000	4	2 1/4	...	...	...	...
2 3/4	2.7500	4	2 1/2	...	...	...	...

APPENDIX D – METRIC THREAD FORM

(External Threads) Approximate Minor diameter = D – 1.2075P   P = Pitch
Preferred sizes for commercial threads and fasteners are shown in boldface type.

Coarse (general purpose)		Fine	
Nominal Size & Thread Pitch	Tap Drill Diameter, mm	Nominal Size & Thread Pitch	Tap Drill Diameter, mm
M1.6 x 0.35	1.25	---	---
M1.8 x 0.35	1.45	---	---
M2 x 0.4	1.6	---	---
M2.2 x 0.45	1.75	---	---
M2.5 x 0.45	2.05	---	---
M3 x 0.5	2.5	---	---
M3.5 x 0.6	2.9	---	---
M4 x 0.7	3.3	---	---
M4.5 x 0.75	3.75	---	---
M5 x 0.8	4.2	---	---
M6 x 1	5.0	---	---
M7 x 1	6.0	---	---
M8 x 1.25	6.8	**M8 x 1**	7.0
M9 x 1.25	7.75	---	---
M10 x 1.5	8.5	**M10 x 1.25**	8.75
M11 x 1.5	9.50	---	---
M12 x 1.75	10.30	**M12 x 1.25**	10.5
M14 x 2	12.00	**M14 x 1.5**	12.5
M16 x 2	14.00	**M16 x 1.5**	14.5
M18 x 2.5	15.50	**M18 x 1.5**	16.5
M20 x 2.5	17.5	**M20 x 1.5**	18.5
M22 x 2.5[*]	19.5	**M22 x 1.5**	20.5
M24 x 3	21.0	**M24 x 2**	22.0
M27 x 3[*]	24.0	**M27 x 2**	25.0
M30 x 3.5	26.5	**M30 x 2**	28.0
M33 x 3.5	29.5	M33 x 2	31.0
M36 x 4	32.0	**M36 x 2**	33.0
M39 x 4	35.0	M39 x 2	36.0
M42 x 4.5	37.5	**M42 x 2**	39.0
M45 x 4.5	40.5	M45 x 1.5	42.0
M48 x 5	43.0	**M48 x 2**	45.0
M52 x 5	47.0	M52 x 2	49.0
M56 x 5.5	50.5	**M56 x 2**	52.0
M60 x 5.5	54.5	M60 x 1.5	56.0
M64 x 6	58.0	**M64 x 2**	60.0
M68 x 6	62.0	M68 x 2	64.0
M72 x 6	66.0	**M72 x 2**	68.0
M80 x 6	74.0	**M80 x 2**	76.0
M90 x 6	84.0	**M90 x 2**	86.0
M100 x 6	94.0	**M100 x 2**	96.0

[*]Only for high strength structural steel fasteners
ASME B1.13M – 2001 Standard. Reprinted from the standard listed by permission of the American Society of Mechanical Engineers. All rights reserved.

APPENDIX E – FASTENERS (INCH SERIES)

Important! All fastener dimensions have a tolerance; each dimension has a maximum and minimum value. Only one size for each dimension is given in this appendix. Refer to the standards noted for the complete listing of values.

Regular Hex Head Bolts

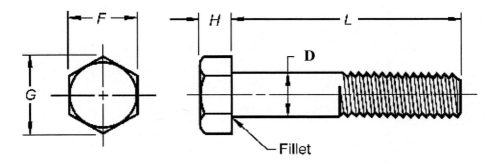

Size (D)	Head Height Basic	Width Across Flats Basic Adjust to sixteenths	Width Across Corners Max.	Thread Length	
				6 in. or shorter	Over 6 in.
1/4	H = 0.625 D + 0.016	F = 1.500 D + 0.062		0.75	1.00
5/16 – 7/16	H = 0.625 D + 0.016			1.00	1.25
1/2 – 7/8	H = 0.625 D + 0.031		G = 1.1547 F	1.25	1.50
1 – 1 7/8	H = 0.625 D + 0.062	F = 1.500 D		2.50	2.75
2 – 3 3/4	H = 0.625 D + 0.125			5.25	5.50
4	H = 0.25 D + 0.188			6.25	6.50

- Radius of Fillet: D less than ½ in.: R 0.01~0.03,
  D larger than ½ in. but less than 1 in.: R 0.02~0.06
  D larger than 1 in.: R 0.03~0.09

Heavy Hex Head Bolts

Size (D)	Head Height Basic[*]	Width Across Flats Basic Adjust to sixteenth	Width Across Corners Max.
1/2 – 3	Same as for regular hex head bolts.	F = 1.500 D + 0.125	Max. G =1.1547 F

[*]Size to 1 in. adjusted to sixty-fourths. 1 1/8 through 2 1/2 in. sizes adjusted upward to thirty-seconds. 2 3/4 thru 4 in. sizes adjusted upward to sixteenths.

ASME B18.2.1 - 1996 Standard. Reprinted from the standard listed by permission of the American Society of Mechanical Engineers. All rights reserved.

APPENDIX E – FASTENERS (INCH SERIES) Continued

Hex Nuts and Hex Jam Nuts

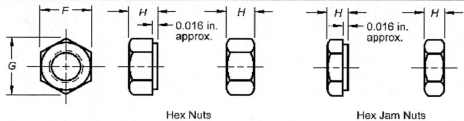

Hex Nuts   Hex Jam Nuts

Nut Size (D)	Nut Thickness Basic	Width Across Flats Basic (Adjust to Sixteenths)	Width Across Corners (Max.)
1/4	H = 0.875D	F=1.500 D + 0.062	Max. G = 1.1547 F
5/6 – 5/8	H = 0.875D		
3/4 – 1 1/8	H = 0.875D – 0.016	F = 1.500 D	
1 1/4 – 1 1/2	H = 0.875D – 0.031		

Hex Thick Nuts

Nut Size (D)	Width Across Flats Basic (Adjust to Sixteenths)	Width Across Corners (Max.)	Nut Thickness Basic
¼	F = 1.500 D + 0.062	Max. G = 1.1547 F	See Table
5/6 – 5/8	F = 1.500 D		
3/4 – 1 ½	F = 1.500 D		

Nut Size (D)	1/4	5/16	3/8	7/16	1/2	9/16	5/8
Nut Thickness Basic	9/32	21/64	13/32	29/64	9/16	39/64	23/32

Nut Size (D)	3/4	7/8	1	1 1/8	1 1/4	1 3/8	1 1/2
Nut Thickness Basic	13/16	29/32	1	1 5/32	1 1/4	1 3/8	1 1/2

Hex Jam Nut

Nut Size (D)	Nut Thickness Basic	Width Across Flats Basic (Adjust to Sixteenths)	Width Across Corners (Max.)
1/4	See Table	F=1.500 D + 0.062	Max. G = 1.1547 F
5/6 – 5/8	See Table		
3/4 – 1 1/8	H = 0.500D – 0.047	F = 1.500 D	
1 1/4 – 1 1/2	H = 0.500D – 0.094		

Nut Size (D)	1/4	5/16	3/8	7/16	1/2	9/16	5/8
Nut Thickness Basic	5/32	3/16	7/32	1/4	5/16	5/16	3/8

APPENDIX E – FASTENERS (INCH SERIES) Continued

Hexagon and Spline Socket Head Cap Screws

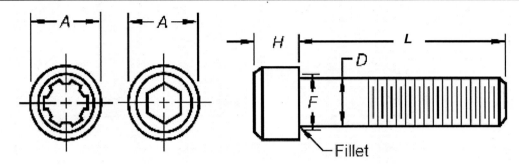

Screw Size (D)	Head Diameter	Head Height
# 0 –- # 10	See Table	Max. H = D
1/4 – 1 1/2	Max. A = 1.50 D	

Screw Size (D)	# 0	# 1	# 2	# 3	# 4	#5	# 6	# 8	# 10
Max. Head Diameter	0.096	0.018	0.140	0.161	0.183	0.205	0.226	0.270	0.312

Hexagon and Spline Socket Flat Countersunk Head Cap Screws

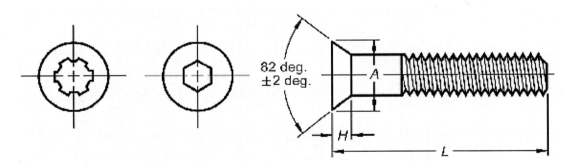

Screw Size (D)	Head Diameter (A) Theor. Sharp	Head Height (H)
# 0 –- # 10	See Table	
# 4 –- 3/8	Max. A = 2 D + 0.031	Max.H = 0.5 (Max. A – D) x cot(41°)
7/16	Max. A = 2 D – 0.031	
1/2 – 1 1/2	Max. A = 2 D – 0.062	

APPENDIX E – FASTENERS (INCH SERIES) Continued

Drill and Counterbore Sizes for Socket Head Cap Screws

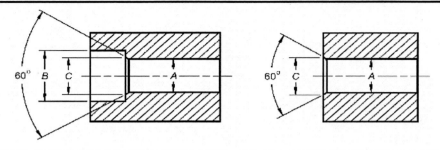

Nominal Size of Screw (D)	Nominal Drill Size (A)		Counterbore Diameter (B)	Countersink (C)
	Close Fit	Normal Fit		
#0 (0.0600)	(#51) 0.067	(#49) 0.073	1/8	0.074
#1 (0.0730)	(#46) 0.081	(#43) 0.089	5/32	0.087
#2 (0.0860)	3/32	(#36) 0.106	3/16	0.102
#3 (0.0990)	(#36) 0.106	(#31) 0.120	7/32	0.115
#4 (0.1120)	1/8	(#29) 0.136	7/32	0.130
#5 (0.1250)	9/64	(#23) 0.154	1/4	0.145
#6 (0.1380)	(#23) 0.154	(#18) 0.170	9/32	0.158
#8 (0.1640)	(#15) 0.180	(#10) 0.194	5/16	0.188
#10 (0.1900)	(#5) 0.206	(#2) 0.221	3/8	0.218
1/4	17/64	9/32	7/16	0.278
5/16	21/64	11/32	17/32	0.346
3/8	25/64	13/32	5/8	0.415
7/16	29/64	15/32	23/32	0.483
1/2	33/64	17/32	13/16	0.552
5/8	41/64	21/32	1	0.689
3/4	49/64	25/32	1 3/16	0.828
7/8	57/64	29/32	1 3/8	0.963
1	1 1/64	1 1/32	1 5/8	1.100
1 1/4	1 9/32	1 5/16	2	1.370
1 1/2	1 17/32	1 9/16	2 3/8	1.640
1 3/4	1 25/32	1 13/16	2 3/4	1.910
2	2 1/32	2 1/16	3 1/8	2.180

(1) Countersink. It is considered good practice to countersink or break the edges of holes that are smaller than F (max.) in parts having a hardness which approaches, equals, or exceeds the screw hardness. The countersink or corner relief, however, should not be larger than is necessary to insure that the fillet on the screw is cleared. Normally, the diameter of countersink does not have to exceed F (max.). Countersinks or corner reliefs in excess of this diameter reduce the effective bearing area and introduce the possibility of imbedment or brinnelling or flaring of the heads of the screws.

(2) Close Fit. The close fit is normally limited to holes for those lengths of screws that are threaded to the head in assemblies where only one screw is to be used or where two or more screws are to be used and the mating holes are to be produced either at assembly or by matched and coordinated tooling.

(3) Normal Fit. The normal fit is intended for screws of relatively long length or for assemblies involving two or more screws where the mating holes are to be produced by conventional tolerancing methods. It provides for the maximum allowable eccentricity of the longest standard screws and for certain variations in the parts to be fastened, such as: deviations in hole straightness, angularity between the axis of the tapped hole and that of the hole for the shank, differences in center distances of the mating holes, etc.

ASME B18.3 -2003 Standard. Reprinted from the standard listed by permission of the American Society of Mechanical Engineers. All rights reserved.

APPENDIX E – FASTENERS (INCH SERIES) Continued

Slotted Flat Countersunk Head Cap Screws

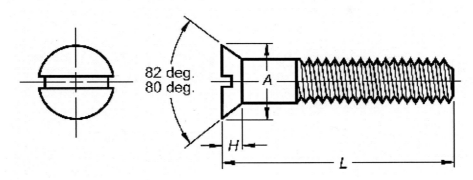

Screw Size (D)	Head Diameter (A) Theor. Sharp	Head Height (H)
1/4 through 3/8	Max. A = 2.000 D	Max. H = 0.596 D
7/16	Max. A = 2.000 D – 0.063	Max. H = 0.596 D – 0.0375
1/4 through 3/8	Max. A = 2.000 D – 0.125	Max. H = 0.596 D – 0.075
1 1/8 through 1 1/2	Max. A = 2.000 D – 0.188	Max. H = 0.596 D – 0.112

ASME B18.6.2 – 1998 Standard. Reprinted from the standard listed by permission of the American Society of Mechanical Engineers. All rights reserved.

Slotted Round Head Cap Screws

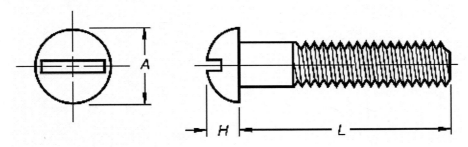

Screw Size (D)	Head Diameter (A) Theor. Sharp	Head Height (H)
1/4 through 5/16	Max. A = 2.000 D – 0.063	Max. H = 0.875 D – 0.028
3/8 through 7/16	Max. A = 2.000 D – 0.125	Max. H = 0.875 D – 0.055
1/2 through 9/16	Max. A = 2.000 D – 0.1875	Max. H = 0.875 D – 0.083
5/8 through 3/4	Max. A = 2.000 D – 0.250	Max. H = 0.875 D – 0.110

ASME B18.6.2 – 1998 Standard. Reprinted from the standard listed by permission of the American Society of Mechanical Engineers. All rights reserved.

APPENDIX E – FASTENERS (INCH SERIES) Continued

Preferred Sizes of Type A Plain Washers

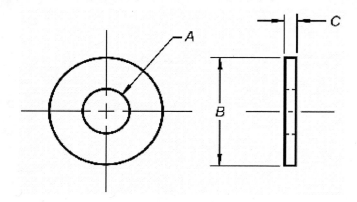

Nominal Washer Size *	Inside Diameter (A) Basic	Outside Diameter (B) Basic	Thickness (C)	Nominal Washer Size *	Inside Diameter (A) Basic	Outside Diameter (B) Basic	Thickness (C)
	0.078	0.188	0.020	1 N	1.062	2.000	0.134
	0.094	0.250	0.020	1 W	1.062	2.500	0.165
	0.125	0.312	0.032	1 1/8 N	1.250	2.250	0.134
#6 (0.138)	0.156	0.375	0.049	1 1/8 W	1.250	2.750	0.165
#8 (0.164)	0.188	0.438	0.049	1 1/4 N	1.375	2.500	0.165
#10 (0.190)	0.219	0.500	0.049	1 1/4 W	1.375	3.000	0.165
3/16	0.250	0.562	0.049	1 3/8 N	1.500	2.750	0.165
#12 (0.216)	0.250	0.562	0.065	1 3/8 W	1.500	3.250	0.180
1/4 N	0.281	0.625	0.065	1 1/2 N	1.625	3.000	0.165
1/4 W	0.312	0.734	0.065	1 1/2 W	1.625	3.500	0.180
5/16 N	0.344	0.688	0.065	1 5/8	1.750	3.750	0.180
5/16 W	0.375	0.875	0.083	1 3/4	1.875	4.000	0.180
3/8 N	0.406	0.812	0.065	1 7/8	2.000	4.250	0.180
3/8 W	0.438	1.000	0.083	2	2.125	4.500	0.180
7/16 N	0.469	0.922	0.065	2 1/4	2.375	4.750	0.220
7/16 W	0.500	1.250	0.083	2 1/2	2.625	5.000	0.238
1/2 N	0.531	1.062	0.095	2 3/4	2.875	5.250	0.259
1/2 W	0.562	1.375	0.109	3	3.125	5.500	0.284
9/16 N	0.594	1.156	0.095				
9/16 W	0.625	1.469	0.109				
5/8 N	0.656	1.312	0.095				
5/8 W	0.688	1.750	0.134				
3/4 N	0.812	1.469	0.134				
3/4 W	0.812	2.000	0.148				
7/8 N	0.938	1.750	0.134				
7/8 W	0.938	2.250	0.165				

*Nominal washer sizes are intended for use with comparable nominal screw or bolt sizes.
ANSI B18.22.1 - 1965 (R2003) Standard. Reprinted from the standard listed by permission of the American Society of Mechanical Engineers. All rights reserved.

APPENDIX E – FASTENERS (INCH SERIES) Continued

Regular Helical Spring-Lock Washers

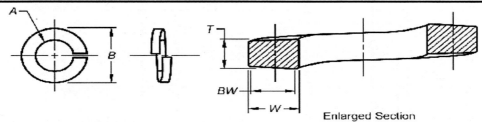

Enlarged Section

Nominal Washer Size	Min. Inside Diameter (A)	Max. Outside Diameter (B)	Mean Section Thickness (T)	Min. Section Width (W)	Min. Bearing Width (BW)
#2 (0.086)	0.088	0.172	0.020	0.035	0.024
#3 (0.099)	0.101	0.195	0.025	0.040	0.028
#4 (0.112)	0.114	0.209	0.025	0.040	0.028
#5 (0.125)	0.127	0.236	0.031	0.047	0.033
#6 (.0138)	0.141	0.250	0.031	0.047	0.033
#8 (0.164)	0.167	0.293	0.040	0.055	0.038
#10 (0.190)	0.193	0.334	0.047	0.062	0.043
#12 (0.216)	0.220	0.377	0.056	0.070	0.049
1/4	0.252	0.487	0.062	0.109	0.076
5/16	0.314	0.583	0.078	0.125	0.087
3/8	0.377	0.680	0.094	0.141	0.099
7/16	0.440	0.776	0.109	0.156	0.109
1/2	0.502	0.869	0.125	0.171	0.120
9/16	0.564	0.965	0.141	0.188	0.132
5/8	0.628	1.073	0.156	0.203	0.142
11/16	0.691	1.170	0.172	0.219	0.153
3/4	0.753	1.265	0.188	0.234	0.164
13/16	0.816	1.363	0.203	0.250	0.175
7/8	0.787	1.459	0.219	0.266	0.186
15/16	0.941	1.556	0.234	0.281	0.197
1	1.003	1.656	0.250	0.297	0.208
1 1/16	1.066	1.751	0.266	0.312	0.218
1 1/8	1.129	1.847	0.281	0.328	0.230
1 3/16	1.192	1.943	0.297	0.344	0.241
1 1/4	1.254	2.036	0.312	0.359	0.251
1 5/16	1.317	2.133	0.328	0.375	0.262
1 3/8	1.379	2.219	0.344	0.391	0.274
1 7/16	1.442	2.324	0.359	0.406	0.284
1 1/2	1.504	2.419	0.375	0.422	0.295
1 5/8	1.633	2.553	0.389	0.424	0.297
1 3/4	1.758	2.679	0.389	0.424	0.297
1 7/8	1.883	2.811	0.422	0.427	0.299
2	2.008	2.936	0.422	0.427	0.299
2 1/4	2.262	3.221	0.440	0.442	0.309
2 1/2	2.512	3.471	0.440	0.422	0.309
2 3/4	2.762	3.824	0.458	0.491	0.344
3	3.012	4.074	0.458	0.491	0.344

APPENDIX F – METRIC FASTENERS

Metric Hex Bolts

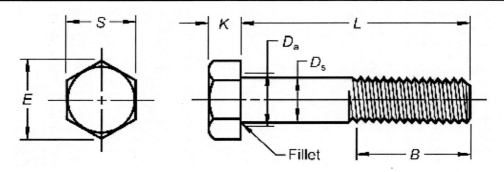

D	Ds	S	E	K	Da	Thread Length (B)		
Nominal Bolt Diameter And Thread Pitch	Max. Body Dia.	Max. Width Across Flats	Max. Width Across Corners	Max. Head Height	Fillet Transition Diameter	Bolt Lengths ≤ 125	Bolt Lengths > 125 and ≤ 200	Bolt Lengths >200
M5 x 0.8	5.48	8.00	9.24	3.88	5.7	16	22	35
M6 x 1	6.19	10.00	11.55	4.38	6.8	18	24	37
M8 x 1.25	8.58	13.00	15.01	5.68	9.2	22	28	41
M10 x 1.5	10.58	16.00	18.48	6.85	11.2	26	32	45
M12 x 1.75	12.70	18.00	20.78	7.95	13.7	30	36	49
M14 x 2	14.70	21.00	24.25	9.25	15.7	34	40	53
M16 x 2	16.70	24.00	27.71	10.75	17.7	38	44	57
M20 x 2.5	20.84	30.00	34.64	13.40	22.4	46	52	65
M24 x 3	24.84	36.00	41.57	15.90	26.4	54	60	73
M30 x 3.5	30.84	46.00	53.12	19.75	33.4	66	72	85
M36 x 4	37.00	55.00	63.51	23.55	39.4	78	84	97
M42 x 4.5	43.00	65.00	75.06	27.05	45.4	90	96	109
M48 x 5	49.00	75.00	86.60	31.07	52.0	102	108	121
M56 x 5.5	57.00	85.00	98.15	36.20	62.0		124	137
M64 x 6	65.52	95.00	109.70	41.32	70.0		140	153
M72 x 6	73.84	105.00	121.24	46.45	78.0		156	169
M80 x 6	82.16	115.00	132.79	51.58	86.0		172	185
M90 x 6	92.48	130.00	150.11	57.74	96.0		192	205
M100 x 6	102.80	145.00	167.43	63.90	107.0		212	225

ASME B18.3 - 2003 Standard. Reprinted from the standard listed by permission of the American Society of Mechanical Engineers. All rights reserved.

APPENDIX F – METRIC FASTENERS (Continued)

Drill and Counterbore Sizes for Socket Head Cap Screws

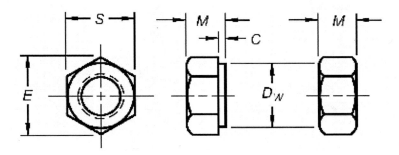

D	S	E	M	DW	C
Nominal Bolt Diameter and Thread Pitch	Max. Width Across Flats	Max. Width Across Corners	Max. Thickness	Min. Bearing Face Diameter	Max. Washer Face Thickness
M1.6 x 0.35	3.20	3.70	1.30	2.3	
M2 x 0.4	4.00	4.62	1.60	3.1	
M2.5 x 0.45	5.00	5.77	2.00	4.1	
M3 x 0.5	5.50	6.35	2.40	4.6	
M3.5 x 0.6	6.00	6.93	2.80	5.1	
M4 x 0.7	7.00	8.08	3.20	6.0	
M5 x 0.8	8.00	9.24	4.70	7.0	
M6 x 1	10.00	11.55	5.20	8.9	
M8 x 1.25	13.00	15.01	6.80	11.6	
M10 x 1.5	15.00	17.32	9.10	13.6	
M10 x 1.5	16.00	18.45	8.40	14.6	
M12 x 1.75	18.00	20.78	10.80	16.6	
M14 x 2	21.00	24.25	12.80	19.4	
M16 x 2	24.00	27.71	14.80	22.4	
M20 x 2.5	30.00	34.64	18.00	27.9	0.8
M24 x 3	36.00	41.57	21.50	32.5	0.8
M30 x 3.5	46.00	53.12	25.60	42.5	0.8
M36 x 4	55.00	63.51	31.00	50.8	0.8

APPENDIX F – METRIC FASTENERS (Continued)

Metric Socket Head Cap Screws

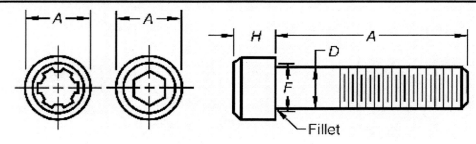

Screw Size (D)	Head Diameter (A)	Head Height (H)
1.6 through 2.5	See Table	
3 through 8	Max. A = 1.5 D + 1	Max. H = D
> 10	Max. A = 1.5 D	

Screw Size (D)	1.6	2	2.5
Max. Head Diameter (A)	3.00	3.80	4.50

ASME/ANSI B18.3.1M - 1986 (R2002) Standard. Reprinted from the standard listed by permission of the American Society of Mechanical Engineers. All rights reserved.

Metric Countersunk Socket Head Cap Screws

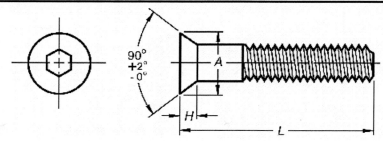

Basic Screw Diameter and Thread Pitch	Head Diameter (A) Theor. Sharp	Head Height (H)
M3 x 0.5	6.72	1.86
M4 x 0.7	8.96	2.48
M5 x 0.8	11.20	3.10
M6 x 1	13.44	3.72
M8 x 1.25	17.92	4.96
M10 x 1.5	22.40	6.20
M12 x 1.75	26.88	7.44
M14 x 2	30.24	8.12
M16 x 2	33.60	8.80
M20 x 2.5	40.32	10.16

ASME/ANSI B18.3.5M - 1986 (R2002) Standard. Reprinted from the standard listed by permission of the American Society of Mechanical Engineers. All rights reserved.

APPENDIX F – METRIC FASTENERS (Continued)

Drill and Counterbore Sizes for Socket Head Cap Screws

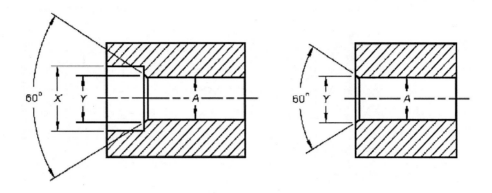

Nominal Size or Basic Screw Diameter	A		X	Y
	Nominal Drill Size		Counterbore Diameter	Countersink Diameter
	Close Fit	Normal Fit		
M1.6	1.80	1.95	3.50	2.0
M2	2.20	2.40	4.40	2.6
M2.5	2.70	3.00	5.40	3.1
M3	3.40	3.70	6.50	3.6
M4	4.40	4.80	8.25	4.7
M5	5.40	5.80	9.75	5.7
M6	6.40	6.80	11.25	6.8
M8	8.40	8.80	14.25	9.2
M10	10.50	10.80	17.25	11.2
M12	12.50	12.80	19.25	14.2
M14	14.50	14.75	22.25	16.2
M16	16.50	16.75	25.50	18.2
M20	20.50	20.75	31.50	22.4
M24	24.50	24.75	37.50	26.4
M30	30.75	31.75	47.50	33.4
M36	37.00	37.50	56.50	39.4
M42	43.00	44.00	66.00	45.6
M48	49.00	50.00	75.00	52.6

APPENDIX F – METRIC FASTENERS (Continued)

Drill and Countersink Sizes for Flat Countersunk Head Cap Screws

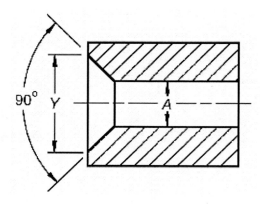

D	A	Y
Nominal Screw Size	Nominal Hole Diameter	Min. Countersink Diameter
M3	3.5	6.72
M4	4.6	8.96
M5	6.0	11.20
M6	7.0	13.44
M8	9.0	17.92
M10	11.5	22.40
M12	13.5	26.88
M14	16.0	30.24
M16	18.0	33.60
M20	22.4	40.32

ASME/ANSI B18.3.5M - 1986 (R2002) Standard. Reprinted from the standard listed by permission of the American Society of Mechanical Engineers. All rights reserved.

APPENDIX G – FASTENERS

BOLT AND SCREW CLEARANCE HOLES

(1) Inch Clearance Holes

Nominal Screw Size	Fit Classes		
	Normal	Close	Loose
	Nominal Drill Size		
#0 (0.06)	#48 (0.0760)	#51 (0.0670)	3/32
#1 (0.073)	#43 (0.0890)	#46 (0.0810)	#37 (0.1040)
#2 (0.086)	#38 (0.1015)	3/32	#32 (0.1160)
#3 (0.099)	#32 (0.1160)	#36 (0.1065)	#30 (0.1285)
#4 (0.112)	#30 (0.1285)	#31 (0.1200)	#27 (0.1440)
#5 (0.125)	5/32	9/64	11/64
#6 (0.138)	#18 (0.1695)	#23 (0.1540)	#13 (0.1850)
#8 (0.164)	#9 (0.1960)	#15 (0.1800)	#3 (0.2130)
#10 (0.190)	#2 (0.2210)	#5 (0.2055)	B (0.238)
1/4	9/32	17/64	19/64
5/16	11/32	21/64	23/64
3/8	13/32	25/64	27/64
7/16	15/32	29/64	31/64
1/2	9/16	17/32	39/64
5/8	11/16	21/32	47/64
3/4	13/16	25/32	29/32
7/8	15/16	29/32	1 1/32
1	1 3/32	1 1/32	1 5/32
1 1/8	1 7/32	1 5/32	1 5/16
1 1/4	1 11/32	1 9/32	1 7/16
1 3/8	1 1/2	1 7/16	1 39/64
1 1/2	1 5/8	1 9/16	1 47/64

APPENDIX G – FASTENERS

BOLT AND SCREW CLEARANCE HOLES (Continued)

(2) Metric Clearance Holes

Nominal Screw Size	Fit Classes		
	Normal	Close	Loose
	Nominal Drill Size		
M1.6	1.8	1.7	2
M2	2.4	2.2	2.6
M2.5	2.9	2.7	3.1
M3	3.4	3.2	3.6
M4	4.5	4.3	4.8
M5	5.5	5.3	5.8
M6	6.6	6.4	7
M8	9	8.4	10
M10	11	10.5	12
M12	13.5	13	14.5
M14	15.5	15	16.5
M16	17.5	17	18.5
M20	22	21	24
M24	26	25	28
M30	33	31	35
M36	39	37	42
M42	45	43	48
M48	52	50	56
M56	62	58	66
M64	70	66	74
M72	78	74	82
M80	86	82	91
M90	96	93	101
M100	107	104	112

APPENDIX H – REFERENCES

- ASME B1.1 - 2003: Unified Inch Screw Threads (UN and UNR Thread Form)
- ASME B1.13M - 2001: Metric Screw Threads: M Profile
- USAS/ASME B4.1 - 1967 (R2004): Preferred Limits and Fits for Cylindrical Parts
- ANSI B4.2 - 1978 (R2004): Preferred Metric Limits and Fits
- ASME B18.2.1 - 1996: Square and Hex Bolts and Screws (Inch Series)
- ASME/ANSI B18.2.2 - 1987 (R1999): Square and Hex Nuts (Inch Series)
- ANSI B18.2.3.5M - 1979 (R2001): Metric Hex Bolts
- ASME B18.2.4.1M - 2002: Metric Hex Nuts, Style 1
- ASME B18.2.8 - 1999: Clearance Holes for Bolts, Screws, and Studs
- ASME B18.3 - 2003: Socket Cap, Shoulder, and Set Screws, Hex and Spline Keys (Inch Series)
- ASME/ANSI B18.3.1M - 1986 (R2002): Socket Head Cap Screws (Metric Series)
- ASME/ANSI B18.3.5M - 1986 (R2002): Hexagon Socket Flat Countersunk Head Cap Screws (Metric Series)
- ASME 18.6.2 - 1998: Slotted Head Cap Screws, Square Head Set Screws, and Slotted Headless Set Screws (Inch Series)
- ASME B18.21.1 - 1999: Lock Washers (Inch Series)
- ANSI B18.22.1 - 1965 (R2003): Plain Washers
- ASME Y14.2M - 1992 (R2003): Line Conventions and Lettering
- ASME Y14.3 - 2003: Multiview and Sectional view Drawings
- ASME Y14.4M - 1989 (R1999): Pictorial Drawings
- ASME Y14.5M - 1994: Dimensioning and Tolerancing
- ASME Y14.6 - 2001: Screw Thread Representation
- ASME Y14.100 - 2000: Engineering Drawing Practices

Notes:

INDEX